ILLINOIS

WILDLIFE ENCYCLOPEDIA

ILLINOIS

WILDLIFE ENCYCLOPEDIA

— AN ILLUSTRATED GUIDE TO —

BIRDS, FISH, MAMMALS, REPTILES, AND AMPHIBIANS

SCOTT SHUPE

Skyhorse Publishing

Skyhorse Publishing books may be purchased in bulk at special discounts for sales promotion, corporate gifts, fund-raising, or educational purposes. Special editions can also be created to specifications. For details, contact the Special Sales Department, Skyhorse Publishing, 307 West 36th Street, 11th Floor, New York, NY 10018 or info@skyhorsepublishing.com.

Skyhorse® and Skyhorse Publishing® are registered trademarks of Skyhorse Publishing, Inc.®, a Delaware corporation.

Visit our website at www.skyhorsepublishing.com.

10 9 8 7 6 5 4 3

Library of Congress Cataloging-in-Publication Data is available on file.

Cover design by Rain Saukas
Cover photos courtesy of the author

Print ISBN: 978-1-5107-2885-1
Ebook ISBN: 978-1-5107-2890-5

Printed in China

ACKNOWLEDGEMENTS

The author gratefully acknowledges the following individuals who contributed to the completion of this book. In no particular order, those individuals are:

Rob Mottice, Senior Aquarist at the Tennessee Aquarium in Chattanooga, TN, for help in identifying freshwater fish species photographed at that facility.

David Wilkins, Curator at the South Carolina Aquarium in Charleston, SC, for his help in identifying fresh water fish species photographed at his facility.

Larry Warner, North Carolina Aquarium on Roanoke Island, NC, for his help in identifying freshwater fish species photographed at his facility.

The staff of the North Carolina Aquarium at Pine Knoll Shores, NC for help in identifying freshwater fish species photographed at that facility.

The staff at the Georgia Fish Center for helping identify minnow species photographed at that facility.

The staff at the Texas Fresh Water Fish Center for help in identifying minnow species photographed at that facility.

Dave Frymire for helping the author secure herp specimens for photography and for allowing me to photograph several snake species in his possesion.

John R. MacGregor, KDFWR, for providing a number of amphibian and mammal photographs used in this book and for providing technical information and scientific advice regarding the reptiles and amphibians.

Matthew R. Thomas, KDFWR, for help in identifying several species of darters and minnows photographed by the author for this book as well as for his technical advice and icthyological expertise; and for providing a large number of fish photographs used in the book.

Amy Berry, Clay Hill Memorial Forest and Nature Center, for providing fish and amphibian specimens for photography.

Dr. Gordon Weddle, Campbellsville University, for providing fish and amphibian specimens for photography.

Dr. Ritchard Kessler, Campbellsville University, for help collecting fish specimens for photography.

Jim Harrison and Kristin Wiley of the Kentucky Reptile Zoo for allowing the author to trap on their property mammal and fish specimens for photography.

Clinton Cunningham for assistance in acquiring and photographing herpetology specimens.

Kathleen Mount for assistance in acquiring and photographing herpetology specimens.

Judy Tipton for alerting me to the presence of and allowing me to photograph nesting birds in her yard.

Tim Johnson for helping secure lizard specimens for photography.

Matt Wagner and John Hardy from the Mississippi Museum of Natural History for helping to ID fishes photographed in aquariums at that facility.

Brainard Palmer-Ball of the Kentucky Ornithological Society for help identifying fall warblers photographed by the author for this book.

Barbara Graham for taking the author spelunking in the sandstone caves of eastern Kentucky searching for bats to photograph.

Candy McNamee for guiding the author on a search for migratory birds along the Texas coast.

Karen Finch for guiding the author in a search for migratory birds in south Florida.

Dr. Tim Spier, Murray State University, for his help in collecting fish specimens for photography.

Jennifer Rader of the Kansas Department of Wildlife, Parks and Tourism for allowing me to photograph freshwater stream fishes at the Southeast Kansas Nature Center.

John Hewlett who accompanied the author in the field and helped locate and collect fish and reptile specimens for photography.

James Kiser for providing several photographs.

Don Martin of Don Martin Bird Photography for contributing several of the more excellent bird photos in the book.

T. Travis Brown for several photo contributions.

David Speiser, www.lilibirds.com, for several professional-quality bird photo contributions.

Jeffrey Offereman for his photo contribution.

David Haggard, naturalist with Tennessee Department of Conservation, for his photo contribution of a rare blue morph Green Treefrog.

Phil Myers, University of Michigan, for his photo contribution.

Konrad Schmidt of North America Native Fish Association for contributions of several fish photos.

Uland Thomas for photo contribution.

Dave Neely for photo contribution.

Brian Zimmerman, www.ZimmermansFish.com, for several fish photo contributions.

Nate Tessler for his fish photo contributions.

John Williams for his photo contribution.

Michael Jeffords of the Illinois Natural History Survey for his photo contribution.

Danielle Ruffato of the Illinois Natural History Survey for her help in locating photographs.

Jean Mengelkoch of the Illinois Natural History Survey for her help in locating photographs.

Greg Lavaty for his photo contributions.

Tom Murray for his photo contribution.

Jeff Poklen for his photo contributions.

Peter Paplanus for his photo contributions.

James H. Harding for his photo contributions.

Roger Tabor, USFWS, for photo contribution.

Nathan Petersen for his photo contribution.

US Fish and Wildlife Service and US Forest Service for photo contributions.

Peter Steenstra, USFWS, for his photo contribution.

Last but certainly not least I would like to thank my publisher, Jason Katzman of Skyhorse Publishing.

In our negotiations, Jason has not only shown patience and a willingness to compromise, but also great faith in this author. He has also exhibited extraordinary entrepreneurial courage in taking on a huge project of which this book is but a first step.

Finally, this book is dedicated to author's three sons, Haydn, Denham, and Kyle Shupe. Though now adults, as youngsters their keen eyes, youthful enthusiasm, and unflinching companionship were responsible for the author getting many of the photographs in this book. More importantly, their presence in this world has consistently provided this author with the motivation to repeatedly bite off more than he can chew.

PHOTOGRAPHERS

Most of the over 600-plus wildlife photographs that appear in this book were taken by the author. However, many of the high-quality photographs were contributed by several wildlife photographers across the US. Those individuals were critical to the completion of this book and their remarkable photographs add much to its content. The names of those photographers and the number of photos each contributed appear below.

Matthew R. Thomas — 23
John R MacGregor — 16
David Speiser, www.lilibirds.com — 9
Don Martin Bird Photography — 9
Brian Zimmerman — 2
Konrad Schmidt — 11
Nate Tessler — 4
Peter Paplanus — 3
James Kiser — 2
Dave Neely — 2
T. Travis Brown — 2
Phil Myers — 1
David Haggard — 1
Jeff Poklen — 2
Uland Thomas — 1
Tom Murray -1
Jeffrey Offermann, www.flickr.com/photos/jeff_offerman — 1
John Williams — 1
Michael Jeffords — 1
Greg Lavaty — 1
James H. Harding — 1
Nathan Petersen — 1
US Fish & Wildlife Service, Roger Tabor — 1
US Fish & Wildlife Service, Peter Steenstra — 1
US Fish & Wildlife Service, Digital Files — 1
US Forest Service — 1

Thank you also to many other photographers who offered their help but whose photographs I was not able to use due to redundancy or time constraints. A complete list of photo credits appears in the back of this book.

TABLE OF CONTENTS

ILLINOIS

WILDLIFE ENCYCLOPEDIA

INTRODUCTION

From the earliest European exploration and settlement of Illinois, the state's wildlife has played and important role. Native Americans living in the region sustained themselves largely by harvesting mammals, birds, and fish for sustenence, and the first Europeans came in search of Beaver and buckskins. While the state's wildlife is still an important resource for trappers, hunters, and fishermen, wildlife is also increasingly important for its intrinsic, aesthetic value. Though the age-old practice of hunting and fishing is the most obvious example of how wildlife can enrich our lives, for many Illinoisans the opportunity to simply observe wildlife and experience nature also serves to enhance our existence.

In more recent history, the pursuit of wildlife has evolved to encompass more benevolent activities such as bird watching and wildlife photography. In fact, the numbers of Americans who enjoy these "nonconsumptive" forms of wildlife-related recreation today exceed the numbers of those who hunt and fish. The range of wildlife-related interests and activities has broadened so considerably that the US Fish & Wildlife Service in its most recent assessment of the economic impact of wildlife in America lists a broad catagory labeled "Wildlife Watching." The economic impact of wildlife watching in America today far exceeds the impact that hunters and fishermen have on the economy.

With interest in wildlife and nature continuing to grow throughout Illinois, the need for a single, simple reference to the state's wildlife has become evident. A number of excellent books that deal specifically with Illinois' birds, reptiles, mammals, and fishes are available, but none combine all the state's wildlife into a comprehensive, encyclopedic reference. This volume is intended to fill that niche. It is hoped that this book will find favor with school librarians, life science teachers, students of field biology classes, and professional naturalists as well as with the general populace.

As might be expected with such a broad-spectrum publication, intimate details about the natural history of individual species is omitted in favor of a format that provides more basic information. In this sense, this volume is not intended for use as a professional reference, but instead as a handy, usable, layman's guide to the state's wildlife. For those who wish to explore the information regarding the state's wildlife more deeply, a list of references for each chapter appears in the back of the book and includes both print and reliable Internet references.

Embracing the old adage that a picture is worth a thousand words, color photographs are used to depict and identify each species. Below each photograph is a table that provides basic information about the biology of each animal. This table includes a state map with a shaded area showing the species' presumed range in the state, as well as general information such as size, habitat, and abundance. The taxonomic classification of each species is also provided, with the animal's Class, Order, and Family appearing as a heading at the top of the page.

The range maps shown in this book are not intended to be regarded as a strictly accurate representation of the range of any given species. Indeed, the phrase "Presumed range in Illinois," which accompanies each species' range map, should be literally interpreted. The ranges of many species in the state are often not well documented. The range maps for some species in this book may be regarded as at best an "educated guess." Furthermore, many wide-ranging species are restricted to regions of suitable habitat. Thus an aquatic species like the Beaver, while found statewide, would not be expected to occur in the middle of an upland crop field. Additionally, other species that may have once been found throughout a large geographic area may now have disappeared from much of their former range. A number of fish species, for example, are rare or extirpated in the state due to water quality degradation of many of the state's rivers and streams.

Further complicating the issue of species distribution is the fact that animals like birds and bats, possessed with the ability of flight, are capable of traveling great distances. Many species of both birds and bats are migratory and regularly travel hundreds or even thousands of miles annually. It is not uncommon for these migratory species to sometimes appear in areas where they are not typically found. The mechanisms of migration and dispersal of many animals is still a bit of a mystery, and the exact reason why a bird from another portion of the country (or even from another continent) should suddenly appear where it doesn't belong is often speculation. Sometimes these appearances may represent individuals that are simply wandering. Other times it can be a single bird or an entire flock that has been blown off course by a powerful storm or become otherwise lost and disoriented. Whatever the cause, there are many bird species that have been recorded in the state that are not really a part of Illinois' native fauna, and their occasional sightings are regarded as "accidental."

On the other hand, some species may appear somewhere in the state once every few years dependant upon weather conditions or availability of prey in its normal habitat. Although these types of "casual species" could be regarded as belonging among Illinois' native bird fauna, their occurrence in the state is so sporadic and unpredictable that deciding which species should be included as a native becomes very subjective. The point is that the reader should be advised that while all the bird species depicted in this volume can be considered to be members of the state's indigenous fauna, *not every bird species that has been seen or recorded in Illinois is depicted in this book.*

For readers who wish to delve into more professional and detailed information about the vertebrate zoology of Illinois, the list of references shown for each chapter should adequately provide that opportunity.

Scott Shupe, 2018.

CHAPTER 1

THE FACE OF THE LAND

— THE NATURAL REGIONS OF ILLINOIS —

Defining and understanding the natural regions of Illinois is the first step in understanding the natural history of the state. Man-made political boundaries such as county lines and state borders are meaningless to wildlife, whereas natural features like rivers can be important elements in influencing the distribution of the state's wildlife.

The major considerations used in determining and delineating natural regions are factors such as elevation, relief (topography), drainages, geology, and climate. All these are important elements that can determine the limits of distribution for living organisms. It follows then that some knowledge of these factors is essential when involved in the study of the state's natural history. The study of natural regions is known as *Physiography*, which means "physical geography" or literally "the face of the land." While the terms geography and physiography are closely related and sometimes used interchangeably, geography is a broader term which includes such things as human culture, resource use, and man's impact on the land, while physiography deals only with elements of geography created by nature.

The term most often used to define a major natural region is "*Physiographic Division.*" There are 10 major physiographic divisions across the United States and Canada, and portions of 3 affect the state of Illinois. The 3 major physiographic divisions of Illinois are the the *Interior Plains Division*, the *Ozark Highlands Division,* and the *Atlantic Plain Division*. Of these, over 90 percent of the state is within the Interior Plains Division. See Figure 1.

Elevation and topography are the major defining characters of the 3 main provinces affecting Illinois, with the highest elevation in Illinois (1,235 feet) occurring in the northwestern corner of Illinois in the *Interior Plains Division*. The lowest elevation is in the *Atlantic Plain Division* in the southern tip of the state (279 feet where the Ohio and Mississippi rivers converge).

The **Interior Plains Division** includes nearly all of the state of Illinois as well as most of the Great Plains states and most of the American Midwest. This large division extends all the way to the Rocky Mountains.

The Interior Plains Division has 4 provinces, 2 of which, the *Interior Low Plateau Province* and the *Interior Lowland Province,* occur in Illinois.

The **Atlantic Plain Division** occurs mostly offshore (the Continental Shelf) and only the *Coastal Plain Province* occurs on mainland America. This province includes much of the southeastern US and extends northward up the Mississippi River Valley into the southernmost tip of Illinois.

The **Ozark Highlands Division** is found mostly in Missouri and Arkansas, but a small sliver of land in southeastern Illinois is contained within this division. The Ozark Highlands Division is divided into 2 smaller provinces, one of which, the *Ozark Plateau Province*, occurs in Illinois.

Figure 1 on the following page shows where the major physiographic divisions occur in the Eastern United States. Meanwhile Figure 2 shows how the major physiographic divisions are divided into smaller provinces and how those provinces affect the state of Illinois.

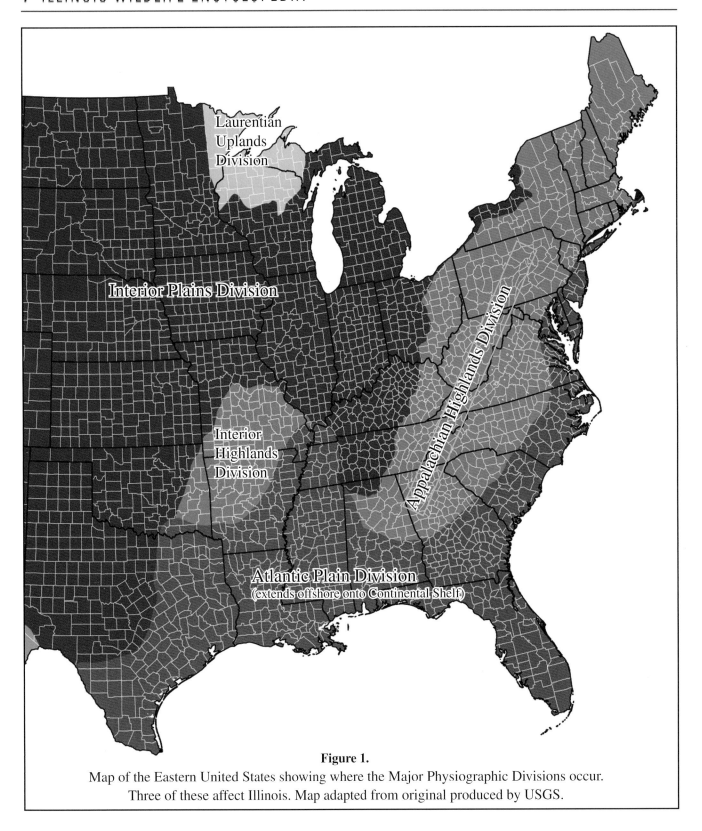

Figure 1.
Map of the Eastern United States showing where the Major Physiographic Divisions occur.
Three of these affect Illinois. Map adapted from original produced by USGS.

Each of these 3 major divisions shown on the map above are further divided into smaller provinces.
The map on the following page (Figure 2) shows how these major divisions are divided into smaller provinces.

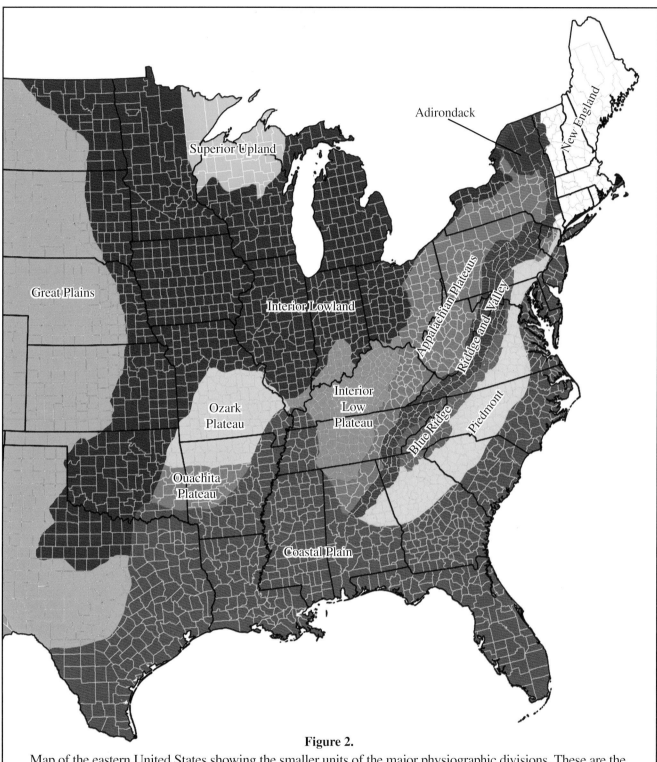

Figure 2.
Map of the eastern United States showing the smaller units of the major physiographic divisions. These are the *Physiographic Provinces* that are contained within each major division. Map adapted from original produced by USGS

The Map above shows how the Physiographic divisions are subdivided into smaller units called *"Physiographic Provinces."*

These provinces shown in Figure 2 above are subdivided further into *Physiographic Sections* (also sometimes called natural regions). Figure 3 on the following page shows the Physiographic Sections of the state of Illinois.

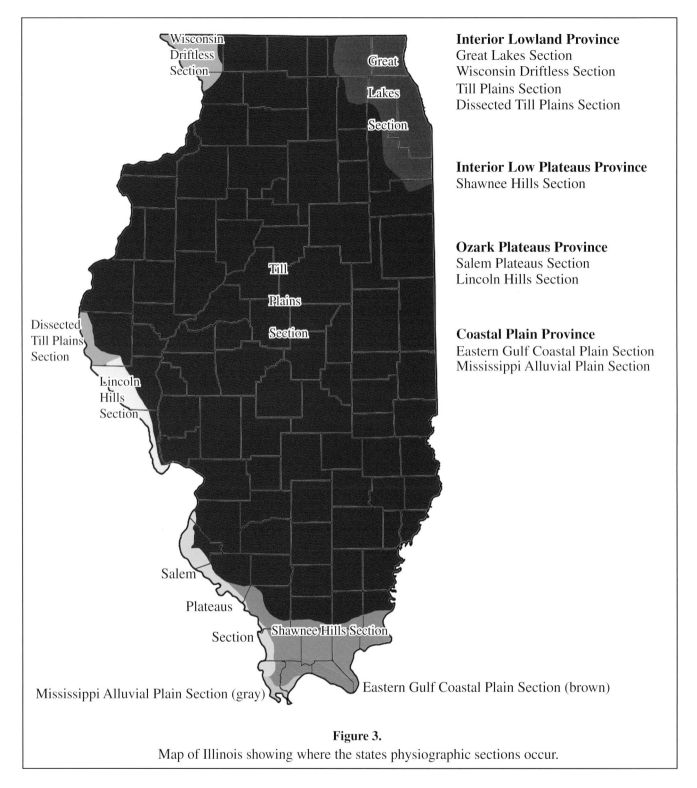

Interior Lowland Province
Great Lakes Section
Wisconsin Driftless Section
Till Plains Section
Dissected Till Plains Section

Interior Low Plateaus Province
Shawnee Hills Section

Ozark Plateaus Province
Salem Plateaus Section
Lincoln Hills Section

Coastal Plain Province
Eastern Gulf Coastal Plain Section
Mississippi Alluvial Plain Section

Figure 3.
Map of Illinois showing where the states physiographic sections occur.

Some appreciation of the physiographic units shown in Figures 1 through 3 will be useful in comprehending the distribution of Illinois' vertebrate wildlife species. For instance, some species may occur in the state only in a small region defined by the state's physiographic divisions, or it may be widespread in a number of regions. Thus when reading species accounts, there may be references to a species range in the state, such as "found in Illinois only in the Mississippi Alluvial Plain" or "widespread throughout the Interior Lowland Province."

Glaciation in Illinois

In the state of Illinois, the history of the state's climate has played and important role in both the state's topography and in differentiating natural regions. Within the relatively recent geological history of Illinois (beginning about one and half million years ago and ending only a few tens of thousands of years ago), most of the state (and much of the northern half of North America) was covered by immense glaciers. These glaciation events impacted the landscape of the region so significantly that naturalists today often refer to regions in the Midwest as "glaciated" or "unglaciated" regions.

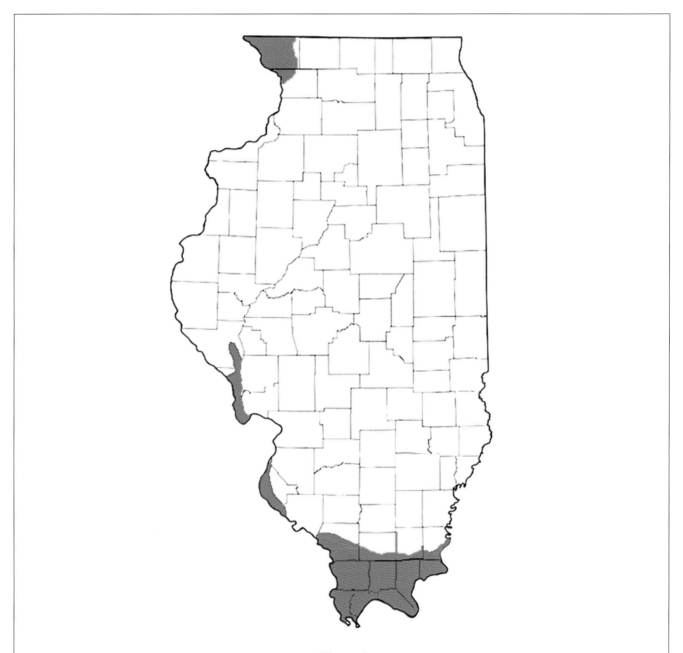

Figure 4.

Map of Illinois showing regions of the state impacted by glaciers (yellow). Non-glaciated regions are in olive green. Notice how closely the glaciated region of Illinois comports with the Interior Lowland Physiographic Province shown in Figure 2. Note also that the non-glaciated regions are nearly synonomous with some of the state's smaller physiographic sections, such as the Wisconsin Driftless, Salem Plateaus, and Shawnee Hills sections.

CHAPTER 2

ECOREGIONS AND WILDLIFE HABITATS OF ILLINOIS

PART 1—ECOREGIONS

First, it should be noted that in ecology, as in the study of most other scientific disciplines, different opinions exist among experts as to the definition of a particular habitat or ecoregion (such as types of forests). Man's understanding of the Earth's ecology continues to evolve, and not every ecologist adopts the same model or criteria in describing habitats and ecosystems. Moreover, different models may be used by different researchers based on the needs of that research. The ecological model adopted here is derived from the ecoregions used by the Environmental Protection Agency (www.epa.gov/wed/ecoregions).

The Environmental Protection Agency recognizes a total of 14 "Level I Ecoregions" in the US and Canada. Each of these Level I Ecoregions consists of several progressively smaller divisions, known respectively as Level

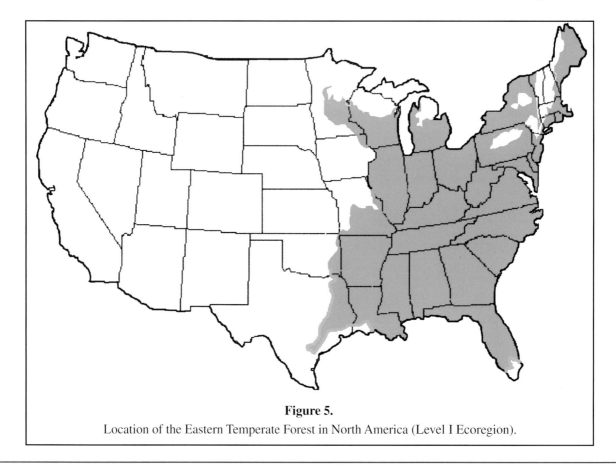

Figure 5.
Location of the Eastern Temperate Forest in North America (Level I Ecoregion).

II Ecoregions, Level III Ecoregions, and Level IV Ecoregions. The entire state of Illinois falls within one of the larger of North America's 14 Level I Ecoregions, known as **Eastern Temperate Forest** (see Figure 5 on previous page).

The designation of Illinois as a forest habitat is based on the state's *naturally occurring wildlife habitats*, i.e., the historical natural conditions found in Illinois prior to the changes wrought by European settlers. Obviously, today much of Illinois is not forested. In fact, even prior to European settlement, the natural habitats of the state included large expanses of Tallgrass Prairie (just over half of Illinois was originally grasslands). Significant but smaller amounts of wetlands in the form of swamps and marshes were also distributed throughout the state. Thus, although the Level I habitat type is designated as forest, Illinois has always contained a variety of other habitats that were embedded within the boundaries of the Eastern Temperate Forest Level I Ecoregion.

The Eastern Temperate Forest (Level I Ecoregion) consists of 5 Level II Ecoregions. The Level II Ecoregions of the Eastern Temperate Forest are the **Ozark-Ouachita-Appalachian Forest,** the **Southeast US Plains,** the **Mississippi Alluvial and Southeast**

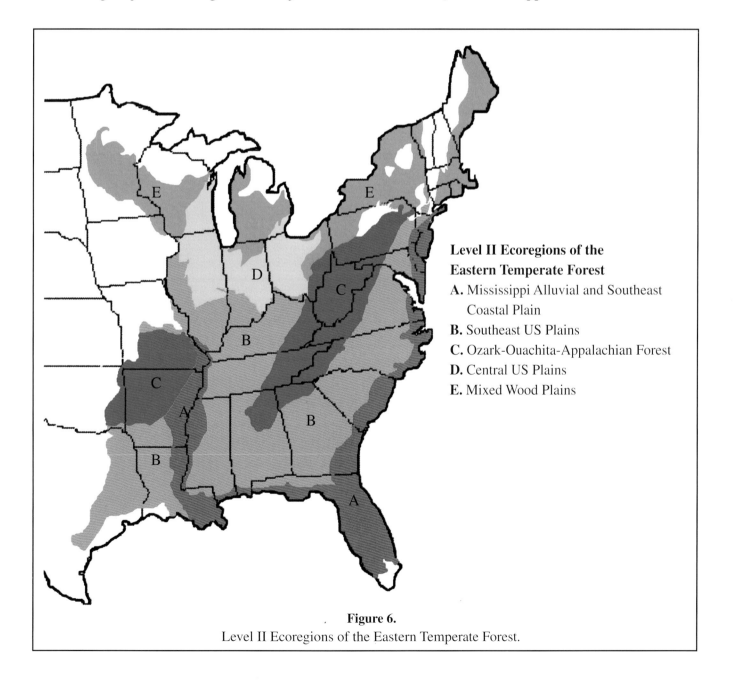

Level II Ecoregions of the Eastern Temperate Forest
A. Mississippi Alluvial and Southeast Coastal Plain
B. Southeast US Plains
C. Ozark-Ouachita-Appalachian Forest
D. Central US Plains
E. Mixed Wood Plains

Figure 6.
Level II Ecoregions of the Eastern Temperate Forest.

Coastal Plains, **Mixed Wood Plains**, and **Central US Plains**. The locations of these 5 Level II Ecoregions are shown in Figure 6 on the previous page.

Four of the 7 Level II Ecoregions shown above occur in Illinois. The Level II Ecoregions that affect Illinois are the **Mississippi Alluvial and Southeast Coastal Plain** (in extreme southwestern Illinois), the **Mixed Woods Plains** (extreme northwest corner of Illinois), the **Southeast US Plains** (southern and western Illinois), and the **Central US Plains** (most of northeastern Illinois).

The Level II Ecoregions shown in Figure 6 above are sometimes referred to differently by other ecological models. The portion of the Mississippi Alluvial and Southeast Coastal Plains Ecoregion in Illinois is also known as "*Mississippi Lowland Forest.*" Similarly, the part of the Southeast US Plains found in Illinois may be referred to as "*Central US Hardwood Forests.*"

A written descripton of the Level II ecoregions affecting Illinois follows on the next page.

Central US Plains

In Illinois, this ecoregion is contained entirely in the physiographic province known as the Interior Lowlands (see Figure 2). Originally this region was primarily hardwood forest with oak, hickory, maple, elm, ash, and beech as the dominant tree species. Significant but scattered areas of tall grass prairies also occurred here, along with wetland areas of marsh and swamp.

Today the region is dominated by agriculture and urban regions.

Southeast US Plains

Hardwoods are dominant in this ecoregion, with more drought tolerant species such as oaks and hickories being more common. Pines also occur in some areas. Grasslands were once sporadic but fairly widespread within this ecoregion, and wetland swamps and marshes dominated river valleys and lowlands. Also widespread are ecotone habitats, successional areas, and most commonly, man-made habitats (see Table 3). This ecoregion supports the highest number of herbaceous plants and shrubs in North American (over 2,500 species). Modern agriculture has drastically altered the natural habitats in this region and in fact pristine examples of the original habitats of this region in Illinois are virtually nonexistent today, with nearly all of this forest type being regenerative growth.

Mixed Wood Plains

This ecoregion includes parts of Ontario and Quebec in Canada as well as much of the New England states. The term "Mixed Woods Plains" is appropriately descriptive as the endemic tree species are a mix of deciduous and coniferous evergreens. In Illinois, this ecoregion corresponds with the Wisconsin Driftless physiographic section (Figure 3). Historically the area was much more heavily forested than what is seen today.

Mississippi Alluvial and Southeast Coastal Plain

This ecoregion barely enters Illinois in the southernmost tip of the state. The portion of this ecoregion that affects Illinois also sometimes goes by the name *Mississippi Lowland Forests.* The original riparian floodplain forests of the Mississippi River floodplain have been devastated by logging and agriculture. Originally stretching from the mouth of the Mississippi to southern Illinois, only a few pockets of this magnificent forest type remain. Wetter areas and river swamps are dominated by Baldcypress, tupelo, and willows. On the higher ground oaks, hickories, gum, Cottonwood, River Birch, Sycamore, Red Maple, and pines are the main forest components. Local habitats are now dominated by open lands (mostly agricultural) and ecotones where pockets of swampland, marsh, and woodlots remain. In addition to mesic floodplain forests and some dry woodlands, swamps and marshes were a common naturally occurring habitat here. Today all these habitats are but a sliver of what once occurred in the ecoregion. At present, human-altered habitats (mostly agricultural areas) are the most widespread, interspersed with some ecotone habitats and successional areas.

Figure 7 on the next page shows how the Level II ecoregions discussed above are subdivided into Level III

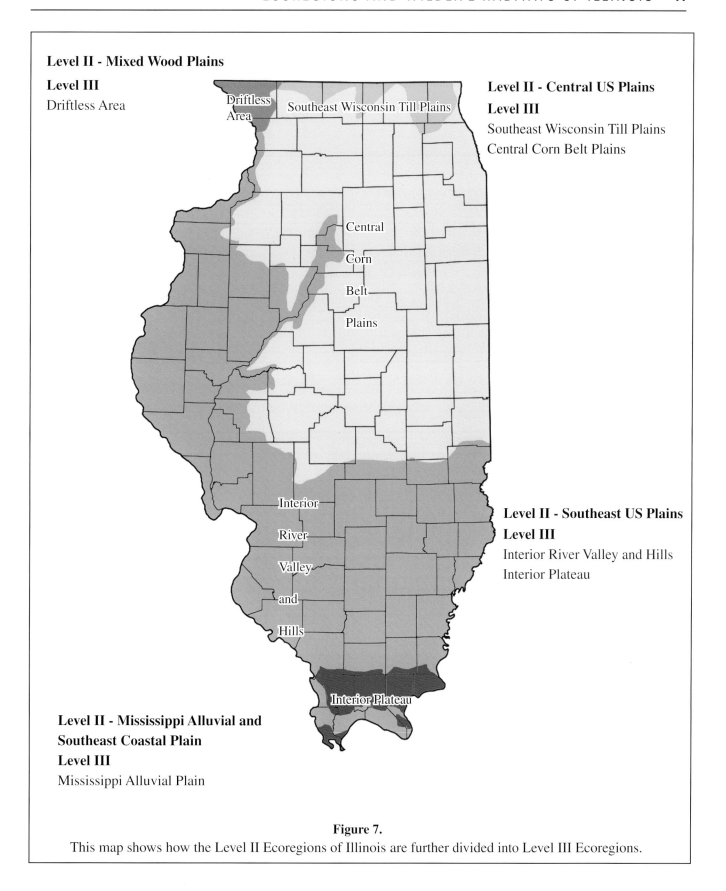

Level II - Mixed Wood Plains

Level III

Driftless Area

Level II - Central US Plains

Level III

Southeast Wisconsin Till Plains

Central Corn Belt Plains

Level II - Southeast US Plains

Level III

Interior River Valley and Hills

Interior Plateau

Level II - Mississippi Alluvial and Southeast Coastal Plain

Level III

Mississippi Alluvial Plain

Figure 7.

This map shows how the Level II Ecoregions of Illinois are further divided into Level III Ecoregions.

ecoregions and where those Level III Ecoregions affecting Illinois are found within the state.

When examining Figure 7, it is instructive to pay attention to how some of the Level III Ecoregions correspond with maps shown in Figures 3 and 4. For example, the Level III Ecoregion known as the Driftless Area corresponds with the physiographic section known as the Wisconsin Driftless (Figure 3). Likewise, the Interior Plateau Level III Ecoregion is also within an unglaciated area of the state (Figure 4), and similarly corresponds to the physiographic province labeled Interior Low Plateau in Figure 2.

These Level III Ecoregions can be divided even further into Level IV Ecoregions. Ecologist and wildlife biologists find these finer ecoregion divisions useful in the study of the natural history of organisms. Some species are dependent upon a specific habitat or ecoregion for survival. Thus, an understanding of the various ecoregions and what factors are important in the designation of that ecoregion are imperative to wildlife management and conservation efforts. To see how the Level III Ecoregions above are further divided into Level IV Ecoregions, consult the Environmental Protection Agency's Ecoregions of North America website.

— PART 2 - HABITATS —

In this book, as in many discussions about the natural environments of America, the terms *habitat* and *ecoregion* are frequently used interchangeably. But strictly speaking, there are differences between the two. The term "ecoregion," as defined by the World Wildlife Fund, means "a large unit of land or water containing a geographically distinct assemblage of species, natural communities, and environmental conditions." A *habitat* meanwhile is usually defined simply as "where an organism lives." Thus, an area of mesic (moist) forest, or xeric (dry) forest, are both *habitats* that are contained within the larger forest *ecoregion*. In many publications, the word biome is sometimes used synonymously with both the term habitat and the term ecoregion.

A description of the habitat types found in Illinois is as follows:

Woodlands

As the Level I Ecoregion of Illinois is the Eastern Temperate Forest, it comes as no surprise that woodlands are one of the most widespread naturally occurring habitat types in the state. Although professional biologists and ecologists recognize a larger number of different woodland habitat types, in this volume woodland habitats have been simplified and combined into two major types of woodland habitats that can *occur in all of Illinois forest ecoregions*. Nearly all of Illinois' woodland habitats are regenerative woodlands, i.e. woodlands that have been logged for timber at some time during the last 150 years. A few enclaves of mature woodlands may remain in the state, but they would be tiny, highly fragmented remnants of what once was a mature forest ecosystem.

Xeric (dry) Woodlands

These woodlands are usually found at the tops of ridges where the soil is thin and runoff is high. They can also occur on the sides of south or west south facing slopes of hills and ridges. Drought tolerant species are dominant in dry woodlands. In some xeric woodlands where trees are widely spaced and shrub growth is reduced, grasses and herbs normally associated with savannas and grasslands can be found on the forest floor. Pines and Red Cedar are the representative conifers in dry woodlands while a variety of oaks and hickories dominate the deciduous tree community. Xeric woodlands occur on ridgetops and steep south or west facing slopes. Steep conditions are condusive to a high rate of rainfall runoff and south or west facing slopes experience a greater amount of sunlight. Dry woodlands are also common in areas where rocky substrate may be near the surface and topsoils are thin or very poor. Many of the tree species are the same as those found in mesic woodlands, but in the xeric woods they are often stunted and gnarly. Xeric Woodland is least common in the *Mississippi Alluvial Plain* but can occur in the few upland areas such as bluffs that border the river floodplain, or in highland areas with sandy soils.

Mesic (moist) Woodlands

Mesic woods are found on north- or east-facing slopes, at the bottoms of deep gorges, and in protected coves and valleys where prolonged direct sunlight is limited and evaporation is low. Mesic Woodlands are also are common in lowlands along major river valleys. Tulip Poplar, Sugar Maple, Beech, Basswood, oaks, hickories, and in historical times the American Chestnut are just a few of the deciduous tree species found in these diverse woodlands. Swamp forests are dominated by species such as Baldcypress, Tupelo, gum, and Red Maple.

Wetlands

Wetlands were once a very significant part of the wildlife habitat of the major river valley in the state and occurred extensively throughout southern Illinois in the Coastal Plain Physiographic Province. Wetlands can be areas that are seasonally flooded or contain permanent standing water. In this book, wetlands are characterized by two basic types, swamps and marshes. Both swamps and marshes are very important habitats for many types of wildlife in Illinois. Today very few of the original wetland habitats remain in Illinois. The various types of wetland habitats occurring in Illinois are outlined on the following page.

Swamps
A swamp is best defined as a wetland area in which the dominant plants are trees. Most of Illinois swamplands have always been found in southern Illinois or in low-lying areas adjacent to rivers and streams. Baldcypress, willows, gums, and Red Maple are common tree species of Illinois swamps. Generally speaking, swamps are permanently flooded, but some habitat models may include seasonally flooded bottomland forest. Swamps are important areas of biodiversity and are critical to the survival of many vertebrate wildlife species in Illinois. Swamps are sometimes categorized by the dominant tree species present (as in Baldcypress Swamp, Gum-Tupelo Swamp, etc.).

Marshes
Marshes are wetlands in which the main plant species are grasses, sedges, and shrubs. Some small trees like willows may be present, but they are never dominant. Cattails, Pickerel Weed, Buttonbush, Rose Mallow, and Water Lily are common plants in marshes. Some marshes may be only seasonally flooded, while others have

permanently standing water. As with swamps, marshes enjoy significant diversity and are vital habitats to many of Illinois' vertebrate wildlife species. Marshes were historically widespread in Illinois in all physiographic provinces in the state.

Bogs
Bogs are shallow depressions that are permanently moist and often contain standing water. The vegetation usually consists of mosses, ferns, sedges, Jewelweed, and other herbaceous plants. Though bogs are widespread in the boreal forests of the far north, in much of the United States they are rare habitats that are often an acre or less in size. Bogs are among the rarest habitats in the United States and they can harbor many rare plant species, but they are too small and rare to be significant for most vertebrate wildlife. However, they do provide important habitats for some amphibian species, especially in upland areas where standing water may be uncommon.

Springs/Seeps
Springs and seeps are areas where underground water reaches the surface. The main difference between the two is the amount of water emerging. In seeps, the amount of water is usually much less than in a spring, with the water literally "seeping" from the ground. Seeps also may encompass a much larger area than a typical spring where the water emerges from a single point. These are small habitats but they can be very important and their influence can extend far downstream from the point of emergence.

Open Lands

The naturally occurring areas of open land in Illinois were historically limited to Savanna, Grasslands, and small forest openings known as Glades and Barrens. Obviously today much of Illinois consists of open land, but present-day open lands are the result of changes wrought by man. A description of the state's *naturally occurring* open lands is as follows:

Glades and Barrens
Glades and Barrens are rare and widely scattered and are found in Illinois mostly in the Interior Low Plateau and

Ozark Plateau Provinces (Figure 2). They are among the smallest (and subsequently the most endangered) habitats in Illinois. These habitats are created when underlying rock or gravels reach the surface. The resulting absence of soils creates an opening where the regions usual assemblage of plant species are lacking. *Glades* are usually associated with woodlands and as there is not enough soil to allow for the growth of large trees, they produce open to semi-open areas within forests. Grasses and herbaceous plants are common within glades and many

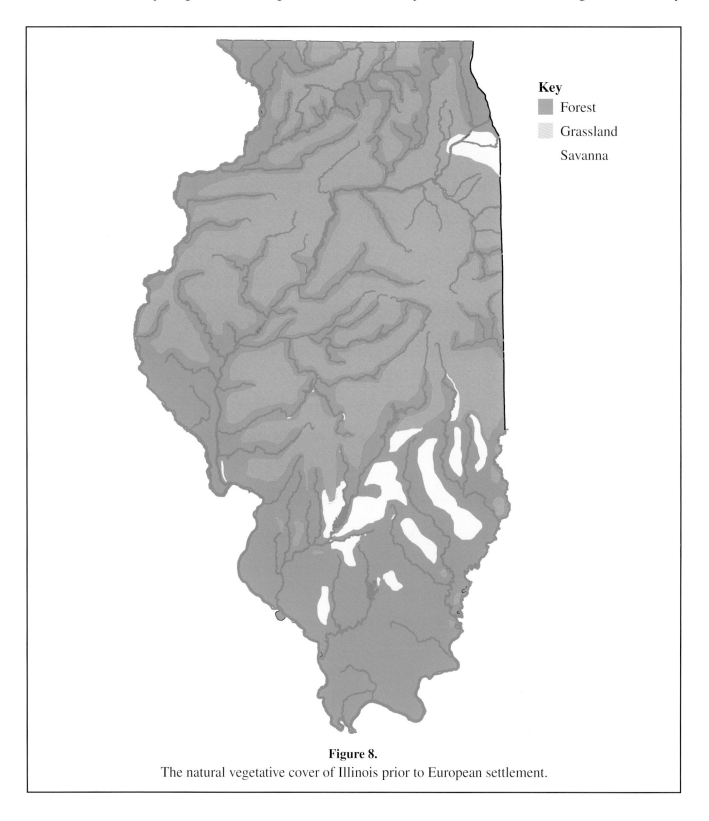

Figure 8.
The natural vegetative cover of Illinois prior to European settlement.

glades are associated with grassland plant communities. Some drought tolerant tree species can occur in these habitats by taking root in deep crevices within the rock. Red Cedar is the most common tree species found in this habitat. *Barrens* are often large slabs of exposed bedrock or underlying gravel and are usually much more "barren" than glades. In some places along cliff faces they consist of exposed bedrock with only the smallest amount of vegetation consisting of an occasional tuft of grass, moss, or lichen clinging to cracks in the rock. Glades and Barrens usually occupy very small areas of land and are thus extremely vulnerable to human disturbance. Although Barrens and Glades support some very unique and extremely rare plant species, most are too small to be a significant habitat for Illinois' vertebrate wildlife species.

Savanna

Savanna habitats are best characterized as grasslands with widely spaced trees. In Illinois, most savanna habitats historically occurred in southern Illinois, although some savanna habitats also once occurred in northeastern Illinois. Figure 8 on the previous page is a map of Illinois showing where savanna habitats historically occurred in Illinois.

Universal Habitats

These habitats occur in virtually all ecoregions throughout North America. The term "universal habitat" is not a commonly used scientific denotation, but rather it is a term created by the author for this book as a way to designate those types of habitats that can and do occur almost everywhere. However, 3 types of universal habitats listed immediately below (ecotones, successional areas, and riparian zones) are scientifically recognized terms.

Ecotones

Ecotones are defined as areas of transition between 2 or more habitats. The term "edge area" is often used synonymously with ecotone. Classic examples of ecotone areas would be a place where a woodland meets an open field or where a swamp or bottomland abuts against a ridge of upland woods. Ecotones are universal habitats found in all regions. These are very productive areas for wildlife, as species from varying habitats can often be found together around ecotones.

Successional Areas

This is another type of habitat that can occur anywhere. Nature is never static. Grasslands are always in the process of becoming woodlands unless the successional process is altered by fire or mowing. Woodlands destroyed by fire may become grassland. A lake subject to sedimentation can become a swamp or marsh. In time, a marsh can fill and become a meadow. Beavers can create a new wetland where before there was a meadow with a small stream. In Illinois, the most familiar successional habitat is the regeneration of a woodland following logging or the reversion to a weedy field of a neglected cropland. These last 2 types of successional areas are favored by wildlife species like the Whitetail Deer and the Eastern Cottontail.

Riparian Zones

A riparian zone is a narrow band of habitat bordering a stream or river. Technically, the term is used to describe the narrow zone of lush growth that accompanies a stream coursing through an otherwise arid landscape (as in the riparian habitats of the desert southwest). In Illinois, where so much of the natural landscape has disappeared, stream courses through open farmlands. Their associated ribbon of trees, shrubs, and forbs are significant zones of natural habitat which can become very important corridors for the movement and dispersal of vertebrate wildlife. Riparian habitats occur throughout the state.

Man-Made Habitats

Man-made habitats usually receive no attention in most scientific discussions regarding *natural* habitats.

However, humans have so altered the natural condition of the land that much of the wildlife habitat that exists in America today has been created by human activities. Although the loss of natural habitats has contributed to the disappearance of many species and continues to be the greatest threat to wildlife worldwide, many species have been able to adapt to man-made habitats and a few actually thrive in these new habitats.

Agricultural Areas

Although some may find it difficult to envision a harvested soybean field as a wildlife habitat, in truth many of Illinois' wildlife species have adapted to occupy or use on a part-time basis the state's abundant agricultural areas. A harvested soybean field in winter is one of the best places to see winter migrant birds like the Snow Bunting or Lapland Longspur. A cattle pasture in summer is home to the Eastern Meadowlark, and flocks of Common Grackles, Starlings, and Red-winged Blackbirds will use both habitats throughout the year. Some species like the White-tailed Deer and the Wild Turkey in part owe their present-day abundance to the ever present food supply provided by grain farmers. In fact, most mammals and many birds found in Illinois have adapted to include agricultural areas in their habitats.

Reclaimed Lands

Strip mining for coal has destroyed many thousands of acres of naturally occurring wildlife habitat in Illinois. Many of these lands have undergone *reclamation* and now constitute radically altered but significant wildlife habitats. Although the reclaimed habitats are quite different from the original habitats, and support a much lower species diversity, they are utilized by several vertebrate species. Sadly, the habitats lost in the mining/reclamation process were many times richer in species diversity than the present-day reclaimed habitats, and those original habitats are now forever gone from the reclaimed areas.

Urban Habitats

As is the case with Agricultural lands, it is sometimes difficult to think of urban landscapes as wildlife habitat.

Again, however, many species adapt well to towns and cities and in fact some will thrive there. The Chimney Swift experienced a population boom in the days when every building in Illinois had a chimney. The Common Nighthawk frequently nests on the flat rooftops of downtown buildings, and everyone is familiar the sight of a Robin plucking worms from a well-manicured

suburban lawn or a Rock Dove (Pigeon) strolling the sidewalks of a large city.

Today most of Illinois' land mass is held in private ownership. Very little of these private lands are managed for wildlife or set aside as areas for the conservation of natural habitats. Fortunately, there are a number of agencies that hold land in public trust with the goal of providing and maintaining natural wildlife habitats. Among these are federal agencies like the US Forest Service, the National Park Service, the US Fish & Wildlife Service, and the Illinois Department of Natural Resources.

A quick look at the map in Figure 8 provides profound insight regarding the scope of the loss of Illinois original vegetative habitats. To anyone with an appreciation of wilderness and nature in its pristine condition, Illinois has become an impoverished place. Many of the state's wildlife species face a perilous and uncertain future. Happily, many species continue to adapt and some thrive in the state's new environments. Thankfully, agencies like the Illinois Department of Natural Resources and the US Fish & Wildlife Service work unceasingly to protect, manage, and enhance the state's wildlife and remaining wild habitats. But there is only so much that these organizations can accomplish. Today only a tiny fraction of Illinois' 57,923 square miles of land area is publicly owned. That means that the real responsibility for stewardship of nature in Illinois falls to individual landowners.

We humans, to a very great degree, have succeeded in altering our natural landscapes so much that we no longer feel an intimate connection to the land. We consider ourselves to be residents of an artificially created locality. We are Illinoisans rather than residents of the formerly great Eastern Deciduous Forest. If asked what part of the state in which our town is located, we may say "Johnson County" rather than reply that our town is located within rugged uplands of the Interior Plateau.

To some extent, natural boundaries have always been utilized by man when creating political boundaries. A prime example is the Mississippi River that serves as the western border of Illinois. Smaller creeks and rivers regularly serve as county lines, and the state's southern border with Kentucky is delineated by the Ohio River.

But we humans have a strong tendency to create regions and boundaries which ignore natural boundaries and instead serve our personal, social, and political needs. While this mind-set serves our society well in many ways, it often does a disservice to our environment. If we could learn to think of ourselves more as a part of the larger ecosystems, we would perhaps show more concern for the stewardship of those ecosystems. At this stage in human history, with our population topping 7 billion people, our natural resources being pushed to the point of exhaustion, our ocean ecosystems possibly on the verge of collapse, mass extinctions just around the corner, and global climate change in the immediate future, a new understanding and appreciation of the natural world by all citizens seems to be the only hope for a promising future.

The pages that follow are intended to introduce Illinoisans to the remarkable diversity, wondrous beauty, and miraculous lives of our state's wildlife species. It is hoped that this introduction will lead to a greater awareness, concern, and appreciation for our natural heritage. It is further hoped that acquiring that awareness and appreciation will lead to a better stewardship of the living things with which we share this planet. And more importantly, the natural ecosystems upon which both they and we ultimately depend.

CHAPTER 3

THE MAMMALS OF ILLINOIS

— THE ORDERS AND FAMILIES OF ILLINOIS MAMMALS —

Note: The sequence in which the mammal orders and families are shown below is a reflection of how they appear on the following pages, and is not intended to represent the phylogenetic relationship of the mammals.

Class - **Mammalia** (mammals)

Order - **Didelphimorpha** (opossums)

Family	**Didelphidae** (opossum)

Order - **Cingulata** (armadillos, anteaters, sloths)

Family	**Dasypodidae** (armadillos)

Order - **Carnivora** (carnivores)

Family	**Procyondidae** (raccoon family)
Family	**Felidae** (cat family)
Family	**Canidae** (canines)
Family	**Mustelidae** (weasel family)
Family	**Mephitidae** (skunks)

Order - **Artiodactlya** (hoofed mammals)

Family	**Cervidae** (deer family)

Order - **Lagamorpha** (rabbits & hares)

Family	**Leporidae** (rabbits)

Order - **Rodentia** (rodents)

Family	**Sciuridae** (squirrel family)
Family	**Geomyidae** (gophers)
Family	**Castoridae** (beaver)
Family	**Muridae** (rats & mice)
Family	**Dipodidae** (jumping mice)

Order - **Soricomorpha** (moles & shrews)

Family	**Soricidae** (shrews)
Family	**Talpidae** (moles)

Order - **Chiroptera** (bats)

Family	**Vespertililionidae** (other bats)

Class - **Mammalia** (mammals)

Order - **Didelphimorphia** (opossums)	Order - **Cingulata**
Family - **Didelphidae**	Family - **Dasypodidae** (armadillos)
Virginia Opossum *Didelphis virginiana*	**Armadillo** *Dasypus novemcinctus*

Size: About 2.5 feet from nose to tail tip. Males can weigh up to 14 pounds, females are smaller.

Presumed range in Illinois

Abundance: Very common. In fact this is one of the most common medium sized mammals in Illinois.

Variation: Opossums are quite variable. In most, the fur is grizzled gray (as in photo above). All white or all black individuals can also occur, along with a cinnamon color.

Size: About 30 inches from snout to tail tip. Can weigh up to 17 pounds.

Presumed range in Illinois

Abundance: Still fairly rare in Illinois, but increasing numbers of Armadillos are being seen in the state.

Variation: There is no significant variation in Armadillos and no subspecies in America. The sexes look alike but males are somewhat larger than females.

Habitat: Virtually all habitats within the state are utilized. Including suburban and even urban areas where there is enough vegetative cover. Opossums are more common in areas altered by humans, such as farmlands and the vicinity of small, rural communities. They are less common in areas of true wilderness.

Habitat: This wide-ranging animal's habitat includes everything from tropical rain forest to arid semi-desert, grassland, and temperate forests. Moist or sandy soils are preferred as they facilitate easier digging of denning burrows as well as rooting for soil invertebrates. In Illinois presently restricted mostly to the southern part of the state.

Breeding: This is America's only member of the mammalian subclass Marsupialia. Young Opossums are born as embryos only 12 days after conception. The newborn babies are just over 0.5 inch in length. At 1 month, they are about the size of a mouse. Litters are large (up to 13) and 2 litters per year is common.

Breeding: Females always give birth to 4 identical twins, all derived from a single fertilized egg that divides in 2, then divides again to form 4 zygotes before beginning to then develop into individual embryos. The young are well developed at birth, which reduces mortality among immatures. 1 litter per year is typical.

Natural History: Opossums are one of the most successful medium size mammals in America, which is somewhat surprising given that they are slow-moving, rather dim-witted animals that rarely survive beyond 2 years in the wild. They are mainly nocturnal and eat most any palatable plant matter (seeds, grains, fruits, berries); and any type of meat they can catch or scavenge. They are known to kill and eat venomous snakes and have a strong resistance to pit viper venoms. They are well known for faking death (playing possum) when stressed. They have strong nocturnal tendencies but they are sometimes active during the day, especially when breeding. When hard pressed they will climb to escape. In trees, they use their prehensile tail to compensate for their somewhat clumsy climbing. Their greatest enemy today is the automobile. Thousands are killed nightly on highways across America.

Natural History: Armadillos first began their northern expansion into the US from Mexico about 150 years ago. 100 years later there were still no records from Illinois, although they were then found as far north as west Tennessee. Today increasing numbers are being seen in southern Illinois. Occasional road-killed specimens from more northerly regions of Illinois may represent stowaways on trains or trucks, or more likely, individuals that have been purposely transported by people. How far north they will spread is unknown. Cold climates may be a limiting factor to their spread. Surprisingly, Armadillos are capable of swimming and they are also known to hold their breath and "bottom walk" short distance across small streams. They are known to sometimes carry the ancient disease of leprosy and have been used in leprosy research.

Class - Mammalia (mammals)

Order - Carnivora (carnivores)

Family - **Procyonidae** (raccon, ringtail, coatis)	Family - **Felidae** (cats)

Raccoon
Procyon lotor

Bobcat
Lynx rufus

Size: Up to 2.5 feet in length. Weights of 15 to 30 pounds. Record 62 pounds. Females are smaller than males.

Presumed range in Illinois

Abundance: Common to very common. Can even be found in urban and suburban environments with cover in the form of trees and shrubs.

Variation: There is little variation in Illinois specimens. A few black indivuals occur occasionally. Most resemble the photo above. As many as 25 subspecies.

Habitat: Found in virtually every habitat in the state, but wetlands, stream courses, and lake shores are favorite haunts.

Breeding: Breeds in late winter with an average of 4 (maximum of 8) young born 2 months later (April or May). Young begin to accompany the mother on foraging trips at about 2 months. They are on their own by 5 months.

Natural History: Raccoons are omnivores that feed on a wide variety of crustaceans, insects, amphibians, reptiles, small mammals, and eggs as well as grains, berries, fruits, acorns, weed seeds, and some vegetables. Although they are mainly nocturnal, they are often active by day, especially in morning and late afternoons. During particularly harsh weather, they may den for days at a time. Summer dens are often tree hollows while old groundhog burrows may be used during the winter. In Illinois, the Raccoon is an important game animal harvested for its fur and to a lesser extent as food. More often they are hunted just for sport and released unharmed after being treed by hounds. Like many other mammals, Raccoons are subject to an interesting phenomena known as "Bergman's Rule." Bergman's rule states that the body size of mammals tends to be larger the farther north the species is found. This phenonmena is the result of the fact that larger bodies are capable of retaining more heat. A really big male Raccoon from northern North America may top the scales at 40 pounds. Meanwhile an adult male Raccoon in Florida may weigh only 10 to 12 pounds.

Size: Length up to 3 feet. Weighs 15 to 35 pounds. Maximum of about 45 pounds. Females are smaller than males.

Presumed range in Illinois

Abundance: Uncommon in Illinois, but recently increasing in numbers. Most common in southern Illinois but could possibly be seen statewide.

Variation: Several subspecies occur in America but there is little variation in Illinois. Some specimens have more pronounced spotting to their fur.

Habitat: Rugged, remote woodlands and impenetrable swamps are preferred sanctuaries.

Breeding: Most breeding occurs in winter or spring with an average of 3 or 4 young born 2 months later. Young Bobcats begin to forage with the mother by late summer and may stay with her for up to a year while perfecting hunting skills.

Natural History: Strictly a meat eater, the Bobcat's food items range from mice to deer. Cottontail Rabbits are a favorite prey as are squirrels, young turkeys, and songbirds. Hunts by ambush or stalking to within close range and making an explosive attack. Although mainly nocturnal, Bobcats can be abroad at any time of day. Their home range can be from one to several square miles, and males have larger ranges than females. Scent marking territory with urine and feces is common. In captivity, Bobcats have lived for over 20 years, but the estimate for wild cats is 12 to 14 years. This species has just begun to return to much of Illinois after being completely extirpated over a hundred years ago. Off and on reports of occasional specimens persisted over the years but stable, breeding populations have only recently begun to return to the state. The range map above shows the species as occurring statewide today, but it is likely still absent from many areas of the state, especially in regions of intensive agriculture and urban areas. They may rarely be seen almost statewide in rural regions where there are large tracts of woodland, swampland, or protected natural habitats.

Class - **Mammalia** (mammals)

Order - **Carnivora** (carnivores)

Family - **Canidae** (canines)

Gray Fox	Red Fox	Coyote
Urocyon cinereoargenteus	*Vulpes vulpes*	*Canis latrans*

Gray Fox

Size: Length 32 to 45 inches. Weight up to 15 pounds.

Presumed range in Illinois

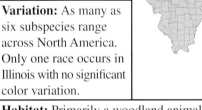

Abundance: Fairly common.

Variation: As many as six subspecies range across North America. Only one race occurs in Illinois with no significant color variation.

Habitat: Primarily a woodland animal that is more common in the forested regions of the state. Tends to avoid expansive open regions like farmlands and prairies.

Breeding: Dens in a burrow, hollow log, or rock cave. 4 pups is usual but up to 7 is known.

Natural History: The Gray Fox is the only American canine with the ability to climb trees. Insects are important food items in summer with mice and rabbits becoming more important in winter. When grapes, persimmons, and other fruits are ripe, they will eat them almost exclusively and in fact this is the most omnivorous canine in America. Home range can vary from a few hundred acres to over a square mile, depending upon habitat quality. Unlike the Red Fox that can be found as far north as the arctic circle, the Gray Fox is a more southerly animal and ranges southward into South America. Gray Foxes have lived for up to 14 years in captivity, but the average life span in the wild is only a few years. Contrary to popular belief, Gray Foxes never interbreed with Red Foxes.

Red Fox

Size: Length 33 to 43 inches. Weight up to 15 pounds.

Presumed range in Illinois

Abundance: Fairly common.

Variation: Red Foxes can occur in several different color phases, the best known of which are red, silver, and cross fox.

Habitat: Although habitat generalists, Red Foxes shows a preference for open and semi-open country over deep woods. In Illinois, they are probably more common in the glaciated regions of the state.

Breeding: About 4 to 5 young are born underground, often in an old groundhog burrow, but they will dig their own hole.

Natural History: The Red Fox is one of the world's most widespread mammals and is found in Europe, Asia, north Africa, and Australia (introduced) as well as throughout North America. They are adaptable, opportunistic omnivores that will eat everything from grasshoppers to grapes. Scavenging carrion is also common. Their fur is such a good insulator that they can sleep atop a snow bank without melting the snow beneath their body. These are important fur-bearing animals and are today often reared in captivity on "fur farms." Red Fox populations have probably increased since European settlement and subsequent clearing of forests for agriculture. The short, summer coat is paler than the luxurious winter fur. All color phases have a white tail tip.

Coyote

Size: Length up to 49 inches. Average about 35 pounds.

Presumed range in Illinois

Abundance: Fairly common.

Variation: Very dark individuals and reddish specimens are known to occur. Most specimens will resemble the photo above.

Habitat: Coyotes have adapted to all habitats in Illinois, but they are most common in the more open agricultural areas in the in the glaciated regions of the state. Occasionally adapts to urban parks.

Breeding: Coyotes are able to breed before their first birthday. Litter size (2 to 10) varies with availability of prey.

Natural History: The Coyote is a relative newcomer to Illinois, having begun their invasion from the west about a half century ago. Today they range all the way to the Atlantic. They are the top predator in much of the state, occupying a niche once held by the wolf and the Cougar. They are extremely intelligent, adaptable canines that quickly learn to thrive in almost any environment. In rural areas where hunters abound they are extremely wary, but in urban areas or protected lands they may become quite bold around humans. The characteristic yipping and howling of these vocal canines has become a common nighttime sound in rural Illinois. Mostly nocturnal, but also active by day. The longevity record is 18 years for a specimen in captivity.

Class - **Mammalia** (mammals)
Order - **Carnivora** (carnivores)
Family - **Mustelidae** (weasel family)

Mink *Mustela vison*	Long-tailed Weasel *Mustela frenata*	Least Weasel *Mustela nivalis*
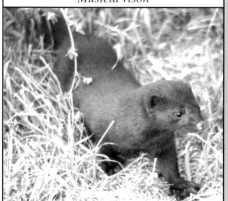	Summer pelage	Summer pelage

Mink	**Long-tailed Weasel**	**Least Weasel**
Size: 20 to 27 inches in length. Weighs 2 to 3 pounds. Presumed range in Illinois	**Size:** 12 to 15 inches from snout to tail tip. Weighs 6 to 11 ounces. Presumed range in Illinois	**Size:** 7 inches. Weighs about 1.5 ounces. Presumed range in Illinois 
Abundance: Fairly common.	**Abundance:** Uncommon.	**Abundance:** Uncommon to rare.
Variation: Males are twice as large as females. Pelage color varies from light brown to very dark brown.	**Variation:** Males are nearly twice the size of females. Specimens in northernmost US may turn white in winter.	**Variation:** Specimens from farther north turn white in winter. Males are about one-third larger than females.
Habitat: Swamps and marshes are the primary habitat. Also frequents creeks, rivers, and lake shores.	**Habitat:** Occupies a wide variety of habitats but favors being near stream courses.	**Habitat:** Avoids deep woods and lives mostly in or around the edges of fields and marshes.
Breeding: 3 to 6 young are born in an underground den that is often an old muskrat house. Young begin to hunt with mother at about 2 months.	**Breeding:** Mating occurs in midsummer but embryo development is delayed until the following spring. 4 to 5 young is typical, and babies have white fur.	**Breeding:** Breeds throughout the year and can produce 2 litters per year of 1 to 6 young. Young develop quickly and can hunt on their own in 6 weeks.
Natural History: Mink are well-known for their luxurious fur. Most mink fur sold in America today is from captive, farm-raised mink. Mink are excellent swimmers and will catch fish in stream pools. They are strict carnivores that feed heavily on amphibians and crayfish during the summer. In winter, their diet turns to mammal prey such as rabbits and rodents. Muskrats are a favorite winter food of the large males who kill their formidable prey with a bite to the back of the neck. As with other members of the Mustelidae family, mink have well-developed musk glands that produce a distinct musky odor when the animal is excited, breeding, or marking territory. The range of the mink extends from the southeastern United States all the way to Alaska, including most of Canada.	**Natural History:** Weasels are known for being, on a pound per pound basis, one of the world's most ferocious predators. Although their prey includes animals as small as insects, they will also take prey the size of a grown Cottontail Rabbit. Mice, voles, and other rodents, along with shrews and small birds make up the bulk of their non-invertebrate diet. Of these, voles are a favorite prey and may make up as much as three-fourths of the diet. They have also been known to scavenge the dead bodies of large animals such as deer. These highly active mammals have a high metabolic rate and they are active by both day and night, consuming up to one third of their body weight in a day. When an animal is killed that is too large to consume at one meal, they will cache the remains and return to finish it later.	**Natural History:** This is one of the world's smallest carnivores. Their tiny, elongated bodies allow them to maneuver easily into rodent burrows, and mice and voles are their primary prey. They hunt day and night, alternating hunts with short naps. They are active year-round and their rapid metabolism means they must consume one-half of their body weight each day. When the opportunity presents, they will kill more than they can eat and store the extra food for later. They are known to line their nest with mouse fur or bird feathers from their prey. Few will ever see this tiny, secretive little predator. In Illinois, they are found only in the northern portion of the state. Winter pelage in Illinois varies from solid white to white with patches of brown. Summer pelage is brown.

Class - **Mammalia** (mammals)

Order - **Carnivora** (carnivores)

Family - **Mustelidae** (weasels)		Family - **Mephitidae** (skunks)

River Otter	Badger	Striped Skunk
Lutra canadensis	*Taxidea taxus*	*Mephitis mephitis*

River Otter		Badger		Striped Skunk	
Size: Length 35 to 45 inches. Up to 25 pounds.	Presumed range in Illinois 	**Size:** To 30 inches. Males to 24 pounds, females smaller.	Presumed range in Illinois	**Size:** Length 23 to 31 inches. Average weight about 8 to 10 pounds.	Presumed range in Illinois 
Abundance: Uncommon in Illinois.		**Abundance:** Uncommon in Illinois.		**Abundance:** Common.	
Variation: As many 7 subspecies range across North America. There is very little variation in Illinois specimens.		**Variation:** No significant variation occurs in this species in Illinois. Males are larger than females.		**Variation:** Varies considerably in the amount of white in the dorsal stripes. Can be nearly all white or solid black.	

Habitat: Any unpolluted aquatic habitat in the state may be suitable for River Otters. They are always in association with rivers, lakes, swamps, or creeks.	**Habitat:** The Badger is primarily an animal of the prairie. They will frequent open pastures and grassy areas in search of ground squirrels, voles, etc.	**Habitat:** Striped Skunks are found in all habitats in Illinois, but they are most common in mixed, semi-open habitats and edge areas.
Breeding: 2 or 3 young are born in an underground den often dug in a stream bank. Births are usually in the spring or summer.	**Breeding:** Breeds in midsummer, with young born in early spring. Average number of young is 2 or 3 but can be as many as 6 or 7.	**Breeding:** Breeding occurs in late winter. Litter size averages 3 or 4 but can be as many as 10. Weanlings follow the mother in single file while foraging.

Natural History: River Otters are semi-aquatic mammals that possess fully webbed toes and waterproof fur. They are excellent swimmers that prey on fish, frogs, crayfish, turtles, and small mammals. Their fur is highly valued, a fact that led to their extirpation from most of the eastern US by the late 1800s. Restocking programs by by state wildlife agencies throughout the Midwest have been successful and today these endearing animals can once again be found in many areas of the Illinois. Although there are still parts of the state where they may not yet have colonized, it is reasonable to consider their range today as being nearly statewide in suitable habitats along the major river drainages. A limited trapping season began in Illinois in 2012 and the species appears secure in the state today.

Natural History: The Badger is a digging machine. It possess long claws, powerful forelegs, and a specialized structure of the eye known as a "nictitating membrane" which keeps dirt from entering the eye sockets. Badgers feed mostly by digging small mammals from their underground burrows. Ground squirrels and gophers are the favorite prey, but almost any type of animal may be eaten, including carrion. In the western US, Badgers have been observed hunting cooperatively with Coyotes. The Coyote guards the escape holes (and catches a few fleeing animals), while the Badger benefits from having the Coyote blocking the escape route long enough for the Badger to dig out the hapless ground squirrel or gopher. Abandoned Badger dens are utilized by a wide variety of other animals.

Natural History: The Striped Skunk's distinctive black and white color is almost as well-known as its primary defense, which of course is to spray an attacker with its pungent, foul-smelling musk. The musk can burn the eyes and membranes, and its odor is remarkably persistent. They can effectively project the musk up to about 15 feet and the odor can be detected hundreds of yards away. A direct hit to the face from the musk glands can cause debilitating nausea and temporary blindness. Striped Skunks dine mainly on invertebrates and as much 75 percent of their diet consists of insects and grubs. They possess well-developed front claws for digging and a powerful sense of smell for locating buried grubs, worms, turtle eggs, etc. Also eats baby mice, eggs, and nestlings of ground nesting birds.

Class - **Mammalia** (mammals)
Order - **Artiodactyla** (hoofed mammals)
Family - **Cervidae** (deer family)
Whitetail Deer - *Odocoileus virginianus*   Buck Doe Fawn

Size: Males up to 40 inches high at shoulder. Females about 20 percent smaller. Mature males can weigh over 200 pounds, females up to 150, though most are smaller. Deer from the northernmost regions of Illinois have larger body size than those in the southern parts of the state. This is due to a phenomena known as "Bergman's Rule." Larger bodies lose heat less rapidly due to the smaller ratio of body volume to surface area, thus in colder regions mammals with a larger body size tend to survive better.

Presumed range in Illinois

Abundance: Very common.

Variation: There are as many as 13 different subspecies of Whitetail Deer recognized in mainland North America, plus several more island races. The Illinois subspecies is the Northern Woodland Whitetail Deer, *Odocoileus virginianus borealis.* Young (fawns) exhibit a pattern of white spots that fade with age. Adults have reddish brown color in the summer and grayish in the fall/winter.

Habitat: Found in virtually every habitat within the state and increasingly common in urban areas. Favorite habitats are a mix of woodland, brushy areas, and weedy fields, especially near farmlands. Successional areas, such as regrowth of woodlands after fires or logging, is also a prime habitat. In Illinois, deer are more common where there is a mixture of agricultural land and woodlands. They are least common in mature, unbroken forests and in areas of intensive agriculture or major urbanization.

Breeding: Breeding begins in early fall and may continue into the winter, with the peak breeding season occurring in November. 1 or 2 (rarely 3 or even 4) young are born in the spring or early summer following a 6-and-a-half-month gestation. Females (does) usually bear their first offspring at 2 years of age. The first pregnancy typically results in a single fawn, the second pregnancy usually is twins, and the third through fifth twins or triplets (rarely quadruplets). Young lie hidden for the first few weeks and are left alone much of the time. The female will visit the hidden fawn about once every 4 hours to allow nursing, then moves away to avoid attracting predators. At about 1 month of age the young will begin to follow the mother and stay close through the summer and into the fall.

Natural History: Bucks (males) shed their antlers each year in late winter and regrow a new set by fall. Growing deer antlers are among the fastest growing animal tissue known. While growing, the antlers are covered in a spongy, fuzzy skin called "velvet." Antlers grow larger each year up to about 6 or 7 years of age, when they begin a gradual decline. Whitetail Deer are browsers and they feed on a wide variety of forbs, leaves, twigs, buds, crops, and mast (especially acorns). Although they are sometimes destructive to farm crops like corn or soybeans, they are an important game animal in Illinois with as many as 144,000 harvested in 2017 for food and sport. The maximum life span is 20 years, but most are dead by age 10. State wildlife agencies like the Illinois Department of Natural Resources are charged with the responsibility of protecting and managing the state's wildlife populations. In Illinois, this means taking into consideration not only the health and well-being of the state's deer herd, but also the cultural aspect of providing food and recreation for the state's hunting population. Additionally, considerations such as crop depredation by deer to the state's farmers, impacts on auto insurance rates by deer-auto collisions, etc. Thus determining how many deer of what sex should be harvested annually involves taking into consideration many factors. Happily, this animal represents one of the world's great wildlife conservation stories. Nearly wiped out by the early 1900s, the Whitetail Deer is today as numerous in America as it was during the time of Daniel Boone. At present, the population in Illinois numbers nearly three quarters of a million deer. Up from a low of only a few thousand a century ago. In recent years these animals have begun to invade urban areas where deer hunting is restricted. In towns and cities they can become a nuisance as they feed in suburban gardens and devour landscape plants. Still, many urban dwellers enjoy their presence.

Class - **Mammalia** (mammals)

Order - **Lagomorpha** (lagamorphs)

Family - **Leporidae** (rabbits, hares)

Eastern Cottontail *Sylvilagus floridanus*	**Swamp Rabbit** *Sylvilagus aquaticus*

Size: Adult length about 17 inches. Weight up to 2.5 pounds.

Size: Adults reach about 20 inches and weigh as much as 5 pounds.

Presumed range in Illinois

Abundance: Typically very common, but populations fluctuate on about 10-year cycles. During years of high abundance they can be extremely common.

Abundance: Uncommon to rare in Illinois. Can be fairly common in some swamplands in southern Illinois, especially along the lower Mississippi and lower Cache Rivers.

Variation: No variation in Illinois, but at least 12 very similar subspecies of this wide ranging rabbit are recognized across the United States.

Variation: No variation in Illinois. There is another subspecies that inhabits the southwestern Gulf Coastal Plain. Illinois Swamp Rabbits are subspecies *aquaticus*.

Habitat: May be found in virtually any habitat within the state except for permanent wetlands. Most common in overgrown fields and edge areas. Fond of briers, honeysuckle, and tall weeds.

Habitat: Swamps, marshes, and bottomlands in the southern tip of the state. Most common in the Deep South, and southern Illinois represents the northernmost extension of the range of this species.

Breeding: Has an amazing reproductive capacity. In fact, this is the most prolific of the 7 rabbit species in America, producing up to 7 litters per year with as many as 5 young per litter.

Breeding: Much less prolific than its smaller cousin the Cottontail. Breeds January through August. 3 young is typical after a 37-day gestation period. Averages 2 litters per year.

Natural History: In the spring and summer, Eastern Cottontails feed on a wide variety of grasses, legumes, and herbaceous weeds. Briers, sapling bark, and other woody materials may make up the bulk of the diet in winter. They can become a nuisance in fruit orchards, where they will eat the bark of sapling fruit trees during the winter. These rabbits are prey for many predators including foxes, coyotes, bobcats, hawks, and owls, especially the Great Horned Owl. Humans hunt them as well and they are one of the most sought-after small game animals in America. Many people regard their flesh as highly palatable, and the German dish known as "Hasenpfeffer" is made from rabbit. The life expectancy for a Cottontail is not high, and only about 1 in 4 will live to see their second birthday. Populations are known to fluctuate, and during years when their numbers are highest, there may be as many as 9 rabbits per acre in good habitat.

Natural History: An excellent swimmer, the Swamp Rabbit will elude hunters hounds by diving into water and swimming for a long distance. This is the largest of the "true" rabbits in America (not including jackrabbits and hares). They are as much as twice as large as the various species of Cottontails. The range of this species has diminished with the loss of wetlands both in Illinois and throughout its core range in the southeast. The occurrence of the Swamp Rabbit in wetlands is easily detected by the presence of droppings on floating logs within the swamp. They are mostly nocturnal but will be active at dusk or even afternoon in warm weather. These large rabbits have correspondly larger ranges than the small Eastern Cottontail and their home range can exceed 10 acres. By contrast the Eastern Cottontail will typically have a home range of less than 3 acres. Bobcats and Horned Owls are probably the biggest predator of swamp rabbits in most areas.

Class - **Mammalia** (mammals)

Order - **Rodentia** (rodents)

Family - **Sciuridae** (squirrel family)

Eastern Chipmunk *Tamias striatus*	**Gray Squirrel** *Sciurus carolinensis*	**Fox Squirrel** *Sciurus niger*
		Black morph 

Eastern Chipmunk	Gray Squirrel	Fox Squirrel
Size: About 10 inches and 4.5 ounces.  Presumed range in Illinois	**Size:** 19 inches and about 1 pounds, 2 ounces.  Presumed range in Illinois	**Size:** 23 inches and about 1 pounds, 12 ounces.  Presumed range in Illinois
Abundance: Fairly common.	**Abundance:** Very common.	**Abundance:** Common.
Habitat: Deciduous forests in upland areas. Avoids wetlands. Fond of rock outcrops, stone fences, etc. Common in urban parks.	**Habitat:** Prefers mature deciduous forests but also found in mixed coniferous forests and second growth areas as well as urban parks.	**Habitat:** Prefers open forests with trees widely spaced and edge areas, overgrown fence rows, etc. Can be common in swamps.
Variation: There are between 5 and 8 subspecies nationwide (experts disagree on the exact number). 2 subspecies are recognized in Illinois but the differences between the subspecies is very subtle and apparent only to trained mammologists. The specimen shown above is a good representative.	**Variation:** At least 6 subspecies occur in the US and some are quite variable. Melanistic (black) populations can be found in some areas of the northern US and albino populations occur in a few locations in Illinois. Some may have reddish brown tails but most resemble the specimen pictured above.	**Variation:** There are a total of 10 subspecies nationwide and they range in color from solid black to reddish to silver-gray. *S. n. rufiventer* occurs in Illinois. Most are like the shown standing specimen above, but solid black color morphs can be seen in some areas of the state (see inset photo).
Breeding: May breed twice per year, first in February and again in April. Produces 4 to 5 young per litter.	**Breeding:** Breeds December through February and again in June/July. 4 to 6 young per litter.	**Breeding:** Produces 4 to 6 young twice annually, breeding in winter and again in summer.
Natural History: While they are excellent climbers, chipmunks are true "ground squirrels," sleeping, rearing young, and wintering in an underground burrow which they dig themselves. They also will use rock crevices or hollow logs. They become less active in winter and will remain below ground living on stored nuts and seeds for long periods during harsh weather. Although Chipmunks are fairly common in much of Illinois, they are usually absent from expansive open areas and areas of extensive agriculture. Like other squirrels, the chipmunk is a vocal animal but its voice is less raspy, sounding at times like the chirping of a bird.	**Natural History:** Feeds on nuts, seeds, fungi, tree buds, and the inner bark of trees as well as bird eggs and hatch-lings. May sometimes even eat carrion. Like most rodents, they will gnaw bones or shed deer antlers for calcium. Well-known for burying and storing nuts. Frequently calls with a raspy "bark," especially when alarmed. Builds summer nests of leaves in tree crotches. Winter dens are in tree hollows. During severe weather may be inactive for several days. Poor mast years may produce mass migrations. Gray Squirrels are extremely athletic little animals and exhibit remarkable agility in trees. They are strictly a woodland animal.	**Natural History:** Fox Squirrels wander frequently into open areas and spend more time on the ground than Gray Squirrels. Their home range is much larger. They are generally less common than the Gray, rarely reaching the population densities of their smaller cousins. In some areas of Illinois, however, they may be more common than the Gray Squirrel, especially in semi-open country. They feed on the same foods of nuts, seeds, buds, berries, etc. But the diet of Fox Squirrels also often includes the seeds of pine cones. Barks and chatters when disturbed but is overall less vocal than the smaller squirrel species which occur in Illinois.

Class - **Mammalia** (mammals)

Order - **Rodentia** (rodents)

Family - **Sciuridae** (squirrel family)

Red Squirrel *Tamiasciurus hudsonicus*	Thirteen-line Ground Squirrel *Spermophilus tridecemlineatus*	Franklin's Ground Squirrel *Spermophilus franklinii*

Size: 12 inches and about 6 ounces. **Abundance:** Uncommon in Illinois. **Variation:** Summer pelage is duller and less red and the prominent "ear tufts" are only seen in fall and winter squirrels.	Presumed range in Illinois 	**Size:** 12 inches and 5 to 8 ounces. **Abundance:** Fairly common in northern Illinois. **Variation:** No variation. They are remarkably similar throughout their range which includes the Midwest and the entire Great Plains.	Presumed range in Illinois 	**Size:** To 15 inches and 34 ounces. **Abundance:** Rare in Illinois. **Habitat:** A grassland species that prefers taller grasses than the smaller Thirteen-lined Ground Squirrel. Burrow is on high ground.	Presumed range in Illinois 

Habitat: Like most tree squirrels, this is a forest species. Any type of northern forest may be inhabited, including deciduous and mixed, but conifer forests are where they are most common.	**Habitat:** Natural habitats are prairies and sandy grasslands. Today, pastures, golf courses, cemeteries, lawns, and even highway right of ways are utilized. Prefers areas of short, sparse grass.	**Variation:** No significant variation and there are apparently no subspecies. Among adults, males are slightly larger than females. Young Squirrels undergo a molt from juvenile to adult pelage.
Breeding: Capable of producing 2 broods per year. 3 to 5 young is typical. In years of good mast crops, they may produce larger litters of 7 or 8.	**Breeding:** Mating takes place soon after emerging from hibernation. The average of 6 to 8 young are blind and naked at birth. They wean at 6 weeks.	**Breeding:** Produces and average of 7 or 8 young born in May. Baby squirrels are hairless and with eyes closed but will be mature by October.
Natural History: Like most tree squirrels, the Red Squirrel is diurnal in habits. While most people find them to be endearing little animals, others regard them as pests and there is a widespread myth among squirrel hunters that Red Squirrels will attack and castrate the males of the more desirable (from the hunters' point of view) Gray Squirrel. Red Squirrels will store huge piles of conifer cones, usually at the base of large tree. These piles are known as "middens" and they can attain an enormous size. Piles 15 feet across and 3 feet high have been recorded. The range of the Red Squirrel includes all of Canada except the Arctic and the Great Plains, and all the northern US and south in the Appalachians to Georgia.	**Natural History:** Although they often go by the nickname "Striped Gopher," the Thirteen-lined Ground Squirrel is a member of the Squirrel Family and not very closely related to the true gophers that inhabit parts of Illinois. This species may have expanded its range from presettlement days. Cutting of forests and clearing of land for agriculture and other human uses seems to have benefited this open country species. They are confirmed burrowers that may excavate several tunnels, which can be 6 feet in length and over a foot deep. Below ground, hibernation begins in October and lasts about 6 months. In addition to grasses and clovers, they will eat seeds and some insects. Range in Illinois is restricted to areas with deep topsoils.	**Natural History:** Although the Franklin's Ground Squirrel is widespread across northern Illinois, it seems to be a rather rare species with spotty distribution. It is often most common along old railroad tracks where the elevated road bed provides an bit of high ground for the burrow. They are diurnal in habits and are primarily vegetarians, but they will eat a wide variety of insects and animal matter, including carrion, often roadkill. These squirrels are not commonly observed in part because they spend so much time in their burrow. They have a rather long period of hibernation that may be more than half the year. In Illinois, they are active from April to early September. Even in summer they spend much time underground.

Class - **Mammalia** (mammals)		
Order - **Rodentia** (rodents)		
Family - **Sciuridae** (squirrel family)		Family - **Geomyidae** (gophers)

Flying Squirrel *Glaucomys volans*	**Groundhog** *Marmota monax*	**Plains Pocket Gopher** *Geomys bursarius*

Size: 10 inches and 2 to 3 ounces.	Presumed range in Illinois 	**Size:** 16 to 26 inches and 6 to 9 pounds.	Presumed range in Illinois 	**Size:** 10 inches and 6.5 ounces.	Presumed range in Illinois
Abundance: Fairly common.		**Abundance:** Common.		**Abundance:** Uncommon in Illinois.	
Variation: There is little variation and the sexes are alike. As many as 8 subspecies nationwide but differences are very subtle.		**Variation:** Individuals vary in color from brown to grayish, reddish, or rarely, nearly black. Most resemble the specimen shown.		**Variation:** There is little variation in Illinois, but Illinois specimens are much darker than populations found elsewhere.	

Habitat: These little squirrels are totally dependent upon trees and make their home in woodlands. Primarily hardwoods but also in mixed pine-hardwood forests. They will live in suburbs and urban areas if sufficient mature trees are present	**Habitat:** Fields and woodland edges. The main habitat requirements are some open ground within the vicinity of the burrow for foraging, as well as some higher ground that is above the floodplain for locating the burrow. They avoid swamps and permanent wetlands.	**Habitat:** Pocket Gophers require loose, loamy, or sandy soils which facilitate easy burrowing. Avoids wet soil regions and fields that are regularly plowed. Will utilize pastures, and in Illinois, are reported to occupy hayfields (especially alfalfa fields).
Breeding: Only 1 litter per year with up to 6 young. Nest is usually within a hollow in a tree. Bluebird boxes and other artificial nest sites are also used.	**Breeding:** Mating occurs in spring with 2 to 4 young typical. 1 litter per year. Young are born below ground and remain there for about 6 weeks.	**Breeding:** Litter size is reported to be as many as 7 or as few as single baby. Young are mature in about 3 months.
Natural History: Dens in tree hollows and old woodpecker holes. Our only nocturnal squirrel. Leaps from tree to tree and glides using flaps of skin between front and hind legs like a parachute. Flattened tail serves as a rudder while gliding. Feeds on nuts, seeds, fruits, fungi, lichens, tree buds, insects, bird eggs, and nestling birds as well as mice. Flying Squirrels are gregarious animals and several may share a den. They can live up to 10 years and will become quite tame in captivity, making reasonable pets. Wild squirrels in rural areas sometimes invade homes and attics where they can become a noisy nuisance as they scramble about in the wee hours.	**Natural History:** These large ground squirrels dig extensive underground burrows where they retreat from danger, spend the night, and overwinter. They accumulate huge deposits of fat during the summer and fall, which sustains them during winter hibernation. During this time, their metabolism slows dramatically with as few as 4 heartbeats per minute. They will sometimes climb small trees and bushes in springtime to eat swelling tree buds, but their primary diet is forbs and grasses. Except during breeding or when rearing, young they are solitary animals and typically only 1 adult occupies a burrow. They can become pests in rural gardens or farmers' croplands.	**Natural History:** Pocket Gopers are truly fossorial mammals that spend nearly all their life in their elaborate underground burrow systems. Burrows up to 500 feet in total length have been recorded. They have well-developed claws on their front feet and very powerful forelimbs for excavation their burrows. Their enlarged incisor teeth are used mainly to sever roots, but are also adapted to allow them to literally chew their way through harder soils. Foods are mostly tuberous roots of a wide variety of forbs, but some leaves are also eaten. These rodents are uncommon in Illinois today as much of their original habitats have been converted to row crops like corn and soybeans.

Class - **Mammalia** (mammals)

Order - **Rodentia** (rodents)

Family - **Castoridae** (beaver family)

Beaver - *Castor canadensis*	Beaver dam (top) - Beaver lodge (bottom)

Size: Up to 43 inches in total length. Can weigh up to 65 pounds.

Abundance: Common. Least common in upland regions, but even there it is common in river valleys and bottomlands.

Variation: The American Society of Mammologists recognizes 24 subspecies in North America. The status of Beavers in the eastern US is difficult to determine due to reintroduction programs using transplanted beavers.

Presumed range in Illinois

Habitat: Beavers are thoroughly aquatic mammals that to a great extent create their own wetland habitats. To construct their ponds and waterways, they require the presence of a stream or spring run with constant or near constantly flowing water which can be dammed. Streams that are subject to fierce flooding or with exceptionally powerful flows are avoided in preference for more easily contained water flows. In addition to creating their own habitats, they will use lakes, rivers, swamps, marshes, and large, deep creeks. In rivers and lakes, the lodge or den is often a burrow into the bank of the lake or river. In dammed streams or swamps and marshes, a stick lodge like the one pictured above is usual.

Breeding: Mating takes place in midwinter, with the young being born about 4 months later. There is only 1 litter per year. Baby beavers are quite precocious and are born with well-developed fur and eyes that open immediately. 4 or 5 young, called kits, is typical. In ideal habitats, more young may be produced. Young beavers are usually weaned in just 2 or 3 weeks, but the young Beavers will remain with the family for up to 2 years before striking out on their own to find new territories. Adult beavers may mate for life.

Natural History: Beavers are primarily nocturnal in habits, but they may be active at dawn and dusk. In remote locations where human intrusion is absent, they are observed active during the day as well. They feed mostly on the inner bark of trees, with willow being a dietary mainstay. They will also consume sedges and other aquatic vegetation, but in winter live exclusively on bark. The dorsal-ventrally flattened tail is hairless and scaly and along with the webbed hind feet provide these animals with powerful swimming tools. They also possess enlarged incisors which grow continually throughout life and are used to gnaw through trunks and fell trees. Most trees cut by Beavers are small saplings which are used as food, but they will also cut large trees up to 2 feet in diameter to open the canopy and promote the growth of new food sources. These largest of the North American rodents are famous for their dam-building abilities and they will also build elaborate living quarters known as "lodges." After many years of use, these lodges may become up to 15 feet across and can house an entire extended family. They have underwater entrances for protection and a hollow "room" that is above the water-line and lined with wood chips or grasses. Other species such as Muskrats and mice may take up residence within these lodges. At one time, Beaver fur was one of the most valuable natural resources in America and the pursuit of Beaver fur led to the exploration of much of the continent. Within a few decades, they were nearly exterminated by trappers. They can sometimes be a pest when their dam-building activities flood farmers' fields, but their wetland creating activities benefit many scores of wetland wildlife species. In fact, the Beaver is one of the most significant players in local ecosystems throughout North America and their value to the overall ecology would be hard to overstate.

Class - **Mammalia** (mammals)

Order - **Rodentia** (rodents)

Family - **Muridae** (rats & mice)

Muskrat *Ondatra zibethicus*	Eastern Woodrat *Neotoma floridana*	Norway Rat *Rattus norvigicus*

Size: 20 inches total length and weighs about 2.5 pounds.

Abundance: Common.

Variation: There is no significant variation among individuals in Illinois. Several subspecies occur elsewhere.

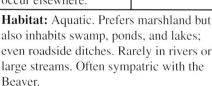
Presumed range in Illinois

Size: Adults reach 16 inches and about 12 ounces.

Abundance: Very rare. Endangered in Illinois.

Variation: There are no subspecies and no variation is known to occur in Illinois, or anywhere within its range.

Presumed range in Illinois

Size: Length can be as much as 15 inches and weigh up to 12 ounces.

Abundance: Very common.

Variation: None in the wild. The well-known laboratory rat is an albino form of this species.

Presumed range in Illinois

Habitat: Aquatic. Prefers marshland but also inhabits swamp, ponds, and lakes; even roadside ditches. Rarely in rivers or large streams. Often sympatric with the Beaver.

Habitat: Woodrats usually associate with rocks and cliff faces where they make their dens in crevices. They will also use logs, derelict buildings, etc. In Illinois uses limestone bluffs.

Habitat: This highly adaptable rodent can live virtually anywhere, including as a stowaway on ships, which is how it immigrated to America from Europe.

Breeding: Prolific. Capable of multiple litters annually and may produce as many as 6 young per litter. Young are weaned in about a month.

Breeding: Breeds spring through fall. 3 to 4 litters per year is possible with 2 young being typical. Litter sizes of up to 6 young have been recorded.

Breeding: The fecundity of the Norway Rat is legendary. From 6 to 8 litters per year with up to a dozen young per litter.

Natural History: Primarily nocturnal but often active during daylight hours in the spring. With webbed hind feet and a laterally flattened tail, muskrats are excellent swimmers. They feed on a variety of aquatic vegetation. The name comes from the presence of well-developed musk glands. These rodents are an important fur-bearer and in the recent past millions were trapped annually across America for their fur. Life span is only 3 to 4 years in the wild. The Mink may be the most important predator on muskrats, especially of the young. Adults build lodges similar to the Beaver, but use grasses rather than sticks. The entrance to the Muskrat lodge is below water level while the chamber of the lodge itself is above the high water mark. Sometimes burrows into banks.

Natural History: The range of this species in Illinois has shrunk to a very small area of limestone bluffs in the Pine Hills Natural Area. This isolated population is over 100 miles from the nearest populations in Missouri and Tennessee. Allegheny Woodrats favor rocky outcrops, talus slopes, boulder piles, and cliff faces where they make their den in crevices or small caves. They are sometimes known as "pack rats," a name derived from their habit of collecting shiny objects that range from aluminum cans to eating utensils. They cache food in large quantities in what are known as "middens." Ancient woodrat nests in caves can persist for centuries and are studied to gain insight into the historical natural history of a region. Dens are occupied by 1 adult (and young).

Natural History: Also called the Brown Rat, this species has followed man to every corner of the globe. They are responsible for an almost unimaginable degree of human suffering. Throughout the history of human civilization, these rodents have destroyed crops and stored foods while spreading devastating diseases, most notably Bubonic Plague. Though less of a threat to modern societies, these rats still shadow the human species. They are common in both urban and rural settings. In cities, they live on human garbage, in rural areas, livestock food and crops. The common laboratory rat is a domestic version of this animal that has somewhat redeemed the species for humans as an experimental animal for medical and scientific research.

Class - **Mammalia** (mammals)
Order - **Rodentia** (rodents)
Family - **Muridae** (rats & mice)

House Mouse *Mus musculus*	Deer Mouse *Peromyscus maniculatus*	White-footed Mouse *Peromyscus leucopus*

Size: 6.5 inches and about 0.75 of an ounce.

Abundance: Very common.

Habitat: A highly adaptable and successful rodent that usually associates with human habitations and man-made structures.

Presumed range in Illinois

Size: 5 to 8 inches and about 1 ounce.

Abundance: Fairly common.

Habitat: Deer Mice use open fields, including agricultural land. Can sometimes be found in wide-open, harvested crop fields.

Presumed range in Illinois

Size: 7 inches and about 1 ounce.

Abundance: Very common.

Habitat: White-footed Mice prefer the woods but may also be found in overgrown fields, fence rows, etc. These mice avoid open areas.

Presumed range in Illinois

Variation: Wild specimens show surprisingly little variation throughout the world, but domesticated laboratory mice come in a variety of colors and patterns. The most well-known color is solid white, and most of the "white mice" seen in labs and pet stores are albinos.

Variation: These 2 species are so similar that most people will not be able to tell them apart. The specimen shown is the White-footed Mouse, but the Deer Mouse (above left) is nearly identical. Both have several subspecies nationwide (over a dozen in the White-footed Mouse and over 50 in the Deer Mouse). In the Deer Mouse, short-tailed, small-eared forms are found in open fields and grasslands and a long-tailed, large-eared variant occurs in woodland habits. Both species exhibit some age-related color variation, with younger mice being darker, more grayish in color.

Breeding: Broods can number from 5 to 12. Young females begin breeding at 6 weeks and produce 14 litters per year.

Breeding: Both these species are prolific breeders that can breed nearly year-round. A typical litter is 4 or 5 young, but can be more. The young mice develop rapidly and are ready to breed themselves when only 2 months old.

Natural History: The House Mouse has adapted to living in close proximity to humans and today they are found wherever there are people throughout the world. As their name implies, they regularly enter into houses where they can become both a pest and a health hazard. They live both in cities and farmlands, and despite their prediliction for human habitations, they are quite capable of living in wilderness. Like the Norway Rat, the House Mouse originated in Eurasia and traveled around the world as a stowaway on sailing ships, eventually populating the entire globe. These mice are primarily nocturnal and their food includes nearly everything eaten by humans plus insects and fungi. The "lab mouse" is an albino version.

Natural History: These common mice serve as prey for a variety of predators, from coyotes and bobcats to weasels, snakes, and birds of prey. Both species are primarily nocturnal. They feed on a wide array of seeds, nuts, and grain as well as berries, insects, snails, centipedes, fungi, and occasionally other mice. One important food item is a fungus known as *Endogone* that is ubiquitous in the soil. They will cache large stores of seeds and nuts in the fall and they remain active throughout the winter. Both can become a nuisance as they will regularly enter human dwellings, often nesting in a little used drawer or cupboard. Several species of *Peromyscus* mice are vectors for tick-born Lyme disease, and in the southwestern United States, some Deer Mice can harbor the deadly Hanta Virus. Humans who experience close contact or prolonged exposure to their feces and urine may be at risk. Both species can be arboreal and they may den or nest well above the ground, or they may live beneath a rotted log or stump. Both are adaptable and successful native rodents. The Deer Mouse is found in every habitat type in America and ranges from near sea level to the high mountains. The White-footed Mouse is nearly as adaptable. Professional mammologists use measurements of the skull, tail, and hind foot to differentiate between these 2 similar and sympatrically occurring species. Together they constitute much of small mammal foods for many of Illinois' predators, and their role in local ecosystems is of great importance.

Class - **Mammalia** (mammals)

Order - **Rodentia** (rodents)

Family - **Muridae** (rats & mice)

Golden Mouse *Peromyscus nuttalli*	**Western Harvest Mouse** *Reithrodontomys megalotis*	**Rice Rat** *Oryzomy palustris*

Golden Mouse		**Western Harvest Mouse**		**Rice Rat**	
Size: Length about 6.5 inches and weighs 0.75 ounce.	Presumed range in Illinois 	**Size:** Length about 5.5 inches and weighs 0.4 of ounces.	Presumed range in Illinois 	**Size:** Up to 9 inches in length and weighing about 2.5 ounces.	Presumed range in Illinois 
Abundance: Rare. Threatened in Illinois.		**Abundance:** Common in northern Illinois.		**Abundance:** Rare. Threatened in Illinois.	
Variation: No variation among adults which are golden brown. Young mice are slightly grayer in color.		**Variation:** No significant varaiation among adults in Illinois. Young mice are darker, more grayish than adults.		**Variation:** No variation in Illinois specimens, but several subspecies are recognized in the southeastern US.	
Habitat: Favors edge areas where there is a profusion of vines such as honeysuckle and greenbriar. Conifers and cedars are often present in the mouse's habitat in Illinois.		**Habitat:** Favors areas of successional growth. Overgrown fields with rank growth of grass or weeds, remnants of Tallgrass Prairie habitats, old railroad beds, edge areas, etc.		**Habitat:** Prefers to be near water. Wet meadow, marsh, and the edges of swamps. Can also be found in uplands where high ground is in close proximity to wetlands.	
Breeding: Breeds from early spring through fall, producing several litters per year. 2 to 4 young is typical. Builds a grass nest above ground.		**Breeding:** Average litter size is 4. Babies are born naked and with their eyes closed but will be weaned and on their own within a month.		**Breeding:** Breeds several time per year and will breed year-round. 3 to 5 babies. Young will reach sexual maturity in 2 months.	
Natural History: Mainly nocturnal. Golden mice have strong arboreal tendencies. They use vines and limbs as highways and will forage for seeds both in the trees and on the ground. The nest is usually in a thicket of vines several feet off the ground. Acorns are also eaten as are invertebrates, and these mice are decidedly omnivorous. These are handsome little mice with fine, golden fur. Unlike many other mice species, the Golden Mouse rarely enters human habitations, preferring a more natural habitat. One captive individual was reported to have lived for 8 years, a very long life span for a mouse. The average life span in the wild is probably less than a year. A very handsome little mouse that is relatively unknown.		**Natural History:** Harvest Mice are very similar to several other mice species found in Illinois. Mammologists can quickly recognize the Harvest Mouse by examining the front incisors, which posses a groove not seen in other species of mice. Their food is thought to be mostly the seeds from various grasses, but they are known to feed on insects and larva as well. There is some belief that these mice have recently expanded their range in Illinois, and may have been rare in the state prior to European settlement. The fact that their favorite habitat is succesional areas means that human activities could have helped open habitat niches for the species in Illinois. Prior to European settlement, burning of grasslands by natives may have helped.		**Natural History:** The name Rice Rat comes from the prevalence of this species in rice fields throughout the southeast. In addition to rice, they consume several other types of seeds and plants but also eat large amounts of animal matter. In fact, this is one of the most carnivorous rodents in America. The list of animal prey includes insects, crustaceans, fish, and baby birds and bird eggs, to name a few. They are accomplished swimmers and will dive and swim underwater to escape a predator. They are also good climbers. They are strictly nocturnal in habits. As with most other rodents, they are preyed upon by a wide variety of raptors, carnivorous mammals, and especially, snakes.	

Class - **Mammalia** (mammals)

Order - **Rodentia** (rodents)

Family - **Muridae** (rats & mice)

Meadow Vole *Microtus pennslyvanicus*	**Woodland Vole** *Microtus pinetorum*	**Prairie Vole** *Microtus ochreogaster*

Meadow Vole	Woodland Vole	Prairie Vole
Size: About 6.5 inches in length and 1.75 ounces.	**Size:** Length can reach 5 inches. Weighs 1 ounce.	**Size:** As much as 6 inches in length and 1.5 ounces.
Abundance: Very common.	**Abundance:** Common.	**Abundance:** Fairly common.
Variation: None in Illinois. As many as 25 subspecies are recognized throughout North America.	**Variation:** 3 subspecies are recognized in Illinois, but differences are indistinguishable to the lay observer.	**Variation:** No significant variation among adults in Illinois. Young voles are usually darker in color.
Habitat: Primarily fields and meadows from the northern US to the Arctic Circle. Shows a preference for damp meadows.	**Habitat:** Primarily deciduous woodlands but also found in mixed hardwood/conifer forests. May sometimes found in overgrown fields.	**Habitat:** This species generally avoids the woods and prefers open, grassy habitats and overgrown fields. Unlike the Meadow Vole, uses dry upland fields.
Breeding: A remarkably fecund animal, young Meadow Voles can breed within 4 weeks after birth. Litter size is 4 to 6.	**Breeding:** Breeds spring through fall with up to 4 litters per year. 1 to 4 young per litter.	**Breeding:** Unlike most rodents, Prairie Voles are monogamous. 3 to 5 young is typical.
Natural History: Generally regarded as one of the world's most prolific mammals. Populations in many areas are cyclical, and during years of high population density, there can be as many as several hundred per acre in prime habitat. Because they can be so common, these voles are an important food source for predatory species ranging from snakes and carnivorous mammals to birds of prey. They can also impact humans by eating crops, garden produce, young trees in orchards, etc. They feed on a wide variety of grasses and plants and will eat seeds, roots, and even bark. They maintain surface runways hidden beneath rank grasses and they may be active both day and night. Their range in Illinois is restricted to the northern half of the state.	**Natural History:** Woodland Voles create networks of tunnels just below the ground or "runways" that are near the surface but beneath the leaf litter on the forest floor. These tunnel systems are utilized by other small mammals such as shrews. They rarely venture far from these tunnels, but do emerge to glean seeds, grasses, and mast. They also eat roots, especially roots of grasses; root crops like potatoes are also eaten. Active both day and night. Their subterranean habits render them less vulnerable to many predators, but they are prey for a wide variety of carnivores, raptors, and especially snakes which are able to enter the burrow systems. Owls are another significant predator. Young exhibit a dark gray color. Adults are more chestnut.	**Natural History:** Coarse, grizzled gray fur and shorter tail distinguish this species from the Woodland Vole. Although insects are eaten, these voles feed mostly on vegetation. Including but not limited to grasses, roots, herbaceous weeds, seeds, leaves, stems, etc. Like other voles, they will create a system of shallow burrows. The North American range of this species approximates the occurrence of the original American prairies. It is probably less common today than in historical times, but it is still a widespread and fairly common species in Illinois. Like many small mammals native to Illinois, the population densities of these voles can fluctuate from year to year or even within a calendar year. The exact cause of these fluctuations is not understood.

Presumed range in Illinois

Class - **Mammalia** (mammals)
Order - **Rodentia** (rodents)

Family - **Muridae** (rats & mice)	Family - **Dipodidae** (jumping mice)
Southern Bog Lemming *Syanptomys cooperi*	**Meadow Jumping Mouse** *Zapus hudsonius*

Size: Adult is 5 inches in length and about 1.25 ounces.

Presumed range in Illinoisv

Size: Total length 8 inches (mostly tail) and 0.75 ounces.

Presumed range in Illinois

Abundance: Uncommon, distribution spotty.

Abundance: Fairly common.

Variation: As many as seven subspecies. Disagreement regarding Illinois specimens but maybe multiple variants.

Variation: There may be as many as three subspecies in Illinois. They are indistinguishable to the average observer.

Habitat: Although they can found in bogs, they occupy nearly all habitat types. The presence of grasses seems to be the only habitat requirement.

Habitat: Meadows and fields that contain dense cover. Generally avoids woodlands but may occur in edge areas, tree-line fence rows, and stream banks.

Breeding: Very prolific. Breeds most of year except for midwinter. Typical litter is 3 with a maximum of 8. Young wean at about 3 weeks.

Breeding: 3 to 6 young are born after an 18-day gestation period. Breeds about 3 times a year from spring to late summer.

Natural History: Primarily nocturnal and crepuscular, they feed on green plants and berries mainly. They often occur in colonies. Bog Lemmings are mainly northern mammals, and the southern Appalachians represent their southernmost distribution today. As with many small mammal species, the numerous subspecies can be told apart only by expert mammologists. The range map above may not be an accurate depiction of this species distribution in Illinois, as it is apparently sporadically distributed in the state. Very similar to in habits and lifestyle the voles of the genus *Microtus* (previous page). Creates runways through dense grass on the surface of the ground and also digs a burrow system below ground. Well adpated to wetlands, Bog Lemmings are good swimmers.

Natural History: This rodent, along with the very similar Woodland Jumping Mouse, comprise the North American representatives of the family Dipodidae. This unique family also ranges into the Old World. The Meadow Jumping Mouse is distinguished from the similar Woodland Jumping Mouse by the uniformly dark tail (as opposed to a white tipped tail). As with the many small mammal species, they are mainly nocturnal. They frequently use runways made by *Microtus* or other small rodents. Food items include fungi, insects, seeds, and berries. Jumping Mice put on heavy layers of fat just prior to their long hibernation, but mortality during hibernation is high and as many as two-thirds may not survive their winter sleep.

Class - **Mammalia** (mammals)

Order - **Soricomorpha** (insectivorous mammals)

Family - **Soricidae** (shrews)

Masked Shrew *Sorex cinereus*	**Southeastern Shrew** *Sorex longirostris*	**Least Shrew** *Cryptotis parva*

Size: Maximum of 3.8 inches in length and 0.375 ounces in weight.

Abundance: Farily common.

Variation: Brownish in summer, grayish in winter. 2 nearly identical subspecies occur in Illinois.

Presumed range in Illinois

Size: Maximum of 3.5 inches in length and 0.14 ounces in weight.

Abundance: Fairly common.

Variation: As many as 3 subspecies are recognized; only 1 (*S. l. longirostris*) is found in Illinois.

Presumed range in Illinois

Size: May reach 3 inches and weigh as much as 0.2 ounces.

Abundance: Common.

Variation: Summer pelage is brownish, turning to slate gray during winter. There are 2 subspecies in Illinois.

Presumed range in Illinois

Habitat: Found in virtually all wild habitats. Primarily a northern species. Prefers mesic microenvironments and may occur in wetlands.

Habitat: Found in a wide variety of habitats. Woods, fields, thickets, etc. May occupy both moist and dry environments.

Habitat: Grassy areas and overgrown fields primarily, but also in woodlands. Uses rotten logs and old stumps as habitat and requires some ground cover.

Breeding: Breeds throughout the summer. At least 2 litters of 4 to 6 annually.

Breeding: 4 to 10 tiny (0.5 inches) young are born from spring to fall.

Breeding: Several litters per year is common averaging 4 to 5 young per litter.

Natural History: Although they are mainly nocturnal animals, these shrews are active both day and night. They dart in and out of leaf litter on the forest floor or move rapidly along runways in overgrown fields. They will make chirping noises as they forage, and some believe these sounds are used to echolocate. Known food items are snails/slugs, caterpillars, grubs, spiders, and ants. They will also eat carrion. Shrews do not hibernate, and must forage year-round. For an animal with such high food requirements, survival in winter would seem a daunting task. But dormant insects and other invertebrates are located and eaten in large quantities. In fact, shrews may be quite beneficial to man by consuming enormous quantities of injurious insects and grubs. The Masked Shrew also frequently goes by the name Cinereous Shrew, a reference to the grayish-brown color of its fur.

Natural History: As with most tiny vertebrates, the Southeastern Shrew has a remarkable metabolic rate and must eat almost constantly to survive. Another characteristic of tiny mammals is a short life span. The maximum life span for the Southeastern Shrew is reported to be about 1.5 years. Spiders are reported as the most important food item, but a wide variety of other invertebrates are also eaten. As the name implies, they are found throughout the southeastern United States. Until recently these shrews were regarded as rare, but increasingly effective trapping/collecting techniques have revealed that they are fairly common in many areas of their range. They can sometimes be discovered beneath cover boards, tin, or other material placed in suitable habitats to attract small, secretive vertebrates. Many locality records come from herpetologists seeking reptiles beneath cover.

Natural History: Possessing an extremely high metabolism, this tiny mammal can consume its own weight in food daily. Like many other shrews, they are known to cache food items. Although these shrews are rarely seen due to their diminutive size and reclusive habits, they are usually a fairly common mammal. Owls are a major predator and in fact the presence of these tiny shrews in a given area is often confirmed by examining owl pellets for skeleton remains. Known food items are caterpillars, beetles, other insects, snails, spiders, and earthworms. One other tiny shrew species, the **Pygmy Shrew** (*Sorex hoyi*), has been recorded from Illinois, but it is much less common and very rarely observed. The local abundance of the Pygmy Shrew is difficult to determine because since they are so tiny, they fail to trip the mechanism on most small mammal traps.

Class - **Mammalia** (mammals)

Order - **Soricomorpha** (insectivorous mammals)

Family - **Soricidae** (shrews)	Family - **Talpidae** (moles)

Short-tailed Shrews
Blarina carolinensis (Southern) *Blarina brevicaudus* (Northern)

Eastern Mole
Zapus hudsonius

Size: Maximum length of about 4.5 inches and weighs 0.5 ounces.	Presumed range in Illinois 	**Size:** Maximum length of about 5.5 inches and weighs 1 ounce.	Presumed range in Illinois 	**Size:** Total length 8 inches (mostly tail) and 0.75 ounces.	Presumed range in Illinois 
Abundance: Common.		**Abundance:** Very common.		**Abundance:** Very common.	
Variation: These 2 species are so much alike that most people will not be able to distinguish them.		**Variation:** Except for attaining a larger size, nearly identical to the Southern Short-tailed Shrew.		**Variation:** These animals are remarkably similar throughout their range. Males are slightly larger than females.	

Habitat: Both species are fond damp woodlands and in fact neither can tolerate excessively dry conditions very well. Both avoid saturated soils, however. Note in the maps above that the combined range of the two species includes most of Illinois.

Habitat: Except for wetlands, these moles can be found in any habitat where soils are suitable for burrowing.

Breeding: Breeding is believed to occur in spring and fall. Up to 4 litters of 4 to 6 young annually.

Breeding: 1 litter per year in early spring. 2 to 5 young.

Natural History: The Short-tailed shrews are so similar that even experts sometimes resort to lab tests to determine species. Until recently, they were regarded as the same species, and apparently the only reliable definition of species is obtained by counting chromosomes! Both species are also easily confused with the Least Shrew, from which they can be distinguished by examining the teeth with the aid of a magnifying glass or dissecting microscope (Least Shrews have 3 visible unicuspids, Short-tail Shrews have 4). Both species of Short-tail Shrews are primarily nocturnal animals and both have very high metabolic rates. They are hyperactive animals that will eat as much as one-half their body weight daily! The ferocity of shrews is legendary among mammologists. Many have learned the hard way never to place a shrew in a container with a mouse if you want to keep both alive! The northern species is known to have periods of intense activity followed by periods of lethargy. Food is a variety of insects, snails, earthworms, millipedes, etc. as well as much larger prey including mice that are as large as themselves. The Northern Short-tailed Shrew is known to possess venomous saliva with which kills its prey. It is presumed that the southern species also possess this ability. Both species have tiny eyes and their vision is quite poor. The northern species is known to utilize echolocation. Some sounds they produce are audible to humans, but others are not. It is believed that these "ultrasonic" sounds act like a form of radar to detect objects in their path, rather like what is known in bats. Except when breeding and rearing young, these are solitary animals. They forage beneath the leaf litter in runways and tunnels and will dig their own tunnels or use those of other small rodents. Piebald and leucistic specimens have been reported from Illinois (Hoffmeister 1989).

Natural History: The most wide-ranging mole in America. Although considered a pest in suburban lawns and rural gardens, Eastern Moles actually perform some helpful tasks. The tunnels they dig help to aerate the soil and allow rainfall to penetrate more easily. They also prey heavily upon destructive grubs such as the Japanese Beetle. The pelage of the Eastern Mole is "reversible" and will lie smoothly against the skin whether mole is moving forward or backward in tight tunnels. The powerful forelegs allow this animal to burrow at an astonishing pace, and the webbed toes help move dirt aside. The eyes are tiny and covered with skin, and there are no external ears. This is an animal that is superbly adapted to a subterrean lifestyle and Eastern Moles will spend 99 percent of their lives below ground. They are sometimes found above ground following heavy rains.

Class - **Mammalia** (mammals)

Order - **Chiroptera** (bats)

Family - **Vespertilionidae** (vesper bats)

Hoary Bat *Lasiurus cinereous*	Eastern Red Bat *Lasiurus borealis*	Big Brown Bat *Eptisicus fuscus*

Hoary Bat	Eastern Red Bat	Big Brown Bat
Size: Maximum 5.5 inches. Wingspan to 16 inches.	**Size:** Maximum 5 inches. Up to 0.5 ounces Wingspan 13 inches.	**Size:** 4.5 inches and nearly 1 ounces. Wingspan 14 inches maximum.
Abundance: Fairly common.	**Abundance:** Common.	**Abundance:** Common.
Variation: Females are on average slightly heavier than males.	**Variation:** Males are red, females are chestnut or yellowish.	**Variation:** No significant variation in Illinois specimens.
Habitat: Forest species primarily.	**Habitat:** Woodlands and edge areas.	**Habitat:** Open fields, vacant lots.
Breeding: Averages 2 pups born in mid-May to mid-June.	**Breeding:** Litter size is 1 to 4 with the pups born in late May or early June.	**Breeding:** Several litters per year is common averaging 4 to 5 young per litter.

Presumed range in Illinois

Natural History: With a wingspan of 16 inches, this is the largest bat species in Illinois. Its name comes from the white-tipped hairs of the fur on its back. Hoary Bats have the greatest distribution of any American Bat. They summer as far north as Canada and winter in the coastal plain of the southeastern United States or in the desert southwest. Most of the Hoary Bats seen in Illinois are migrating to and from summer/winter residences. Although they are not rare in Illinois during spring and fall migrations, they are not usually seen at other times of the year. Oddly, the sexes segregate themselves following breeding and most of those seen in the eastern United States in summer are females. Males summer farther west in the Great Plains, Rocky Mountains, or west coast. Like the Red Bat, these bats are mostly solitary and roost among the foliage in trees. Moths are reported to be their primary food.

Natural History: In summer, this species usually roosts in trees by hanging from a limb. Usually solitary but sometimes more than 1 bat will roost together. Roosting bats resemble dead leaves. Trees chosen for roosting are often at the edge of a woodland bordering an open field. Red Bats are migratory; they summer in Illinois while wintering farther to the south. They may linger well into the fall and begin arriving in Illinois as early as late March. Their total range in America is quite large and includes most of the United States east of the Rocky Mountains and much of southeastern Canada. Hibernation takes place in hollow trees or beneath leaf litter on the forest floor, a very unusual tactic for a bat! Though mainly nocturnal, this species often flies in daylight, especially in late afternoon or early evening. Their habit of roosting on low-hanging branches at woodland edges makes them fairly conspicuous.

Natural History: Stays year-round in Illinois. Winters in caves or derelict buildings. Summer roosts are usually associated with human structures (buildings, eaves, bridges). Also known to use hollow trees and abandoned mines. The primary food is reported to be beetles. These are the large, brown bats that are common around human habitations and they range throughout the state. These bats seem to tolerate cold fairly well and they remain active well into the fall. They can sometimes even be seen flying around on warm days in winter. Small flying beetles are a favorite food item, but a wide variety of insects are eaten. This bat is a useful consumer of insect pests and is thus a valuable friend to man. Like many bats in America, it as been hard hit by "White-nose Syndrome." The impact of this devastating disease on ecosystems is yet to be determined, but it will almost certainly be detrimental.

Class - **Mammalia** (mammals)

Order - **Chiroptera** (bats)

Family - **Vespertilionidae** (vesper bats)

Genus - *Myotis* (myotis bats)

Gray Bat *Myotis grisescens*	**Northern Bat** *Myotis septentrionalis*	**Little Brown Bat** *Myotis lucifugus*

Size: All *Myotis* are somewhat small bats, ranging in size from 3 to 3.5 inches and weighing from 0.2 to 0.34 ounces. The Gray Bat is the largest (3.5 inches), with one America's smallest being the Eastern Small-footed Bat (3 inches in length and about 0.2 ounces).

Presumed range of Myotis Bats in Illinois

Abundance: The 5 species of Myotis Bats found in Illinois range in abundance from common to rare. The rarer species are the Gray Bat (federally endangered) and the Indiana Bat (not shown, federally endangered). The Southeastern Bat (not shown) is endangered in Illinois. Both the Little Brown Bat and the Northern Bat are fairly common. The Gray Bat is an uncommon species in Illinois found only in southern and southwestern portions of the state.

Variation: Most bats present an identification problem for the average person, but the Myotis bats can be especially confusing. Confirming the exact species usually requires looking very closely and may sometimes mean having the bat in hand. An exception would be the Gray Bats, which can be differentiated from *other Myotis bats* by their decidedly grayish coloration.

Habitat: Gray Bats are true cave dwellers, using caves for hibernation, roosting, and rearing young. Other *Myotis* species may hibernate in caves but will also use other places such as hollow trees or buildings for summertime roosts. Some species are sometimes seen roosting in clumps by day beneath the shelter of roof overhangs, roofs of picnic pavillions, inside old barns, etc. A wide variety of habitats are utilized by these bats during warmer months. Forests, fields, wetlands, and especially stream courses. Some species, like the Little Brown Bat, will sometimes roost in buildings, including attics of inhabited houses. The Northern Bat has been known to use buildings as a winter refuge.

Breeding: Mating occurs in the fall with fertilization delayed until early spring. Young are born in late spring or early summer and all species form "maternity colonies" of females with young which may be in caves, buildings, hollow trees, or other structures. *Myotis* bats produce a single baby annually (except for the Southeastern Bat which can give birth to twins).

Natural History: Virtually the entire population of Gray Bats in America hibernate in a handful of caves scattered across the southeastern United States. Indiana Bats are also known for their huge hibernating colonies that tend to concentrate in only a few select caves during winter. Both species are thus vulnerable to human or natural disturbance of their select hibernating locales. Some Myotis Bats are migratory, moving south during winter months. Most feed in flight on flying insects, but one species (Northern Bat) feeds by gleaning insects from leaves while hovering. Some like to forage primarily over water above ponds, creeks, and wetland areas (Little Brown Bat, Gray Bat, Southeastern Bat). Throughout America, many bat species are in steep decline and many once common species have been hard hit by a fungal disease known as "White Nose Syndrome." The Little Brown Bat, once perhaps the most common *Myotis* in America, has been especially hard hit by this disease. All bats are remarkable little animals that consume untold numbers of injurious insect species, including many millions of mosquitoes, and they are thus extremely useful to man. Their reputation for harboring the rabies virus is factual, but the threat to the average person is usually overstated. There is a common myth that any bat seen abroad during daylight is rabid. In fact, some bats will fly in late afternoon or on warm days in winter, and their appearance in daylight does not mean a rabid bat. Bats found on the ground, however, should not be handled. Though some bats will roost or even hibernate beneath leaf litter on the forest floor, bats on the ground and out in the open may in fact be sick and infected.

Class - **Mammalia** (mammals)
Order - **Chiroptera** (bats)
Family - **Vespertilionidae** (vesper bats)

Silver-haired Bat *Lasionycterius noctivagans*	**Eastern Pipistrelle** *Pipistrellus subflavus*	**Evening Bat** *Nycticeius humeralis*
	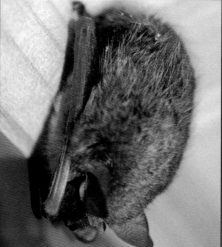	

Size: Maximum length of 4 inches and weighs 0.34 ounces.	Presumed range in Illinois	**Size:** 3.5 inches. Weight about 0.25 ounces. Wingspan 9 inches.	Presumed range in Illinois	**Size:** Maximum length 4 inches. Weighs about 0.5 ounces.	Presumed range in Illinois
Abundance: Fairly common.		**Abundance:** Common.		**Abundance:** Common.	
Variation: None		**Variation:** None.		**Variation:** None	
Habitat: A forest species that hides tree hollows or beneath peeling bark during daylight.		**Habitat:** Woodlands, stream courses, and edges of fields bordering woodlands.		**Habitat:** Swamps, stream corridors, woodlands, woods openings, and edge areas are used.	

Breeding: Young are born in late spring. 2 pups are typical.	**Breeding:** Litter size is 1 to 4 with the pups born in late May or early June.	**Breeding:** Several litters per year is common averaging 4 to 5 young per litter.
Natural History: This is a widespread species that ranges from coast to coast in North America. In summer this species ranges as far north as Canada and southeastern Alaska. In fact, this species is more common in summer months in northern regions. In Illinois, this is a apparently a migrant species that leaves the state in summer for more northerly forests. It is probably most common in Illinois in spring and fall and is known to overwinter in the southern part of the state. Unlike many bat species, the Silver-haired Bat is mostly a solitary animal that roosts singly, although some colony activity is reported among females with young. Silver-haireds derive their name from the "frosted" appearance of their pelage, a unique and identifying characteristic among Illinois bats. Feeding flights are mostly near water (streams, bogs, lakes, etc.).	**Natural History:** Eastern Pipistrelles are widespread and common throughout the eastern United States. They will leave the roost before dark and are often seen hunting at dusk. Like many bats, the females form maternal colonies where young are reared, often in buildings or sheds. Unlike many other species, however, these maternal colonies are usually small, numbering only one or two dozen individuals. Hibernation begins in late fall (October) and lasts until April or May. Hibernating bats may lose as much as 25 to 30 percent of their body weight before emerging in the spring. Uniquely among bats, hibernating Pipistrelles accumulate water droplets on their fur. Why this happens is not fully understood. When flying, these little bats move slowly in a very erratic manner and in flight they resemble a large moth. They typically forage around the tops of trees for all manner of flying insects.	**Natural History:** Evening Bats in Illinois are summer residents that winter farther south where hibernation is not necessary. Most leave by early fall, but some may stay into late fall. Summer roosts include hollow trees as well as buildings, and they do not seem to utilize caves as is the habit of many bat species. A wide variety of small insects are eaten, including species that are injurious to farm crops. Though widespread across much of the southeast, these are lowland and low plateau animals that avoid the higher elevations of the Appalachian Mountains. Most of these bats found in the northern portions of their range in the summer are females, with the males apparently staying farther to the south. This separation of sexes during certain times of the year is not an uncommon trait among some bat species. The reasons why the sexes separate are not well understood.

Class - **Mammalia** (mammals)
Order - **Chiroptera** (bats)
Family - **Vespertilionidae** (vesper bats)
Rafinesque's Big-eared Bat *Corynorhinus rafinesquii*

Size: 3.75 inches and 0.4 ounces.

Abundance: Uncommon in Illinois.

Variation: None.

Habitat: Woods, riparian areas. For roosting uses tree hollows, caves, beneath loose bark, and derelict buildings.

Breeding: Breeds in fall and gives birth to a single baby in spring.

Presumed range in Illinois

Natural History: Rafinesque's Big-eared Bat hibernates in the state and is thus found here year-round. It may roost communally or singly, and like many bats it will sometimes roost among other species. In the Appalachian region, this species shows a preference for sandstone caves. Food is mostly moths (as much as 90 percent). More nocturnal than many bats, these bats do not fly at twilight, instead waiting for full darkness. Females congregate in "nursery roosts" in the spring to give birth. Young bats can fly at about 3 weeks and may live more than 10 years. This bat occurs rather sporadically throughout its range and the map above is an estimation of its range in llinois.

CHAPTER 4

THE BIRDS OF ILLINOIS

— THE ORDERS AND FAMILIES OF ILLINOIS BIRDS —

Note: The sequence in which the bird orders and families are shown below is a reflection of how they appear on the following pages, rather than a representation of the phylogenetic relationship of the birds.

Class - **Aves** (birds)

Order - **Passeriformes** (songbirds)

Family	**Tyrannidae** (flycatchers)
Family	**Turdidae** (thrushes)
Family	**Lanidae** (shrikes)
Family	**Aluidae** (larks)
Family	**Mimidae** (thrasher family)
Family	**Motacillidae** (wagtails)
Family	**Bombycillidae** (waxwings)
Family	**Certhidae** (creepers)
Family	**Paridae** (chickadee family)
Family	**Regulidae** (kinglets)
Family	**Sittidae** (nuthatches)
Family	**Troglodytidae** (wrens)
Family	**Poliptilidae** (gnatcatchers)
Family	**Hirundinidae** (swallows)
Family	**Corvidae** (crows & jays)
Family	**Vironidae** (vireos)
Family	**Parulidae** (warblers)
Family	**Icturidae** (blackbirds)
Family	**Thraupidae** (tanagers)
Family	**Sturnidae** (starling)
Family	**Passeridae** (European sparrows)
Family	**Emberzidae** (sparrows)
Family	**Cardinalidae** (grosbeaks)
Family	**Fringillidae** (finches)

Order - **Apodiformes** (swifts & hummingbirds)

Family	**Apodidae** (swifts)
Family	**Trochylidae** (hummingbirds)

Order - **Coraciiformes**

Family	Alcedinidae (kingfishers)

Order - **Piciformes**

Family	Picidae (woodpeckers)

Order - **Cuculiformes**

Family	Cuculidae (cuckoos)

Order - **Columbiformes**

Family	Columbidae (doves)

Order - **Galliformes** (chicken-like birds)

Family	Phasianidae (grouse)
Family	Odontophoridae (quail)

Order - **Caprimulgiformes**

Family	Caprimulgidae (nightjars)

Order - **Strigiformes** (owls)

Family	Strigidae (typical owls)
Family	Tytonidae (barn owl)

Order - **Falconiformes** (raptors)

Family	Accipitridae (hawks, eagles, kites)
Family	Falconidae (falcons)

Order - **Ciconiiformes** (wading birds)

Family	Ardeidae (herons)

Order - **Gruiformes** (rails & cranes)

Family	Rallidae (rails)
Family	Gruidae (cranes)

Order - **Chariidriformes** (shorebirds)

Family	Charidriidae (plovers)
Family	Scolapacidae (sandpipers)
Family	Laridae (gulls & terns)

Order - **Pelicaniformes**

Family	Pelecanidae (pelicans)

Order - **Gaviiformes**

Family	Gaviidae (loons)

Order - **Podicipediformes**

Family	Podicipedidae (grebes)

Order - **Anseriiformes** (waterfowl)

Family	Anatidae (ducks, geese & swans)

Order - **Suliformes**

Family	Phalacrocoracidae (cormorants)

Class - **Aves** (birds)

Order - **Passeriformes** (songbirds)

Family - **Tyrannidae** (flycatchers)

Eastern Wood Pewee	Olive-sided Flycatcher	Eastern Phoebe
Contopus virens	*Contopus cooperi*	*Sayornis phoebe*

Size: 6.5 inches.

Abundance: Common.

Variation: None. Sexes are alike.

Habitat: Wood Pewees are forest birds but they favor small openings in the woods or edge areas where marshes or fields border woodlands.

Presumed range in Illinois

Size: 7.5 inches.

Abundance: Uncommon to rare.

Variation: None. Sexes are alike.

Habitat: The summer habitat is coniferous forests of mountains and northern North America where it associates with small forest openings.

Presumed range in Illinois

Size: 7 inches.

Abundance: Common.

Variation: None. Sexes are alike.

Habitat: Woodlands and woods openings. Also in rural yards or parks in wooded regions. Can be common around rural homesteads.

Presumed range in Illinois

Migratory Status: Wintering in South America, the Eastern Wood Pewee arrives in North America in late spring (peak arrival in Illinois mid-May). They are a summer/breeding resident across the state that stays throughout the summer. They beginning leaving in late August with a few lingering into early October.

Migratory Status: A spring and fall passage migrant in Illinois. Birds that pass through Illinois spend the summer in the boreal forests of Canada and winter from southern Mexico to South America. Spring migrants begin to arrive in state in May and have moved on by mid-June. Fall migration through state is mid-August through September.

Migratory Status: Eastern Phoebes begin to arrive in the Midwest as early as March, perhaps a little later in the northernmost portion of Illinois. They are summer residents that will nest in the state. Fall migration begins late September through October and in the southernmost region of the state a few may linger into the winter.

Breeding: Nests are usually built high in trees in a terminal fork. Nest material consists of grasses and lichens. 2 to 4 eggs are laid.

Breeding: Nest is typically on a branch of a conifer and built of sticks, lichens and rootlets. 1 clutch per year. 3 to 4 eggs per clutch.

Breeding: Phoebes are early nesters in Illinois. Nesting can occur by early April and there will often be a second nesting later in the summer.

Natural History: These nondescript little brown birds often go unnoticed except for the distinctive call from which they derive their name. Their "pee-a-weee" song is a common summer sound in the woodlands throughout Illinois. Like other members of the flycatcher family, they hunt flying insects from high perches, swooping out to catch their food on the wing. They are typically fairly tolerant of humans and can sometimes be closely approached. They are very similar to Eastern Phoebe, but note orange lower bill and pale wing bars on the Eastern Wood Pewee.

Natural History: These flycatchers are quite acrobatic in the air. They feed in typical flycatcher fashion by sallying forth from a high perch to snatch flying insects. Bees and wasps are reportedly a favorite food. This species avoids deep forest in favor of openings such as bogs, meadows, or second growth and may benefit from forest fires or human activities such as logging. Paradoxically, the species has been declining in recent decades. This decline is possibly tied to changes in the winter habitat in tropical America. They are federally listed as Species of Concern by the USF&WS.

Natural History: The Eastern Phoebe is most easily told from other Flycatchers by its habit of constantly wagging its tail down and up. Its nests are also distinctive, being constructed of mud and lined with mosses. Nests are placed beneath some form of overhang, most often the eaves of buildings. The cup-shaped nest is plastered to the surface in the manner of many swallows. These are normally tame little birds that will allow humans to approach to within a few yards before flying off only a short distance. Similar to the Wood Pewee but has a dark bill and lacks wing bars.

Class - **Aves** (birds)

Order - **Passeriformes** (songbirds)

Family - **Tyrannidae** (flycatchers)

Empid Flycatchers
genus - *Empidonax* (5 nearly identical species in Illinois)

Acadian Flycatcher *Empidonax virescens*	**Willow Flycatcher** *Empidonax traillii*	**Least Flycatcher** *Empidonax minimus*

Alder Flycatcher *Empidonax alnorum*	**Yellow-bellied Flycatcher** *Empidonax flaviventris*	

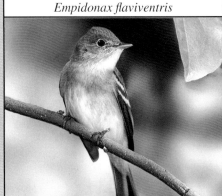 

Combined range of all 5 *Empidonax* Flycatchers in Illinois

Size: Range in size from 5.25 to 5.75 inches.

Abundance: Least Flycatcher is fairly common throughout its broader range but has declined in some regions of the Midwest. Alder Flycatcher may be the least common of the group. Acadian is probably the most common. Willow and Yellow-bellied are probably fairly common.

Variation: Five species of *Empidonax* flycatchers may be seen in Illinois. All 5 species are so similar in appearance that even expert bird-watchers have trouble identifying individual species. Most people must content themselves with calling them all "Empid Flycatchers."

Migratory Status: The Yellow-bellied Flycatcher is a spring and fall migrant that merely passes through the state. All other *Empidonax* flycatchers in Illinois will breed in the state. All winter far to south, some as far as South America. *Empidonax* species return to Illinois from early or mid-May to mid-June. All begin to leave in August and are gone by mid-September.

Habitat: All are woodland species. Acadian and Willow Flycatchers are fond of streamside habitats, swamps, and marshes. Least Flycatchers prefer regenerative woodlands and edge areas. Yellow-bellied Flycatchers summer in the boreal forests of the far north. Both the Alder Flycatcher and the Least Flycatcher also range well to the north of Illinois but breeding has been confirmed in Illinois for all but the Yellow-bellied Flycatcher. All 5 species may be seen throughout the state during migration.

Breeding: The Acadian Flycatcher weaves a flimsy nest of grass on a low branch and lays 2 to 4 eggs. Willow Flycatchers build their nest in the fork of a low branch or bush and lay 2 to 4 eggs. Least Flycatcher breeds mostly to the north of Illinois but a few will breed in the northern part of the state. They usually lay 4 eggs in a nest woven of grasses and fibers and placed in a fork of a tree branch. Alder Flycatcher nests are coarsely woven cups typically placed in low bushes with 4 eggs.

Natural History: Some species, like the Acadian Flycatcher, may be less numerous in Illinois today due to the decline in forested habitats. The Willow Flycatcher, on the other hand, may be helped by the regeneration of successional forests. Serious bird-watchers find that the most reliable way to identify these small flycatchers is to learn their songs. In fact, Willow and Alder Flycatchers are so similar in appearance that visual identification alone is unreliable.

Class - **Aves** (birds)

Order - **Passeriformes** (songbirds)

Family - **Tyrannidae** (flycatchers)

Eastern Kingbird	Great Crested Flycatcher
Tyrannus tyrannus	*Myiarchus crinitus*

Size: 8.5 inches

Abundance: Common.

Variation: None. Sexes alike.

Migratory Status: A summertime resident of Illinois that nests in the state. Winters entirely in South America, mainly in Amazonian regions of Columbia and Ecuador. Movement north begins in late April with some birds not arriving until early May. Departs in September.

Presumed range in Illinois

Habitat: Prefers open fields and pastures in rural areas. In urban settings it likes open parks and large empty lots. Commonly seen perched on fences.

Breeding: The nest is built of twigs and grass high in trees. The average clutch size is 3 to 5 eggs. 1 clutch per year. Sturdy nest is placed on limb near the top of large tree.

Natural History: The name "Kingbird" is derived from this species aggressive defense of territory against other birds, including even large hawks! They hunt flying insects from an open perch, which is frequently a fence or power line. When flying insect prey is spotted, they will launch themselves into an attack that often results in an aerial "dogfight" between bird and insect. They will also hunt flying insects by hovering. Berries are an important food item, especially mulberrys. Serviceberries, blackberries, and Elderberrys are also eaten. These are conspicuous birds. Their charcoal gray upper parts contrast strongly with a whitish breast and belly. The bright reddish-orange blaze on the top of the head is usually not visible to the casual observer. Winters in South America, as far south as Argentina. Some populations in the eastern United States have shown declines in the last few decades.

Size: 8.75 inches.

Abundance: Fairly common.

Variation: None. Sexes alike.

Migratory Status: A summertime resident of Illinois. Arrives in the state in early May. Some birds will winter in peninsula Florida, but most winter in Central America or Mexico. Some migrate through the Carribean. Others up the coast of Texas or across the Gulf of Mexico.

Presumed range in Illinois

Habitat: Openings in deciduous and mixed woodlands. Edge areas and open woodlands are also used. Winter habitat is tropical forests of many types.

Breeding: Unlike most flycatchers this bird is a cavity nester, often using old woodpecker holes. 3 to 5 eggs, laid in mid-May, is typical.

Natural History: The name comes from the "crested" look of the head, which may not be readily apparent. Reddish underside of the tail and wing primaries, along with the distinctly yellowish belly contrasting with gray breast, is unique among Illinois flycatchers. These features plus large size make it one of the more recognizable members of the flycatcher family. However, they are a rather unobtrusive species that can be easily overlooked. Food is large insects captured in flight from its perch, which is often high in the canopy. Returns in late April from wintering grounds in Central America. Forages for insects in treetops and catches flying insects on the wing. Also consumes some berries. More common in the southeastern United States than in Illinois and the Midwest. Breeding success may be tied to woodpecker populations since old woodpecker holes are a favorite nesting site.

Class - **Aves** (birds)

Order - **Passeriformes** (songbirds)

Family - **Turdidae** (thrush family)

Robin *Turdus migratorius*	Eastern Bluebird *Siala sialis*	Wood Thrush *Hylocichla mustela*

Size: 10 inches.	**Size:** 7 inches.	**Size:** 7 inches.
Abundance: Very common.	**Abundance:** Fairly common.	**Abundance:** Uncommon.
Variation: Male is more brightly colored, female more subdued.	**Variation:** Significant sexual dimorphism. See photos above.	**Variation:** No significant variation in Illinois specimens.
Migratory Status: Although migratory, Robins can be seen year-round in Illinois. They move if weather is harsh.	**Migratory Status:** Summer resident in north, but may stay year-round in southern Illinois.	**Migratory Status:** A summer resident that winters in Central America and South America. April to September in Illinois.

Presumed range in Illinois

Habitat: Virtually all habitats in the state may be utilized. Most common in areas of human disturbance, especially older suburbs. They are fond of hunting earthworms in suburban lawns.	**Habitat:** Field edges, woods openings, and open fields, marshes, and pastures. Savanna like habitats, i.e. open spaces interspersed with large trees, are a favorite habitat.	**Habitat:** Woodlands. May be found in both mature forests and successional areas. In both it likes thick undergrowth. On wintering grounds uses tropical rainforest.
Breeding: The 3 to 4 "sky blue" eggs are laid in a nest constructed of mud and grass, often in the crotch of a tree in an urban yard.	**Breeding:** Bluebirds are cavity nesters that readily take to man-made nest boxes. 2 broods per summer is common. 3 to 6 eggs per clutch.	**Breeding:** Nest is mud, twigs, and grass similar to that of the Robin. Nest may be in understory or at mid-level. Lays 2 to 5 blue-green eggs.
Natural History: Despite the fact that the Robin is a migratory species, individuals are seen in Illinois year-round. It is likely that the state's summer residents retreat south during winter and are replaced by southward-moving individuals that have summered much farther to the north. In winter they are sometimes seen in large migratory flocks numbering over 100 birds. Perhaps the best known of America's bird species, Robins are commonly seen on both urban and rural lawns throughout the state. They may also been seen in remote wilderness areas. The Latin name *migratorius* is appropriate for this species and its summer range extends all the way to the Arctic. Feeds heavily on earthworms.	**Natural History:** The Eastern Bluebirds habit of readily adapting to artificial nest boxes has helped bring them back from alarmingly low numbers decades ago, when rampant logging of eastern forests depleted nest cavities. They are primarily insect eaters and are vulnerable to exceptionally harsh winters. Harsh winter weather will prompt a mass movement south and prolonged periods of very cold weather can literally wipe out entire populations that are caught too far north. In winter, Bluebirds eat many types of berries and will readily eat raisins from feeders. Their popularity among humans has lead to the establishment of The North American Bluebird Society, dedicated to Bluebird conservation.	**Natural History:** The Wood Thrush feeds on insects, spiders, earthworms, and other invertebrates found by foraging beneath leaf mold on the forest floor. They will also feed on berries which can be an important food during fall migration. Like many songbirds, this species is threatened by the fragmentation of forest habitats throughout North America. Smaller forest tracts make it easier for Cowbirds to find Wood Thrush nests. Consequently nest predation by Cowbirds is increasing and may be one reason for recent population declines. This threat is especially pronounced in the Midwest. The exceptional song of the Wood Thrush is usually described as "flute-like" or "ethereal" and is heard mostly at dawn and dusk.

Class - **Aves** (birds)		
Order - **Passeriformes** (songbirds)		
Family - **Turdidae** (thrush family)		
Hermit Thrush *Catharus guttatus*	**Veery** *Catharus fuscescens*	**Swainson's Thrush** *Catharus ustulatus*

Size: 7 inches.	**Size:** 7 inches.	**Size:** 7 inches.
Abundance: Fairly common.	**Abundance:** Uncommon.	**Abundance:** Fairly common.
Variation: Varies slightly from reddish brown to grayish brown.	**Variation:** Illinois birds are reddish, those from farther west are duller.	**Variation:** No significant variation in Illinois specimens.
Habitat: Damp woodlands, thickets, and successional areas with heavy undergrowth of bushes and shrubs.	**Habitat:** Understory of deciduous woodlands. Most common in second growth forest with thick undergrowth.	**Habitat:** Moist to wet woodlands and swamps with heavy underbrush and cool, heavily shaded woods.

Presumed range in Illinois

Migratory Status: Mostly a spring fall migrant. Lingers in northern Illinois in fall. May be seen throughout the winter extreme southern Illinois.	**Migratory Status:** Spring and fall migrant throughout most of the state. A few will summer in northern Illinois, mostly in the northernmost portion.	**Migratory Status:** Spring and fall migrant. Winters in South America and summers quite far to the north in Canada and even Alaska.
Breeding: 3 to 5 blueish-green eggs are laid in a nest built just above ground level. Most will nest in the boreal forests of Canada. No nesting in Illinois.	**Breeding:** Breeds mostly farther north, but some nesting in northern Illinois. Nest is hidden in thickets on or near the ground. From 3 to 5 eggs are laid.	**Breeding:** Builds its moss lined nest in a coniferous tree in boreal forest well to the north of Illinois. Lays 3 to 5 eggs that are blue with brown spots.
Natural History: Any Thrush seen in Illinois during the winter will be this species. They are rather shy but less so than other *Catharus* and they will sometimes visit feeders for suet or raisins. They feed mainly on insects found on the forest floor and beneath leaf mold, but berries are also an important element in the diet, especially in winter. The song of the Hermit Thrush is regarded by many as one of the more beautiful summer sounds in the northern forests. Although secretive, their presence during winter makes them more conspicuous. Unlike most other thrush species, populations of the Hermit Thrush appear stable. As with other thrush species, the Hermit Thrush is known for the quality of its song.	**Natural History:** Although the Veery is widespread during migration, they are hard to observe in much of Illinois since most are usually just passing through and they migrate mostly at night. One of the more secretive of the thrushes, they stay mostly in thick undergrowth where they feed on a variety of insects, earthworms, spiders, and berries. Bird-watchers often confirm this bird's presence by recognizing its distinctive call, which has been described as "hauntingly beautiful." This species has shown a downward population trend in many regions of its range in North America. Factors cited as possibly contributing to this trend are loss of wintering habitat in South America and fragmentation of breeding habitats in North America.	**Natural History:** Another secretive, difficult-to-observe thrush that in migration flies by night and spends its days resting and feeding in heavy undergrowth. As with many of the thrushes, positive identification can be difficult. This species and the Gray-cheeked Thrush are easily confused. The buff-colored cheeks are a good identification character. Like others of its kind, the Swainson's Thrush feeds on insects and invertebrates as well as berries. Unlike others of its genus, however, this thrush is known to feed higher in trees (most other thrushes feed mostly on the ground). Spring migration in Illinois begins in late April and runs through mid-May. Fall migration peaks in September.

Class - **Aves** (birds)

Order - **Passeriformes** (songbirds)

Family - **Turdidae** (thrush family)	Family - **Lanidae** (shrikes)	Family - **Alauidae** (larks)
Gray-cheeked Thrush *Catharus minimus*	**Northern Shrike** *Lanius excubitor*	**Horned Lark** *Eremophila alpestris*

Size: 7.25 inches.

Presumed range in Illinois

Abundance: Fairly common.

Variation: Overall coloration varies from grayish to brownish.

Migratory Status: A secretive spring and fall nighttime migrant that is easily missed.

Habitat: Summer habitats are boreal forests. Winters in South America. May be seen in woodlands throughout the state during migration.

Breeding: Breeds in remote tundra and taiga in northern Canada and Alaska. Lays 3 to 6 eggs.

Natural History: Secretive and uncommon, the biology of the Gray-cheeked Thrush is poorly known. Its summer habitats are dense spruce forests and willow-alder thickets in the far north. Breeding range extends well into the Arctic Circle and winter range is at least as far south as northern South America. Differentiating between the various thrush species can be challenging. The Gray-cheeked Thrush is easily confused with both the Swainson's Thrush and the Hermit Thrush but can be told by the gray color of the cheek. The Bicknell's Thrush, one of America's newest bird species, was once regarded as a subspecies of the Gray Cheeked Thrush. Some data suggests that the Gray-cheeked is outnumbered by other thrushes by a ratio of as much 5 to 1.

Size: 10 inches.

Presumed range in Illinois

Abundance: Rare in Illinois.

Variation: Sexes alike. Juveniles have stronger barring on breast.

Migratory Status: A winter resident only. Summers in northern Canada and Alaska.

Habitat: Summer habitat is the taiga-tundra ecoregion of the far north. In Illinois frequents edge areas and semi-open regions near woodlands or brush.

Breeding: Nest is proportionately large Built of twigs and rootlets lined with feathers, hair, or fur. Lays 4 to 6 eggs.

Natural History: These fierce little birds are much like a miniature raptor. They hunt mostly insects, but will also attack and kill lizards, mice, small snakes, and birds as large as themselves. Sometimes called "Butcher Bird," they kill with a powerful beak and have the unusual habit of caching food items by impaling the bodies of prey onto a thorn or fence barb. They will form permanent territories, which they defend from other shrikes. Northern Shrikes range across the northern portions of North America south to the central Rocky Mountains in the west, the Great Lakes region of the Midwest, and all of New England. Sadly, this unique species is declining throughout its range. A similar species, the **Loggerhead Shrike** (*L. Lanius ludovicianus*), occurs in parts of southern Illinois.

Size: 7.5 inches.

Presumed range in Illinois

Abundance: Fairly common.

Variation: Sexes similar. Males more vividly colored.

Migratory Status: Year-round, but much more common during spring and fall.

Habitat: This is a prairie species that is seen only in expansive, open fields. Large, harvested crop fields are the primary habitat for this bird in winter.

Breeding: Nests on barren ground. Lays 3 to 5 eggs. Breeds throughout most of Illinois.

Natural History: This prairie species needs open ground and has probably benefited from human activity in the eastern United States as a result of land clearing and agricultural operations. Closely cropped pastures or tilled lands are used almost exclusively in Illinois. Except during nesting, these are gregarious birds that are nearly always seen in flocks. They feed on small seeds and tiny arthropods gleaned from what may appear to be nearly barren ground. Harvested agricultural fields, gravel bars, and other open lands are utilized, especially in winter. Like the American Pipit, with which it sometimes associates, the Horned Lark is a species that is often overlooked by the average Illinoisan. During outbreaks of severe winter weather, flocks may move farther south.

Class - **Aves** (birds)

Order - **Passeriformes** (songbirds)

Family - **Mimidae** (thrasher family)

Mockingbird *Mimus polyglottis*	**Gray Catbird** *Dumetella carolinensis*	**Brown Thrasher** *Toxostoma rufum*

Size: 10.5 inches. Presumed range in Illinois	**Size:** 8.5 inches. 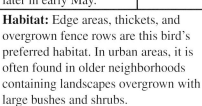 Presumed range in Illinois	**Size:** 11.5 inches.  Presumed range in Illinois
Abundance: Common.	**Abundance:** Common.	**Abundance:** Fairly common.
Variation: None.	**Variation:** None.	**Variation:** None.
Migratory Status: Summer-only resident in northern Illinois, but is a year-round resident in most of the rest of the state.	**Migratory Status:** Spring, summer, and fall only. A few reach the shores of Lake Michigan by late April, most arrive later in early May.	**Migratory Status:** A summer resident in most of Illinois. A few will winter in the southern tip of the state if the weather is mild.
Habitat: Prefers semi-open habitats with some cover in the form of bushes and shrubs. Found in both rural and urban environments. During colder months, they are usually found in the vicinity of berry producing plants.	**Habitat:** Edge areas, thickets, and overgrown fence rows are this bird's preferred habitat. In urban areas, it is often found in older neighborhoods containing landscapes overgrown with large bushes and shrubs.	**Habitat:** Edges of woods, thickets, fence rows, overgrown fields, and successional areas. Suburban lawns that have adequate cover in the form of bushes and shrubs may also be used. Avoids deep woods.
Breeding: The nest is made of sticks and is usually in a thick bush or small tree. 3 to 4 eggs are laid and more than 1 nesting per season is usual.	**Breeding:** The loosely constructed nest is made of sticks, vines, and leaves placed in dense bushes. 3 to 4 eggs is common.	**Breeding:** Builds a stick nest in the heart of a dense shrub, usually within a few feet of the ground. Lays 2 to 5 eggs in late spring.
Natural History: The name "Mocking Bird" is derived from this bird's habit of mimicking the calls of other birds, and they have a huge repertoire of songs. They are known to mimic the calls of everything from warblers to blue jays and even large hawks. New songs are learned throughout their life, and the number of different songs recorded by this species is up to 150. They feed largely on insects, but in the winter they switch to berries and fruits. Mockingbirds have a reputation among rural folk as a useful bird that will chase away other pesky birds such as blackbirds and other species that can be garden pests. Appears to be expanding its range northward into southern Canada.	**Natural History:** The Gray Catbird is much more secretive than its relative the Mockingbird. Food includes all manner of insects, spiders, larva, and berries. Feeds both in the trees and on the ground. When feeding on the ground will use the bill to flip over dead leaves. Named for their call which sounds remarkably like a meowing cat, these shy birds are often heard but unseen as they "meow" from beneath a dense shrub. Like their cousins the Mockingbirds, Gray Catbirds have a large repertoire of songs and they are accomplished mimics of other bird species. They winter along the lower coastal plain of the US, Florida, the Caribbean, Mexico, and Central America.	**Natural History:** During warm weather, the Brown Thrasher feeds on insects and small invertebrates of all types. It uses its long bill to overturn leaves and debris beneath trees and shrubs and also actively hunts in the grass of urban lawns. In winter, they will eat berries and sometimes come to feeders for raisins or suet. During the breeding season, males perch atop bushes or small trees and serenade all within earshot with their song. Though the Brown Thrasher lacks the repertoire of its cousin the Mockingbird, it does possess one of the most varied song collections of any bird in America. Migrates at night. A few will remain in southern Illinois throughout the winter if the winter is mild.

Class - **Aves** (birds)

Order - **Passeriformes** (songbirds)

Family - **Motacillidae** (wagtails)	Family - **Bombycillidae** (waxwings)	Family - **Certhiidae** (creepers)
American Pipit *Anthus rubescens*	**Cedar Waxwing** *Bombycilla cedrorum*	**Brown Creeper** *Certhia americana*

summer plumage

American Pipit	Cedar Waxwing	Brown Creeper
Size: 6.5 inches.	**Size:** 7 inches.	**Size:** 5.25 inches.
Abundance: Uncommon.	**Abundance:** Fairly common.	**Abundance:** Uncommon.
Presumed range in Illinois	Presumed range in Illinois	Presumed range in Illinois
Variation: Seasonal plumage changes.	**Variation:** No variation. Sexes alike.	**Variation:** No variation, sexes alike.
Migratory Status: Mostly a migrant seen during spring and fall and in winter.	**Migratory Status:** Year-round resident but usually more common during migration.	**Migratory Status:** Mainly a winter resident, but year-round some parts of the state.
Habitat: In migration, the American Pipit is usually seen in expansive open areas such as harvested croplands or mud flats.	**Habitat:** Found both in forests and semi-open country including overgrown fields, orchards, etc. May be seen in both rural and urban settings.	**Habitat:** This is a forest species that prefers mature woodlands with large trees for breeding. In winter, they are seen in a variety of wooded habitats.
Breeding: Breeds in tundra areas and southward into the higher altitudes of the Rocky Mountains. Lays 3 to 7 eggs in a nest on the ground.	**Breeding:** Builds a nest of grasses. Nest site is typically high on a tree branch. Nesting in Illinois occurs in June. Lays 3 to 5 eggs.	**Breeding:** The nest is nearly always built behind a piece of loose bark on the trunk of a large dead tree. 5 or 6 eggs is typical.
Natural History: The American Pipit is a hardy species that nests in America's coldest climates. They move south in the winter where they are easily overlooked. Their mottled brown winter plumage is highly cryptic, especially where they usually reside in expansive, open fields or mud flats. During migration and in winter, they may be seen in the company of flocks of Horned Larks or rarely with Lapland Longspurs (another winter migrant from the far north). Characteristically wags its tail up and down. Despite being widespread (their range includes all of North America) they are relatively unknown birds to many. Another similar species, the **Sprague's Pipit** (*Anthus spragueii*) is an uncommon winter visitor to Illinois from the western prairies.	**Natural History:** Waxwings are named for the peculiar red-colored waxy feathers on their wings. The name "Cedar" Waxwing comes from their propensity for Eastern Red Cedar trees where they consume large quantities of cedar berries. These birds are highly social and are usually seen in large flocks. They feed mostly on berries and wander relentlessly in search of this favored food item. During the summer, insects, mulberries, and serviceberries are important food items. Crabapples and other fruiting trees are also favored. They are highly irregular in occurrence but are frequently seen across the state as they rove around in search of food sources. Large flocks are known to descend on a fruiting bush and consume every berry. Rarely seen singly or in pairs.	**Natural History:** Brown Creepers feed on small insects, spiders, etc., found in tree-trunk bark crevices. They have the peculiar foraging habit of landing on the trunk at the base of the tree and "creeping" upward, spiraling around the tree as they go. When they reach a certain height, they fly down to the base of another nearby tree and begin again. In Illinois, the Brown Creeper is a bit of a loner, and it is rare to see more than 1 or 2 in any one area. This is the only representative of the creeper family (Certhidae) found in North America. Several other species occur in Eurasia and Africa. Population declines in regions where mature forests have been reduced suggests a dependence upon that habitat type. Has probably declined in Illinois since European settlement.

Class - **Aves** (birds)

Order - **Passeriformes** (songbirds)

Family - **Paridae** (chickadee family)

Carolina Chickadee *Poecile carolinensis*	**Black-capped Chickadee** *Poecile atricapillus*	**Tufted Titmouse** *Baeolophus bicolor*

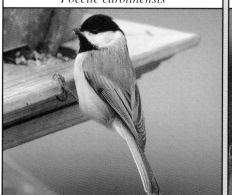

Carolina Chickadee

Size: 4.75 inches.

Abundance: Very common.

Variation: None. Sexes alike.

Migratory Status: Carolina Chickadee is year-round resident in the southern two-thirds of the state.

 Presumed range in Illinois

Black-capped Chickadee

Size: 5.25 inches.

Abundance: Common.

Variation: None. Sexes alike.

Migratory Status: Black-capped Chickadee is year-round resident in the northern half of the state.

Presumed range in Illinois

Tufted Titmouse

Size: 6 inches.

Abundance: Very common.

Variation: None. Sexes alike.

Migratory Status: A year-round resident. Like Chickadees, this species is common at feeders during winter.

  Presumed range in Illinois

Habitat: Carolina Chickadee is primarily a deciduous woodland species but may be found anywhere so long as at least a few trees are present. Black-capped Chickadee adds coniferous woodlands to its habitat types. Both may be found in urban and rural areas, and both show a preference for edge areas.

Habitat: Small woodlots and successional areas. Favors edge habitats. Common in both rural and urban habitats.

Breeding: Both species are cavity nesters that will use hollows in limbs, rotted fence posts, etc. or very often, old woodpecker holes. Man-made nest boxes may also be used, but are natural cavities are preferred. Carolina Chickadee lays 4 to 6 eggs in April or May. Black-capped lays 6 to 7 eggs from late April to early June.

Breeding: This species is a cavity nester that will utilize natural cavities as well as old woodpecker holes. Average of 5 eggs.

Natural History: Among our smallest songbirds, the Chickadees are a familiar bird at feeders throughout the state. They will become quite acclimated to people, and with some patient coaxing, they may be induced to land upon an outstretch hand containing sunflower seeds. An acrobatic little bird when searching for insect prey, they can dangle upside down from tiny branches. Their whistling song and their "chick-a-dee-dee-dee" call is distinctive and they can be quite noisy at times. In winter they will form mixed flocks with other small birds. They are hyperactive, tiny birds that have high energy requirements. Winter mortality can be high. The ranges of these 2 very similar species are generally mutually exclusive, with the Black-capped occupying the more northerly regions. In fact, the Black-capped ranges as far north as northern Canada and Alaska. The Carolina, on the other hand, is a southern bird that ranges across the southeastern United States (except for the highest elevations in the Appalachian Mountains). In harsh winter weather, Black-cappeds may move a little farther south into the range of the Carolina Chickadee, and hybrids between these 2 species are known to occur where the ranges meet in the eastern United States. Of the 2, the Black-capped is slightly larger and has more of a white "frosting" on the wings. The range maps above are at best close approximations of the ranges of these 2 species rather than exact depictions of where they might occur in the state.

Natural History: Primarily a seed eater in winter, the Tufted Titmouse is one of the first birds to find a new bird feeder. Sunflower seeds are favored, but they also love peanuts. Like Chickadees, they are sometimes quite bold around humans servicing feeders. In warm months, they forage for small insects and spiders among the foliage of trees. They can sometimes be seen hanging upside down on a small branch or leaf as they search for prey. Their familiar song is a melodic "birdy-birdy-birdy." In the winter, they mix readily with Chickadees and other small birds. Their range corresponds closely to the Eastern Temperate Forest Level I Ecoregion. Recently this species appears to be expanding its range farther to the north.

Class - Aves (birds)

Order - Passeriformes (songbirds)

Family - Regulidae (kinglets)

Ruby-crowned Kinglet *Regulus calendula*	Golden-crowned Kinglet *Regulus satrapa*

Male

Female

Female

Size: 4.25 inches.

Presumed range in Illinois

Abundance: Fairly common. During periods of peak migration they can be quite common, especially during fall cold fronts.

Variation: Male has red stripe on head that is most visible when the male is excited. Females lack this red stripe on the crown. Otherwise sexes are very similar. Spring birds and juveniles are grayer above and less yellowish below.

Migratory Status: Spring and fall migrant that passes through the state. They summer well to the north. A few may spend the winter in the southernmost parts of the state, but will move south if the weather gets to harsh.

Habitat: Summer habitat is undisturbed boreal forest across all of Canada from the Atlantic to the Pacific and well into Alaska. Also summers in the higher elevations of the Rocky Mountains. Winter habitats much more generalized to include deciduous and mixed woodlands as well as swamps and lowlands.

Breeding: Breeds in old growth conifers in the far north. Produces enormous clutches of up to 12 eggs. Nest is built near the tops of spruce trees or fir trees. Nest is constructed of a wide variety of materials including mosses, lichens, blades of grass, and conifer needles. Fur, feathers, or animal hair are used to line the nest.

Natural History: This is one of America's smallest songbird species, smaller even than the Chickadee. The bright red blaze on the top of the head of the male is usually not visible unless the feathers of the crown are erected. Males most often display the red feathers on the crown when issuing a challenge to other males, displaying to females, or singing their territorial song. Otherwise their bright red crown feathers will remain hidden from view. In summer they prey on arthropods and their eggs. In winter they will also feed on berries and some seeds. They are hyperactive little birds that forage throughout the canopy as well as along lower branches. Clumps of dead leaves hanging from a tree limb are like magnets to these tiny hunters who will find small spiders, insects, and other diminutive arthropods hiding within the clumps. They are constantly in motion and regularly flick the wings open as they hop quickly from tiny branch to tiny branch at the terminal end of boughs of trees and bushes. Hunts mostly along the tips of smaller branches. Some studies suggest this species may be declining in the eastern United States. Some suggest this decline may be due to logging and forest fragmentation in the breeding range. Birds that pass through Illinois are true latitudinal (north-south) migrants. Populations in the living in the Rocky Mountains of the western United States migrate from high elevations to lower elevations (altitudinal migration).

Size: 4 inches.

Abundance: Fairly common.

Variation: Males have orange crown, females (shown) have yellow crown.

Migratory Status: A winter resident that usually arrives in September or October.

Habitat: This is a forest species that prefers mature woodlands with large trees for breeding. In winter they are seen in a variety of wooded habitats.

Breeding: Builds its nest in the top of a spruce or fir in northern woodlands. Lays a large clutch of up to 11 eggs and may produce 2 broods per year.

Natural History: Even smaller than its cousin the Ruby-crowned Kinglet, the Golden-crowned is a hardier bird that can tolerate colder winter weather. However, severe winter conditions can lead to near 100 percent mortality in localized areas. Amazingly, this little carnivore manages to find arthropod prey throughout the winter and does not switch to seeds and berries in colder weather. Hyperactive and always in motion. They often feed by "leaf hawking" (hovering while picking tiny insects from beneath a leaf). In winter they are often seen in small groups or mixed flocks. There are a few records of Golden-crowned Kinglets in northern Illinois in summer, but that is very rare.

Class - **Aves** (birds)

Order - **Passeriformes** (songbirds)

Family - **Sittidae** (nuthatches)

White-breasted Nuthatch *Sitta carolinensis*	Red-breasted Nuthatch *Sitta canadensis*

Size: 5.75 inches.

Abundance: Fairly common.

Variation: None. Sexes alike.

Migratory Status: A year-round resident in Illinois

Habitat: This is a bird of deciduous and mixed woodlands. Mature forests are preferred, but they also occupy regrowth.

Breeding: Nests in natural tree cavities or woodpecker holes. Averages 6 eggs per clutch. Only 1 brood per year is produced, and young fledge in late May.

Presumed range in Illinois

Size: 4.5 inches.

Abundance: Fairly common.

Variation: None. Sexes alike.

Migratory Status: Mostly a fall and winter resident in Illinois.

Habitat: Summers in the spruce-fir forests of the north and west. Occupies deciduous woodlands in Illinois.

Breeding: Cavity nester that excavates their own nest holes in the manner of woodpeckers. Average of 6 eggs. Some breeding has been recorded in Illinois.

Presumed range in Illinois

Natural History: Nuthatches are famous for foraging tree trunks in an upside down position. This behavior gives them the opportunity to occupy a different feeding niche from woodpeckers and other bark hunting birds that hunt from an upright position. By creeping down the trunk in an upside down position, the nuthatches may see tiny prey hidden in crevices visible only from an above perspective and therefore missed by woodpeckers and creepers. This is an example of different species partitioning habitat by exhibiting different foraging behavior. In addition to insects, they also eat seeds and are regulars at most bird feeders in the state. They will cache seeds in bark crevices and they tend to be quite territorial. Pairs will stake out a territory and typically live within that area throughout the year. 1 of 4 species of nuthatch found in North America and the only one that is a full-time inhabitant of deciduous woodlands. Other species occupy boreal forests, southern pine forests, and western pine forests.

Natural History: These birds have a tendency to make "irruptive" migrations far to the south in winter every few years, and the exact mechanism of their irruptive movements remains something of a mystery. It is believed to be related to cone production in northern coniferous forests where this species usually lives. During the spring and summer, the Red-breasted Nuthatch feeds entirely on small arthropods. Seeds are the staple food during winter, and Sunflower seeds are a favorite item at bird feeders. They will wedge seeds into bark crevices to hold them fast while using the beak to hammer open the shell in characteristic "nuthatch" fashion. They will glean insects from bark in the same upside down manner as their larger cousin the White-breasted Nuthatch. Unlike many cavity nesters, the Red-breasted Nuthatch seems to avoid using man-made nest boxes. It may take over 2 weeks to excavate their nest hole. They will reportedly line the entrance of the nest cavity with resin from conifers, possibly to deter other cavity nesters or potential predators.

Class - **Aves** (birds)

Order - **Passeriformes** (songbirds)

Family - **Troglodytidae** (wrens)

Carolina Wren *Thryothorus ludovicianus*	Marsh Wren *Cistothorus palustris*	Sedge Wren *Cistothorus platensis*

Size: 5.5 inches.	**Size:** 5 inches.	**Size:** 4.25 inches.
Abundance: Common.	**Abundance:** Uncommon.	**Abundance:** Uncommon.
Migratory Status: Carolina Wrens are a year-round resident in all of Illinois.	**Migratory Status:** Summer resident in all but southern Illinois, where it is a migrant.	**Migratory Status:** Migrant in southern Illinois. Summer resident elsewhere in the state.
Variation: No population variations, and the sexes are alike.	**Variation:** No population variations, and the sexes are alike.	**Variation:** No populattion variations and the sexes are alike.

Presumed range in Illinois

Habitat: Carolina Wrens are very flexible in habitat choices. They can be seen in remote wilderness or in suburban backyards.	**Habitat:** Pastures, marshes, and lowland meadows as well as open, grassy edges of wetlands or ponds. Coastal salt marshes are widely used in winter.	**Habitat:** This is a wetland species that enjoys marshes and wet meadows. Unlike the Marsh Wren, it does not occupy cattail marsh but prefers grassy areas.
Breeding: A nest of fine twigs and grass is built in a sheltered place, often provided by man. Eggs number 3 to 6. Will produce at least 2 clutches per year.	**Breeding:** Nest is low in grasses or small bush. Nest is built of grasses woven into a ball with an entrance hole in the side. Several unused "decoy" nests are built. 7 eggs is typical.	**Breeding:** Nest is built low to the ground, often in a clump of sedges or a small bush. 6 or 7 eggs is typical and some may produce 2 broods per year. Does nest in Illinois.
Natural History: Along with the House Wren, this is one of the most common wrens in Illinois. The Carolina Wren adapts well to human-influenced habitats and is well-known for building its nest in an old pair of shoes or in a vase of flowers left on the back porch for a few days. They will become quite tame around yards and porches and frequently endear themselves to their human neighbors. They are voracious consumers of insects, spiders, and caterpillars and help control insect pests around the home. They are also incessant singers whose musical song serves as a dawn alarm for many residents throughout the state. They are most common in the southern half of the state. In northern regions, they are vulnerable to harsh winters.	**Natural History:** Marsh Wrens winter to the south of Illinois but they are an uncommon summer resident in the much of the state. They may be seen anywhere in Illinois where suitable habitat exists during migration periods. These are secretive birds that can be very difficult to observe, even in areas where they are common. They spend most of their time hidden in thick stands of cattails or other vegetation deep in the marsh. Like most wrens, they will sing continuously in the breeding season and most bird-watchers confirm their presence by learning to recognize their song. Marsh Wrens will build one or more "decoy" nests that are never used, and they are also known to destroy the eggs of other birds that may be nesting in the vicinity of their own nests.	**Natural History:** This is another secretive species that is difficult to observe. Like the Marsh Wren, it winters well to the south of Illinois but it is an uncommon summer resident in the state. The natural history of this species is poorly known, but it is known that nesting dates vary considerably from one region of the country to another. Nesting can occur from May to as late as September. Some birds may produce 2 broods per year in 2 different regions. The diet is spiders and insects. Sedge Wrens winter in the coastal plain of the southeastern United States from the Carolinas all the way to northwestern Mexico. Fall migration begins in September and most birds are usually gone from the northern portions of their range by late October. Spring migration is in April and May.

Class - **Aves** (birds)

Order - **Passeriformes** (songbirds)

Family - **Troglodytidae** (wrens)		Family - **Poliptilidae** (gnatcathers)
House Wren *Troglodytes aedon*	**Winter Wren** *Troglodytes hiemalis*	**Blue-gray Gnatcatcher** *Polioptila caerulea*

House Wren	Winter Wren	Blue-gray Gnatcatcher
Size: 4.75 inches.	**Size:** 4 inches.	**Size:** 4.25 inches.
Abundance: Very common.	**Abundance:** Uncommon.	**Abundance:** Common.
Variation: Sexes are alike.	**Variation:** No variation, sexes alike.	**Variation:** No significant variation.
Migratory Status: A spring/summer resident that begins to arrive in Illinois in April and departs in the fall.	**Migratory Status:** Mostly a winter resident and migrant. Lingers then moves farther south in harsh winter weather.	**Migratory Status:** One of the earliest returning summer migrants, arriving in southern Illinois as early as late March.

Presumed range in Illinois

Habitat: Prefers open and semi-open habitats. These wrens readily associate with humans and are most common in small towns and suburbs. They can also be common in more natural habitats.

Habitat: Mature, old growth forests are the primary summer habitat, often near a stream or bog. Deciduous and mixed woodlands are utilized in winter, but conifers are preferred.

Habitat: Occupies a wide variety of forested or successional habitats. Most common along wooded streams and bottoms. Shows a definite preference for deciduous woodlands.

Breeding: A cavity nester, the House Wren readily takes to artificial nest boxes. In fact, this species may owe its increase in population to man-made "birdhouses." Lays up to 8 eggs.

Breeding: Breeds to the north of Illinois, mainly in the boreal forests of Canada. Nest is often constructed in the root wad of an upturned tree. Lays 5 to 9 eggs.

Breeding: Nest is a cuplike structure built with lichens and plant fibers glued together with spider web. Nest usually placed at mid-level near the terminus of a branch. 4 to 5 eggs is average.

Natural History: Although the House Wren may be seen anywhere in Illinois, it may be more common in the northern portions of the state during the breeding season. It is perhaps least common in the southern tip of the state, but it does breed statewide. They are more common today than in historical times, as they favor open and semi-open habitats over dense forests. They also have a strong affinity for human-altered habitats and settlements. They feed on a wide variety of insects, spiders, snails, caterpillars, etc. When feeding large broods of young, they catch huge quantities daily. House Wrens range from coast to coast across America and northward into the prairie provinces of Canada.

Natural History: Much shyer and more secretive than other wrens, the Winter Wren skulks about under dense bushes and shrubs where it tends to stay close to the ground. This species has likely declined since presettlement times due to the destruction of ancient forests. Like other wrens, these birds are strictly carnivorous and feed on a wide variety of small insects, larva, arachnids, amphipoda, etc. As with many other invertivorous birds, they are vulnerable to exceptionally harsh winters. Their stubby, upturned tail makes identification easy, but they are more often heard than seen as they are persistent, loud singers. Winter Wrens are holarctic in distribution, being found in Europe and northern Asia as well as North America.

Natural History: As their name implies, gnatcatchers feed on tiny prey. Any type of small arthropod is probable food item. They hunt the tips of tree branches and sometimes pick off prey while hovering. Despite their small size, they will chase away larger birds and will mob predators such as hawks, snakes, or house cats. The gnatcatchers are a unique family that is probably most closely related to the wrens. Like many small songbird species, the Blue-gray Gnatcatcher is often the victim of nest parasitism by the Brown-headed Cowbird, which lays its eggs in other birds nests. Despite cowbirds, they seem to be a thriving species and their range has been expanding northward in recent times.

Class - **Aves** (birds)

Order - **Passeriformes** (songbirds)

Family - **Hirundinidae** (Swallows)

Barn Swallow	Cliff Swallow	Bank Swallow
Hirundo rustica	*Petrochelidon pyrrhonota*	*Riparia riparia*

Size: 7 inches.

Abundance: Very common throughout most of the state.

Variation: Males are slightly more vivid.

Migratory Status: A summer resident that returns to the state in April.

Presumed range in Illinois

Habitat: Open and semi-open habitats. Most common in agricultural areas but found virtually everywhere in the state. Least common in forest areas.

Breeding: Nest is bowl-shaped and made of mud and grasses, plastered to roof joists of a barn or eaves of buildings, beneath concrete bridges, etc.

Natural History: A familiar bird to all who grew up on rural farmsteads, Barn Swallows are common throughout most of North America in summer. They summer in the US and winter in Central and South America. European breeders winter in the Mediterranean, Africa, and the Middle East while Asian breeding birds winter throughout southeast Asia to Australia, making this one of the most widespread bird species in the world. Its long association with humans throughout the world has led to the invention of many legends. Barn Swallows nesting in your barn was considered by pioneers as good luck, while destroying a nest in the barn would cause the milk cow to go dry. Flying insects are the main food, including pesky flies and even wasps. This is the world's most common swallow species.

Size: 5.5 inches.

Abundance: Fairly common in most of Illinois.

Variation: No variation. Sexes alike.

Migratory Status: Summer resident. Seen in Illinois from April to September.

Presumed range in Illinois

Habitat: Open areas near large bodies of water are the preferred habitat for this species. Breeding habitat was historically limited to regions with cliff faces.

Breeding: Conical mud nests are plastered beneath sheltered overhangs of concrete structures such as bridges or dams. 4 eggs is typical.

Natural History: The Cliff Swallow is primarily a western species that nested historically on cliff faces in the Rocky Mountains. They are more numerous today than even a few decades ago. Man-made structures such as dams and bridges have likely helped this species expand its range in the eastern United States. These birds are colony animals that seem to always nest in groups. A source of mud for building nests is required, and there seems to be a preference for nesting near water. Colony size varies from a few dozen to a few hundred nests. Farther west, where the species is more common and widespread, colonies consisting of several thousand nests are known. Like other swallows, they feed almost entirely upon airborne insects, and they are adept at locating swarms of airborne prey.

Size: 5.25 inches.

Abundance: Uncommon in much of Illinois.

Variation: No variation. Sexes alike.

Migratory Status: Summer resident. Seen in Illinois from April to September.

Presumed range in Illinois

Habitat: Open country near large rivers. In migration may be seen in a wide variety of habitats but most often observed in valleys, near lakes, etc.

Breeding: Historically nested in high steep banks along major rivers. Nest hole is dug by the parents and may be as much as 2 to 3 feet deep. 4 to 6 eggs.

Natural History: Although widespread across America during migration, this species is rather rare in much of the state. Like many swallows, the Bank Swallow nests in large communities. Nest colonies are usually associated with large river systems with exposed cliff faces. Despite being somewhat uncommon in Illinois, these birds are found throughout the world; in fact, they are one of the most widespread bird species on Earth. The natural nesting habitat has always been riverbanks and bluffs, but today they utilize the banks created by man-made quarries or road cuts through hillsides. During migration, Bank Swallows can be seen in the company of other species of migrating swallows. Food is exclusively flying insects caught on the wing. Mostly flies, flying ants, small beetles, and mayflies.

Class - **Aves** (birds)

Order - **Passeriformes** (songbirds)

Family - **Hirundinidae** (Swallows)

Northern Rough-winged Swallow *Stelgidopteryx serripennis*	Tree Swallow *Tachycineta bicolor*	Purple Martin *Progne subis*

Northern Rough-winged Swallow		Tree Swallow		Purple Martin	
Size: 5.5 inches.	Presumed range in Illinois	**Size:** 5.75 inches.	Presumed range in Illinois	**Size:** 8 inches.	Presumed range in Illinois
Abundance: Fairly common.		**Abundance:** Fairly common.		**Abundance:** Fairly common.	
Variation: No variation, sexes alike.		**Variation:** Sexes alike. Immatures are gray.		**Variation:** Sexually dimorphic (see photos).	
Migratory Status: Summer resident. Winters in south Florida and in Central America. In Illinois from April to October.		**Migratory Status:** A warm-weather bird. Arrives in Illinois as early as March after wintering well to the south.		**Migratory Status:** Summer resident. The first arriving birds are males and they may arrive as early as late March.	

Habitat: Mainly open and semi-open areas, but can be found in forested regions along rivers or cliffs.	**Habitat:** Open and semi-open habitats. Fond of being near water, including small farm ponds and Beaver swamps.	**Habitat:** Inhabits both rural areas and suburbs. Artificial nest boxes near water in open areas are attractants.
Breeding: Nests in crevices in rock faces, cliffs, etc. Today often uses man-made situations such as road cuts, quarries, etc. Not a colony nester. Lays 4 to 8 eggs.	**Breeding:** A cavity nester, Tree Swallows will use old woodpecker holes or tree hollows. They also use artificial nest boxes and sometimes nest in close proximity to Purple Martins.	**Breeding:** Originally nested in natural cavities but today nearly all use artificial nest sites. 3 to 6 eggs is typical but may lay as many as 7 or 8. Purple Martins are colony nesters.
Natural History: As with other swallows, the Rough-winged Swallow feeds by catching flying insects in midair. All swallows in America are diurnal hunters whose predatory role is replaced at dusk by the bats. Although this swallow is found from coast to coast across America, it is not extremely common anywhere. Unlike the similar Bank Swallow, Rough-winged Swallows are not known to dig their own burrow, and availability of nest burrows may be one reason why these swallows tend to be solitary nesters. They will use burrows dug by other species of birds or small mammals as well as natural cavities in cliff faces. They are also known to use man-made structures. In mountainous regions, this species is usually associated with river valleys.	**Natural History:** Tree Swallows are more numerous today than in historical times and are increasing in numbers in the state. Human activities have benefited this species by creating more open lands and also by creating more ponds and lakes throughout the landscape. The proliferation of artificial nest boxes has also helped (they take readily to Bluebird Boxes) and the resurgence of Beaver populations is also credited with helping this species. Flying insects are the primary food items, but they species also eats bayberries during the winter. They are also known to eat snails during the breeding season to obtain calcium for eggshell production. The Tree Swallow winters along the southeastern coastline of the US, Florida, Mexico, and the Caribbean.	**Natural History:** Our largest swallow and perhaps the most beloved bird in America. Many people anxiously await the return of Purple Martins each spring to nest boxes erected in their yard. This bird's relationship with humans extends at least as far back as the 18th century and today there are at least 2 national organizations dedicated to Purple Martin enthusiasts. House Sparrows and Starlings sometimes take over "martin houses" unless the landowner is vigilant. Mainly a warm-weather species that is dependent upon flying insect prey, Purple Martins are vulnerable to spring cold fronts in the more northern reaches of the summer range. This species is so adapted to nesting in man-made nest boxes that today it is rare to find one nesting in natural cavities.

Class - **Aves** (birds)

Order - **Passeriformes** (songbirds)

Family - **Corvidae** (jays & crows)

Blue Jay *Cyanocitta cristata*	**American Crow** *Corvus brachyrhynchos*	**Fish Crow** *Progne subis*

Blue Jay

Size: 11 inches.

Abundance: Common.

Variation: No variation, sexes alike.

Migratory Status: Although some populations may migrate, Blue Jays can be seen in Illinois year-round.

Presumed range in Illinois

Habitat: Statewide from dense woodlands to semi-open farmlands. They can also be common in suburban and urban neighborhoods.

Breeding: Builds a stick nest fairly high up on a tree branch, often in a fork. Lays an average of 4 eggs usually in April. Blue Jays in the southern United States may produce two clutches.

Natural History: The Blue Jay's handsome blue, black, and white feathers and distinctive crest make it one of the most recognizable birds in the state. They mainly eat insects, acorns, and grains, but also eat eggs and young of other songbirds. They will aggressively mob much larger birds like hawks and owls, as well as snakes and house cats. Members of this family are relatively long-lived. The record life span for a wild Blue Jay is 18 years, but a captive specimen was reported to have lived for 26 years. An endemic American bird, Blue Jays are found throughout the eastern half of the United States from about the Rocky Mountains eastward. They also range northward into Canada but well below the Arctic Circle. They may be very common in suburban areas.

American Crow

Size: 17.5 inches

Abundance: Common.

Variation: No variation, sexes alike.

Migratory Status: This is one of our year-round birds, but migrant crows from Canada increase the population in winter.

Presumed range in Illinois

Habitat: Occurs in virtually all habitats including urban areas. Favors regions where there is a patchwork of woods and open spaces.

Breeding: Crows build a bulky stick nest high in the fork of a tree, well hidden by thick foliage. The nest is quite large and may be 2 feet across. 4 eggs is a typical clutch.

Natural History: Crows are omnivores that will eat virtually anything, including the young and eggs of other birds. They are among the most intelligent and resourceful of birds. They may be seen in pairs, small groups, or large flocks numbering in the hundreds. Highly adaptable, crows have fared well in human-altered habitats and the species is more common today than prior to European settlement. It is almost certain to remain a common species. As a testament to the crow's intelligence, in rural areas where hunting is commonplace, they are extremely wary of humans; while in protected parks and urban regions, they will become quite accepting of the presence of humans. In such environments they will raid suburban yards for pet food and garbage.

Fish Crow

Size: 15 inches.

Abundance: Uncommon.

Variation: No variation, sexes alike.

Migratory Status: Summer migrant that winters in the lower coastal plain. Seen in only in southern Illinois.

Presumed range in Illinois

Habitat: Restricted to the floodplains of the Mississippi and Ohio Rivers, as well as near the mouths of tributaries. May be expanding range northward.

Breeding: Large stick nest is placed in a tree crotch. Averages clutch size is about 4 eggs. Only a single clutch is produced annually. Breeding in Illinois has been recorded.

Natural History: Identical to the America Crow but smaller (17 inches), the Fish Crow occurs in Illinois only along the major rivers in the southern tip of the state. They are often seen in the company of their larger cousin and when seen together the Fish Crow can be distinguished by its smaller size. Expert bird-watchers can identify this species by its call, which is higher pitched than that of the American Crow. A southern species that historically was found in coastal areas and lowlands of the lower coastal plain, the Fish Crow has expanded its range northward over the last few decades. They were first recorded in the Mississippi Alluvial Plain of Kentucky about 50 years ago. Today they range well up into southern Illinois during summer.

Class - **Aves** (birds)
Order - **Passeriformes** (songbirds)
Family - **Vironidae** (vireos)

Yellow-throated Vireo *Vireo flavifrons*	White-eyed Vireo *Vireo griseus*	Blue-headed Vireo *Vireo solitarius*

Size: 5.5 inches.  Presumed range in Illinois	**Size:** 5 inches.  Presumed range in Illinois	**Size:** 5.5 inches.  Presumed range in Illinois
Abundance: Mostly uncommon.	**Abundance:** Common.	**Abundance:** Uncommon in Illinois.
Variation: No variation, sexes alike.	**Variation:** No variation, sexes alike.	**Variation:** No variation, sexes alike.
Migratory Status: A long-range migrant that winters as far away as northern South America. Returns in April.	**Migratory Status:** Winters from the lower coastal plain into Mexico, Cuba and Bahamas. Returns in April.	**Migratory Status:** Another spring/fall migrant that passes through Illinois in April and in September.
Habitat: A woodland bird that will inhabit a wide variety of forest types excluding stands of pure conifers. In Illinois, more common in areas of extensive forest where it prefers edge areas.	**Habitat:** Dense thickets and early successional hardwoods are favored. May also be seen in later stage successional deciduous woodlands and in overgrown fields with small saplings and thickets.	**Habitat:** This vireo likes expanses of mature forests, and is also partial to conifers for its summer habitat. It thus summers mostly well to the north of Illinois in the boreal forests of Canada.
Breeding: The nest is a woven basket usually suspended from the fork of a small branch at the mid-story level. 4 eggs is typical.	**Breeding:** Nest is a woven, hanging basket held together with silk from caterpillars or spiders placed in a fork very low to the ground. 3 to 5 eggs.	**Breeding:** Nest construction is similar to other vireos. A tightly woven cup is suspended from a horizontal fork. 4 eggs is typical.
Natural History: The nest is usually located in a branch overhanging a forest opening such as a lane or a stream. Feeds on a wide variety of arthropods with caterpillars being a mainstay. Also eats small amount of berries and seeds in the fall. The biology of this species is not as well understood as with many other vireos, but it is known that it has decreased in numbers in areas of deforestation. As with many small woodland songbirds, the nest of the Yellow-throated Vireo is subject to parasitism by cowbirds. The summer range of this species coincides closely with the Eastern Temperate Forest Level I Ecoregion. The winter range is from southern Mexico to northern South America. Migrants regularly cross the Gulf of Mexico.	**Natural History:** This is the only vireo with a white iris, making identification easy. Nest parasitism by Brown-headed Cowbirds is estimated to be as high as 50 percent, with no young surviving in parasitized nests. Highly insectivorous. Caterpillars are a favorite food item. Will also eat fruit. White-eyed Vireos winter along the lower coastal plain of the US, the Caribbean, and the Yucatan Peninsula. Like the previous species, nest parasitism by Brown-headed Cowbirds posses a potential threat. Deforestation contributes to the problem. Brown-headed Cowbirds tend to avoid deep woods in favor of more open habitats. Loss of large tracts of woodland makes life easier for the cowbirds and more difficult for the species which they parasitize.	**Natural History:** Also known as the Solitary Vireo. Most Blue-headed Vireos summer to the north of Illinois in Canada, but breeding has been recorded in Illinois. They winter from the lower coastal plain of the southeastern US all the way to Central America. They are quite common in peninsular Florida throughout the winter. Food is mostly insects, with moths and butterflies and their larva being a major portion of the diet. Most foraging is done in trees well above the forest floor. As is the case with many of America's migrant songbirds, the Blue-headed Vireo is highly dependent upon large tracts of forest. Deforestation negatively impacts local populations; but forest regeneration in many areas of its summer range has helped this species in recent years.

Class - **Aves** (birds)
Order - **Passeriformes** (songbirds)
Family - **Vironidae** (vireos)

Red-eyed Vireo *Vireo olivaceus*	**Warbling Vireo** *Vireo gilvus*	**Philadelphia Vireo** *Vireo philadelphia*

Red-eyed Vireo

Size: 6 inches.

Abundance: Very common.

Presumed range in Illinois

Variation: Sexes alike but males are slightly larger.

Migratory Status: A summer resident that winters in the Amazon Basin. Arrives from early to late April.

Habitat: Although a woodland species, the Red-eyed Vireo is very generalized in its habitat requirements. Mature forests, regenerating woodlands and forest fragments are all occupied.

Breeding: 2 to 4 eggs are laid in May. May have 2 broods per summer with 2nd brood fledging in late August.

Natural History: This is one of the most common summer songbirds in America forests and woodlots, but it is not readily observed due to its habit of staying high in the forest canopy. It is however regularly heard, as it sings incessantly throughout the spring. While on their breeding grounds they are primarily insectivorous feeders, but they do consume some fruits while wintering in the tropics. The population health of the Red-eyed Vireo may be due to its less stringent dependence upon large tracts of forest. This species can subsist happily in small woodlands and regenerative areas. However, in these habitats it is more susceptible to the parasitic nesting of the Brown-headed Cowbird. Their red eye color is unique among vireos.

Warbling Vireo

Size: 5.5 inches.

Abundance: Fairly common.

Presumed range in Illinois

Variation: No variation between sexes or annual molts.

Migratory Status: Appears in Illinois in late April to early May. Winters in Mexico and Central America.

Habitat: Although this species likes mature trees in its habitat, it avoids dense forest in favor of areas with a mosaic of small woodlands. Riparian woodlands are also utilized.

Breeding: Nesting takes place in midsummer. Nests are placed high in trees. 4 eggs is typical.

Natural History: The Warbling Vireo is less common than the Red-eyed Vireo in Illinois. But, like the similar Red-eyed Vireo, they are persistent singers that are more often heard than seen. They feed by gleaning small insects and other arthropods from canopy foliage. A few seeds and berries are also sometimes eaten. This is one of the most widely distributed members of the North American Vironidae family. Their breeding range extends from coast to coast across the northern two-thirds of the United States as well as much of Canada. By contrast, the winter range is much smaller and restricted to the western half of Mexico and western Central America from northern Costa Rico northward.

Philadelphia Vireo

Size: 5.5 inches.

Abundance: Fairly common.

Presumed range in Illinois

Variation: Sexes alike. Juveniles brownish above.

Migratory Status: Migrant. Passes through in late spring or very early summer. Winters in Central America.

Habitat: Philadelphia Vireo can be found in large tracts of forest, but it seems to favor successional woodlands over mature forest. Uses mixed conifer and deciduous woodlands.

Breeding: The breeding range of the Philadelphia Vireo is contained mostly in Canada. 4 eggs is typical.

Natural History: The Philadelphia Vireo migrates through most of Illinois each spring but it does not nest in the state. They are a somewhat rarely observed bird and are difficult to distinguish from the more common Warbling Vireo, but they usually have more yellowish wash below. They are also very similar to the Red-eyed Vireo and their song also closely resembles that species. Their food is mostly caterpillars. As with many other neotropical migrant songbirds that can be seen in Illinois, this species is a trans-gulf migrant that makes epic non-stop flights across the Gulf of Mexico during migration. The **Bell's Vireo** (*V. belli*) is another similar species of *Vireo* that will spend the summer in Illinois and breeds widely, though it is uncommon in the state.

Class - **Aves** (birds)

Order - **Passeriformes** (songbirds)

Family - **Parulidae** (warblers)

Canada Warbler *Cardellina canadensis*	Wilson's Warbler *Cardellina pusilla*	Yellow-breasted Chat *Icteria virens*
	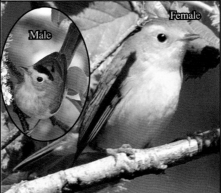 	

	Presumed range in Illinois		Presumed range in Illinois		Presumed range in Illinois
Size: 5.25 inches. **Abundance:** Uncommon. **Variation:** Females have less black. **Migratory Status:** Winters in South America. A few nest in northeast Illinois but most are just passing through in route to breeding grounds in Canada.		**Size:** 4.75 inches. **Abundance:** Uncommon. **Variation:** Black "cap" more prominent in males **Migratory Status:** A passage migrant in Illinois. Most spring migrating birds will have passed through the state by the end of May. Fall migration in September.		**Size:** 7.5 inches. **Abundance:** Fairly common. **Variation:** None. Sexes alike. **Migratory Status:** Summer resident. Winters in southern Mexico and throughout Central America. Arrives in Illinois for breeding in late April to early/mid-May.	

Habitat: Favors moist northern forests with thick understory shrubs. Known to associate with conifers on breeding grounds.

Habitat: Summer breeding habitat is in the boreal forests of Canada, Pacific Northwest, northern Rockies, and Alaska. Winter habitat is tropical forests.

Habitat: This warbler likes overgrown fields, second growth areas, and early successional regenerating woodlands. It avoids the deep woods.

Breeding: Nest is on the ground and hidden amid dense vegetation. In Canada nest is often placed amid carpet of moss. 4 to 5 eggs is typical.

Breeding: Nest is on the ground. Uniquely, the nest of this warbler is usually placed in a small depression. From 2 to 7 eggs may be laid.

Breeding: Nests low to the ground in brier thickets or a dense shrub such as a multiflora rose. Nest is cuplike. Lays 2 to 5 eggs.

Natural History: A few will nest in parts of the Midwestern US, but most (over 80 percent) will nest in Canada. Although they do migrate through most of the Illinois, they do so mostly at night and pass through quickly en route to breeding grounds farther to the north. The Canada Warbler has been in decline for several decades. Loss of breeding habitat in North America as well as wintering habitat in South America is probably to blame. Future threats include the Woolly Adelgid, and alien insect that is decimating hemlock forests throughout the eastern US. Formerly this species was placed in the genus *Wilsonia*.

Natural History: Wilson's Warbler is a not a common species in Illinois Although they may migrate through any part of the state, the bulk of this species population occurs and migrates to the west of Illinois. They are probably more numerous in the Pacific states than they are in the eastern United States. However, some studies indicate that they are declining in the west. Most blame the loss of riparian habitat for decline in western populations. They range as far north as the Arctic Ocean in summer and as far south as Panama in winter. The species name *"wilsonia"* is for early naturalist and ornithologist Alexander Wilson.

Natural History: The Yellow-breasted Chat is America's largest wood warbler and some question its status in the family Parulidae. They are fairly common in suitable habitats in Illinois in summer months but are not easily observed due to their secretive nature and preference for dense vegetation. Foods are a wide variety of arthropods with a preference for crickets, grasshoppers, caterpillars, and spiders. They are also known to eat some fruits and berries. These birds are probably more numerous today than prior to deforestation. Their breeding range in eastern North America corresponds closely to the Eastern Temperate Forest level I ecoregion.

Class - **Aves** (birds)

Order - **Passeriformes** (songbirds)

Family - **Parulidae** (warblers)

Swainson's Warbler *Lymnothlypis swaisonii*	Hooded Warbler *Setophaga citrina*	Northern Parula *Setophaga americana*

Size: 5.5 inches.	Presumed range in Illinois	**Size:** 5.25 inches.	Presumed range in Illinois	**Size:** 4.5 inches.	Presumed range in Illinois
Abundance: Very rare in Illinois.		**Abundance:** Fairly common.		**Abundance:** Fairly common.	
Variation: No variation and the sexes are identical.		**Variation:** Black "hood" on head and face is reduced in females.		**Variation:** Females lack black on breast but otherwise sexes are similar.	
Habitat: In Illinois, reportedly uses swamps and deep ravines in upland woods. In the Deep South, often associates with Giant Cane.		**Habitat:** A forest species. Most common in heavily forested regions but may be found anywhere that there is significant woodlands.		**Habitat:** Habitat is forest. Mostly bottomland woods or swamps or along streams and rivers. In Illinois, this species is seen mostly in the south.	

Migratory Status: Winters on the Yucatan Peninsula and in the northern Caribbean. They may be seen in Illinois from April through September. Believed to migrate across the Gulf of Mexico in spring.	**Migratory Status:** After wintering in Central America and parts of the Caribbean, the Hooded Warbler returns in late April (southern Illinois) or as late as mid-May (northern Illinois). Leaves for wintering grounds by September.	**Migratory Status:** Summer resident. Winters from south Florida to Central America. Arrives in April and begins to leave in August or September. All are gone by early October. Migrates at night.
Breeding: The nest is built on the ground and is made of dead leaves, rendering it quite cryptic and difficult to locate. Lays 3 to 4 eggs. Very few nests have been discovered in Illinois.	**Breeding:** Cup-shaped nest of grasses, bark, and dead leaves is woven into two or more upright limbs of a small bush near the ground. Nest sites are usually associated with dense shrubs. 4 eggs.	**Breeding:** Nests high in trees. Sycamores, Baldcypress, and Hemlocks are reported as favorite nest trees. In the Deep South nests are often built in Spanish moss. 4 or 5 eggs.
Natural History: This is the rarest warbler in Illinois. in fact it is one of the rarest birds in the state and one of the rarest warblers in America. A few pairs have been recorded in Illinois in Alexander, Jackson, and Johnson counties and they may occur in other southern Illinois counties. The Swainson's Warbler is primarily a ground dweller. In Illinois (and in much of its range in the Deep South,) this is a lowland species that is usually found in dense cane thickets. Some birds do summer and nest in upland regions of the southern Appalachian Mountains.	**Natural History:** Like many small, woodland birds, the Hooded Warbler is more likely to be heard than seen. On their breeding grounds in the eastern US they require large tracts of woodlands, and they have declined in areas where intensive agriculture or development has resulted in the loss of this habitat. This handsome little warbler is a good example of why the protection of extensive tracts of forest can be so important in the conservation of neotropical migrant songbirds. With the largest eyes of any warbler, this species is adapted to a life spent in heavy shade.	**Natural History:** The Northern Parula feeds by gleaning tiny arthropods from tree branches. They tend to feed and spend much time in the middle an upper story of the forest. This habit couple with their small size make them difficult to observe. These handsome little warblers are most common in deep forests and are least common in the northeast. They can be common breeding birds north of Illinois in Canada, but they seem to avoid most of the northern half of the state for nesting. They are one of the smallest warblers, but are strikingly colored, especially the males.

Class - **Aves** (birds)

Order - **Passeriformes** (songbirds)

Family - **Parulidae** (warblers)

Yellow Warbler *Setophaga petechia*	Black-throated Blue Warbler *Setophaga caerulescens*	Cerulean Warbler *Setophaga cerulea*

Size: 5 inches.	**Size:** 5.25 inches.	**Size:** 4.75 inches.
Presumed range in Illinois	Presumed range in Illinois	Presumed range in Illinois
Abundance: Common.	**Abundance:** Uncommon in Illinois.	**Abundance:** Uncommon in Illinois.
Variation: Chestnut streaks on breast reduced on female.	**Variation:** Female is olive brown above, drab olive-yellow below.	**Variation:** Female is blueish green with faded gray streaks.
Habitat: Thickets of willow or buttonbush in wet lowlands are the classic habitat for this species. Mesic upland woods may also be used.	**Habitat:** Summer habitat consists of large, contiguous tracts of mature northern forests. During migration seen in a variety of habitats.	**Habitat:** Summer habitat is primarily deciduous forests. Both bottomland forest and moist upland woods. requires mature forests.
Migratory Status: Summer resident. Winters in Mexico and Central America. Birds nesting in Illinois arrive in late April and early May. Fall migration is early. In fact, this is one of the earliest fall migrators, leaving in mid-July.	**Migratory Status:** A passage migrant in Illinois. May be seen in Illinois in late April or May as it moves through headed north. Departs breeding grounds in early fall and spends the winter in the Caribbean. Fall migration mostly east of Illinois.	**Migratory Status:** Winters in the Andes Mountains. Flies across the gulf to the southeastern US coast then northward into interior, arriving in Illinois by mid-April to early May. A few will reside in the state all summer.
Breeding: Nest is built in the upright fork of a sapling and averages four or five eggs. Nest is a cuplike structure made mostly from grasses. Breeds throughout the state.	**Breeding:** Nest is strips of bark lined with finer materials such as moss. Usually placed in an upright fork of dense shrub. Clutch size typically 4. Does not breed in Illinois.	**Breeding:** Nest is a tight cup woven around forked branches in the mid- to upper canopy level. Average clutch size is 3 or 4 to as many as 5. Breeding habitat includes thick understory.
Natural History: This is one of North America's most wide ranging of the warblers. Their summer breeding range encompasses the entire northern two thirds of North America, from the Atlantic to the Pacific and extends as far north as the Arctic Circle and they can be seen statewide in Illinois. Feeds on a variety of insects and other arthropods and uses a variety of foraging techniques including gleaning of leaves and branches, flying from perch to seize airborne prey and picking insects from leaves and branches while hovering. Caterpillars are an important food item during breeding.	**Natural History:** Most of this warblers summer/breeding habitat is to the north and east of Illinois. Summers mostly in the northeastern US and eastern Canada. In Illinois, it is seen only as a migrant and then only in spring as the fall migration is usually to east of Illinois. This species forages mostly in shrubs and branches at the mid-story level for caterpillars and other small arthropod prey. Deforestation and forest fragmentation in both summer and winter habitats are the greatest threats. These threats may be compounded by habitat degradation from alien species like the Woolly Adelgid.	**Natural History:** The Cerulean Warbler hunts high in the canopy, gleaning tiny invertebrates from small branches and leaves. Searches both upper and lower surface of leaves for food. Like many species dependent upon forests, this warbler experienced significant population declines following the European settlement of America. Today many states list it as a threatened species, including Illinois. Protection of large tracts of deciduous woodlands is probably the best conservation action that can be taken to help the species. Unfortunately, not enough of this type conservation takes place in Illinois.

Class - **Aves** (birds)

Order - **Passeriformes** (songbirds)

Family - **Parulidae** (warblers)

Magnolia Warbler *Setophaga magnolia*	**Yellow-rumped Warbler** *Setophaga coronata*	**Blackpoll Warbler** *Setophaga striata*

Size: 5 inches.	**Size:** 5.5 inches.	**Size:** 5.5 inches.
Abundance: Common.	**Abundance:** Common.	**Abundance:** Uncommon.
Variation: Sexually dimorphic. See above.	**Variation:** Sexually dimorphic. See above.	**Variation:** Sexually dimorphic. See above.
Migratory Status: Migrant that passes through in spring and fall. Most conspicuous in during spring migration.	**Migratory Status:** Mostly a spring/fall migrant but also a winter resident in southern part of the state.	**Habitat:** Summer habitat is taiga and tundra-taiga transition zones; often well above the arctic circle.
Habitat: Summer habitat for most is in spruce forests in Canada. In Illinois can be seen statewide during migration. Winters in Mexico, Central America, and the Caribbean.	**Habitat:** Outside its breeding range this warbler is a habitat generalist. It can be seen virtually anywhere in the state during spring or fall migrations. Summer habitat is boreal forests.	**Migratory Status:** This is a springtime migrant that passes through Illinois in April and May en route to breeding grounds in northern Canada. Fall migration is mostly east of Illinois.
Breeding: Nests in evergreen trees. The nest is usually well concealed amid dense vegetation. 4 eggs laid. Individuals that nest south of Canada will use stands of Eastern Hemlock exclusively.	**Breeding:** Breeds in the boreal forest of Canada and Alaska. Nest is built on the branch of a conifer. Clutch size is usually 4 or 5 eggs. 1 clutch per year. Vulnerable to cowbirds.	**Breeding:** Nest is an open cup built on a branch near the tree trunk, usually in a spruce and often only a few feet off the ground. Eggs number 3 to 5. Young fledge as early as within 8 to 10 days.
Natural History: Feeds on insects (including large numbers of caterpillars) that are caught near the ends of branches in dense conifer trees. Known to feed on the Spruce Budworm and may enjoy greater survival of offspring during years of budworm outbreaks. This is an abundant species that appears to be stable in population numbers. Leaves Central American wintering grounds in February and arrives in Illinois from mid-April to mid-May. They are fairly common migrants throughout the state in spring. Fall migration begins in September and may last into October. Fall migration routes generally more easterly than spring, thus they are usually observed in Illinois during spring migration.	**Natural History:** There are 2 morphologically distinct forms of this common warbler, one in the eastern US and one in the western US. The form seen in Illinois is sometimes called the "Myrtle Warbler." This species also exhibits seasonal plumage changes, with winter birds resembling females. In summer feeds mainly on insects, but if bad weather necessitates it is capable of surviving on berries during the winter. Unlike most warblers that will winter in the tropics, the Yellow-rumped is a hardy species and in mild winters can be seen as far north as southern Illinois, Indiana, and Ohio in the Midwest and New Jersey on the east coast. Populations of this bird seem fairly stable and it is probably in less jeopardy than many other warblers.	**Natural History:** This is one of the great long distance migrants among America's songbird species. In fall migration some may travel non-stop over the Atlantic Ocean from Newfoundland (Canada) all the way to South America. Considering that this is a bird that weighs less than 0.5 ounces, that is a remarkable feat of endurance. To accomplish this remarkable flight they will pack on a heavy layer of fat during summer. Although some individuals will pass through Illinois during the spring, they tend to stay hidden high in the forest canopy. The fall migration is mostly along the east coast. Thus this is a rarely seen bird in the state except by those who train themselves to look for it during spring migration.

Presumed range in Illinois (each column)

Class - **Aves** (birds)

Order - **Passeriformes** (songbirds)

Family - **Parulidae** (warblers)

Bay-breasted Warbler *Setophaga castenea*	Pine Warbler *Setophaga pinus*	Black-throated Green Warbler *Setophaga virens*
		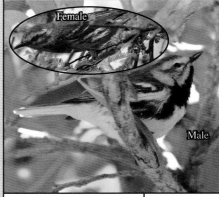

Bay-breasted Warbler	Pine Warbler	Black-throated Green Warbler
Size: 5.5 inches.	**Size:** 5.5 inches.	**Size:** 5 inches.
Abundance: Uncommon.	**Abundance:** Uncommon in Illinois.	**Abundance:** Fairly common.
Variation: See photos above. Female resembles fall male.	**Variation:** Males brighter, females and immatures are drabber.	**Variation:** Females have less black, more yellow on throat.
Migratory Status: Spring migrant. Fall migration is mostly east of the Appalachians.	**Migratory Status:** Mainly a summer resident, a few may linger into late fall or winter.	**Migratory Status:** Mostly a migrant. A few will summer and nest in northern Illinois.
Habitat: Summer habitat is spruce/fir woodlands of Canada. During migration it is found in a variety of habitats. Winter habitats are tropical forests of Central and South America.	**Habitat:** Pine forests are the primary habitat, but they are also seen in deciduous and mixed woodlands, especially during migration. In Illinois, they occur mostly in the southern part of the state.	**Habitat:** This warbler requires significant tracts of unbroken forests. Except for migration, it is an inhabitant of conifer and mixed conifer/deciduous forests, especially those containing hemlock.
Breeding: Nests in dense conifer trees on horizontal limb. Nest is cup-shaped and made of woven twigs, pine needles and grasses. Average clutch size is 5 or 6 eggs.	**Breeding:** Builds its nest high in pine trees. This is one of the earliest nesting warblers, with 3 or 4 eggs laid as early as mid-April. Breeding range is limited to regions where pines occur.	**Breeding:** Does not breed in Illinois. Most nesting occurs in the northern Great Lakes and in the Appalachian Mountains. Lays 4 eggs in nest usually built in a conifer.
Natural History: This long distance migrant is not commonly seen by residents of Illinois, as they pass through rather quickly. They migrate later than most other warblers and don't appear in northern Illinois until mid- to late May. Their primary food in summer is the Spruce Budworm caterpillar, and their populations may rise and fall with the availability of this insect. Populations have declined possibly due to spraying of Canadian forests to control spruce budworms. These birds are less common today than decades ago. They winter from southern Central America to northwestern South America. In the winter, they will eat fruit.	**Natural History:** As its name implies, this species is always found in association with pine trees. This is the only warbler whose range is contained entirely within the United States and Canada. It is also the only one of its kind to regularly change its diet from insects to seeds in the winter, thus it is one of the few warblers seen at bird feeders. These birds can reach high densities in winter in the southern pine forests, when resident populations are supplemented by northern migrants. Pine Warblers are much more tolerant of cold weather than other warblers, perhaps because they are able to switch from insects to seeds as a food source.	**Natural History:** Like others of its kind, this small, handsome warbler faces many threats. Red Squirrels are reportedly an important nest predator in the boreal forests of Canada and New England. In places the major threat may come from other birds like the Blue Jay, and from the common and widespread Midland Rat Snake. Sharp-shinned Hawks are always a threat to the adults, while Brown-headed Cowbirds parasitize the nest. Human activities such as forest fragmentation threaten populations as a whole. Add to that the impact of Woolly Adelgid insects on hemlock trees and you have an uncertain future for this and many other warbler species.

Class - **Aves** (birds)		
Order - **Passeriformes** (songbirds)		
Family - **Parulidae** (warblers)		
Blackburnian Warbler *Setophaga fusca*	**Palm Warbler** *Setophaga palmarum*	**Yellow-throated Warbler** *Setophaga dominca*

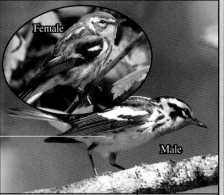

Blackburnian Warbler

Size: 5 inches.

Abundance: Fairly common migrant.

Variation: Bright orange of males reduced to yellowish wash on females and immatures.

Migratory Status: A spring/fall migrant in Illinois.

Presumed range in Illinois

Habitat: Summers mostly in mature coniferous and mixed forests. Migration habitat is highly variable. Birds that breed in the Appalachians favor groves of Eastern Hemlock.

Breeding: Does not nest in Illinois. Elsewhere nest is usually in a conifer and well concealed amid foliage. Average of 4 to 5 eggs.

Natural History: The beautiful blaze orange coloration on the head, throat, and breast of the Blackburnian Warbler is unmistakable. They are probably fairly common during migration. However, this is a difficult species to observe due to the fact that it is primarily a treetop dweller. Thus few people who are not trained to look for them will see them. They feed mostly on caterpillars. Blackburnian Warblers seen in Illinois are merely passing through en route to boreal forests far to the north. Some will nest in the southern Appalachians as far south as Alabama, but those that pass through Illinois are on their way to more northerly regions. Forest fragmentation on wintering grounds in South America may pose a threat.

Palm Warbler

Size: 5.5 inches.

Abundance: Fairly common migrant.

Variation: Does exhibit seasonal variation, but winter plumaged birds are not seen in Illinois.

Migratory Status: A spring and fall migrant in Illinois.

Presumed range in Illinois

Habitat: Summer habitat consists of bogs and woods openings in boreal forests. Transient in a variety of habitats during migration. Winter habitat is open woodlands, mangroves, and thickets.

Breeding: Nests of moss is on the ground in a northern bog, usually at the base of a conifer tree. Clutch size is 4 or 5. Many nest in remote wilderness.

Natural History: This species nests in the boreal forests of Canada and winters along the southeastern US coast (including all of Florida) and throughout the Caribbean. Unlike most warblers that spend most of their time high in the canopy, the Palm Warbler is a decidedly terrestrial species that hunts primarily on the ground or in low shrubs. It is one of the most northerly wintering of the warblers, with many staying in the southeast US or Florida (thus the name Palm Warbler). Their summer habitats are very far to the north, well into northern Canada. Food is mainly insects, mostly caught on the ground. Includes grasshoppers, beetles, lepidopterans, flies and bee larva. Some berries and nectar may be consumed in winter.

Yellow-throated Warbler

Size: 5.5 inches.

Abundance: Fairly common.

Variation: Sexes similar. No significant variation between adults and juveniles.

Migratory Status: A summertime resident in most of the state.

Presumed range in Illinois

Habitat: In Illinois found mostly along wooded stream corridors. Also uses bottomland forest and mature woodlands with open understory. Known to often associate with Sycamore trees.

Breeding: Nest is placed high in a tree, often a Sycamore. Nest is made of grasses and spider web and lined with soft materials. Four eggs is typical.

Natural History: This warbler species can be seen all summer in southern Illinois and a few begin arriving in early to mid-April. It winters in south Florida and the Caribbean. This is another "treetop" species that spends most of its time high in the canopy. It feeds on diminutive arthropods gleaned in a very deliberate fashion from branches, bark, leaves and petioles. This species retreated from the northern portions of its breeding range several decades ago, but is now showing a resurgence back into those areas. The cause of this population fluctuation is unknown, but possibly relates to habitat alterations by man, and a subsequent recovery of those habitats. They are a very rare species in northern Illinois in summer.

Class - **Aves** (birds)
Order - **Passeriformes** (songbirds)
Family - **Parulidae** (warblers)

Prairie Warbler *Setophaga discolor*	**Chestnut-sided Warbler** *Setophaga penslyvanica*	**American Redstart** *Setophaga ruticilla*

Prairie Warbler
Setophaga discolor

Size: 4.75 inches.

Abundance: Fairly common in southern Illinois.

Variation: Females less vividly marked, immatures paler.

Migratory Status: Summer resident. Occurs rarely north of area shown on map above.

Presumed range in Illinois

Habitat: Semi-open habitats. Old, overgrown fields, shrubby successional areas, second growth woodlands and cedar glades. Very rare to absent in intensive agricultural areas. Uses coastal dunes during winter.

Breeding: Breeds throughout the southern two-thirds of the state. An average of 4 eggs (3 to 5) are laid May to June.

Natural History: Insects, spiders, slugs, and other soft-bodied arthropods are listed as food items. Feeds from the ground all the way up to tree-tops, but mainly gleans lower bushes and shrubs. Tail-bobbing is a common behavior in this species. The Prairie Warbler winters farther north than many warbler species. While some fly as far as the Yucatan Peninsula, others stay in the northern Caribbean or Florida. They can be fairly common in the Florida Everglades during winter. Despite having benefited from clearing of forests the last century, there are unexplained declines in some populations in recent years.

Chestnut-sided Warbler
Setophaga penslyvanica

Size: 5 inches.

Abundance: Fairly common migrant.

Variation: Female like male but colors more subdued.

Migratory Status: Summer resident in most of the state. Migrant in the southern tip.

Presumed range in Illinois

Habitat: The Chestnut-sided Warbler is a bird of successional areas and shrubby, second-growth. Forest edges, early regenerative timber harvest areas, and forest clearings are favored for nesting. In migration also seen in mature woods.

Breeding: Nests fairly low to the ground in thick cover of dense sapling growth. 3 or 4 eggs are laid in late spring or early summer.

Natural History: This is one of the few warbler species that has benefited from deforestation. They are probably more common now than they were in the days prior to the European settlement of America. Despite their overall increase in population, they are negatively impacted by modern agricultural practices. The clearing of fence rows and overgrown field corners, and conversion of successional habitats into cropland eliminates their preferred habitat. They are thus absent from most agricultural regions except as a migrant. As with many other warbler species that travel through Illinois, the Chestnut-sided warbler breeds mostly far to the north in Canada or New England.

American Redstart
Setophaga ruticilla

Size: 5.75 inches.

Abundance: Fairly common.

Variation: Sexually dimorphic (see photos above).

Migratory Status: Summer resident. Arrives in April, departs in September.

Presumed range in Illinois

Habitat: Prefers deciduous woodlands over conifers. More common in second growth areas and riparian thickets. Larger woodlands are preferred over small woodlots. In winter range uses mangroves and tropical forests.

Breeding: The nest woven of thin fibers of grass or bark strips and placed in the crotch of an upright branch or trunk. Usually 4 eggs.

Natural History: The striking bright orange-on-black colors of the male flash like neon in the heavily shaded forests where this species makes its home. They are active little birds that display their bright colors by regularly spreading their tail feathers and drooping their wings. They hunt tiny insects among the foliage and often catch flying insects in mid-air. In Illinois, this species is much more common in forested regions and it may be absent from expansive agricultural regions. Small numbers winter in coastal Louisiana, the lower Rio Grande valley an the everglades region of south Florida. Most winter from northwest Mexico to northern South America. Clearing of tropical forests is a threat.

Class - **Aves** (birds)
Order - **Passeriformes** (songbirds)
Family - **Parulidae** (warblers)

Cape May Warbler *Setophaga tigrina*	**Orange-crowned Warbler** *Oreothlypis celata*	**Nashville Warbler** *Oreothlypis ruficapilla*

Size: 5 inches.	Presumed range in Illinois
Abundance: Uncommon.	
Variation: Females and immatures are less vividly colored.	
Migratory Status: Transient spring migrant. Not seen in fall.	

Size: 5 inches.	Presumed range in Illinois
Abundance: Uncommon in Illinois.	
Variation: Female slightly duller. Varies regionally.	
Migratory Status: Passage migrant in both spring and fall.	

Size: 4.75 inches.	Presumed range in Illinois
Abundance: Common migrant.	
Variation: Little variation. Sexes and immatures are all quite similar.	
Migratory Status: A pasage migrant in both spring and fall.	

Habitat: This is another species that summers in boreal forests, primarily in the vicinity of spruce bogs and other forest openings. Winter habitat is mostly in the West Indies.

Habitat: Summers in northern woodlands (Canada and Rocky Mountains) where it prefers habitats with significant understory. Also found old weedy fields, brier thickets, etc. during migration.

Habitat: Summer habitat includes tamarack bogs and boreal forests. Prefers second growth and open woodlands with shrubby undergrowth. Avoids the deep woods.

Breeding: Nest is near the trunk in the top of a spruce or fir. 5 or 6 eggs are laid in early to mid-June. 1 clutch per year.

Breeding: Breeds in northern Canada and as far north as Alaska and well into the Arctic Circle. Western subspecies breeds along west coast. Lays 4 to 5 eggs.

Breeding: Nests on the ground under bushes or in hummocks of grasses or sphagnum moss. Clutch size ranges from 3 to 6.

Natural History: On summer breeding grounds far to the north the Cape May Warbler spends its time high in the trees. Feeds heavily on Spruce Budworm caterpillars. Their breeding cycle corresponds to the timing of maximum availability of budworm caterpillars and the population density of this species is known to be closely tied to the presence of this food source. In years of heavy budworm infestations they will rear large broods. On wintering grounds they are known to feed heavily upon nectar and fruits and they have a specialized tubular tongue for extracting nectar from flowers and juices from fruit. The fall migration back to the Carribean is mostly well to the east of Illinois, thus they are only seen in the state for a short time each spring.

Natural History: Like most warblers, this species is highly insectivorous, but in winter it also eats some fruit and is known to feed at the sap wells created by sapsucker woodpeckers. Feeds deliberately in the lower branches of trees and in bushes. These can be very common birds on their northern breeding grounds, but they are seen in Illinois only briefly during migration. Their range coincides with the North American Continent. Theys sometimes linger well north of their summer range have been seen very rarely in northern states in winter. Orange streak on crown from which it derives its name is not typically visible in the field. Winters across the southern US from the Carolinas to California, and south to northernmost Central America.

Natural History: This warbler species has benefited from human alterations to the American landscape (they prefer logged over, second growth habitats). However, some human alterations have also had a very negative effect. As with many other migrant songbirds, they are vulnerable to towers, power lines, and antennas. No one knows exactly how many birds are killed during migration each year by flying into these obstacles, but some estimate the number to be in the millions. Insects are eaten almost exclusively by this warbler. Summers in northern US and Canada, winters in Mexico. Ornithologists recognize two distinct subspecies in North America. One migrates through the Rocky Mountain west, the other subspecies stays east of the Great Plains.

Class - **Aves** (birds)

Order - **Passeriformes** (songbirds)

Family - **Parulidae** (warblers)

Tennessee Warbler *Oreothlypis peregrina*	Blue-winged Warbler *Vermivora cyanoptera*	Golden-winged Warbler *Vermivora crysoptera*

Tennessee Warbler		Blue-winged Warbler		Golden-winged Warbler	
Size: 4.75 inches.	Presumed range in Illinois	**Size:** 4.75 inches.	Presumed range in Illinois	**Size:** 4.75 inches.	Presumed range in Illinois
Abundance: Common migrant.		**Abundance:** Rare in Illinois.		**Abundance:** Generally uncommon.	
Variation: Females and fall plumages more greenish overall.		**Variation:** Hybrids with Golden-winged produces 3 different variants.		**Variation:** See photos above. Juveniles similar to female.	
Migratory Status: Passage migrant in both spring and fall.		**Migratory Status**: Summer resident in most of the state.		**Migratory Status:** Passage migrant in both spring and fall.	

Habitat: Summer habitat is the boreal forest of Canada. Winter habitat in Central America is semi-open forest and forest edges. In migration may be seen anywhere.	**Habitat:** Overgrown weed fields with ample brushy undergrowth and early successional woodlands constitute this birds primary habitat. Least common in areas of intensive agriculture.	**Habitat:** Second growth woodlands and overgrown fields. Summer range is in the boreal forest of Canada and in the higher elevations of the Appalachian Mountains.
Breeding: Nest is on the ground at the base of a tree or among upturned roots. Nest is usually well hidden. Clutch size ranges from 3 to 8.	**Breeding:** Nest is near the ground in or under a low bush often at the edge of a woodland/field interface. From 4 to 6 eggs are laid in May.	**Breeding:** Nests on the ground near the ground at the base of a bush, hidden in thick grass and weeds. Nest is a cryptic bowl of dead leaves and grass. 4 to 5 eggs.
Natural History: The numbers of this species passing through Illinois each spring and fall fluctuates depending upon the previous years abundance of its primary summer food, the Spruce Budworm. In the northern forests of Canada in good budworm years, this is one of the most common bird species. In years of diminished budworm populations, the population of these birds also crashes. This relationship provides a valuable insight into the intricate interdependencies of unrelated organisms. This is an inconspicuous bird as it feeds high in trees and migrates later in the spring after trees are fully leaved. Thus it is difficult to detect despite being common. The name comes from the fact that first scientifically collected specimen was from Tennessee.	**Natural History:** A shrub land specialist, the Blue-winged Warbler has experienced an upswing in populations as a result of deforestation by pioneering Europeans settlers of eastern North America. In recent years there has been a decline in their numbers in the northeastern US as forests have begun recovering from the rampant logging of the last century. In North America they are most common in the Appalachian Plateau Province and rare in the agricultural regions of the Interior Lowlands Province (including Illinois). These birds sometimes hybridize with the similar Golden-winged Warbler and produce at least 3 additional forms of difficult to identify hybrid birds. Populations of this species have declined in recent years due to loss of habitat.	**Natural History:** The northernmost tier of counties in Illinois may be within the summer/nesting range of the Golden-winged Warbler. Actual sightings of of this bird in Illinois may be difficult, but they are a highly sought species with the state's bird-watchers. Loss of winter habitat and nest parasitism by the Brown-headed Cowbird are possible reasons for a recent population decline. But hybridization with Blue-winged Warblers which are now expanding their range northward may be the main reason for the increasing rarity of the Golden-winged. They winter in a variety of forest habitats in Mexico, Central America and northern South America from sea level to 7,000 feet. Like many other warblers, this species migrates across the Gulf of Mexico in spring.

Class - **Aves** (birds)		
Order - **Passeriformes** (songbirds)		
Family - **Parulidae** (warblers)		

Ovenbird	**Louisiana Waterthrush**	**Worm-eating Warbler**
Seiurus aurocapilla	*Parkesia motacilla*	*Helmitheros vermivorus*

Ovenbird	**Louisiana Waterthrush**	**Worm-eating Warbler**
Size: 6 inches.	**Size:** 6 inches.	**Size:** 5.5 inches.
Abundance: Fairly common.	**Abundance:** Fairly common.	**Abundance:** Uncommon in Illinois.
Variation: Females and fall plumages more greenish overall.	**Variation:** Two nearly identical species of Waterthrush (see below).	**Variation:** This species shows no variation and the sexes are alike.
Migratory Status: Summer resident in most of the state.	**Migratory Status**: Louisiana Waterthrush is a summer resident.	**Migratory Status:** Summer resident and passage migrant.
Habitat: Mature, contiguous forests. Seems to prefer upland woods. A substrate of abundant leaf litter is an important element to this birds habitat. Probably absent from many areas of Illinois where forests no longer exist.	**Habitat:** Louisiana Waterthrush uses forested streams as the preferred habitat. In migration they may also be seen along the edges of swamps or small woodland ponds. Northern Waterthrush uses similar habitats.	**Habitat:** This is a woodland species, but it seems to avoid lowland forests. It is more common in summer in rugged regions with steep slopes. It may occur in a wide variety of habitats during migration.
Breeding: Nests is on the ground and is constructed of leaves and grass. Nest is unique in that it has a domed roof with an opening in front. 3 to 6 eggs.	**Breeding:** Nesting can occur as early as May. 4 to 6 eggs are laid in a nest placed in tree roots along a the banks of a stream.	**Breeding:** Nests are built on the ground in deep woods and are often hidden beneath overhanging vegetation. 4 to 5 eggs is typical.
Natural History: This large warbler is a ground dweller, and is usually observed on the ground or in low foliage. Food is a wide variety of insects and arthropods taken mostly on the ground among the leaf litter. The song of the Ovenbird is distinctive and has been variously described as "emphatic" and "effervescent." Often two nearby birds will sing at once, with their overlapping songs sounding like a single bird. This species has experienced a decline in the last few decades. Forest fragmentation and Brown-headed Cowbird nest parasitism may be to blame. The name "Ovenbird" is derived from the fact that the nest is shaped rather like the old fashioned brick ovens that had a domed roof and opened to the front.	**Natural History:** This species is famous for its incessant "tail bobbing" behavior. The entire rear half of the body constantly wags up and down when foraging in stream side habitats. Requires ecologically healthy stream habitats and this species may be a barometer of overall stream health. *Similar Species:* The **Northern Waterthrush** (*P. noveboracensis)* is so similar to the Louisiana Waterthrush that most casual observers will not be able to tell them apart. The Northernjust passes through Illinois while the Louisiana breeds in much of the state. Northern breeds in bogs and beaver ponds in boreal forests of Canada and Alaska. Both species associate with wetland habitats. Northern favors boreal bogs.	**Natural History:** The map above is at best an estimation and this species may be seen elsewhere during migration. They are rather rare in northern Illinois and especially rare in the northeastern portion of the state. This is a species that specializes in feeding amid low bushes, searching the dead leaf clusters and low hanging foliage for insects, spiders and primarily, caterpillars. Like many of America's neotropical migrant songbirds, the Worm-eating warbler is highly dependent upon deciduous forests for breeding habitat. They need large tracts of woodland. They winter in Mexico, Central America and the West Indies. Despite their name, earthworms are not an important item in their diet.

Class - **Aves** (birds)		
Order - **Passeriformes** (songbirds)		
Family - **Parulidae** (warblers)		

Prothonotary Warbler *Protonotaria citrea*	**Common Yellowthroat** *Geothlypis trichas*	**Kentucky Warbler** *Geothlypis formosus*
 Male	 Male	 Male

Prothonotary Warbler
Protonotaria citrea

Size: 5.5 inches.

Abundance: Uncommon in Illinois.

Variation: Females are slightly less vivid in their colors.

Migratory Status: Summer resident throughout most of state.

Presumed range in Illinois

Habitat: Prothonotary Warblers always nest near water. They are most common in swamps and marshes but can also be seen along lake shores, riparian areas, and in the vicinity of small ponds.

Breeding: Unlike other warblers that build a nest, the Prothonotary Warbler nests in tree cavities. They will also use artificial nest boxes. Lays 4 or 5 eggs.

Natural History: The dredging and draining of swamplands throughout the eastern United States significantly reduced breeding habitat for this warbler in the first half of the 20th century. Loss of wetlands in the US has stabilized somewhat in the last few decades, but the species now faces threats from habitat loss on its wintering grounds in northern South America. Most of the swampland habitats in Illinois disappeared with European settlement. In Illinois today, this warbler occurs sporadically throughout the state where suitable habitat still exists. In some areas of its range it has recently benefited from the placement of artificial nest boxes. Feeds on aquatic insects, snails and tiny crustaceans. In winter they will also eat fruits and nectar.

Common Yellowthroat
Geothlypis trichas

Size: 5 inches.

Abundance: Fairly common.

Variation: Female lacks the prominent black mask.

Migratory Status: A summer resident that nests throughout Illinois.

Presumed range in Illinois

Habitat: Likes thick vegetation in wetland areas. Cattails and sedges in marshes and swamp edges are especially favored. Avoids deep woods but may be seen around edges of woods, especially near streams.

Breeding: The nest is woven from wetland grasses among cattails or sedges. 4 to 6 eggs are laid in late May or early June. Cowbird parasitism occurs.

Natural History: The Common Yellowthroat is one of the more abundant warblers in America and their summer range includes most of North America south of the Arctic. They do avoid the desert southwest and dry southern plains. Not surprising since they are mainly a wetland loving species. They feed low to the ground on almost any type of tiny invertebrate. Their behavior when foraging is rather "wren-like" as they negotiate dense stands of cattails, reeds, and tall grasses. They tend to stick to heavy cover and when flushed make short flights into deep cover. Nearly all of Illinois' Common Yellowthroats move south in the fall, but a few have been been known to linger in the southern part of the state well into late fall.

Kentucky Warbler
Geothlypis formosus

Size: 5.5 inches.

Abundance: Fairly common.

Variation: Female has reduced black mask, otherwise very similar.

Migratory Status: A summer resident that nests throughout Illinois.

Presumed range in Illinois

Habitat: Throughout its summer range the Kentucky Warbler enjoys deciduous bottomland forests and wooded riparian habitats. Within this macrohabitat it requires a microhabitat of dense undergrowth.

Breeding: A ground nester. The nest is constructed of dead leaves and grasses and is usually well hidden. 4 to 5 eggs are laid by mid-May.

Natural History: Kentucky Warblers are an abundant and widespread bird in suitable habitats throughout the southern summer. Although widespread across Illinois in summer, they become increasingly scarce northward and in regions of intensive agriculture. They are probably most common in the southern portion of the state. Like other small warblers they are easily overlooked. The Cornell Laboratory of Ornithology (birds online) website reports that this species appears to be in decline. Destruction of mature tropical forests may be to blame. It is also possible that fragmentation of large forests tracts in North America could be a threat. A handsome warbler, it feeds low to the ground on a wide variety of invertebrates.

Class - **Aves** (birds)
Order - **Passeriformes** (songbirds)
Family - **Parulidae** (warblers)

Mourning Warbler *Geothlypis philadelphia*	Connecticut Warbler *Oporonis agilis*	Black-and-white Warbler *Mniotilta varia*

Size: 5.25 inches.	Presumed range in Illinois	**Size:** 5.75 inches.	Presumed range in Illinois	**Size:** 5.25 inches.	Presumed range in Illinois
Abundance: Uncommon in Illinois.		**Abundance:** Very rare in Illinois.		**Abundance:** Fairly common.	
Variation: Female has less contrasting head color.		**Variation:** Females are duller without gray head of male.		**Variation:** Female has more white on face and breast.	
Migratory Status: Passsage migrant that may be seen statewide.		**Migratory Status:** Moves quickly through the state in spring.		**Migratory Status:** Summer resident in much of Illinois.	

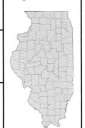

Habitat: The Mourning Warbler's summer/breeding habitat is mostly in the boreal forests and bogs of Canada. In migration they are most likely to be seen in dense regenerative woodlands. Usually seen on or near the ground.	**Habitat:** Summer/breeding habitat is boreal forest. There it prefers edges of coniferous woodlands bordering wetland habitats like tamarack bogs and muskeg. Winter habitat is forests in Central and South America.	**Habitat:** Found in a wide variety of forest types, but mature and second-growth deciduous forests are the primary habitat. Mixed conifer-hardwood forests are also used. Likes woodlands with dense understory.
Breeding: Nests on the ground in dense vegetation or a clump of grass. Lays an average four eggs. Does not breed in Illinois but passes through the state in route to more northerly regions.	**Breeding:** Nest is hidden in thick undergrowth on or near the ground. Three to five eggs are laid in late June. Young birds fledge in late July or early August. Does not breed in Illinois.	**Breeding:** Nest is constructed of dry leaves, dead grasses, and the bark of grapevines. Placed in a depression on the ground at the base of tree or stump. Lays 3 to 5 eggs.
Natural History: This warbler likes second growth areas with lush undergrowth. It prefers these conditions both in its summer breeding grounds in boreal forests as well as its wintering grounds in tropical forests. Thus it is one of the few neotropical migrant warblers that has actually benefited from mans insatiable appetite for wood products. They are not easily observed as they are a secretive bird that "skulks" in dense thickets. Unlike many neotropical migrant songbirds that make long distance flights across the Gulf of Mexico, this warbler follows the coastline north though Mexico, Texas, and Louisiana before flying inland up the Mississippi Valley and dispersing across northern regions.	**Natural History:** This shy warbler is rarely observed. In part due to its secretive nature (migrating birds are typically observed low to the ground in dense undergrowth). In addition, it occurs in Illinois only briefly during migration. Finally, this is one of the rarest of America's warblers. Even on the breeding grounds they favor remote regions where they are difficult to locate. Most breeding in Canada is, but they do breed in parts of northern Wisconsin and Minnesota. Despite its name, this species is quite rare in Connecticut, where it may only occasionally be seen during fall migration. Due to its secretive nature and relative rarity, this is one of the least understood and least commonly observed of America's warbler species.	**Natural History:** Feeds by plucking tiny creatures from tree bark and branches. Its feeding habits are more similar to that of woodpeckers, nuthatches, and creepers than to most warblers. This species is dependent upon deciduous and mixed conifer forests, and it can be sensitive to deforestation in Illinois. But overall it does not appear to have been significantly impacted throughout its wider range. While this species can be seen throughout the state during migration, it nests in Illinois mostly in the southern part of the state where ample woodlands still remain. Like many warblers it spends much of its time in the canopy, which makes it difficult to observe. When seen its black and white color is distinctive.

Class - **Aves** (birds)

Order - **Passeriformes** (songbirds)

Family - **Icturidae** (blackbirds)

Brown-headed Cowbird *Molothrus ater*	**Red-winged Blackbird** *Agelaius phoeniceus*	**Common Grackle** *Quiscalus quiscula*

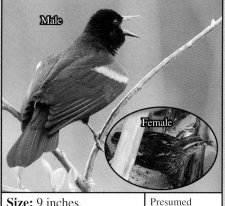

Brown-headed Cowbird	**Red-winged Blackbird**	**Common Grackle**
Size: 7.5 inches.	**Size:** 9 inches.	**Size:** 12.5 inches.
Presumed range in Illinois	Presumed range in Illinois	Presumed range in Illinois
Abundance: Common.	**Abundance:** Common.	**Abundance:** Very common.
Variation: Sexually dimorphic. See photos above.	**Variation:** Sexual and seasonal plumage variations.	**Variation:** 2 color morphs, "bronze" and "purple."
Migratory Status: Year-round resident most conspicuous in winter.	**Migratory Status**: Although migratory, seen year-round in Illinois.	**Migratory Status:** Although migratory, seen year-round in Illinois.
Habitat: Open fields and agricultural areas primarily, but can also be common in towns and suburbs. Inhabits edge areas and woods openings but avoids deep forest.	**Habitat:** The Red-wing Blackbirds favorite breeding habitat is marsh or wet meadows. They are also found along roadside ditches and the edges of ponds in open areas.	**Habitat:** Grackles favor agricultural areas and open fields/croplands. They are also common in urban areas where they inhabit lawns, parks, etc. In winter roosts in large flocks in small woodlots.
Breeding: Female cowbirds lay their eggs in the nest of other bird species, a unique nesting strategy known as "brood parasitism" (see below). As many as 40 eggs may be laid in dozens of songbird nests.	**Breeding:** The nest of the Red-winged Blackbird is a woven basket usually suspended from two or three cattail blades and is most often positioned over water. 2 to 4 eggs are laid. Young are fed enormous quantities of insects.	**Breeding:** Grackles often nest in groups that may consist of a dozen or more pairs. The nest is built in the upper branches of medium size trees and several nests can be in the same tree, or in adjacent trees.
Natural History: This species is unique among Illinois birds in that the adults play no role in rearing their young. Instead the female lays an egg in another species' nest and the adoptive parents rear the young cowbird, usually to the detriment of their own offspring. The disappearance of extensive forest tracts has allowed the cowbird to parasitize many more woodland songbirds than was possible prior to settlement. As a result, this species now poses a real threat to many smaller songbird species, especially the warblers. In winter Cowbirds will join with mixed flocks of other blackbird species. They can become an unwelcome nuisence at backyard bird feeders during harsh weather.	**Natural History:** In winter Red-winged Blackbirds often join large mixed flocks that can include all the birds shown on this page. All together the blackbirds are probably the most numerous birds in Illinois in winter. Males sing conspicuously in spring. Like the other blackbirds on this page, the Red-winged has benefited from human alterations to Illinois' natural habitats, thriving in open land and agricultural areas. Food is almost entirely insects and the along with the Common Grackle this species plays an important role in insect control. The bright red and yellow "epaulets" on the wing of the male are greatly reduced in winter, but some color is still visible on the wing.	**Natural History:** Grackles are known for forming large flocks during the winter that will roost communally and can number in the thousands. When these large congregations move into a town or neighborhood they can become a messy nuisance, but their reputation for spreading disease is exaggerated. Throughout most of the year they are busy consuming millions of insect pests. In harsh winter weather they may descend on backyard bird feeders in large flocks that overwhelm the regular residents, creating consternation among backyard bird-watchers. The two color morphs known as "bronze" and "purple" reflect the color of the iridescence of the plumage. Illinois birds are typically purple morphs.

Class - **Aves** (birds)

Order - **Passeriformes** (songbirds)

Family - **Icturidae** (blackbirds)

Bobolink *Dolichonyx oryzivorus*	Rusty Blackbird *Euphagus carolinus*	Brewer's Blackbird *Euphagus cyanocephalus*

Size: 7 inches.	Presumed range in Illinois	**Size:** 9 inches.	Presumed range in Illinois	**Size:** 9.5 inches.	Presumed range in Illinois
Abundance: Uncommon.		**Abundance:** Uncommon.		**Abundance:** Uncommon in Illinois.	
Variation: Females and winter males are sparrow-like in color.		**Variation:** Significant seasonal plumage variations. See photos above.		**Variation:** Females are drab brown. Males are iridescent blue-black.	
Migratory Status: Summer resident in northern Illinois, migrant in southern Illinois.		**Migratory Status:** Both a seasonal migrant and a winter resident. Most will winter to the south.		**Migratory Status:** A winter/spring migrant visitor from the western US.	

Habitat: Boblinks are open country birds and they are usually seen in pastures and hayfields. Their original habitats in the state were probably tallgrass prairies, which no longer exist in any significant amount.	**Habitat:** Wintering Rusty Blackbirds favor wetland habitats. Floodplain forests, edges of swamps and woods bordering marshes make up the bulk of this birds winter habitat. Summers in wet boreal woodlands and tundra edges.	**Habitat:** Favors open country. In Illinois it is usually seen in harvested or plowed agricultural fields, pastures, etc. It may also frequent feedlots where it feeds on waste grain. In the bulk of its range out west it inhabits grasslands.
Breeding: Females breed with a number of males and a clutch of 5 eggs may have several fathers. Nest is woven of grasses and placed on the ground.	**Breeding:** Breeding occurs far to the north (as far as the arctic). An average of four eggs are laid in a bulky nest of twigs, lichens and grass.	**Breeding:** As many as 8 eggs may be laid, but 5 or 6 is probably average. Nests on the ground Some nesting has been recorded in northern Illinois.
Natural History: Boblinks are one of the greatest migrators of any bird seen in Illinois. They will nest in the northern US and Canada and winter in southern South America in the open grasslands of the Pampas region of Uruguay and Argentina. Thats a round trip of nearly 20,000 miles! In Illinois they are more common in the northern half of the state and uncommon to rare as a nesting bird in the southern portions of the state. This species has experienced population declines in the last half century, but has recently benefited from CRP programs. Food items include seeds, grains and many invertebrates during breeding. Many people are surprised to learn that these handsome birds are in the blackbird family.	**Natural History:** In the last few years Rusty Blackbirds have garnered the attention of bird-watchers and conservationists concerned about an apparently significant decline in the population of this species. The loss of wet woodlands to agriculture throughout much of their wintering grounds in the southern US may be partly to blame. Unlike many blackbirds that regularly intermingle with other species, the Rusty Blackbird seems to remain mostly segregated from the large winter flocks of grackles, cowbirds, starlings and Red-wingeds. These birds summer far to the north and are seen in Illinois mostly in winter. They will migrate farther to the south if the winter weather gets harsh. Food is insects, seeds, grains, etc.	**Natural History:** The Brewer's Blackbird is a western species that historically inhabited the Great Plains and Rocky Mountain Regions all the way to the Pacific Ocean. With the clearing of land brought on by human activities, the Brewer's Blackbird began to invade the Eastern Temperate Forest Level I Ecoregion in the early 1900s. Although they are still uncommon in Illinois compared to our other blackbirds, bird-watchers report sightings nearly every winter. Feeds mostly on grains and seeds of grasses or weeds in winter. Summer diet is largely insects. The stomach of one bird reportedly contain over 50 tiny grasshoppers! This is a very common blackbird in the western half of North America.

Class - **Aves** (birds)

Order - **Passeriformes** (songbirds)

Family - **Icturidae** (blackbirds)

Yellow-headed Blackbird *Xanthocephalus xanthocephalus*	**Eastern Meadowlark** *Sturnella magna*	**Western Meadowlark** *Sturnella neglecta*

Yellow-headed Blackbird

Size: 9.5 inches.

Abundance: Rare in Illinois.

Variation: Sexually dimorphic. See photos above.

Migratory Status: Rare summer resident in northernmost Illinois. Migrant in eastern Illinois.

Presumed range in Illinois

Habitat: A marsh specialist. Throughout most of their range in the western US they are common around "prairie potholes" lakeshores, marshes, beaver ponds and creeks where cattails and sedges dominate.

Breeding: A cuplike nest is woven around several upright stalks of cattail or sedge. Averages 3 to 5 eggs and produces only one clutch per season.

Natural History: Feeds heavily on aquatic insects during the breeding season and feeds them to the young exclusively. In fall and winter switches to weed seeds and grains. When engaged in territorial displays and singing the males are quite conspicuous. Females are more discreet and sometimes difficult to observe. Illinois populations are migratory. Adult males migrate separately from females and juveniles. They are seemingly less tolerant of cold than most other blackbirds as they will arrive on northern breeding grounds later and depart earlier than other blackbirds. Winters in the southwestern United States and most of Mexico. Greatest abundance in summer is in the Dakotas.

Eastern Meadowlark

Size: 9.5 inches.

Abundance: Common.

Variation: Breeding adults exhibit slightly brighter plumage colors.

Migratory Status: Eastern Meadowlarks are year-round resident birds throughout the state.

Presumed range in Illinois

Habitat: Open, treeless pastures and fields that are kept closely grazed or mowed. They like short grasses and avoid overgrown areas. In winter they are often seen in harvested croplands or emerging wheat fields.

Breeding: Nest is on the ground and well hidden beneath overhanging grasses or under the edge of a grass tussock. 3 to 5 eggs.

Natural History: As might be expected of a bird that loves open spaces, the Eastern Meadowlark is least common in Illinois in forested regions of the state. Even in the heavily wooded regions such as the Shawnee Hills, however, this bird can be found in areas of open habitat. They feed mostly on insects in warmer months, with grasshoppers and crickets being a dietary mainstay in the summer. During winter they will eat seeds and grain. They tend to occur in small flocks during the winter, but pair off and scatter in the breeding season. The following species (Western Meadowlark) is nearly identical. Expert birders rely on listening to the birds songs to make a positive identification.

Western Meadowlark

Size: 9.5 inches.

Abundance: Less common than Eastern.

Variation: Breeding adults exhibit slightly brighter plumage colors.

Migratory Status: Western Meadowlarks are summer residents and migrants in Illinois.

Presumed range in Illinois

Habitat: Open, treeless pastures and fields that are kept closely grazed or mowed. They like short grasses and avoid overgrown areas. In winter they are often seen in harvested croplands or emerging wheat fields.

Breeding: Nest is on the ground. Woven from grass stems and may be open or domed, with or without tunnel-like entrance. Lays 5 or 6 eggs.

Natural History: In appearance (and most other respects) the Western Meadowlark is very similar to the eastern species. Visually, the yellow on the throat of the Western extends farther beneath the lower jaw (malar). One might reasonably wonder how two so similar species can coexist without interbreeding. The answer is likely in the fact that their songs are decidedly different. Thus breeders respond only to the songs of their own species. Northern Illinois is near the eastern edge of this species range. The bulk of the population resides in the Great Plains region. They also range westward through the Rocky Mountains all the way to the Pacific Ocean.

Class - **Aves** (birds)

Order - **Passeriformes** (songbirds)

Family - **Icturidae** (blackbirds)

Baltimore Oriole *Icturus galbula*	Orchard Oriole *Icturus spurius*

Size: 8.75 inches.

Size: 7 inches.

Baltimore Oriole	Orchard Oriole
Abundance: Common. Most common in northern Illinois.	**Abundance:** Fairly common statewide.
Migratory Status: A summer resident that begins to return to southern Illinois in late April with migrants arriving through late May in northern Illinois. Winters in Florida, Cuba, Jamiaca, and southern Mexico south to northern South America.	**Migratory Status:** Summer resident that breeds throughout Illinois. Returns in late April through mid-May. Departs from northern portions of breeding range early as late July. Winters from southern Mexico to northern South America.
Variation: Significant sexual and age related dimorphism (see photos above). Immature male less vividly colored.	**Variation:** Significant sexual and ontogenetic plumage variation. Immature males resemble female (see photos).
Habitat: Savanna-like habitats are preferred. Pastures with scattered large trees, parks and lawns in urban areas, or farms and ranches in rural areas. During migration may be seen in a variety of habitats.	**Habitat:** This species shows a preference for semi-open habitats and narrow strips of woodland bordering rivers and streams. Their name comes from the fact that they are fond of orchards and they will often nest fruit trees.
Breeding: The nest is an easily recognizable "hanging basket" woven from grasses and suspended from a tree limb. 4 to 6 eggs is typical.	**Breeding:** The nest is a rounded basket woven from grasses and suspended from a forked tree branch. 4 eggs is typical, but can be as many as 6.
Natural History: These handsome orange and black birds are a favorite with backyard bird-watchers. They will come to nectar feeders and fruits such as oranges, and they relish grape jelly. In addition to nectar and fruit they feed heavily on insects. In some areas of their range they have adapted well to human activities. Small town neighborhoods and city parks are among their habitats today. Although they are fond of semi-open habitats and avoid dense forests, they do like the presence of some mature trees in their habitat. Thus, they may decline from areas where intensive agriculture reduces the presence of woodland patches and large trees.	**Natural History:** Like the larger Baltimore Oriole, Orchard Orioles will eat fruit. They also feed on a wide variety of arthropods gleaned from tree branches and leaves, as well as from weedy fields. Immature males resemble females but have a large black throat patch. These birds are somewhat gregarious and they often occur in flocks on tropical wintering grounds. They are also known to nest in small colonies where ideal habitat exists. Spraying for insects in orchards can be dangerous for these insect and fruit eaters as it can be for other bird species, many of which are highly susceptible to insecticides.

Class - **Aves** (birds)
Order - **Passeriformes** (songbirds)
Family - **Thraupidae** (tanagers)

Scarlet Tanager *Piranga ludoviciana*	**Summer Tanager** *Piranga rubra*

Female
Male

Male

Female

Juvenile male

Size: 7 inches.

Abundance: Uncommon in Illinois.

Migratory Status: A summer resident that breeds in Illinois and winters in tropical America. Begins to arrive in mid- to late April. Leaves for wintering grounds in September.

Presumed range in Illinois

Variation: Sexual and ontogenetic plumage variations. Juvenile males resemble females for the first year of their lives. See photos above.

Habitat: The summer habitat for the Scarlet Tanager closely coincides with the Eastern Temperate Forest Level I ecoregion. It prefers large tracts of unbroken woodlands.

Breeding: The thin, saucerlike nest of the Scarlet Tanager is placed on the fork of an outer branch. 4 eggs is typical. Only one brood is produced.

Natural History: The Scarlet Tanager is one of the most strikingly colored birds in America. Unfortunately, this species dependence upon larger tracts of forested land means that its future is uncertain. Forest fragmentation leads to vulnerability to cowbird nest parasitism. Throughout much of the Midwest, where deforestation and fragmentation of forests has been rampant, this species is in decline. In Illinois it has become an uncommon to rare species except where large tracts of deciduous woodlands remain. Food in summer is mostly insects, including wasps and hornets, a habit that makes them a valuable bird to have around the rural homestead. Add to that their gaudy black and red plumage and you have a bird that all Illinoisans should strive to protect. Winters from Panama to northwestern South America.

Size: 7.75 inches.

Abundance: Fairly common except in agricultural areas.

Migratory Status: Well named, this bird is seen in Illinois only during summer. It winters in the tropics. Spring arrival is usually late April to early May. Fall migration in September.

Presumed range in Illinois

Variation: Sexual and ontogenetic dimorphism. See photos above. The mottled yellow-green and bright red of the juvenile male entering its second year can be seen in early spring.

Habitat: Like their like their Scarlet Tanager cousins, Summer Tanagers are birds of the eastern forests. However, this species is more likely to occupy fragmented forests and edge areas.

Breeding: The rather flimsy nest is on a terminal fork of a branch that is usually low over an opening such as a creek bed. The typical clutch size is 3 to 4.

Natural History: Summer Tanagers feed on a variety of woodland insects and larva, but they also eat some berries and fruits. One of their primary food items however is bees and wasps, a fact that makes them an attractive species to have around the rural homestead. Immature males resemble females their first summer. By the following spring they begin transformation into the bright red plumage of the adult male. During this transformation they are one of the most colorful birds in Illinois woodlands (see photos above). Breeding bird surveys in recent years have detected a slight decline in populations of this species. Landscape changes in their wintering grounds may be the reason. They will winter from southern Mexico to northern South America. Like many migratory songbirds they often migrate at night.

Class - **Aves** (birds)

Order - **Passeriformes** (songbirds)

Family - **Sturnidae** (mynas)	Family - **Passeridae** (weaver finches)

European Starling
Sturnis vulgaris

Breeding Adult

Juvenile

House Sparrow
Passer domesticus

Male

Female

Size: 8.75 inches.

Abundance: Very common.

Migratory Status:
A nonmigratory year-round resident throughout the state.

Variation: Breeding plumage iridescent dark purple, nonbreeding has white speckles. Immatures are drab brown.

Presumed range in Illinois

Habitat: Urban and suburban areas as well as farms and ranches. Starlings are closely tied to human activity and are rarely seen in true wilderness. By contrast, they can be quite common in large cities and small towns.

Breeding: Nest is made of grass, leaves, etc., stuffed into a cavity. Often uses cracks or holes in man-made structures. Also old woodpecker holes. Clutch size is typically 5 eggs.

Natural History: The Starling is one of the most familiar birds in America, but ironically it is a non-native species. All the Starlings in America are descendant from a handful of birds released in New York City in the 1890s. Contrary to popular belief, the Starling is not related to the blackbirds. Instead they belong to the same family as the Old World mynas. These birds have enjoyed remarkable success since being introduced to North America and they are now found throughout the continent. They represent a real threat to many of our native species, especially those that nest in cavities. In winter they often join grackles and blackbirds in large mixed flocks that can become a messy nuisance in urban and suburban areas. Along with the blackbirds, these birds are sometimes regarded as a threat to humans due to the avian-borne disease Histoplasmosis. In truth, this threat is exaggerated. The statewide population in Illinois is probably several million birds.

Size: 6.25 inches.

Abundance: Very common.

Migratory Status: Nonmigratory, the House Sparrow is year-round resident of Illinois.

Variation: Males have distinctive gray crown with black face mask. Females are a plain drab brown. See photos.

Presumed range in Illinois

Habitat: The House Sparrows name comes from its affinity for human habitations. These are mostly urban birds and when they do occur in rural areas it is always near farms and homesteads.

Breeding: House Sparrows build bulky nests of grass, feathers, paper strips, etc. placed in hollows or crevices of barns, outbuildings or even occupied homes. 5 to 6 eggs on average.

Natural History: A European immigrant, the House Sparrow was released into the United States about 150 years ago. They have spread across the continent and they are now perhaps the most familiar bird species in America. They roost communally in dense vegetation. Roosting sites are often in yards or foundation plantings next to houses. They are common scavengers around outdoor restaurants and fast food parking lots. They are often considered to be a nuisance bird, but their tame demeanor endears them to many. Despite being extremely common in urban areas, they are quite rare in wilderness. These highly successful birds may nest up to four times in a season. Despite their common name, House "Sparrow," they are not closely related to sparrows. They belong to an Old World family known as the Weaver Finches. Another Weaver Finch species that is found in the St. Louis vicinity is the **Eurasian Tree Sparrow**, *Passer montanus* (also introduced).

Class - **Aves** (birds)		
Order - **Passeriformes** (songbirds)		
Family - **Emberzidae** (sparrows)		

Swamp Sparrow *Melospiza georgiana*	**Song Sparrow** *Melospiza melodia*	**Lincoln's Sparrow** *Melospiza lincolnii*

Swamp Sparrow — *Melospiza georgiana*

Size: 5.75 inches.

Abundance: Fairly common.

Variation: Breeding males are richer in color with a reddish crown.

Migratory Status: Summer resident in northern Illinois, winter in southern Illinois.

Presumed range in Illinois

Habitat: Summers in wetlands. Swamps, marshes (including salt marsh) and wet meadows. More diverse habitats may be used in winter, including upland fields.

Breeding: Nest is made of grasses and placed in cattails, grasses, or low bush. 3 to 6 eggs, 4 on average.

Natural History: Secretive and elusive, the Swamp Sparrow is less familiar to Illinoisans than most of its kin. They will visit feeders during the winter, but they are rarely a commonly seen bird at feeders. These birds are highly dependent upon wetlands for breeding, and they may be negatively impacted by loss of wetlands. At this time however populations appear stable. Grassy fields are also heavily used and can be an important winter refuge. Although they can be quite common in summer habitats and in the bayous of of the Deep South in winter, they do not flock and are nearly always seen singly. There are three distinct subspecies of Swamp Sparrow recognized by professional orinithologists.

Song Sparrow — *Melospiza melodia*

Size: 5.5 inches.

Abundance: Common.

Variation: Many subspecies nationwide with light and dark morphs.

Migratory Status: Year-round resident but numbers may be bolstered in winter by migrants.

Presumed range in Illinois

Habitat: Overgrown fields, dense underbrush, and rank weeds are the preferred habitat of the Song Sparrow throughout their range. They are especially common in edge habitats.

Breeding: Nests are built low to the ground in weeds or shrubs. 4 eggs is typical.

Natural History: Both the common and scientific names of the Song Sparrow are references to its distinct and melodic song. Primarily seed eaters, these sparrows migrate in response to heavy snow cover, and they are common at bird feeders throughout the southern United States each winter. Sharp-shinned and Cooper's Hawks are major predators of adults, and the young and eggs are vulnerable to a variety of snake predators. However, they remain a thriving species. There are dozens of subspecies nationwide with light and dark color morphs. Most Illinois specimens resemble the photo above. One of the earliest and most comphrehensive studies of bird biology was conducted on this species.

Lincoln's Sparrow — *Melospiza lincolnii*

Size: 5.5 inches.

Abundance: Uncommon to rare.

Variation: No significant variation between sexes or juveniles.

Migratory Status: Spring and fall migrant. Possibly seen statewide during migrantion.

Presumed range in Illinois

Habitat: Summer habitat is boreal regions of Canada and northern Rockies where it occupies damp woodlands with dense brush, such as willow. Spruce bogs and wetlands are favored.

Breeding: Nests on the ground amid sedges or at the base of willow in boreal wetlands. Lays 3 to 5 eggs.

Natural History: Lincoln's Sparrows are more common west of the Mississippi and are rather rare in Illinois. In addition it is shy and secretive and tends to stick to heavy cover. Add to this the fact that it is a transient species in Illinois and sightings are uncommon. During migration they are believed to be fairly widespread across the state. When excited they will raise the feathers on the back of the head giving them a "crested" look. Due to their secretive habits the biology of these sparrows is not well understood. Feeds on insects in summer and seeds in winter. Unlike many sparrows they rarely visit feeders except during periods of harsh winter weather. Very similar to the Song Sparrow, but has finer streaking.

Class - **Aves** (birds)

Order - **Passeriformes** (songbirds)

Family - **Emberizdae** (sparrows)

Chipping Sparrow *Spizella passerina*	Clay-colored Sparrow *Spizella pallida*	Field Sparrow *Spizella pusilla*

Chipping Sparrow
Spizella passerina

Size: 5.5 inches.

Abundance: Common.

Variation: Females and winter males are sparrow-like in color.

Migratory Status: A summer resident that returns to Illinois in March and April.

Presumed range in Illinois

Habitat: Edge areas and woods openings. Thrives in human altered habitats including farmsteads, suburban yards, and parks.

Breeding: Breeds earlier than most other Illinois songbirds. Nests may be complete and eggs can being laid as early as mid-April in southern Illinois.

Natural History: Chipping Sparrows move to the Deep South in winter. Nesting has been recorded throughout the state, but they are more common as breeding birds in the central and northern parts of the state. They adapt well to the human disturbance of natural habitats and they are undoubtedly more common today than prior to settlement. They can be quite common in areas of intensive agriculture and also in urban/ suburban environments. In fact, this is one of the most common sparrows in the state during summer months. The Chipping Sparrow feeds mostly on the seeds of grasses and forbs, and does most of its foraging on the ground. Insects are eaten during the breeding season and are fed to the young. They can also be a common bird at feeders, especially in early spring.

Clay-colored Sparrow
Spizella pallida

Size: 5.5 inches.

Abundance: Uncommon in Illinois.

Variation: Nonbreeding birds are paler. No sexual dimorphism.

Migratory Status: seasonal migrant and very rare summer breeder in northern Illinois.

Presumed range in Illinois

Habitat: This is an open country species that prefers grasslands. In Illinois uses abandoned fields taken over by weeds, grass, and brush.

Breeding: Typically nest is close to the ground in grassy or brushy environments. 4 eggs is typical. Most breeding is well to the north of Illinois.

Natural History: This species is may be a newcomer to the Midwest. In Ohio, the first observations occurred in the 1940s. The core range for this species is in the Great Plains region Range expansion eastward into the Great Lakes region apparently began in the 1920s. Illinois of course has always had grassland habitats and the species may have always been here. Despite the fact that the Great Plains ecosystem is one of the most damaged of all America's natural habitats, this species continues to maintain healthy population numbers and it is one of the more common birds in the northern plains of Canada and North Dakota in summer. Winter range includes south Texas and Mexico. They sometimes flock with other sparrows and they have been known to hybridize with the Field Sparrow.

Field Sparrow
Spizella pusilla

Size: 5.75 inches.

Abundance: Common.

Variation: Immature birds have dark streaks on the breast.

Migratory Status: Year-round in southern Illinois. Summer resident in northern Illinois.

Presumed range in Illinois

Habitat: Open and semi-open areas with good cover in the form of weeds and taller grasses. Also shrubby, early regenerative woodland areas.

Breeding: Nest is on the ground usually at the base of a clump of grass or in a low bush. Two broods per year is common. Two to five eggs.

Natural History: Another species that has adapted well to man-made changes in natural landscapes, the Field Sparrow is probably more numerous today than in historical times. Unlike many sparrows however, the Field Sparrow is a "country" sparrow that prefers rural regions over towns and suburbs. Although they are seen year-round in southern Illinois, some southerly movement occurs in populations in winter. Food is mostly grass seeds. Insects are also eaten, especially during the breeding season. Very similar to the American Tree Sparrow, but has all pink bill instead of dark upper mandible. Although still a common species the Field Sparrow has experienced population declines in recent years. Perhaps due to habitat changes in much of its range.

Class - **Aves** (birds)

Order - **Passeriformes** (songbirds)

Family - **Emberzidae** (sparrows)

American Tree Sparrow *Spizelloides arborea*	Lark Sparrow *Chondestes grammacus*	Savannah Sparrow *Passerculus sandwichensis*

American Tree Sparrow
Spizelloides arborea

Size: 6.25 inches.

Abundance: Fairly common in winter.

Variation: Immatures have dusky streaks on the sides and breast.

Migratory Status: A winter resident throughout Illinois. Summers in the far north.

Presumed range in Illinois

Habitat: In winter they use overgrown fields, edge areas and brushy patches with weeds and grasses. Tallgrass Prairies are a favorite refuge. Summer habitat is typically open tundra and taiga.

Breeding: Nest is on the ground. 4 to 6 eggs. These hardy sparrows will nest as far north as the Arctic Circle and well above the tree line.

Natural History: The American Tree Sparrow is a northern species that is only seen in Illinois in the winter when heavy snow cover in the northern regions pushes migrating flocks southward. Like most sparrows, seeds are the staple food in winter. Seeds are also eaten in summer months but insects are more important, especially when rearing young. Seeds of a wide variety of grasses and weeds are consumed, and this species is regularly seen at bird feeders in northern states. Despite its name, this species can be found in summer on treeless, arctic tundra. Winter migrants begin to arrive in the northern US by late October and may reach southernmost Illinois by November. Degree of southerly movement can be dictated by weather conditions.

Lark Sparrow
Chondestes grammacus

Size: 6.25 inches.

Abundance: Uncommon in Illinois.

Variation: Immatures have dark streaks on the breast.

Migratory Status: Summer migrant that is a rare breeder in the central regions of the state.

Presumed range in Illinois

Habitat: The Lark Sparrow is restricted to open habitats and is most common in dry grasslands of the southwestern US It favors open field/brushy ecotones and dry uplands in Illinois.

Breeding: Nest is usually on the ground but may be in a low bush. 3 to 6 eggs is typical. Known to sometimes use the abondoned nest of another bird.

Natural History: A western species that ranges into Illinois but rather sporadically, mostly occurring in the western part of the state. Although they are an uncommon breeding bird in Illinois, in their core range west of the Mississippi River they are a common sparrow species. Males are reported to perform a courtship "dance" that resembles that of a turkey's strutting behavior. The Lark Sparrow's facial pattern of vivid black and white stripes with chestnut cheek patch is distinctive. As with most sparrows, seeds are the primary food in winter. During warmer months both seeds and insects are eaten. Grasshoppers are reported to be a major food item for both young birds and summer adults.

Savannah Sparrow
Passerculus sandwichensis

Size: 5.5 inches.

Abundance: Fairly common.

Variation: Highly variable with as many as 28 subspecies.

Migratory Status: Summer resident in northern Illinois. Winter resident in south.

Presumed range in Illinois

Habitat: Pastures, grasslands, mowed areas, cultivated fields, and vacant lots in urban areas are all used in Illinois. Elsewhere, salt marsh, tundra, and bogs are habitats.

Breeding: Nests on the ground beneath overhanging vegetation. 4 to 5 eggs is typical. Nesting in Illinois is mostly in glaciated regions of the state.

Natural History: This is one of the most widespread sparrow species in America. Between breeding range, winter range, and migration routes the Savannah Sparrow may be seen anywhere on the continent. In Illinois, they are a summer resident in all but the southern tip of the state, where they can be seen in winter. They feed on arthropods in summer and seeds in winter. The name comes from the Georgia town of Savannah (where the first specimen was described) rather than from the habitat type. As with many grassland animals the Savannah Sparrow has experienced population declines in areas of intensive agriculture or urbanization. Delaying cutting of hayfields benefits by allowing young time to fledge.

Class - **Aves** (birds)
Order - **Passeriformes** (songbirds)
Family - **Emberzidae** (sparrows)

Henslow's Sparrow *Ammodramus henslowii*	**Grasshopper Sparrow** *Ammodramus savannarum*	**Vesper Sparrow** *Pooecetes gramineus*

Henslow's Sparrow

Size: 5 inches.

Abundance: Uncommon.

Variation: Females and winter males are sparrow-like in color.

Migratory Status: Summer resident that winters in the lower Gulf Coastal Plain.

Presumed range in Illinois

Habitat: Undisturbed, overgrown grassy/weedy fields in open areas. Unmowed hayfields and reclaimed strip mines are used today. Original habitat is Tallgrass Prairie.

Breeding: Nest is on the ground in thick grass and well concealed. 2 to 5 eggs are laid in May. Double-broods are known.

Natural History: Henslow's Sparrow is nowhere a common species and its relative scarcity and secretive nature make it one of the least familiar birds in the state. This is a species in decline throughout its range. Not surprising since the tallgrass prairies that once provided ample nesting habitat are all but gone. Insects, especially grasshopper and crickets, are important food items in the summer. In winter eats mostly seeds, especially small grass seeds. Snakes are reported to be a major predator on nests, along with a variety of carnivorous mammals. Breeds sparingly across much of Illinois but presumably can be seen throughout most of the state. A Threatened Species in Illinois.

Grasshopper Sparrow

Size: 5 inches.

Abundance: Fairly common.

Variation: No sexual dimorphism and no significant variation.

Migratory Status: Summer resident. Arrives in late April and departs in late August or September.

Presumed range in Illinois

Habitat: A grassland species, the Grasshopper sparrow likes shortgrass and midgrass prairie. In Illinois it uses heavily grazed pastures and hayfields.

Breeding: Nest is on the ground and well hidden beneath overhanging grass. 2 broods per summer is usual with 4 to 5 eggs per clutch.

Natural History: In many ways similar to the preceding species, but much more common. Its name is derived from the sound of its song which mimics the buzzing sound made by some types of orthopteran insects. Throughout its range (which includes most of the US east of the Rocky Mountains) it is a rather inconspicuous bird. Though unfamiliar to most Illinoisans, in the high plains region of the north-central US it is commonly seen (and heard). Feeds entirely on the ground. Food is mostly grasshoppers and other insects in summer. In winter eats both insects and seeds, especially tiny grass seeds. Most range maps show the entire state within Grasshopper Sparrow's summer range.

Vesper Sparrow

Size: 6.25 inches.

Abundance: Fairly common.

Variation: No sexual dimorphism and no significant variation.

Migratory Status: Summer resident in northern Illinois. Winter resident in southern tip.

Presumed range in Illinois

Habitat: This is a bird of open country. Its natural habitats are grasslands and today it also uses agricultural fields. Prefers dry areas.

Breeding: Nest is on the ground in open fields, sometimes concealed by grass tussock. 3 to 5 eggs. May to produce 2 broods per year.

Natural History: The Vesper Sparrow is much more common in the western region of North America, but they are a fairly common breeding bird in the northern portion of Illinois. They are declining in the eastern portions of their range which includes much of the Midwest and Great Lakes region. They winter across the southern US and southward to northern Central America. In Illinois this species may nest in crop fields. Thus it may be fairly common in agricultural regions of the state. By contrast, it is uncommon, rare, or absent in much of the more heavily wooded regions of the state, although it may occur there in reclaimed strip mine areas.

Class - **Aves** (birds)

Order - **Passeriformes** (songbirds)

Family - **Emberzidae** (sparrows)

LeConte's Sparrow *Ammodramus leconteii*	Nelson's Sparrow *Ammodramus nelsoni*	Harris's Sparrow *Zonotrichia querula*
		 Breeding / Non-breeding

Size: 5 inches.

Abundance:
Uncommon in Illinois.

Variation: No sexual dimorphism and no significant variation.

Migratory Status: Migrant in most of the state, rare resident in the southern tip of Illinois.

Presumed range in Illinois

Habitat: Winter habitat is wet meadows, damp hayfields and marshy areas as well as grassy, upland fields. Summer habitat is the prairie regions of Canada.

Breeding: 4 to 5 eggs are laid in a nest woven from grass and placed in a clump of grass. Nests widely across south central Canada and Great Lakes region.

Natural History: This is a small and secretive sparrow that eludes attempts to study it closely. Little is known about many aspects of its biology. For instance only a small number of nests have ever been found. Usually remains hidden from view in dense grasses, and when flushed flies only a short distance before diving back into cover. Food items listed include small grass seeds and arthropods. There is even less information available regarding the habits of birds that winter in the southern tip of Illinois. Most migrate west of the Mississippi River and sightings of this sparrow in Illinois during migration are usually in the western half of the state.

Size: 5 inches.

Abundance:
Rare in Illinois.

Variation: No sexual dimorphism and no significant variation.

Migratory Status: Migrant in most of Illinois, but a few reside in southern Illinois in winter.

Presumed range in Illinois

Habitat: Primary habitat is marshes, both fresh (in summer) and both brackish and salt marshes in winter. Also may use grassy fields during migration.

Breeding: Nest is a cuplike structure placed amid and supported by upright grass stems. 3 to 5 eggs is typical, with a minimum of 2 and maximum of 6.

Natural History: Nelson's Sparrow winters along the southeastern coastline of the US from the Chesapeake Bay to Texas. Most spend the summer in the Canadian plains or along the southern shore of Hudson Bay. A few will pass through western Illinois en route to and from summer breeding grounds in Canada and winter range along the Gulf Coast. Until recently this species was considered conspecific with the Salt Marsh Sparrow. This species requires large tracts of undisturbed marshland or grassland habitat and both habitats have experienced significant alteration or outright destruction. Subsequently, loss of grassland habitat in central Canada and loss of coastal marshes poses a significant threat to this species.

Size: 7.5 inches.

Abundance:
Rare in Illinois.

Variation: Seasonal and ontogenetic plumage variations.

Migratory Status: A seasonal migrant through the western portions of Illinois.

Presumed range in Illinois

Habitat: Primarily a western species whose core range is in the southern plains in winter and the Arctic tundra in summer. Migrants use a variety of open habitats, fields, pastures, etc.

Breeding: Nest is tightly woven from grasses and placed on the ground, usually at the base of a small bush. 4 eggs is typical.

Natural History: Harris's Sparrows in breeding plumage have a distinctly jet black face, throat, and crown, that contrast strongly with the whitish breast. In nonbreeding birds the black is reduced and infused with brown. Juveniles have a white throat and a crown that is heavily speckled with black. The sexes are alike. This species breeding range is contained entirely in the arctic regions of Canada. Its winter range by contrast is the semi-arid brushlands of the southern Great Plains from Nebraska south to Texas. The map above is an approximation of where this sparrow might be seen in the state. Some range maps indicate it may be seen much farther to east, perhaps as far as central Illinois.

Class - **Aves** (birds)
Order - **Passeriformes** (songbirds)
Family - **Emberzidae** (sparrows)

White-throated Sparrow *Zonotrichia albicollis*	**White-crowned Sparrow** *Zonotrichia leucophrys*
 White-striped morph - adult  White-striped morph - juvenile	 Adult  Juvenile

Size: 6.75 inches.	Presumed range in Illinois	**Size:** 7.75 inches.	Presumed range in Illinois
Abundance: Common in winter.		**Abundance:** Fairly common to common in winter.	
Migratory Status: A winter resident and seasonal migrant throughout the state. Arrives from northern breeding grounds in November and stays through early to mid-May. Movements may be dictated by weather.		**Migratory Status:** A winter resident throughout most of the state, migrant elswhere. Seen in Illinois from October through early May. Like the preceding species will move with changing weather patterns.	

Variation: 2 adult morphs. One has bright white eye stripe, other has tan. Immatures have striped breasts.	**Variation:** First-year birds have chestnut and beige head stripe as opposed to black and white (see photos above). Sexes alike.
Habitat: Brushy thickets, fence rows, weedy fields, edges areas, and regenerative woodlands. Both in upland and lowland areas. Can be seen in both rural and urban areas but always in the vicinity of bushes, shrubs, tall weeds, or other cover.	**Habitat:** White-crowned Sparrows may be seen in any area where there are weeds, grasses, or brush in sufficient amount to provide good cover for roosting and escape from predators. Woodland edges and overgrown fence rows are best.
Breeding: Breeds in a broad band across Canada and the northeastern US, as well as northern Great Lakes states (Michigan, Wisconsin, Minnesota). Nest is on the ground in open areas, forest edges, etc. 4 eggs is typical. As many as 7 recorded.	**Breeding:** Breeds in boreal regions, tundra, and mountain meadows. Nest is in a low bush with about 4 eggs. Breeds very far to the north in northern Canada and Alaska. Will summer well into the Arctic Circle beyond the tree-line.
Natural History: This is one of the state's more common sparrows during winter. In early spring just before flying north to summer breeding grounds, the White-throated Sparrow serenades the fields and woodlands with its distinctive whistling song. As these birds are ground foragers, snow cover is one of the most important conditions that influence migratory patterns. Feeds mostly on insects in summer and switches to seeds in winter. When feeding uses both feet with a backwards thrusting motion to clear away leaf litter. They are well represented at bird feeders throughout the Midwest in winter. A short-distance migrator, this species winters mostly within the US.	**Natural History:** Similar in many respects to the White-throated Sparrow to which it is closely related. But the White-crowned ranges farther west (all the way to the Pacific) and farther north. White-crowned Sparrows produce multiple broods (as many as 4 per season in some western populations). Most will have at least two broods annually. Some summer well into the Arctic Tundra and make annual migrations of over 4,000 miles up and down the continent. Eats insects and seeds in summer, mostly seeds in winter. Forages on the ground near cover. Less common than the White-Throated Sparrow, but still a familiar bird at winter feeders. This is one of the most highly studied songbirds in America.

Class - **Aves** (birds)
Order - **Passeriformes** (songbirds)
Family - **Emberzidae** (sparrows)

Dark-eyed Junco *Junco hyemalis*	**Eastern Towhee** *Pipilo erythrophthalmus*
 Typical  Pink-sided morph	 Male  Female

Size: 6 inches.

Abundance: Very common in winter.

Migratory Status: A common winter resident throughout the state Winter migrants have typically all arrived by early December. They often first appear at bird feeders with the seasons first snowfall.

Presumed range in Illinois

Variation: Highly variable. Several different color morphs nationwide Most birds seen in Illinois are the typical "Slate-colored" morph shown in top photo.

Habitat: Occupies a wide variety of habitats in winter, but is most fond of semi-open areas or woods openings. Summer habitat is boreal forests.

Breeding: Nest is on the ground, often concealed in a clump of ferns. 4 eggs is usual. Compact nest is made of dead leaves and grasses with finer grasses as an inside liner. Nesting occurs well to the north of Illinois. Some populations may produce 2 broods in a summer.

Natural History: Juncos are a familiar wintertime bird at feeders throughout America. They arrive with the colder weather fronts and are often associated with snowstorms. In fact a common nickname in much of America is "Snowbird." Northern migrants arrive in Illinois in October/November and most are gone by mid-March. Those that summer in the southern United States do so only at the highest elevations in the Appalachian Mountains (above 3,500 feet). The combined summer, winter, and migratory ranges of the Dark-eyed Junco includes nearly all of the North American continent except Florida.

Size: 8 inches.

Abundance: Common. Less common in northern Illinois.

Migratory Status: A year-round resident in the southern half of Illinois and a summer resident in the northern half of the state. All northern Illinois birds and some southern birds migrate south in winter.

Presumed range in Illinois

Variation: Sexually dimorphic. Males are black on back, head, and wings whereas females are reddish brown. No seasonal variation.

Habitat: Succesional woodlands, overgrown fields/fence rows, edges of stream courses and woodlots where honeysuckle, briers, weeds, and saplings are predominate.

Breeding: Nests are low to the ground or even on the ground. Usually 4 eggs. Nesting in Illinois can occur throughout the state. Nest may be located in a thick bush several feet off the ground or sometimes on the ground, but it always well hidden.

Natural History: Our largest member of the sparrow family. Sometimes called "Rufous-sided Towhee." Its "tow-wheee" song is a familiar sound beginning as early as March. The widespread range of the Eastern Towhee corresponds closely to the Eastern Temperate Forest ecoregion, but they normally do not occur in dense populations. Most bird feeders in rural areas of the eastern US will have a pair for the winter, but rarely more than two pairs. The similar Spotted Towhee (*P. maculatus*) replaces the Eastern Towhee in the western half of America.

Class - **Aves** (birds)

Order - **Passeriformes** (songbirds)

Family - **Emberzidae** (sparrows)

Snow Bunting *Plectrophenax nivalis*	Fox Sparrow *Passerella iliaca*	Lapland Longspur *Calcarius lapponicus*

Size: 6.75 inches.

Abundance: Uncommon.

Variation: Sexual and seasonal plumage variations not seen in Illinois.

Migratory Status: Winter migrant. Usually seen only in harsh winter weather.

Presumed range in Illinois

Size: 7 inches.

Abundance: Uncommon.

Variation: Highly variable. Includes reddish, grayish, and sooty morphs.

Migratory Status: A fall/ winter migrant in northern Illinois. Winter resident in southern Illinois.

Presumed range in Illinois

Size: 6.25 inches.

Abundance: Fairly common in winter.

Variation: Sexual and seasonal plumage variations (not seen in Illinois).

Migratory Status: A winter migrant or resident from the far north. Seen in Illinois only in winter.

Presumed range in Illinois

Habitat: Winter habitat in Illinois is mostly harvested crop fields. Also weedy patches around field edges, roadsides, farmsteads, etc. Summer habitat is rocky areas in tundra.

Habitat: The Fox Sparrow is a lover of dense cover and thickets. Thick weeds and shrubs bordering woodlands or thickets. A mixture of brier, saplings, weeds, regenerating timberlands, etc.

Habitat: Winter migrants use very open areas with nearly bare ground. Large acreage harvested crop fields are the primary habitat for flocks wintering in the Midwestern US.

Breeding: One of the most northerly breeding songbirds in the America. Builds its nest in rock crevices in the high arctic. Lays 4 to 6 eggs.

Breeding: Nests are low to the ground or even on the ground. Breeding is in the boreal forests of Canada and in the northern Rockies. Usually 4 eggs.

Breeding: Nests on the ground in Arctic Tundra. In places it may be the only nesting songbird. Eggs (3 to 7) are not laid until early June.

Natural History: After summering as far north as the shores of the Arctic Ocean, Snow Buntings will move south to winter as far south as northern half of Illinois. In years of exceptional snowfall or extreme cold they may be seen as far south as Kentucky. They are obviously very cold hardy birds, but they can be succeptible to winter die-offs if deep snows conceal their food source of seeds and grain. Winter migrants may be seen in mixed flocks with Lapland Longspurs and Horned Larks. Circumpolar in distribution, there are some indications are that this species is recently experiencing a sharp drop in North American populations.

Natural History: The Fox Sparrow is widespread across the North American Continent, summering in the far north (Canada, Alaska, and the northern Rockies) and wintering across much of the southern United States. Several distinct subspecies are recognized. Illinois specimens usually resemble the photo above. They feed on a variety of insects and other arthropods in summer and subsist mainly on seeds in winter. They can be an occasional to regular visitor at bird feeders during winter, especially during periods of snowy weather. Unlike many other sparrows, the Fox Sparrow is never seen in large flocks and it is rare to have more than one or two at a time visiting feeders.

Natural History: This hardy sparrow breeds and summers in Arctic Tundra and is circumpolar in its distribution. It is very common on its breeding grounds where it is sometimes the only songbird present. In winter they move far to the south, but are not very abundant east of the Mississippi River. Birds seen in Illinois are in winter plumage (as above). A similar species (the **Smith's Longspur**, *Calcarius pictus*) may also been seen in Illinois in winter. In habits it mirrors the Lapland Longspur but its winter range is restricted mostly to prairie regions, while the Lapland Longspur can be seen across most of the northen half of the United States in winter.

Class - **Aves** (birds)

Order - **Passeriformes** (songbirds)

Family - **Cardinalidae** (grosbeaks)

Dickcissel *Spiza americana*	**Northern Cardinal** *Cardinalis cardinalis*	**Rose-breasted Grosbeak** *Pheucticus ludovicianus*

Size: 6.25 inches.

Abundance: Failry common.

Variation: Females are duller and lack the black "bib" of the male.

Migratory Status: Summer resident. Winters from Mexico to northern South America.

Presumed range in Illinois

Habitat: Fallow lands with weeds, saplings, and grasses. Weedy fields in open areas are the preferred habitat. Original range was probably natural prairie regions.

Breeding: Breeds across much of Illinois. Produces only one brood per year. Nest is in a shrub low to ground. 4 eggs is usually but may be as many as 6.

Natural History: The bulk of the Dickcissel's summer range is in the central Great Plains. It probably always nested in Illinois' natural prairies but today has expanded its range farther east into suitable habitats created by deforestation and subsequent conversion of woodlands to cropland and pasture. Outside their core breeding range they are distributed sporadically and they are also known to wander well outside their core range. Flocks numbering in the thousands have been recorded during migration. Eats seeds almost exclusively during migration and on winter range. During breeding is more omnivorous, consuming insects and seeds. An open country bird, the Dickcissel avoids the more heavily forested regions of the state.

Size: 8.75 inches.

Abundance: Very common.

Variation: Pronounced sexual dimorphism. See photos above.

Migratory Status: A year-round resident throughout the state.

Presumed range in Illinois

Habitat: From undisturbed natural areas to suburbs, the Northern Cardinal favors edge areas with shrubs and brush. Avoids areas of extensive forests in favor of successional habitats.

Breeding: Nest is usually in a thick shrub or bush. About 4 eggs on average. Most nesting is from mid-April to August. Two broods per year.

Natural History: Conspicuous and highly recognizable, the Northern Cardinal enjoys the distinction of being the state bird for a total of seven states (including Illinois). They are mainly seed and berry/fruit eaters, but they will eat insects and feed insects to the young. They are common birds at feeders throughout their range, especially during winter, and they are equally abundant in rural and urban regions. In the last century, they have expanded their range farther to the north into the Great Lakes region and New England. Today they are seen throughout much of the United States east of the Rockies. The southern extent of their range is northern Central America. Throughout their range they are often known by the name "Redbird."

Size: 8 inches.

Abundance: Fairly common.

Variation: Sexually dimorphic. See photos above.

Migratory Status: A summer resident that winters from the Yucatan to South America.

Presumed range in Illinois

Habitat: A forest species primarily, but enjoys edge areas and regenerative woodlands with thick shrubby cover. May be fairly common in suburbs with adequate cover in the form of bushes.

Breeding: 3 to 5 eggs are laid in a nest of twigs, grass, and plant fibers. Nesting begins in late May. May rarely produce 2 broods per year.

Natural History: Many Rose-breasted Grosbeaks seen in Illinois are passage migrants that nest farther to the north. But nesting is widespread in the northern two-thirds of the state where they will reside throughout the summer. Those that nest to the north will pass through the state in spring and again in the fall en route to wintering habitats in Central and South America. Food in summer about 50/50 insects and plant material such as seeds, fruits, flowers, and buds. During migration they are readily attracted to bird feeders where sunflower seeds are a favorite food. Bird-watchers throughout the state enthusiastically await the return of migrant songbirds each spring, and the Rose-breasted Grosbeak is a favorite.

Class - **Aves** (birds)

Order - **Passeriformes** (songbirds)

Family - **Cardinalidae** (grosbeaks) | Family - **Fringillidae** (finches)

Blue Grosbeak *Passerina caerulea*	**Indigo Bunting** *Passerina cyanea*	**Pine Siskin** *Spinus pinus*

Blue Grosbeak

Size: 6 inches.

Abundance: Uncommon.

Migratory Status: Summer resident. Winters in Mexico and Central America.

Presumed range in Illinois

Variation: Sexually dimorphic. Female is chestnut brown.

Habitat: On summer range the Blue Grosbeak enjoys overgrown fields dominated by forbs and saplings. Also uses fencerows, thickets, brambles, etc.

Breeding: Nest is a tightly woven cup placed in a low bush or tangle of vines, brush. About 4 eggs. Double brooding is known in the southern part of range.

Natural History: Although the Blue Grosbeak can probably be found throughout much of Illinois in spring and summer, it is most common in the southernmost portion of the state and rarest farther north. However, recent breeding bird surveys suggest that this species is expanding its range northward and they may sooon become more common in northern regions. During summer they feed mostly on crickets, grasshoppers, and other insects, but eat mostly seeds in the early spring and fall. They often will visit bird feeders at these times. These birds are more common in the eastern United States today than they were in historic times, but they are still uncommon birds in the Great Lakes region.

Indigo Bunting

Size: 5.5 inches.

Abundance: Very common.

Migratory Status: A summer resident that arrives in late April and leaves in early fall.

Presumed range in Illinois

Variation: Sexually dimorphic. See photos above.

Habitat: Edge areas, fence rows, rural roadsides with substantial brushy/weedy cover, and overgrown fields or early successional woodlands.

Breeding: 2 broods are common. Lays 2 to 4 eggs in a nest of woven grasses that is usually placed in thick cover only a few feet above the ground.

Natural History: Indigo Buntings are common in summer throughout the eastern half of America. Probably more so today than in historical times when forests dominated the state's habitats. The neon blue color of the male is makes it one of the most striking of North American birds. These birds are found throughout the eastern United States in summer, generally ranging from the short grass plains eastward to the Atlantic and as far north as southern Canada. They are most common in the southeastern US. Their annual migration may encompass up to 2,500 miles and many make the long flight across the Gulf of Mexico. Seeds and berries are the primary food with insects eaten during the breeding season.

Pine Siskin

Size: 5 inches.

Abundance: Fairly common.

Migratory Status: Winter resident. Exhibits erratic north/ south movement in winter.

Presumed range in Illinois

Variation: Sexually dimorphic. See photos above.

Habitat: Pine Siskins prefer coniferous woodlands but in winter they are often seen in mixed or even pure hardwood forests.

Breeding: Nest is woven of grasses, twigs, rootlets, etc. and lined with mosses or fur. 3 to 4 eggs is typical. May nest in loose colonies.

Natural History: The Pine Siskin is a coniferous forest species. Though it is also found in mixed deciduous/ coniferous woodlands and in pure deciduous woods during winter irruptions. It is mostly a bird of the far north and the Rocky Mountains. They sometimes range as far south as the Gulf Coast in winter. In Illinois, they are most common in the northern part of the state, but their erratic movement means they may be common in one area and rare in another. Feeds on seeds of coniferous trees, grass seeds, and weed seeds and will regularly visit feeders in winter and where thistle seeds are favored. Insects are also eaten during breeding. They are often seen in the company of Goldfinches.

Class - **Aves** (birds)

Order - **Passeriformes** (songbirds)

Family - **Fringillidae** (finches)

Goldfinch	Purple Finch	House Finch
Spinus tristis	*Haemorhous purpureus*	*Haemorhous mexicanus*

Summer Male / Winter Male

Male / Female

Male / Female

Goldfinch	Purple Finch	House Finch
Size: 5 inches.	**Size:** 6 inches.	**Size:** 6 inches.
Abundance: Common.	**Abundance:** Fairly common.	**Abundance:** Very common.
Migratory Status: Year-round resident.	**Migratory Status:** Winter migrant	**Migratory Status:** Year-round resident.
Variation: Exhibits sexual and seasonal plumage variations. See above. Female resembles winter male.	**Variation:** Significant plumage differences between the sexes. See photos above.	**Variation:** Plumage differences between males and females make sexes easily recognizable. See photos above.

Presumed range in Illinois (for each species)

Goldfinch	Purple Finch	House Finch
Habitat: Edge areas and successional habitats, fence rows, overgrown fields, and floodplains in open and semi-open areas.	**Habitat:** Summer habitat is moist coniferous forests. In the winter, they are seen in almost all habitats across the eastern half of the US.	**Habitat:** As implied by the name, House Finches are usually associated with human habitation. Found both in cities and rural areas.
Breeding: 4 to 6 uniformly white eggs are laid. Nest is a tightly woven cup of grasses usually wrapped around a triad of upright branches.	**Breeding:** Nest of twigs, roots, and grasses is built in a fork on the outer portion of a branch of a conifer. 3 to 6 eggs per clutch. 2 broods per year.	**Breeding:** Typical woven nest of grasses is usually placed in dense evergreen shrub, cedar, or conifer tree. Lays 3 to 5 eggs and multiple broods are common.
Natural History: This well-known species is widespread across North America. The transition of the male Goldfinch into its strikingly yellow breeding plumage in spring is a profound example of a condition that is common in male birds in which they acquire bright colors. The Goldfinch is a common visitor to bird feeders and is especially attracted to thistle seeds. Unlike many other species that eat seeds in winter and insects in summer, the Goldfinch is mainly a seed eater. Weed seeds, grass seeds, and especially seeds from forbs like thistles, sunflowers, and coneflowers are consumed. This species is apparently immune to parasitism by the Brown-headed Cowbird, as young cowbirds cannot develop on a diet that contains no insects.	**Natural History:** The Purple Finch seems to a be declining species in the eastern United States. Competition with the House Finch may be to blame. Although Purple Finches are seen in Illinois every winter, they may move well south in some years; all the way to the Gulf Coast in years of poor cone production. Seeds are the major food item, including seeds of trees (elm, maples, ash) and seeds of fruits. Buds are also eaten. Insects are also consumed. As with most other seed eaters, the Purple Finch will frequent bird feeders in winter. It may be fairly common at feeders one year, but rare or absent the next. Most likely to be seen at feeders during or following snowstorms. Easily confused with the House Finch, but is larger headed and has a heavier bill.	**Natural History:** House Finches have extended their range into the eastern United States over the last few decades. Originally native to the southwestern United States, the first House Finches appeared in the Midwest in the 1960s. Today they are found throughout the United States including all of Illinois. Primarily a seed eater, these birds can be very common at urban feeders. Weed seeds, fruit, buds and flowers are also reported to be eaten. Birds seen at feeders sometimes exhibit signs of a disease (mycoplasmal conjuctivitis) that causes swelling of the eyes with occasional blindness or death. Similar to and easily confused with the less common Purple Finch, which has a larger head and lacks dark streaking on the belly of the males.

Class - **Aves** (birds)
Order - **Passeriformes** (songbirds)
Family - **Fringillidae** (finches)

Common Redpoll *Acanthis flammea*	**Evening Grosbeak** *Coccothraustes vespertinus*	**Red Crossbill** *Loxia curvirostra*

Common Redpoll

Size: 5 inches.

Abundance: Rare in Illinois.

Migratory Status: Winter migrant.

Variation: Shows varying amounts of reddish or pinkish. Females are darker. Juveniles have brown streaks.

Presumed range in Illinois

Habitat: Summer habitat is in the far north where they occupy edge areas of coniferous forests, open subarctic tundra, arctic tundra, and taiga.

Breeding: Nest is on a branch (forest) or in low vegetation (tundra). Lays 5 eggs. May double brood in good years.

Natural History: Circumpolar in distribution (northern hemisphere), this is one of the world's most northerly songbirds and some will stay through the winter in the far north. Many will move south, some as far northern Illinois. Very rarely they may be seen as far south as Arkansas or Tennessee. Though some Common Redpolls can be seen every winter in northern Illinois, they only approach being a fairly common bird in years of major eruptions. These eruptions are thought to be associated with poor cone production in boreal forests, which is the major winter food source for this species in boreal regions. In addition to conifer seeds they also eat small seeds produced by other trees and shrubs such as birch, willow, and alder. Grass seeds are also eaten and arthropods are fed to the young.

Evening Grosbeak

Size: 8 inches.

Abundance: Rare in Illinois.

Migratory Status: Winter migrant.

Variation: Female is gray-brown with yellowish wash. Male is brighter with yellow stripe on forehead.

Presumed range in Illinois

Habitat: Boreal type forests of conifer and mixed conifer/deciduous. Summer habitat includes the forested regions of Canada and the Rocky Mountains.

Breeding: Saucerlike nest of twigs and rootlets is placed high in a tree at or near the trunk. Lays 3 to 4 eggs.

Natural History: The Evening Grosbeak is a northern species. The main food in winter is the seeds of trees like maples, Box Elder, etc. as well as conifer seeds and weed seeds. In a year of exceptionally poor seed production they will migrate southward great distances in a phenomenon known to bird-watchers as an "irruption." In irruption years they may rarely be been seen as far south as the southern US. During these rare "irruption events" they might be seen anywhere in the state. However, in typical winters northernmost Illinois represents the southern edge of their winter range. Thus sightings of this bird in the state are rare and usually elicit excitement from the state's birdwatching community. The map above is an average winter range for Illinois.

Red Crossbill

Size: 6.5 inches.

Abundance: Very rare in Illinois.

Migratory Status: Winter migrant.

Variation: Males show a decidedly reddish color. Females are more yellowish. Juveniles are heavily streaked.

Presumed range in Illinois

Habitat: Birds seen in Illinois in winter use taiga forests in Canada as their summer habitat. Western populations exist in the conifer forests of the Rockies.

Breeding: Nest is made of twigs and lined with lichens, grass, or conifer needles. 3 eggs are usual.

Natural History: The unique scissorlike beak of the crossbills is an adaptation for feeding on the seeds of conifers. The curved, crossed beak is used to pry open cones enough to allow the tongue to scoop out the seed. Seeds of pine, hemlock, spruce, and fir are the primary foods, but a variety of other seeds are also eaten and they will visit feeders for sunflower seeds. Their foraging habits are nomadic and small flocks wander through the forests searching for cone bearing trees. Like the other boreal species on this page they are prone to nomadic "irruptions." In years of poor cone production they may show up well south of their normal range. In a typical year northern Minnesota, northern Wisconsin, and northern Michigan, represents the southernmost edge of their range in the Midwestern US.

Class - **Aves** (birds)

Order - **Apodiformes** (swifts & hummingbirds)

Family - **Apodidae** (swifts)	Family - **Trochylidae** (hummingbirds)

Order - **Coraciiformes** (kingfishers)

Family - **Alcedinidae** (kingfisher)

Chimney Swift
Chaetura pelagica

Ruby-throated Hummingbird
Archilochus colubris

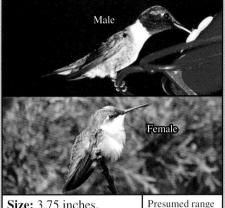

Male

Female

Belted Kingfisher
Megaceryle alcyon

Male

Female

Size: 5.5 inches.

Presumed range in Illinois

Abundance:
Fairly common.

Migratory Status:
Summer resident that winters in the Amazon basin.

Variation: No sexual dimorphism. Immatures slightly lighter.

Habitat: Mainly seen in open and semi-open country and in urban/suburban areas.

Breeding: Nest is a flimsy cup plastered to the inside of a chimney. 2 to 5 eggs are laid.

Natural History: This is a species that has benefited from human population expansion. Historically, the Chimney Swift nested mainly in hollow trees. These birds require a vertical surface within a sheltered place for nesting. When people began to build houses and large structures like schools, churches, and factories equipped with chimneys, their populations exploded. Today they are perhaps less common than a few decades ago when most dwellings and other buildings had chimneys. Some nesting in natural hollows still occurs. Swifts have long, narrow, pointed wings that allow for extreme maneuverability and these birds feed entirely on the wing. Small flying insects are their prey. During migration they are sometimes seen in large flocks that can contain over 1,000 birds. Today, the greatest population densities occur in the vicinity of urban centers.

Size: 3.75 inches.

Presumed range in Illinois

Abundance:
Common.

Migratory Status:
A summer resident that winters mostly in Central America.

Variation: Female lacks ruby throat patch. See photos above.

Habitat: Woodlands. Both deciduous and mixed forests are utilized. Edge areas and open fields are used for feeding.

Breeding: Nest is a tiny cup of fine plant fibers and lichens glued together with spider webs. 2 eggs is typical.

Natural History: The tiny hummingbirds are ounce for ounce one of the world's greatest travelers. Many fly across the Gulf of Mexico each year during migration! Considering that they weigh barely more than 0.1 ounces that is a remarkable feat of endurance. The range of the Ruby-throated Hummingbird includes all of the Eastern Deciduous Forest Level 1 Ecoregion, as well as portions of the Boreal Forest and Great Plains Ecoregions. Nectar is the major food item for hummingbirds and they show a preference for red, tubular flowers. They possess a highly specialized beak and tongue for reaching nectar deep within flowers. They will also eat some small, flying insects caught on the wing, and are known to pluck tiny invertebrates from foliage or small spiders from their webs. These birds will readily use artificial nectar feeders containing a 1 to 4 mix of sugar water.

Size: 13 inches.

Presumed range in Illinois

Abundance:
Uncommon.

Migratory Status:
Year-round resident. Some may move south in winter.

Variation: Female has a rust-colored band across belly.

Habitat: Kingfishers require water and they thus haunt creeks, rivers, lakes, swamps, and farm ponds.

Breeding: Kingfishers nest in burrows they excavate into vertical banks of dirt or sand that are at least 8 feet high.

Natural History: The Belted Kingfisher is one of the most widely distributed birds in North America. In fact they range throughout the continent from Alaska and northern Canada south to Panama. Although widespread (breeding records exists from every county in the state) they are widely dispersed. They are least common in the intensive agricultural regions of Illinois. The presence of suitable nesting habitat in the form of vertical earthen cliffs may be a limiting factor in their abundance. Human activities such as digging of quarries and road cuts through hills and mountains may have helped this species in modern times by providing the requisite vertical banks for nest sites. Small fish are the primary food item. They are known for diving headfirst into the water from either a perch or while hovering to catch fish near the surface.

Class - Aves (birds)

Order - Piciformes (woodpeckers)

Family - Picidae (woodpeckers)

Pileated Woodpecker *Dryocopus pileatus*	Northern Flicker *Colaptes auratus*	Red-headed Woodpecker *Melanerpes erythrocephalus*

Pileated Woodpecker	Northern Flicker	Red-headed Woodpecker
Size: 16.5 inches.	**Size:** 12.5 inches.	**Size:** 9.25 inches.
Abundance: Uncommon.	**Abundance:** Fairly common.	**Abundance:** Uncommon.
Migratory Status: Year-round resident in forested regions of Illinois.	**Migratory Status:** Year-round resident but less common in winter.	**Migratory Status:** Year-round resident. Northern birds may migrate.
Variation: Male has a red cheek patch and more extensive red on the head.	**Variation:** Male has black "mustache." Two color morphs but only one occurs in Illinois.	**Variation:** No sexual variation. Juveniles have gray-brown heads and brown wings.
Habitat: A forest species, the Pileated Woodpecker prefers mature woodlands. It is also seen in semi-open areas where large tracts of woods occur nearby. Floodplain forests are a favorite habitat.	**Habitat:** Semi-open areas and open lands with at least a few large trees. Farmlands, older urban neighborhoods and parks are also used. Least common in dense, mature woodlands.	**Habitat:** Savanna like habitats with widely spaced, large trees are the preferred habitat of the Red-headed Woodpecker. They seem to show a preference for areas near lakes or rivers.
Breeding: Nest is a hollow cavity excavated into the trunk of a tree (usually a dead tree, but sometimes living). Nests are usually fairly high up. 4 eggs.	**Breeding:** Nest is usually excavated in a fairly large diameter dead tree. Also known to use natural hollows. Averages 6 to 8 eggs.	**Breeding:** Nest hole is usually in a dead tree but it is also fond of using utility poles. 5 eggs is typical and some may produce two broods per summer.
Natural History: By far America's largest woodpecker, Pileated Woodpeckers play an important role in the mature forest ecosytem. Their large nest cavities are utilized as a refuge by many other woodland species including small owls, Wood Ducks, bluebirds and squirrels. In the boreal forests of Canada the Pine Marten is reported to use their holes. Using their powerful, chisel-like beaks to break apart dead snags and logs they also help accelerate decomposition of large dead trees. In addition to mast and fruit such as wild cherries, they eat insects, mainly Carpenter Ants and beetle larva. In Illinois, they occur statewide in regions where ample forests exist. Succesional forest are used but they do need mature trees and especially, large dead trees and logs.	**Natural History:** In addition to feeding on insects (mainly ants) usually caught on the ground, the Flicker also eats berries and in winter, grains (including corn). Two distinct subspecies of Northern Flicker occur in North America. The "Yellow-shafted Flicker" is native to Illinois and the rest of the eastern US. In the Rocky Mountain west the "Red-shafted Flicker" occurs. The two are distinguished by the dominant color on the underneath side of the wing, which is visible only in flight. As with Illinois' other large woodpecker (Pileated), the Northern Flicker is regarded as a "keystone" species that is important to other species which use its excavations for shelter and nesting. Thus recent declines in the population of this species is cause for concern.	**Natural History:** Once regarded as very common, this handsome woodpecker has declined significantly in the last century. It eats large amounts of acorns and other mast, especially in fall and winter, and may move about in fall and winter in search of areas with good mast crops. Insects are regularly eaten in warmer months and some may be caught on the wing, but they also commonly forage on the ground. Although they may be found throughout the state they seem to be relatively uncommon. and overall this species has experienced a nationwide population decline. The Red-headed Woodpecker was apparently well known to many native Americans, and was a war symbol of the Cherokee.

Class - **Aves** (birds)
Order - **Piciformes** (woodpeckers)
Family - **Picidae** (woodpeckers)

Red-bellied Wood Pecker *Melanerpes carolinus*	**Downy Woodpecker** *Picoides pubescens*	**Hairy Woodpecker** *Picoides pubescens*

Size: 9.75 inches.

Presumed range in Illinois

Abundance: Common.

Migratory Status: Year-round resident.

Variation: Female has gray crown.

Habitat: A woodland species that inhabits all forest types in the eastern US.

Breeding: Nests in holes excavated by the adults. 4 to 5 eggs are laid in mid-April to early June.

Natural History: Feeds on all types of tree dwelling arthropods as well as seeds, nuts, fruit and berries. Widespread and common throughout the eastern half of the US, generally east of the Rocky Mountains. These woodpeckers are known to take over the nest holes of the endangered Red-cockaded Woodpecker where their ranges overlap in the southern United States. Conversely, the introduced Starling sometimes takes over the nest hole of the Red-bellied Woodpecker. Due to its fairly large size and its tendency to be quite vocal year-round, the Red-bellied Woodpecker is a fairly conspicuous bird in both rural and urban area throughout Illinois. Because both males and females have a significant amount of red on the head they are often misidentified as the much rarer Red-headed Woodpecker. Like other woodpeckers they will come to bird feeders for suet or sunflower seeds.

Size: 6.75 inches.

Presumed range in Illinois

Abundance: Very common.

Migratory Status: Year-round resident.

Variation: Male has red spot on nape.

Habitat: Occupies a wide variety of woodland habitats throughout the state.

Breeding: Nests is usually excavated in a dead limb. Eggs range from 3 to as many as 8. Eggs hatch in 12 days.

Natural History: Ranging across all of North America except the far north and the desert Southwest, the Downy is one of the most widespread woodpeckers in American and is the most common woodpecker in Illinois. These appealing little woodpeckers are well known and frequent visitors to bird feeders where they eat suet and seeds. Arthropods are the most important food item making up as much as 75 percent of the diet. Fruit and sap is also eaten. Like other woodpeckers, the Downy's nest holes in dead limbs and trunks may be utilized by a wide array of other species as a home and shelter. Many small cavity nesting birds may use old woodpecker holes, and mice, lizards, snakes, treefrogs, spiders, and insects can often be found using their abandoned nests. The Downy Woodpecker is very similar to the Hairy Woodpecker but is smaller and has a thinner beak. It is also much more common.

Size: 9.25 inches.

Presumed range in Illinois

Abundance: Fairly common.

Migratory Status: Year-round resident.

Variation: Male has red spot on nape.

Habitat: A forest species that likes woodlands with larger, more mature trees.

Breeding: Nest hole may be in dead snags or living trees with heart rot. 4 eggs is typical.

Natural History: The range of the Hairy Woodpecker closely coincides with that of the smaller Downy Woodpecker. The two are often confused but the Hairy is a much larger bird and has a heavier, longer bill. Like the Downy, this woodpecker excavates nest holes that may be used by a variety of other species, making it an important species in forest ecosystems. A wide variety of insects and other arthropods are eaten along with seeds and fruits. This species can be seen at feeders throughout Illinois, and although it is less common than its smaller cousin it can often be seen in the company of the smaller Downy Woodpecker. When both are seen together, size differences become more apparent. The Hairy Woodpecker varies somewhat geographically in both size and coloration. Western specimens have few white spots ont he wings. Specimens shown above are typical for the eastern United States.

Class - **Aves** (birds)

Order - **Piciformes** (woodpeckers)	Order - **Cuculiformes** (cuckoos, anis & roadrunner)	
Family - **Picidae** (woodpeckers)	Family - **Cuculidae** (cuckoos)	
Yellow-bellied Sapsucker *Sphyrapicus varius*	**Black-billed Cuckoo** *Coccyzus erythropthalmus*	**Yellow-billed Cuckoo** *Coccyzus americanus*

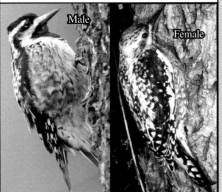

Size: 8.5 inches.

Presumed range in Illinois

Abundance: Uncommon.

Variation: Male has red patch on throat.

Migratory Status: Winter resident in southern Illinois. Migrant elsewhere in the state.

Habitat: In winter this woodpecker occupies a wide variety of woodland habitats. Birds that winter in Illinois use decidous and mixed woodlands.

Breeding: Nest is an excavated hole in dead tree or a living tree with heart rot. Clutch size ranges from 2 to 7 eggs.

Natural History: The Yellow-bellied Sapsucker is unique among Illinois woodpeckers in that it creates feeding opportunities by drilling small holes into the bark of trees. These holes, called "sap wells" fill with sap which the sapsucker then drinks. Sapsuckers regularly visit the "sap wells" to maintain them and defend them from other sapsuckers. Many other bird species benefit from the sapsuckers activities, especially the Ruby-throated Hummingbird which will also drink sap from the woodpeckers holes. The sap also attracts insects which in turn feed many species of insectivorous birds. In addition, the nest holes excavated by the sapsucker may be used other birds, flying squirrels, etc. Though widespread across Illinois in during migration, they are not a common bird anywhere in the state.

Size: 12 inches.

Presumed range in Illinois

Abundance: Uncommon in Illinois.

Variation: Sexes alike. No significant variation.

Migratory Status: Migrant in southern Illinois. Summer resident elsewhere in the state.

Habitat: Successional areas, thickets, and mature woodlands with some open areas. Shows a preference for being near water (riparian areas, lakes, etc).

Breeding: Breeds sparingly throughout Illinois north of the Shawnee Hills. Clutch size averages 2 to 4 eggs.

Natural History: Although once common, the Black-billed Cuckoo has declined in abundance over the past several decades. Widespread use of pesticides may be to blame. Caterpillars are a primary food and pesticide depleted caterpillar numbers results in a scarce food source for the birds. Ironically, large flocks of these handsome birds once acted as a natural control of caterpillars and historical observers reported seeing flocks of Black-billed Cuckoos descend on a tree full of caterpillars and eat every caterpillar on the tree! Today it is rare to see more than one or two of these birds at a time. Cicadas are another important insect food, and in years of cicada outbreaks cuckoos (and many other birds species) will produce larger clutches and successfully rear more young.

Size: 12 inches.

Presumed range in Illinois

Abundance: Fairly common.

Variation: Sexes alike. No significant variation.

Migratory Status: Summer resident throughout the state. More common than Black-billed Cuckoo.

Habitat: Open woodlands, edge areas, regenerative woodlands near open fields, overgrown fence rows, etc. Uses similar habitats on winter range.

Breeding: Breeds from early June through the summer. Nest is flimsy and placed in thick vegetation. 2 to 4 eggs.

Natural History: The Yellow-billed Cuckoo is one of the latest arriving of Illinois' neotropical migrant songbirds. They often go by the nickname "Raincrow" and folklore states that they call right before a rain. Although much more common than the Black-billed Cuckoo, Yellow-billed Cuckoos are not abundant birds today. Like our other cuckoo, their numbers have diminished significantly in modern times. Caterpillars are an important food and widespread pesticide use is likely the major contributing factor in their decline. These are secretive birds that are heard more often than seen. Their call is quite distinctive and is heard most frequently during the "dog days" of mid- to late summer. The young of this species develop rapidly and may leave the nest within 17 days of hatching.

Class - **Aves** (birds)
Order - **Columbiformes** (doves)
Family - **Columbidae** (doves)

Rock Pigeon *Columba livia*	**Mourning Dove** *Zenaida macroura*	**Eurasian Collared-Dove** *Zenaida decaocto*

Rock Pigeon		Mourning Dove		Eurasian Collared-Dove	
Size: 13 inches.	Presumed range in Illinois	**Size:** 12 inches.	Presumed range in Illinois	**Size:** 13 inches.	Presumed range in Illinois
Abundance: Very common.		**Abundance:** Very common.		**Abundance:** Rare but increasing.	
Migratory Status: Year-round resident.		**Migratory Status:** Year-round resident.		**Migratory Status:** Year-round resident.	
Variation: Highly variable.		**Variation:** No variation among adults.		**Variation:** No variation among adults.	
Habitat: Farms and ranches in rural areas and parks and streets in urban environments.		**Habitat:** Agricultural areas and open lands with short grass or areas of bare ground.		**Habitat:** Open and semi-open lands. Agricultural areas and small towns are favored.	

Breeding: Nests on man-made ledges and beneath overhangs in cities. Bridges and barns are used in rural areas. Multiple nesting with 2 eggs per clutch.

Breeding: Builds a flimsy nest of small sticks in sapling or low branch usually from 6 to 15 feet above ground. 2 eggs is usual with multiple broods per year.

Breeding: Usually nests in trees or bushes near human habitation. Lays 2 eggs per clutch but can nest several times per year.

Natural History: Although the Rock Pigeon is about the same overall length as the Mourning Dove and Collard Dove, the pigeon is a much stockier, heavier bird that weighs over twice as much as the Mourning Dove. Despite the fact that this familiar bird ranges from coast to coast across North America, the Rock Pigeon is not a native species. It was introduced into North America by the earliest European settlers in the 1600s. Pigeons followed the first settlers into the west (including Illinois) colonizing towns and settlements and living in close proximity to rural farms and livestock. Today they are one of the most familiar urban birds in America and are also common around farms and ranches. Young pigeons known as "Squab" are eaten in many places throughout the world. Rock Pigeons are incredibly variable and can exhibit almost any color or pattern.

Natural History: Although these birds are found year-round in Illinois their numbers swell each fall with migrants from farther to the north. Mourning Doves are regarded as a game species throughout much of the United States, including Illinois. The US Fish & Wildlife Service estimates that as many as 20 million are killed each fall during America's dove season. While that seems an appallingly high number, the Mourning Dove is actually one of the most numerous bird species in America and the total population is estimated at around 350 million birds! Seeds are the chief food item. They will eat everything from the tiniest grass seeds to every type of seed crop produced by man, including corn, wheat, sorghum, millet and sunflower as well as peanuts and soybeans. This abundant species may face competition from the invasive Eurasian Collard Dove, which occupies a similar ecological niche.

Natural History: Originally native to Eurasia, the Collared-Dove has colonized much of the southern United States since its release in the Bahamas in the 1970s. Since then they have rapidly expanded their range north and west. Today they have colonized the entire state of Illinois. In food habits and other aspects of its biology the Collard-Dove is similar to the Mourning Dove. Young Collard-Doves disperse widely and this species continues to increase across North America. Cold weather does not seem to be a limiting factor but food availability may limit range expansion. How far this species will extend its range in North America is still unknown. As with all other members of the Columbidae family, young birds are fed a semi-liquid "crop milk" regurgitated from the adults crop.

Class - **Aves** (birds)

Order - **Galliformes** (chicken-like birds)

Family - **Phasianidae** (grouse)

Greater Prairie Chicken	Wild Turkey	Ring-necked Pheasant
Tympanuchus cupido	*Meleagris gallopavo*	*Phasianus colchicus*

Size: 17 inches.	Presumed range in Illinois	**Size:** To 47 inches.	Presumed range in Illinois	**Size:** To 35 inches.	Presumed range in Illinois
Abundance: Very rare in Illinois.		**Abundance:** Fairly common.		**Abundance:** Uncommon.	
Migratory Status: Nonmigratory bird that is a year-round resident.		**Migratory Status:** Nonmigratory bird that is a year-round resident.		**Migratory Status:** Nonmigratory bird that is a year-round resident.	
Variation: Sexes very similar. Males have well developed air sacs on the side of the neck.		**Variation:** Females are smaller, duller, have less red on head and neck and lack the "beard."		**Variation:** Females are smaller and cryptic mottled brown. Males are strikingly colored.	

Greater Prairie Chicken	Wild Turkey	Ring-necked Pheasant
Habitat: Prairies. In Illinois a resident of two small remnants of Tallgrass Prairie in Marion and Jasper counties.	**Habitat:** Inhabits all major habitats in the state except for urban areas. Most common in mixture of woods and farms.	**Habitat:** Prefers a mosaic of crop lands interlaced with cover such as wetlands, grassy patches, overgrown fence rows.
Breeding: The nest is a shallow scraped depression lined with grasses. From 5 to 17 eggs have been recorded per clutch.	**Breeding:** Nests on the ground in thick cover such as thickets, honeysuckle, Multiflora Rose, or tall grasses. Lays up to 14 eggs.	**Breeding:** Nests on the ground in thick cover such as tall grasses, cattails, etc. Lays up to 15 eggs. Rarely, two females will use the same nest.
Natural History: The Greater Prairie Chicken is a prime example of a species that is totally dependant upon a particular habitat. Illinois once boasted tens of millions of acres of Tallgrass Prairie. Today that acreage has been converted to agricultual operations and native Tallgrass Prairie has been reduced to tiny, isolated pockets scattered across the the state. The population of Greater Prairie Chickens in Illinois prior to European settlement has been estimated to have been as high as 14 million birds. Today that number is less than 200. As Illinois' prairie habitats dissappeared, so did the Greater Prairie Chicken. Males perform elaborate courtship "dances" on small patches of bare ground known as "leks." The bouncing, fluttering "dance" is accompanied by a deep, resonant vocalization in which the air sacs of the throat are inflated.	**Natural History:** The courtship of the male Wild Turkey includes a "strutting" display that involves spreading the tail feathers, drooping the wings and producing a low frequency "drumming" sound. When attempting to attract females in the spring breeding season males become quite vocal and regularly emit a loud "gobble" that can be heard for a mile. The saga of the disappearance and resurgence of the Wild Turkey in America is one of wildlife managements greatest success stories. In pioneer days turkeys were found throughout Illinois but by the early 1900s they had disappeared from the state. Restocking efforts by the Illinois Department of Natural Resources, aided by sportsmen groups, has been highly successful and Wild Turkeys are now found in suitable habitats throughout the state.	**Natural History:** Ring-necked Pheasants are an alien species from Asia that were introduced into America in the late 1800s. The species has thrived in the Great Plains region where adequate natural habitats still exist. It was once a common bird in northern Illinois, but began to decline as more land was cleared for row crops. Despite conservation efforts by the Illinois Department of Natural Resources, recovery to the numbers seen prior to modern agriculture has not occurred. More recent conservation efforts aimed at restoring patches of natural grasslands should help this and many other wildlife species. This is a popular game bird throughout its range in America and sportsmen's organizations such as "Pheasants Forever" are actively involved in raising money for habitat conservation and restoration.

Class - **Aves** (birds)

Order - **Galliformes**

Family - **Odontophoridae** (quail)

Northern Bobwhite
Colinus virginianus

Size: 10 inches.

Abundance: Uncommon.

Variation: Sexually dimorphic. See photos.

Migratory Status: Year-round resident.

Habitat: Small woodlands, edge areas and overgrown fields bordering agricultural land are the favorite habitats.

Presumed range in Illinois

Breeding: Ground nester. Clutch size averages about 15 eggs but nest failure due to predation is high. Multiple nestings are common.

Natural History: Bobwhite have always been an important game bird in the United States. In recent decades however the species has experienced significant population declines, especially in the northern portions of its range (including Illinois). Some blame a resurgence in predators for the decline, and that is undoubtably part of the problem. But the real culprit is modern agricultural practices that have eliminated fence rows and created expansive crop fields with no ground cover. This is the main factor contributing to the decline of the Bobwhite. Through fall and winter they will stick together in family groups known as a "covey." In spring adults pair off for breeding with the resultant offspring and their parents producing the next falls covey. Mortality through the winter is high and survivors from more than one covey will often join together as winter wanes.

Order - **Caprimulgiformes**

Family - **Caprimulgidae** (nightjars)

Common Nighthawk
Chordeiles minor

Size: 9.5 inches.

Abundance: Fairly common.

Variation: Sexes alike. No significant variation.

Migratory Status: Summer resident

Habitat: Open and semi-open areas. Can be common around cities and towns but also in rural areas.

Presumed range in Illinois

Breeding: No nest is constructed and 2 eggs are laid on bare gravel. Most nests are on flat, gravel covered rooftops.

Natural History: These birds sometimes go by the nickname "Bullbat." They are can be quite common in urban areas in summer but they are also seen in open and semi-open rural areas. Like our other nightjars the Common Nighthawk feeds on the wing, catching moths and other flying insects. But unlike the others this bird is active both at night and at dawn and dusk, or sometimes on cloudy days. Around towns and cities they chase airborne insects attracted to streetlights at night. This is one of the great travelers of the bird world, wintering in South America. Their summer range includes nearly all of North America south of the Arctic. Nighthawks are usually seen in flight, but they will occasionally be spotted resting atop a fence post in open country. They often migrate in large flocks, sometimes nubering over 1,000 birds. They have experienced a precipitous decline in recent years.

Whip-poor-will
Antrostomus vociferus

Size: 12 inches.

Abundance: Uncommon

Variation: Sexes alike. No significant variation.

Migratory Status: Summer resident

Habitat: Forest edge, power-line cuts through wooded areas and xeric woods. Favors thickets for daytime roosting.

Presumed range in Illinois

Breeding: Nests on the ground amid leaf litter. No nest is built and the eggs (usually 2) are laid on the ground.

Natural History: Few animals exhibit a more cryptic color and pattern than this species. When resting on the forest floor during the day they are nearly invisible. A very similar species, the **Chuck-wills-widow** (*A. carolinensis*) is a rare summer resident in extreme southern Illinois. It is smaller (9.75 inches) and browner than the Whip-poor-will. The two are easily differentiated by the their songs, usually described as *whip,prrr-weel* for the Whip-poor-will and as *chuk-wills wee-dow* for the Chuck-will's-widow. Both calls are usually repeated rapidly and at times incessantly. Equipped with a very large mouths for feeding on moths and other large flying insects, both species are nocturnal and catch most of their food in midair. Both species have experienced an unexplained decline in populations over the last decade.

Class - **Aves** (birds)

Strigiformes (owls)	Order - **Strigiformes** (owls)	
Family - **Tytonidae** (barn owl)	Family - **Strigidae** (typical owls)	
Barn Owl *Tyto alba*	**Eastern Screech Owl** *Megascops asio*	**Snowy Owl** *Bubo sciandiacus*

Gray morph

Female

Barn Owl	Eastern Screech Owl	Snowy Owl
Size: 16 inches. 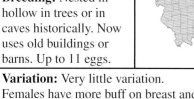 *Presumed range in Illinois*	**Size:** 8.5 inches. *Presumed range in Illinois*	**Size:** 24 inches.  *Presumed range in Illinois*
Abundance: Endangered in Illinois.	**Abundance:** Common.	**Abundance:** Very rare in Illinois.
Migratory Status: Year-round resident.	**Migratory Status:** Year-round resident.	**Migratory Status:** Winter migrant.
Breeding: Nested in hollow in trees or in caves historically. Now uses old buildings or barns. Up to 11 eggs.	**Breeding:** Nest is in tree hollows and old woodpecker holes. Four to six eggs are laid and young fledge in June.	**Breeding:** Nest is on the ground in open tundra. Often built atop small mounds or ridges. Lays 5 to 15 eggs.
Variation: Very little variation. Females have more buff on breast and sides. Also more buff spotting on breast and belly. Males appear nearly pure white below, but do have a few spots.	**Variation:** Two distinct color morphs occur. Gray phase (inset), is more common in the Appalachian Mountains but both red and gray morphs can occur in Illinois.	**Variation:** Females and juveniles have extensive black barring on white background. Adult males are nearly pure white below with reduced dark bars and spots dorsally.
Habitat: Prefers open and semi-open habitats. Short grass pastures are a favorite hunting ground. Probably more common around farms and small towns.	**Habitat:** All types of habitats within the state may be used, including suburban areas and in the vicinity of farms. Favors edge areas, fence rows, etc.	**Habitat:** Summer habitat is the high Arctic and open tundra. Birds that wander south in winter to Illinois favor expansive open fields.
Natural History: The Barn Owl is one of the most widespread owl species in the world, being found throughout most of North America south of Canada, all of Central and South America, most of Europe and sub-saharan Africa, parts of southern Asia and all of Australia. In spite of its wide range they are usually not common anywhere. Small rodents are the primary prey, especially mice and voles. When feeding a large brood of young a pair of Barn Owls may catch over two dozen mice in a single night. Like other owls their hearing is so acute they can catch mice unseen beneath leaves by homing in rustling sounds. Ironically, man's attempts to control rodents with poisoned baits may be in part responsible for the demise of rodent eating species like the Barn Owl.	**Natural History:** The eerie call of the Screech Owl is often described as "haunting and tremulous." Despite being at times vocal birds, these small owls often go unnoticed. They may even live in suburban yards and small towns, especially if older, large trees with hollow limbs and trunks are present. They feed on insects such as crickets and grasshoppers and on a wide variety of small vertebrate prey including mice, voles and songbirds that are plucked from their roosts at night. These wide-ranging birds are found throughout the eastern United States as from the Altlantic to the Rocky Mountains and from southern Canada to Florida and Mexico. Birds in the northern portions of their range can be negatively impacted by severe winters.	**Natural History:** A true icon of northern wilderness, the sight of a Snowy Owl in Illinois is often met with excitement. Winter migrants appear fairly regularly in the northernmost portion of the state and in rare winters they can be seen as far south as the Ohio River. Every now and then large numbers of these giant owls appear in winter in the northern United States in a phenonmena known as an "irruption." The exact cause of these irruptions are not completely understood, but they may relate to food availability in the far north. One of this birds primary food items is lemmings. Populations of these rodents vary considerably from year to year in what amounts to a boom-bust cycle. In years of low lemming numbers many owls will move south.

Class - **Aves** (birds)

Order - **Strigiformes** (owls)

Family - **Strigidae** (typical owls)

Barred Owl *Strix varia*	**Great Horned Owl** *Bubo virginianus*

Fledgling

On nest

Size: 21 inches.

Abundance: Uncommon.

Variation: No sexual variation. Three subspecies are known in America with a fourth in central Mexico, only one (Northern Barred Owl-*S. v. varia*) occurs in Illinois.

Migratory Status: Year-round resident.

Habitat: Woodlands primarily. Especially in bottomlands, swampy areas, and riparian corridors, but also upland woods.

Presumed range in Illinois

Breeding: Nest is usually in tree cavities but known to nest tree crotches or old hawk nests. Usually 2 (rarely 3 or 4) eggs are laid.

Natural History: The Barred Owl ranges throughout the eastern half of the United States from the eastern edge of the Great Plains eastward. The eight noted call of the Barred Owl is described as "Hoo-hoo-hoo-hoo, hoo-hoo-hooaahh." In addition the species is capable of a wide array of hoots, screeches and coarse whistles. Small vertebrates are the main prey, especially rodents like voles, mice and flying squirrels. Birds, lizards, small snakes, and amphibians are also eaten. In the eastern United States the range of the Barred Owl closely coincides with that of the Red-shouldered Hawk and the two predators are often regarded as ecological counterparts occupying the same niche at different times. In Illinois this species is most common along the major river valleys of the state, in the southern tip of Illinois, and in regions where significant woodlands exist.

Size: 23 inches.

Abundance: Fairly common.

Variation: Males are slightly smaller and have a larger white patch on throat. There are 10 subspecies in North America. The Eastern subspecies (*B. v. virginianus*) is found in Illinois.

Migratory Status: Year-round resident.

Habitat: Woodlands, semi-open and open habitats are all utilized, but most common in mosiac of upland woods and fields.

Presumed range in Illinois

Breeding: One of the earliest nesting birds in America. Horned Owls may be sitting on eggs by late January. Nest is often an old hawk nest. 2 eggs is usual.

Natural History: This widespread species occurs throughout the Americas from Alaska to southern South America. In the US specimens from the western portions of the country are much paler than those seen in the east. In the eastern United States Red Cedars and other evergreen trees are a favorite roosting site. The Great Horned Owl is the ecological counterpart of the Red-tailed Hawk, hunting much the same prey in the same regions; with the hawk hunting by day and the owl at night. These powerful predators eat a wide variety of small animals. Rabbits are a favorite food item. They are also known to eat larger mammals like muskrats, groundhogs, and even skunks or rarely, domestic cats! They can be a problem at times for those who raise chickens and leave them out in the open at night. But they also consume many rodents. Once regarded as a varmint, they are now federally protected.

Class - **Aves** (birds)
Order - **Strigiformes** (owls)
Family - **Strigidae** (typical owls)

Short-eared Owl *Asio flammeus*	**Long-eared Owl** *Asio otus*	**Northern Saw-whet Owl** *Aegolius acadicus*

Size: 15 inches.	Presumed range in Illinois	**Size:** 15 inches.	Presumed range in Illinois	**Size:** 8 inches.	Presumed range in Illinois
Abundance: Uncommon.		**Abundance:** Rare in Illinois.		**Abundance:** Rare in Illinois.	
Variation: Females tend to be slightly darker.		**Variation:** Female is darker, more rusty facial disk, and slightly larger.		**Variation:** Immature has buff belly, dark facial disk, white eyebrow.	
Migratory Status: Mostly a wintertime resident or winter migrant, but some breeding has been recorded in Illinois.		**Migratory Status:** Mostly a wintertime migrant, or less commonly a winter resident.		**Migratory Status:** Occurs mainly as a fall and winter migrant but also as a winter resident. Very rare as a breeder.	

Habitat: These are open country birds and the primary habitat is prairie, marsh, and tundra. In forested regions they haunt fields, pastures, meadows, etc.	**Habitat:** Prefers open and semi-open woodlands and riparian habitats in open regions. Breeds and summers in boreal regions and mountains.	**Habitat:** Spruce-fir-pine dominated forests in the north and in the Rocky Mountain west. In the east uses mostly mixed deciduous/conifer forests.
Breeding: Nest is on the ground. A slight depression is scraped out by the owl and lined with grasses. 5 or 6 eggs is typical.	**Breeding:** Usually nests in trees in abandoned stick nests built by hawks, crows or other large bird species. 5 or 6 eggs is typical.	**Breeding:** Uses old woodpecker holes almost exclusively for nesting. 5 or 6 eggs is typical with a survival rate to fledging of about 50 percent.
Natural History: In Illinois, the Short-eared Owl is most likely to be seen in open regions during winter, but a few have nested in the state. Reclaimed strip mines are used as a winter refuge in the Shawnee Hills region of the state. The food is mostly small rodents. Voles are the most significant item in their diet. Rodent prey is located mostly by sound while flying low and slow over open, grassy fields. Most hunting is done at night or dusk and dawn, but these owls are more diurnal than most and may hunt during the day. The erectile feathers on the face that form the "ears" are not usually visible unless the owl is agitated or defensive. They appear to be in decline in much of America and are an endangered species in Illinois.	**Natural History:** Although this rare owl could possibly be seen anywhere in the state, most sightings in Illinois are in the northern portions of the state. They are most likely to be seen in winter, and are not known to breed in Illinois. They are considered a declining species in Illinois. Their name comes from the well developed feather tufts on the head which are erected when resting. These "ear tufts" are folded against the head and not visible on owls in flight. Long-eared Owls during winter can sometimes be seen in small flocks that roost in close proximity to each other. Their food is almost exclusively small mammals, mostly voles and mice of the *Peromyscus* genus.	**Natural History:** Small mammals (mice, voles, and shrews) make up the bulk of this little owls diet. Mice of the genus *Peromyscus* make up as much as three-fourths of the food consumed. Insects are oddly not listed as a major food item, but songbirds are known to be eaten. Small and secretive, the Saw-whet Owl roosts in thick evergreens and is typically silent except during the breeding season. Thus these birds are difficult to observe in the wild. Within its range in the Rockies and Appalachians, seasonal migration is mostly vertical, with the owls moving to lower elevations in winter. These are uncommon owls in Illinois, but some nesting has apparently occurred in the state.

Class - **Aves** (birds)
Order - **Falconiformes** (raptors)
Family - **Accipitridae** (hawks, eagles, kites)
Red-tailed Hawk - *Buteo jamiacensis*

Presumed range in Illinois

Size: 19 inches.

Abundance: Common throughout the state. Perhaps slightly more common in glaciated regions.

Migratory Status: Year-round resident. Numbers are supplemented in winter with migrants from farther north.

Variation: Highly variable. Can vary from nearly solid dark brown to very pale (almost white). Most adult birds are like the typical adult specimen pictured on top left above. Light and dark morphs are mostly winter migrants in Illinois. Females are about 20 percent larger than males. Juveniles have brownish tails with dark crossbars. Some experts recognize as many as 16 subspecies throughout North America.

Habitat: Found in virtually all habitats within the state. Likes open and semi-open areas and is least common in continuous forest, although they do occur there. Favors a mosiac of woodlands, farmland, fencerows, overgrown fields, etc.

Breeding: In Illinois the large stick nest is built high in trees. Nest is usually situated in place that is remote from human activities. Lays 2 to 4 eggs. Young fledge at six weeks.

Natural History: This is the most common and widespread large *Buteo* hawk in America. Their range includes all of North America south of the Arctic and much of the Caribbean and Central America. The Red-tailed Hawk is generally regarded as the daytime counterpart of the Great Horned Owl, hunting by day many of the same species in the same habitats utilized by the owl at night. "Red-tails" prey mostly on rodents (mice, voles, and ground squirrels). Much larger prey like rabbits may also be taken on occasion. In some areas ground dwelling birds like pheasants and quail are taken, and they have been known to attack large flocks of blackbirds. In summer they also take large snakes such as the Woodland Rat Snake (*Pantherophis*). Large examples of these snakes (which are strong constrictors) have been known to turn the tables and end up killing a hungry hawk. During winter these large hawks sometimes resort to eating carrion and can sometimes be seen feeding on road kills. In Illinois (and in much of the eastern US), the Red-tailed Hawk is often known by the nickname "Chicken Hawk" in the mistaken belief that they prey on chickens. Although they may certainly catch a few chickens occasionally, their main food is rats, mice and other rodents, making them an overall useful species to man. Their habit of perching conspicuously in dead trees, snags and power poles along highways makes them one of the more easily observed of America's hawk species. Historically, the Red-tailed Hawk and other raptors were regarded as varmints and for many decades they were shot on sight by uninformed individuals. By the 1950s many birds of prey were becoming scarce in America. Since the passage of the migratory bird treaty act in the early 1970s providing federal protection to all of America's raptor species, Red-tailed Hawks have become common.

Class - **Aves** (birds)

Order - **Falconiformes** (raptors)

Family - **Accipitridae** (hawks, eagles, kites)

Broad-winged Hawk	Rough-legged Hawk	Red-shouldered Hawk
Buteo platypterus	*Buteo lagopus*	*Buteo lineatus*

Size: 16 inches.

Presumed range in Illinois

Abundance: Uncommon in Illinois.

Migratory Status: Summer resident.

Variation: First year plumage is mottled brown (similar to juvenile Red-shouldered Hawk on this page).

Habitat: Favors large tracts of unbroken deciduous woodlands in upland areas. More common in Illinois in the southern part of the state.

Breeding: Stick nest is in a tree crotch, usually in deep woods. Lays 2 to 3 eggs on average.

Natural History: A decidedly woodland raptor whose breeding range in North America closely mimics the Eastern Temperate Forests Level I ecoregion. This species is more common in the Appalachian Highlands and Interior Highlands Divisions as those regions are more heavily forested. They may be seen as a migrant throughout the Interior Lowland Province but the lack of large tracts of forest in this region precludes nesting in much of that area. They are less conspicuous than most hawks except during the migration when they band together in large flocks known as "kettles." Extremely large flocks that may contain 200 birds are usually seen during fall migrations. Food includes insects, but consists mostly of small vertebrates like rodents as well as a large amount of reptile and amphibian prey.

Size: 21 inches.

Presumed range in Illinois

Abundance: Uncommon in Illinois.

Migratory Status: Winter migrant.

Variation: Two distinct color morphs, a dark (nearly black) phase and a lighter morph with paler head and shoulders.

Habitat: This is a northern species that summers as far north as the Arctic. Favors tundra in summer and farmlands and prairies in winter.

Breeding: Nests well to north in Arctic or subarctic regions of tundra and tiaga. Clutch size (3 to 7) is prey dependent.

Natural History: The Rough-legged Hawk is an arctic species that moves south in winter. In Illinois they are most likely to be seen in the northern part of the state. Their migrations are sporadic depending upon weather, snow cover and prey availability, but they can be seen every winter in Illinois. They prey primarily on small mammals and lemmings are an important food on the breeding grounds. During years of high lemming populations more eggs will be laid and more young fledged. In winter they take mice, voles, and shrews mostly. Hunts by soaring and hovering over open country. They can face into the wind and remain in a stationary hover for over a minute. While these are fairly large hawks, they have relatively small feet and small beaks, and are thus unable to take the larger prey taken by hawks like the Red-tailed Hawk.

Size: 17 inches.

Presumed range in Illinois

Abundance: Fairly common.

Migratory Status: Year-round resident.

Variation: 4 subspecies. Ours is the eastern race (*B. l. lineatus*). Female is larger. Ontogenetic variation (see above).

Habitat: Woodlands of all kinds, but especially likes woods bordering swamps or rivers, or along wooded creek-sides. Less common in uplands.

Breeding: Bulky stick nest is in the fork of a tree about 20 to 40 feet high and often near water. 2 to 4 eggs in April.

Natural History: The Red-shouldered Hawk is the daytime counterpart of the Barred Owl, and the two species often occur in the same territory. These are vocal birds. Their call, described as "kee-ah, kee-ah, kee-ah" is rapidly repeated about a dozen times. They can be fairly tame if unmolested and their raucous calling will not go unnoticed when the nest is nearby. They feed on a wide variety of small vertebrates but mostly eat reptiles, amphibians and rodents. The range of the Red-shouldered Hawk coincides closely with the level 1 ecoregion known as the Eastern Temperate Forest. However, a disjunct population (subspecies *elegans*) is found on the west coast of North America in the Mediterranean California Ecoregion. In Illinois this hawk is most comon in portions of the state that are more heavily forested.

Class - **Aves** (birds)

Order - **Falconiformes** (raptors)

Family - **Accipitridae** (hawks, eagles, kites)

Golden Eagle	Bald Eagle	Osprey
Aquila chrysaetos	*Haliaeetus leucophalus*	*Pandion haliaetus*

Presumed range in Illinois

Golden Eagle

Size: 30 inches.

Abundance: Very rare in Illinois.

Migratory Status: Winter migrant. October to April.

Variation: Sexes are similar but female is about 20 percent larger. Juveniles have white in tail.

Habitat: Rugged mountains, deserts, and open plains of the western US and rugged regions of Canadian tundra.

Breeding: A large stick nest up to 6 feet across is usually built on the face of a steep cliff. Usually lays 2 eggs.

Natural History: Although they are slightly smaller than the Bald Eagle, Golden Eagles are probably the most fearsome hunting bird in America. Ground squirrels and other small mammals make up to bulk of their prey, with larger species like jackrabbits and the young of wild sheep, goats, and Pronghorn also being taken. They are sometimes persecuted by sheep ranchers in western North America, who blame them for killing young lambs in the spring. Indigenous to the entire northern hemisphere, in America the Golden Eagle is found mostly in the west. Like many large raptors they are capable of significant seasonal movements. Although very rare east of the Great Plains, they may sometimes show up almost anywhere in North America, including Illinois, especially during winter months.

Bald Eagle

Size: 31 inches.

Abundance: Uncommon in Illinois.

Migratory Status: Both a year-round resident and winter migrant.

Variation: May not acquire the characteristic white head and tail until five years of age.

Habitat: In Illinois Bald Eagles are associated with large rivers and lakes, especially Lake Michigan.

Breeding: Extremely bulky stick nest is reused and gets larger each year. Usually only 2 eggs per clutch.

Natural History: One of the great conservation success stories, Bald Eagles were highly endangered just a few decades ago. Strigent protection, banning of the pesticide DDT, and a widespread education campaign has lead to a remarkable recovery. They first began to recover as a breeding species in most of the country in the 1980s followiing years of strict protection and banning of DDT. Bald Eagles feed largely on fish and carrion but are also capable hunters. Some birds specialize in hunting migratory waterfowl in winter, picking off birds wounded by hunters. Bald Eagles wander widely in the winter and may be seen virtually anywhere in the state, but they are nowhere numerous. Most nesting is around large rivers, lakes or expansive wetlands. Adopted as the national emblem of the United States by congress in 1782.

Osprey

Size: 30 inches.

Abundance: Uncommon.

Migratory Status: Summer resident. Winters in the southern US.

Variation: No variation. Females are slightly larger than males.

Habitat: Typically seen in the vicinity of large lakes and rivers. Increasing in numbers throughout the Midwest.

Breeding: Bulky stick nest is often built on man-made structures like bridges and power line towers. 2 to 4 eggs.

Natural History: Subsists mainly on fish. Hunting tactics consist of a steep dive that ends with the Osprey plunging feet first into the water, allowing them to catch fish up three feet below the surface. Most fish caught in fresh water are non-game species, thus they have little to no impact on sport fisheries. Like the Bald Eagle, Osprey populations in the mid-United States plummeted dramatically in the first half of the 20th century. The same types of conservation efforts that restored the Bald Eagle (including reintroduction programs), have brought Osprey numbers back to respectable levels. Once regarded as an endangered species, the Osprey has recovered enough to have recently been de-listed. Most states now boasts healthy populations of nesting Ospreys and they continue to increase across the country.

Class - **Aves** (birds)		
Order - **Falconiformes** (raptors)		
Family - **Accipitridae** (hawks, eagles, kites)		

Northern Goshawk *Accipiter gentilis*	**Sharp-shinned Hawk** *Accipiter striatus*	**Cooper's Hawk** *Accipiter cooperi*

Northern Goshawk

Size: To 24 inches.

Abundance: Rare in Illinois.

Migratory Status: A rare winter migrant in extreme northern Illinois.

Variation: Females are larger. Juveniles are heavily streaked with dark brown.

Presumed range in Illinois

Habitat: A bird of coniferous and boreal forests. In winter sometimes uses in mixed deciduous/conifer woodlands.

Breeding: Large stick nest can be 3 feet across, usually built in the largest tree in the area. 2 to 4 eggs on average.

Natural History: This is a bird of wilderness. It inhabits most of Canada and the Rocky Mountains. Their primary food consists several species of grouse, but they also take smaller birds as well as squirrels, rabbits, and animals as large as the Snowshoe Hare. Known for fearlessness, the Goshawk has been known to attack humans who venture to close to its nest. It is equally couragous on the hunt and will crash headlong into thickets in pursuit of fleeing prey. This characteristic coupled with its speed and large size have made the Goshawk a favorite bird among those who practice the ancient art of Falconry. Although this species is widespread across the northern half of North America, they are an uncommon bird even within their core range. In Illinois they are seen only very rarely in the northernmost section of the state.

Sharp-shinned Hawk

Size: 9 to 13 inches.

Abundance: Fairly common.

Migratory Status: Both a winter and a year-round resident, but many move north in summer.

Variation: Ontogenetic plumage variation (see photos). Females can be twice the size of males.

Presumed range in Illinois

Habitat: Forests and thickets. Found in both rural and urban areas where vegetative cover is present.

Breeding: Pine trees are a favored locale for placing the nest. Lays as many as 8 eggs, with 5 to 6 being the average.

Natural History: A relentless hunter of small songbirds, the Sharp-shinned Hawk is sometimes seen raiding backyard bird feeders, and they are known to pluck baby songbirds from nests. These small raptors are capable of rapid, twisting flight while pursuing their small songbird prey through woodlands and thickets. In Illinois they are more common during migration periods when birds that summer farther north move southward. Although some birds are breeding residents in the state, most nest far to north, some as far north as Alaska and the Yukon Territory. The Sharp-shinned Hawk is a widely distributed species that ranges across all of North America south of the arctic region and southward all the way to southern Central America. These small hawks are easily overlooked since they favor dense thickets and woodland habitats.

Cooper's Hawk

Size: 14 to 19 inches.

Abundance: Fairly common.

Migratory Status: Year-round resident; but some winter birds may be migrants from farther north.

Variation: Ontogenetic plumage variation (see photos). Females can be 30 percent larger than males.

Presumed range in Illinois

Habitat: Woodlands, regenerative areas, and edge habitats are favored. Can also be seen in tree-lined urban yards.

Breeding: Stick nest is built high in tree and eggs are laid in April or May. Clutch size averages 4 to 6.

Natural History: Feeds almost exclusively on birds and is known to haunt backyard bird feeders. These hawks are a major predator to the Bobwhite, an important game species that is in decline throughout most of its range. Cooper's Hawks are fierce hunters that will fearlessly attack birds as large or larger than themselves, including grouse, waterfowl and domestic chickens. Although quite widespread and fairly common, they are not as observable as the Buteo hawks. Cooper's Hawks tend to stay in wooded areas and thickets with heavier cover than their bulkier cousins. These birds are fast fliers and capable of great maneuverability, an adaptation to hunting in forest and thickets. They have adapted well to human activities and they sometimes exist in urban areas, especially in parks and heavily wooded neighborhoods.

Class - **Aves** (birds)
Order - **Falconiformes** (raptors)
Family - **Accipitridae** (hawks, eagles, kites)

Northern Harrier *Circus cyaneus*	**Mississippi Kite** *Ictina mississippiensis*

Size: To 24 inches.	Presumed range in Illinois 	**Size:** 14 inches.	Presumed range in Illinois
Abundance: Failry common.		**Abundance:** Fairly common.	
Migratory Status: Winter migrant and winter resident.		**Migratory Status:** Summer resident in southern tip of Illinois.	
Variation: Females are mottled brown above and below. Males are gray-brown above and pale gray below.		**Variation:** Juveniles are streaked with brown on the breast. Adults very similar but males have lighter gray heads.	

Habitat: Open country. Pastures, marshes, agricultural fields, wet prairies, and grasslands.	**Habitat:** In Illinois the Mississippi Kite mostly frequents the low-lying regions in the southern tip of the state.
Breeding: Nests on the ground in thick grass. Builds a nest of grasses and weed stems. Lays 4 to 6 eggs.	**Breeding:** Builds a stick nest high up in a large tree. Nesting in Illinois is rare but increasing. Lays 2 eggs.
Natural History: The range of the Northern Harrier is holarctic and includes Europe and northern Asia as well as North America. Unlike most diurnal raptors that hunt entirely by sight, the Northern Harrier mimics the technique used by owls and hunts largely by sound. A special "parabola" of feathers surround the face and direct sound waves to the ears. It hunts by flying low to the ground with a slow, buoyant flight that resembles a giant butterfly. Food is mostly small mammals and birds but reptiles and amphibians are also listed as food items. Roosting and nesting on the ground and hunting as much by sound as by sight, the Northern Harrier is unique among America's diurnal raptors. In historical times before the draining of America's marshes, this was a more common species.	**Natural History:** With their small beaks and feet the Mississippi Kite appears somewhat delicate looking compared to other raptors. In flight they are one of the most graceful. The several species that make up the raptor group known as kites are mainly tropical birds. The Mississippi Kite is the most northerly ranging of the kites, and can be seen as far north as southern Illinois in summer months. Long distance migrants, they arrive in southern Illinois by early May and leave for South America by mid-September. These are gregarious birds that may nest communally and in some parts of their range it is not uncommon to see several nests in close proximity or see groups of birds soaring together. They feed on insects and small vertebrates.

Class - **Aves** (birds)

Order - **Falconiformes** (raptors)

Family - **Falconidae** (falcons)

American Kestrel *Falco sparverius*	Merlin *Falco columbarius*	Peregrine Falcon *Falco peregrinus*

American Kestrel		Merlin		Peregrine Falcon	
Size: 10 inches.	Presumed range in Illinois	**Size:** 11 inches.	Presumed range in Illinois	**Size:** 17 inches.	Presumed range in Illinois
Abundance: Fairly common.		**Abundance:** Uncommon in Illinois.		**Abundance:** Rare.	
Variation: Sexually dimorphic. Male has gray wings, female brown.		**Variation:** Male has blue-gray back, female and immatures brown.		**Variation:** Several variants. Specimen above is typical.	
Migratory Status: A year-round resident. Winter migrants increase the population in winter.		**Migratory Status:** A rare spring/fall migrant and very rare winter migrant.		**Migratory Status:** A few nest and live year round in parts of the state, most are migrants.	
Habitat: Throughout its range the Kestrel is seen in open country. Least common in forested regions.	**Habitat:** Habitat is open regions. Most likely to be seen along major river valleys, especially the larger rivers.	**Habitat:** Prefers cliffs in remote wilderness areas but has adapted to living among skyscrapers in many cities.
Breeding: Usually nests in tree cavities or old woodpecker holes within trees situated in open fields. May also nest in man-made structures. 4 to 5 eggs.	**Breeding:** Breeds far to the north in Canada, Alaska and parts of the north-central Rockies and plains. Uses old crow or hawk nests as well as cliffs.	**Breeding:** Nests on ledges of cliff faces and on man-made structures like skyscrapers and bridges. 4 eggs is typical, sometimes up to 6.
Natural History: While the Kestrel is a fairly common bird in open regions throughout Illinois, there has been some decline in populations in the eastern United States in recent years. Though they are sometimes called "Sparrow Hawk," these are small falcons. The Kestrel is widespread throughout North and Central America and as many as 17 subspecies are recognized. They are often seen perched on power lines and poles along roadways in rural farmlands throughout the state, but they are uncommon in the heavily forested regions. Insects are the major food in summer (especially grasshoppers). In winter they eat small mammals and rarely, small birds. Hunts both from a perch and by hovering over open fields.	**Natural History:** The Merlin is seen in Illinois during migration (or as an occasional wandering bird). These small falcons are only slightly larger than the Kestrel and they are easily confused with that species. The facial markings of the Merlin are less distinct than the Kestrels. Summering mostly far to the north and wintering along coastlines, their migration routes are mostly in the western United States or to the east along the Atlantic coast. Like most falcons however, these birds are prone to wander widely. Although they may occur almost anywhere in the state they are an uncommon to rare bird in Illinois. Food is mostly small birds, especially shorebirds.	**Natural History:** Falcons are fast flying birds and the Peregrine is among the fastest. Hunts pigeons, waterfowl, grouse, etc. Hunting technique usually involves soaring high above and diving in on birds in flight, or diving towards resting birds and panicking them into flight. Once airborne, no other bird can match the Peregrines speed. Diving Peregrines may reach speeds approaching 200 mph, making them perhaps the fastest animal on Earth. In Illinois this species has been reintroduced after being extirpated as a breeding bird many decades ago. The name "peregrine" means "wanderer," and these birds may be seen almost anywhere in the state, albeit quite rarely.

Class - **Aves** (birds)

Order - **Cathartiformes** (vultures)

Family - **Cathartidae**

Turkey Vulture *Cathartes aura*	Black Vulture *Coragyps altratus*
	 Young

Size: 26 inches.	 Presumed range in Illinois	Size: 25 inches.	 Presumed range in Illinois
Abundance: Common.		**Abundance:** Fairly common.	
Migratory Status: Year-round in the southerntip of the state. Summer only in north.		**Migratory Status:** Year-round in the southern tip of the state, but most will go south in winter.	
Variation: Skin on face is pinkish gray on immature birds, bright pink on adult.		**Variation:** Older birds have lighter gray heads with more wrinkles on skin than immatures.	

Habitat: Seen in all habitats throughout the state. Less common in urban areas and regions of intensive agriculture.	**Habitat:** Found in a wide variety of habitats within its range. Mainly restricted to the southern tip of Illinois.
Breeding: Nests on cliff faces, in large tree hollows or on the ground in hollow logs. Almost always lays 2 eggs.	**Breeding:** No nest is built and the 2 eggs are laid on a bare surface. The nest site is often in a derelict building.
Natural History: The absence of feathers on the head and neck of vultures is an adaptation for feeding on carrion. Vultures may stick the head deep inside a rotting carcass and feathers would become matted with filth. The bare skin on the neck and face on the other hand is constantly exposed to the sterilizing effects of sunlight. Turkey Vultures are one of the few birds with a well developed sense of smell, and food is often located by detecting the odor of rotting flesh. Sight is also important and they are quick to notice a fresh carcass on a roadway. Newly mowed fields and other disturbed areas within their range are closely scanned for small animal victims. Highly social, they roost communally, sometimes with Black Vultures. Vultures have benefited from a constant supply of road-killed animals.	**Natural History:** America's vultures are named for the color of the skin on the face. Turkey Vultures have reddish skin (like a turkey), Black Vulture has dark gray or black facial skin. Black Vultures also have shorter tails and lesser wing span, giving them a much "stubbier" look than the Turkey Vulture. Vultures were once regarded as a threat to livestock by spreading disease. In fact, the powerful digestive juices of the gut of vultures destroys bacteria. Both the Turkey Vulture and the Black Vulture have the unappealing habit of defecating on the legs and feet as a way of disinfecting the feet (which can become quite nasty and the birds feed on rotted carcasses). Black Vultures lack the well developed sense of smell of Turkey Vultures, but they do have keen eyesight. Although smaller than the Turkey Vulture, they are more aggresive.

Class - **Aves** (birds)

Order - **Ciconiiformes** (wading birds)

Family - **Ardeidae** (herons)

Great Blue Heron *Ardea herodias*	**Great Egret** *Ardea alba*	**Snowy Egret** *Egretta thula*

Great Blue Heron		Great Egret		Snowy Egret	
Size: 47 inches.	Presumed range in Illinois	**Size:** 39 inches.	Presumed range in Illinois	**Size:** 24 inches.	Presumed range in Illinois
Abundance: Fairly common.		**Abundance:** Uncommon in Illinois.		**Abundance:** Rare in Illinois.	
Migratory Status: Year-round resident. Northern birds may migrate south in winter.		**Migratory Status:** Summer resident along the major river valleys in the state.		**Migratory Status:** Summer migrant, but a few will nest along the Mississippi River.	
Variation: See Natural History below.		**Variation:** Breeders acquire plumes.		**Variation:** Breeders acquire plumes.	

Habitat: Along rivers and streams, swamps, marshes, ponds and wet meadows and floodplains.	**Habitat:** Along major streams, lakes, swamps and marshes. Also low lying areas subject to flooding.	**Habitat:** Along major streams, lakes, swamps and marshes. Also low lying areas subject to flooding.
Breeding: Nests in colonies. Most nesting in Illinois is in wetland areas. Nest is a platform of sticks in tree or bush above water. Nest is a bulky platform of sticks. 3 to 4 eggs is typical.	**Breeding:** Most nesting in Illinois is along the Mississippi and Illinois Rivers. Sporadic nesting occurs elsewhere. Nest is a platform of sticks in tree or bush above water. Lays 3 or 4 eggs.	**Breeding:** Nesting in Illinois occurs only in the southern portion of the state. They will nest in colonies with other heron species. Nest is made of sticks and twigs. 3 to 5 eggs is average.
Natural History: The largest heron in North America, the Great Blue Heron will eat almost anything it can swallow. Fish and frogs are major foods, but it also eats snakes, salamanders, small mammals and even small turtles. Birds are sometimes eaten, including other, smaller heron species. All food items are swallowed whole. Large prey is killed by stabbing repeatedly with the beak or by bashing against a hard object. Smaller prey is often swallowed alive. Hunts both day and night and reportedly has good night vision. Great Blue Herons are found throughout most of the United States and much of Canada, including in riparian habitats in desert regions. Sexes are alike but juveniles will have streaked breast and neck and are duskier overall than adults. A solid white subspecies is found in parts of southern Florida.	**Natural History:** This heron species (along with the Snowy Egret and several other herons) was nearly hunted to extinction during the last half of the 19th century. The long, wispy feathers (known as "plumes") were once used to adorn the hats of fashionable ladies. The plumes are most pronounced during the breeding season. Thus the catastrophic impact of the plume hunters was magnified as hunters killed birds at their nesting colonies. Killing of parent birds doomed nestlings as well. Efforts to save this and other plume bird species lead to some of Americas earliest laws to protect wildlife. Today this species is still a symbol of conservation efforts and is the logo of the National Audubon Society. It is also known by the names Common Egret or Great White Egret. As with many other herons, it often nests in colonies.	**Natural History:** As with several other heron species, the Snowy Egret during breeding season sports long "plume" feathers on the back. As with other plume bird species the Snowy Egret was nearly wiped out by the feather trade of the late 1800s. Today the species has recovered to healthy numbers but remains under threat due to its dependence upon coastal wetlands. This species feeds on smaller prey such as worms, insects, crustaceans, amphibians and small fish. It is an active feeder that often chases prey through the shallows rather than using the stealth method employed by its larger cousins. It also often feeds by swishing its feet in the mud to disturb benthic organisms. The range map above shows the approximate range of summer migrants in the state.

Class - **Aves** (birds)

Order - **Ciconiiformes** (wading birds)

Family - **Ardeidae** (herons)

Little Blue Heron *Egretta cearulea*	**Cattle Egret** *Bulbulcus ibis*	**Green Heron** *Butorides virescens*

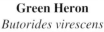

Little Blue Heron
Egretta cearulea

Cattle Egret
Bulbulcus ibis

Green Heron
Butorides virescens

Size: 24 inches.

Presumed range in Illinois

Abundance: Uncommon in Illinois.

Migratory Status: Summer migrant. Very rare breeder in southern Illinois.

Variation: First year birds have white plumage (see inset photo).

Habitat: Wetlands. In Illinois seen mostly along the Mississippi River valley in the southwestern part of the state.

Breeding: Builds a stick nest platform in bushes and low trees in wetlands. Lays 2 to 5 eggs.

Natural History: Even within the heart of its range along the lower coastal plains of the southeastern US, the Little Blue Heron is generally less common that other heron species. In Illinois it is a rather uncommon bird. In addition, the dark plumage of adults and its rather secretive nature make it one of the least observable of our herons. Like most herons, it is an opportunistic feeder that eats almost anything it can swallow. Food is mostly frogs, fish, crustaceans and insects. It is a daytime hunter that hunts by stalking slowly through wetland habitats. The transitional plumage of the juvenile Little Blue Heron is unique, and produces for a brief time a white bird with blue splotches. Blue increases throughout the molt ending in a solid blue adult. The range map approximates the range of summer migrants.

Size: 19 inches.

Presumed range in Illinois

Abundance: Uncommon in Illinois.

Migratory Status: A rare summer migrant and very rare breeder.

Variation: Orange on crown and throat during breeding.

Habitat: Unlike other herons, these birds are usually seen in open pastures and fields in association with cattle.

Breeding: Stick nest built in trees or bushes. Nests in large colonies. 3 or 4 eggs is average.

Natural History: The Cattle Egret is one of our most interesting heron species. Originally native to Africa, Cattle Egrets began an inexplicable range expansion in the early 1800s. They first migrated across the Atlantic to South America and then appeared in North America around 1950. The species continues to expand its range and is today an uncommon summer migrant in the southern half of Illinois. Their name is derived from their habit of associating with cattle herds in pastures. Before expanding their range out of Africa they associated with herds of Cape Buffalo, Hippopotamus and wild ungulates. They feed mostly on insects that are disturbed by the large grazers they follow through pastures and grasslands. The map above shows the approximate range of summer migrants in Illinois. Some nesting has occurred in the state.

Size: 19 inches.

Presumed range in Illinois

Abundance: Fairly common.

Migratory Status: A summer resident that breeds widely across the state.

Variation: Juvenile birds are browner above and have streaked throat.

Habitat: Usually seen in the vicinity of wetlands or rivers and streams. Also common around lakes and small ponds.

Breeding: Usually nests singly rather than in colonies. Nest is a stick platform in a tree fork. Lays 3 to 5 eggs.

Natural History: In many areas the Green Heron often goes by the name "Shy-poke." This is one of our most familiar herons and its range encompasses all of the eastern United States as well as the west coast. It also ranges southward throughout Central America. When flushed it nearly always emits a loud "squawking" alarm call. Feeds mostly in shallow water and often feeds from a perch on a floating log or a limb just above the waters surface. Hunts by stealth and may remain frozen for long periods as it watches and waits for prey. Fish is the primary food item with small frogs probably being the next most common prey. Amazingly, this species has been reported to catch insects and worms to use as bait for luring in fish. While the Green Heron is one of our most common wading birds, it is dependant upon wetlands.

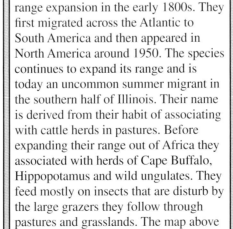

Class - **Aves** (birds)
Order - **Ciconiiformes** (wading birds)
Family - **Ardeidae** (herons)

Yellow-crowned Night Heron *Nyctanassa violacea*	**Black-crowned Night Heron** *Nycticorax nycticorax*	**Least Bittern** *Ixobrychus exilis*

	Presumed range in Illinois		Presumed range in Illinois		Presumed range in Illinois
Size: 25 inches.		**Size:** 25 inches.		**Size:** 13 inches.	
Abundance: Uncommon in Illinois.		**Abundance:** Uncommon in Illinois.		**Abundance:** Uncommon.	
Migratory Status: Summer resident.		**Migratory Status:** Summer resident.		**Migratory Status:** A summer resident.	
Variation: Juveniles are heavily streaked with brown and white.		**Variation:** Juvenile birds are heavily streaked with brown (see inset).		**Variation:** Male has black cap and black back. See both sexes above.	

Habitat: Swamps and marshes. Favors heavier cover than many herons.	**Habitat:** Wetlands, river valleys, and in the vicinity of large impoundments.	**Habitat:** Favors marshes with dense growths of tall grasses and sedges.
Breeding: Breeds very sporadically across Illinois, mostly in glaciated regions. Flimsy stick nest is fairly high in tree, usually over water. 3 to 5 eggs.	**Breeding:** Nests in colonies that are usually situated over swamps or on an island. Colonies may contain hundreds of birds, with 3 or 4 eggs per nest.	**Breeding:** Nest is a well concealed platform built amid dense growth of cattails or other sedges/grasses. Up to 6 eggs are laid.
Natural History: These birds are often active at night, hence the name "night heron." Food is mostly crustaceans. Crabs are important foods in coastal regions, while crayfish are eaten in freshwater areas. A classical ambush predator, the Yellow-crowned Night Heron does most foraging from a stationery position, sitting like a statue and waiting for prey to wander into striking range. They will also stalk slowly and methodically with slow, deliberate movements that are largely undetectable to prey. Diet may be supplemented with fish and invertebrates, but this heron is mainly a crustacean specialist. Has recovered nicely from low numbers decades ago and now seems to be expanding its range farther to the north. The range map above is an approximation an may not be accurate. They are regarded as an Endangered Species by the Illinois Department of Natural Resources.	**Natural History:** Although the Black-crowned Night Heron may be locally common near breeding colonies, it is a rarely seen bird in most of Illinois. Surprisingly, this is a widespread species that is found not only in much of the US, but in fact throughout most of the world. They can be found on every continent except Australia and Antarctica. As its name implies this species is often active at night. The food is primarily fish. However, the list of known foods is quite long and includes, insects, leeches, earthworms, crustaceans, gastropods, amphibians, snakes, small turtles, small mammals, and even birds! Prefers to feed in shallow water along the margins of weedy ponds, marshes, and swamps. A few breed in widely scattered locales across Illinois. Today they are regarded as an Endangered Species in Illinois.	**Natural History:** This smallest of American herons is also a secretive bird that often stays hidden in dense marsh grasses and sedges. When alarmed they point their bill skyward and freeze, mimicking the vertical vegetation of their habitat. These small herons move with ease through thick stands of marsh vegetation. When flushed they fly only a short distance just above the vegetation before dropping back down. Despite their seemingly weak flying abilities, they migrate great distances from wintering areas in south Florida and the Carribean to summer breeding grounds that may be as far north as northern Minnesota. They have very long toes for grasping stems of grass and sedge. Feeds on small fish, insects, crayfish, and amphibians. This species has declined significantly over the last century. Today they are regarded as a Threatened Species in Illinois.

Class - **Aves** (birds)

Order - **Ciconiiformes** (wading birds)	Order - **Gruiformes** (rails & cranes)	
Family - **Ardeidae** (herons)	Family - **Rallidae** (rails)	
American Bittern *Botaurus lentiginosus*	**King Rail** *Rallus elegans*	**Virginia Rail** *Rallus limicola*

American Bittern	King Rail	Virginia Rail
Size: 26 inches.	**Size:** 16 inches.	**Size:** 9.5 inches.
Abundance: Endangered in Illinois.	**Abundance:** Rare in Illinois.	**Abundance:** Uncommon in Illinois.
Migratory Status: Both a migrant and a rare summer resident.	**Migratory Status:** Transient migrant and rare summer resident.	**Migratory Status:** Transient migrant and rare summer resident.
Habitat: Large freshwater marshes are used in summer, coastal marshlands in winter.	**Habitat:** Marshes. Found mostly along coasts but a few move inland in summer.	**Habitat:** Primarily a marsh dweller. In migration may visit ponds, swamps, wet meadows.

(Presumed range in Illinois maps shown for each species)

Variation: None. Sexes alike.	**Variation:** None. Sexes alike.	**Variation:** None. Sexes alike.
Breeding: Nest is in dense emergent vegetation of the marsh and is well hidden. 3 to 5 eggs is typical. Densest breeding occurs in western North America.	**Breeding:** Builds a loosely woven cup from marsh vegetation. Breeds sporadically and breeding has been recorded in Illinois, but very rarely.	**Breeding:** Builds a nest platform of aquatic vegetation a few inches above water level. Nest is usually well hidden among vegetation. Lays 8 or 9 eggs.

Natural History: The biology of this species is not well known. Presumably they may be seen anywhere in Illinois during migration and migrants have been known to use tiny ponds or small pockets of wetlands choked with emergent vegetation like cattails. Few Illinoisans will ever see one, as they are usually quite secretive. Hunts by stealth and may remain motionless for long periods of time. The eyes of this heron are situated with a downward slant, better facilitating the birds ability to see into the water. When startled they will throw the head back and point the beak straight up. The streaked brown pattern of the neck and breast is remarkably cryptic amid vertical stalks of marsh grasses and sedges, and an individual in "frozen" posture becomes almost invisible. Like most herons, an opportunistic feeder. Eats fish, amphibians, crayfish, small mammals, and some insects.

Natural History: Rails are well adapted to life in the marsh. They move with ease through thick grasses and rarely fly except when migrating. They can run quite fast through the grass and rarely offer more than a glimpse. They can also swim and dive beneath the surface, using the wings to swim underwater. Despite the fact that rails are listed as a game bird by most state wildlife agencies, almost no one hunts them, due probably to their scarcity and secretiveness. They feed mostly on aquatic insects and their larva, spiders, and other invertebrates. Some plant material is also eaten. Although they may occur across much of Illinois during migration, they are never common and are rarely observed. While breeding has been recorded in Illinois, the species has declined from its historical breeding range and today this is one of the rarest breeding birds in the state. Regarded as endangered by IDNR.

Natural History: The Virginia Rail is more common in Illinois than the larger King Rail, both as a migrant and as a breeding bird. Nesting has been recorded in much of northern Illinois. Still, this is not a common bird in the state and this fact coupled with its secretive nature means that it is a species that remains unfamiliar to most Illinoisans. Historically, this species was much more common in the state. But today very little of the wetland habitats that once occurred in Illinois remain. As a result, this species along with its larger cousin the King Rail are both species being monitored by the Illinois Department of Natural Resources. The King Rail is an Endangered Species in Illinois, while the Virginia Rail is a classified as being on the "Watch List." A third species of Rail, the **Black Rail** (*Laterallus jamiacensis*) has been observed in the state, but sightings in Illinois are extremely rare.

Class - Aves (birds)

Order - Gruiformes (rails & cranes)

Family - Rallidae (rails)

American Coot *Fulica americana*	Common Gallinule *Gallinula galeata*	Sora *Porzana carolina*

American Coot		Common Gallinule		Sora	
Size: 15 inches.	Presumed range in Illinois	**Size:** 14 inches.	Presumed range in Illinois	**Size:** 9 inches.	Presumed range in Illinois
Abundance: Fairly common.		**Abundance:** Rare in Illinois.		**Abundance:** Uncommon.	
Migratory Status: Year-round in northern Illinois. Winter resident in southern Illinois.		**Migratory Status:** Rare summer resident. Arrives mid-April. Leaves in September.		**Migratory Status:** Summer resident in northern Illinois. Migrant in south.	
Variation: Sexes alike. Juvenile paler gray with yellowish beak.		**Variation:** Sexes alike. Juvenile paler gray without red bill and forehead.		**Variation:** Juvenile lacks black on face and throat. Sexes are alike.	

American Coot	Common Gallinule	Sora
Habitat: Rivers, lakes, large ponds, marshes and wetlands.	**Habitat:** Wetlands and lake shores with abundant vegetation.	**Habitat:** Primarily a marsh dweller. Favors heavily vegetated wetlands.
Breeding: Breeds mostly to the north and to the west of Illinois, but does nest sporadically in northern Illinois. Nest is a platform built amid emergent vegetation. About 6 eggs are laid.	**Breeding:** Nest is a platform of vegetation slightly above the water line and usually well concealed. A very rare nester in Illinois. Will lay as many as 10 eggs.	**Breeding:** Builds a nest platform of aquatic vegetation a few inches above water level. Nest is well hidden in dense upright plants. Breeds in northern Illinois. Lays 8 to 11 eggs.
Natural History: During migration and in winter American Coots gather in large flocks on open water and behave more like ducks than rails. During the breeding season they act more like rails and live among cattails and reeds in freshwater marshes. But they are not as elusive as the rails and are usually easily observed even in summer. They are considered a game species, but rarely hunted as most waterfowl hunters regard them as a "trash" species. They sometimes go by the nickname "Mud Hen." Although the feet are not webbed as with ducks and geese, their long toes are equipped with lateral lobes which flare out when swimming and create an ample surface for pushing against the water. Thus they are good swimmers. They feed both on land (on grasses) and in the water (aquatic plants, algae, and aquatic invertebrates).	**Natural History:** Sometimes known as the Common Moorhen, but that name is properly reserved for a very similar bird that lives in Europe. Although these birds may be seen in suitable habitat throughout of the state, they are rare in Illinois. Farther south in places like Louisiana and Florida they can be quite common. They feed largely on seeds of aquatic plants but also eats animal matter including most predominately snails and insects. Although similar to the American Coot in size and appearance, the Common Gallinule is rarely seen in the open and prefers to stay close to heavy cover. Additionally, they don't form large flocks as do American Coots. However, they are sometimes quite tame and approachable, especially within the heart of their range in Florida and the lower Coastal Plain. Regarded as a Threatened Species in Illinois.	**Natural History:** The Sora is one of the more observable of America's rails. Still, it is fairly secretive, especially during fall migration. They are usually observable on both breeding and wintering grounds, but catching a glimpse of this species is difficult. They are vocal birds however, and their whinnying call can be heard for a long distance. They feed on a variety of aquatic invertebrates but also eat seeds of aquatic plants, particularly wild rice. Soras have exceptionally long toes, an adaptation that allows for walking across floating vegetation. This is the most widespread rail species in America and its combined breeding, migratory and winter range includes the entire continent south of Alaska and the northernmost Canadian provinces. When disturbed it usually runs into deeper cover and flies reluctantly.

Class - **Aves** (birds)

Order - **Gruiformes** (rails & cranes)	Order - **Chariidriformes** (shorebirds)	
Family - **Gruidae** (cranes)	Family - **Charadriidae** (plovers)	
Sandhill Crane *Grus canadensis*	**Killdeer** *Charadrius vociferus*	**Semipalmated Plover** *Charadrius semipalmatus*

Sandhill Crane	Killdeer	Semipalmated Plover
Size: 42 inches. **Abundance:** Uncommon in Illinois. **Migratory Status:** Rare seasonal migrant. **Variation:** Juveniles are splotched with large amounts of rusty brown. See photos above.	**Size:** 10.5 inches. **Abundance:** Common. **Migratory Status:** Year-round resident. **Variation:** None. Sexes are alike and there is no significant seasonal or ontogenic plumage variations.	**Size:** 7.25 inches. **Abundance:** Fairly common. **Migratory Status:** Spring/fall migrant. **Variation:** See photos above. Both winter and summer plumages may be seen in Illinois.

Presumed range in Illinois (for each species)

Habitat: Open lands, farm fields, mudflats, marshes and shallow water areas. In migration uses harvested crop fields.	**Habitat:** Open lands. Mudflats, agricultural fields, lake shores, sandbars, and even gravel parking lots.	**Habitat:** Winter habitat is along coastlines. Summer habitat is open tundra. Migrants favor mud flats and shorelines.
Breeding: Typically lays 2 eggs on a platform nest built of vegetation (see photo above). Most nesting takes place in the far north, but there are breeding populations in the southern US.	**Breeding:** Lays 4 eggs directly on the ground. Nest is often in gravelly or sandy situations in wide-open spaces. Young are very precocial and they will run about within hours of hatching.	**Breeding:** Nests on the ground, usually near water. Nesting grounds are in northern Canada and Alaska. 4 eggs. Chicks are precocious and able to feed themselves immediately.
Natural History: Standing over 3 feet tall, the Sandhill Crane is one of the largest birds seen in America. Populations were seriously depleted by the beginning of the 20th century, but the species has recovered dramatically in the last few decades. The largest populations are seen west of the Mississippi River and number tens of thousands. Eastern populations have been slower to recover but are now reasonably healthy. Several states including nearby Kentucky treat them as a game species and have regulated hunting seasons. Some conservationists question the wisdom of hunting seasons on this species. They often form into large flocks that can be vulnerable to natural disasters such as tornados.	**Natural History:** Although the Killdeer is found statewide, they are much more common in where open habitats are more widespread. This is a species that has likely benefited significantly from human alterations of natural habitats. The creation of open spaces where there was once grassland or forest has resulted in a habitat boom the Killdeer. They are found all over North America south of the Arctic Circle. They were once hunted for food and their populations suffered a serious decline in the days of "market hunting." They feed on the ground and earthworms are a major food source along with grasshoppers, beetles and snails. A few seeds are also consumed. Baby Killdeer are highly precocious and can walk immediately.	**Natural History:** Most Semi-palmated Plovers migrate along the coasts of North America, but a few travel overland and they are occasionally seen in Illinois Most sightings will likely be along the Lake shorelines as they tend to favor shorelines and other open spaces. The food of the Semi-palmated Plover is mostly invertebrate animals plucked from the mud. They hunt these "benthic" organisms along the edges of marshes, lakes, seashores, etc. Aquatic food items include insect larva (especially fly larva), polychaete worms, crustaceans, and small bivalves. On dry land these plovers will eat spiders, flies, and beetles. Most foraging is done along waters edge or in very shallow water or on exposed mudflats.

Class - **Aves** (birds)

Order - **Chariidriformes** (shorebirds)

Family - **Charadriidae** (plovers)

Black-bellied Plover	Golden Plover
Pluvialis squatarola	*Pluvialis dominica*

Size: 11.5 inches.

Abundance: Uncommon in Illinois.

Presumed range in Illinois

Migratory Status: Spring and fall migrant. Spring migration in Illinois is mainly in May. Fall migration is more protracted, from September through early November. May be seen anywhere in the state where suitable habitat exists.

Variation: Seasonal plumage variations (see above). Both plumages may be seen in Illinois.

Habitat: Beaches are the preferred winter habitat. Inland migrants will use shorelines, mudflats and bare fields.

Breeding: Nest is a shallow cup scraped into the Arctic tundra and lined with lichens. 4 eggs are laid.

Natural History: Black-bellied Plovers occur in both the New and Old Worlds and in fact they are one of the most widespread shorebirds in the world. They occur throughout much of the Old World as well as most of the western hemisphere. North American birds winter along both coastlines from just south of Canada to South America, including the Caribbean. Summers are spent within the Arctic Circle of Alaska and Canada. During migration they are seen mostly along America's coastlines and in the Great Plains region, but a some will pass through Illinois. Unlike many shorebirds, the Black-bellied Plover exhibits nocturnal tendencies and will often feed at night. Food items are marine worms and small clams and mussels plucked from the mud at low tide. On the breeding grounds in the far north they will eat insects, small freshwater crustaceans, and berries. Climate change may be a threat if tundra nesting habitat undergoes transformation.

Size: 10.5 inches.

Abundance: Uncommon in Illinois.

Presumed range in Illinois

Migratory Status: Spring and fall migrant. Spring migration in peaks in late April and early May. Fall migration peaks in September and early October. Golden Plovers are more common in Illinois in spring than fall. Could be seen anywhere.

Variation: Sexes similar with seasonal plumage variations (see above). Both plumages may be seen in Illinois.

Habitat: Beaches are the preferred winter habitat. Inland migrants will use shorelines, mudflats, and bare fields.

Breeding: Nest is a scrape on tundra soil. 4 eggs are laid and young are highly precocial, able to walk immediately.

Natural History: Like the similar Black-bellied Plover, the American Golden Plover is a long distance traveller that nests in the Arctic and spends its winters in southeastern South America. Its epic migrations sometimes include extensive flights over vast expanses of open ocean. Many migrate through inland regions and they are known for their propensity to appear almost anywhere during migrations. Food items include some plant material (berries, seeds, foliage) as well as a wide variety of invertebrate prey. Like many shorebirds the American Golden Plover was hunted relentlessly during the days "market hunting" throughout the 1800s. Tens to perhaps hundreds of thousands were killed annually. Today, they are still legally hunted hunted in some South American countries. Habitat loss remains an ever present threat and some scientists have expressed concern about potential changes on tundra breeding grounds due to climate change.

Class - **Aves** (birds)

Order - **Chariidriformes** (shorebirds)

Family - **Scolopacidae** (sandpipers)

Sanderling	Pectoral Sandpiper	Dunlin
Calidris alba	*Calidris melanotus*	*Calidris alpina*

Size: 8 inches.

Abundance: Fairly common.

Migratory Status: Spring/fall migrant. Most common from late July to mid September.

Variation: Significant seasonal variation (see photos above).

Presumed range in Illinois

Size: 8.5 inches.

Abundance: Fairly common.

Migratory Status: Spring/fall migrant. Most common from late July through October.

Variation: Male breeding plumage is darker brown and more vivid.

Presumed range in Illinois

Size: 8.5 inches.

Abundance: Fairly common.

Migratory Status: Spring/fall migrant. Seen April/May and in September/October.

Variation: Significant seasonal plumage changes (see above).

Presumed range in Illinois

Habitat: Shorelines. In winter lives on the beach. During migration frequents lake shores and river bars.

Breeding: Nests on arctic tundra on bare ground. Lays 4 eggs.

Natural History: Unlike most members of the sandpiper family, which are more likely to be found on mudflats, the Sanderling is commonly found on seashores. Except during migration or when breeding, these birds inhabit sandy beaches throughout the Americas. Any person who has been to the seashore has probably been amused by watching this species running back and forth in front of the waves. On beaches it feeds by running just in front of oncoming wave and chasing right behind receding wave, picking up tiny marine crustaceans, bivalves, and polychaetes. On the breeding ground it will eat both terrestrial and aquatic invertebrates and insects. Most Sanderlings migrate along the coastlines of America or through the Great Plains. Some will be seen in Illinois however, especially along the shores of Lake Michigan.

Habitat: Migrants use wet meadows, flooded fields, marshes and lake or pond shorelines, as well as mud flates.

Breeding: Nests on the ground in the arctic coastal plain. Lays 4 eggs.

Natural History: Breeding males of this species perform displays in which they erect the feathers of the breast, droop the wings, raise the tail feathers and emit soft "hooting" sounds. They are the only member of the sandpiper family that vocalizes in this manner. They also perform flight displays above the heads of grounded females. These birds are remarkable travelers that breed in the high arctic and winter in the "Pampas" region of southern South America. Some individuals will cross the Arctic Ocean to breed in Siberia, then migrate back to South America, a round-trip journey of over 18,000 miles each year! The food is mostly small mud dwelling invertebrates. In Illinois this species is most likely to be seen during migration in flooded crop fields in agricultural regions or open areas where receding waters leave mud flats.

Habitat: During migration uses flooded agricultural fields, mud flats, and seasonally flooded lowland pastures.

Breeding: Another high arctic breeder. Lays 4 eggs on ground in open tundra.

Natural History: The Dunlin winters along both coasts of North America where it haunts estuaries and intertidal regions. In southern Louisiana and Gulf Coastal Texas, it often uses rice fields in winter. Various clams, insects, worms, and amphipods are picked from the mud or plucked from vegetation with its moderately long, probing bill. Like other shorebird species it is usually seen in flocks, sometimes numbering in the thousands or even tens of thousands. In the early 1800s market hunters killed these birds in enormous numbers. Using cannon-like shotguns known as "punt guns" that were loaded with bird shot, a single blast could kill scores of shorebirds in a closely packed flock. Todays threats include pesticides and other contaminants and loss of wintering habitat. Widespread across Illinois during migration.

Class - **Aves** (birds)
Order - **Chariidriformes** (shorebirds)
Family - **Scolopacidae** (sandpipers)

The "Peep" Sandpipers
Genus - *Calidris* (5 species in Illinois pictured below)

Least Sandpiper *Calidris minutilla*	**White-rumped Sandpiper** *Calidris fuscicollis*	**Semipalmated Sandpiper** *Calidris pusilla*

Baird's Sandpiper *Calidris bairdi*	**Western Sandpiper** *Calidris mauri*	
		Presumed combined range of the "peep sandpipers" in Illinois

Size: Least Sandpiper 6 inches. Semipalmated Sandpiper 6.25 inches; Western Sandpiper 6.5 inches. White-rumped and Baird's Sandpipers both reach 7.5 inches.

Abundance: The Least Sandpiper and the Semipalmated are probably the most commonly seen of the "Peep" Sandpipers in Illinois. White-rumped and Baird's are both uncommon in the state, while the Western is an uncommon to rare species in Illinois.

Migratory Status: Semipalmated Sandpiper, Least Sandpiper, and White-rumped Sandpiper are all spring/fall migrants in Illinois. Both the Western Sandpiper and the Baird's Sandpiper are seen mainly during fall migrations.

Variation: All five of these species exhibit seasonal plumage changes. All are comparably paler in winter than in summer.

Habitat: The name "Mudpiper" would be a more appropriate name for these birds as they favor mud flats and flooded fields over sandy beaches. All can be seen along the coastlines but many migrate through the interior of North America.

Breeding: All "peep" sandpipers nest on the ground in the barren arctic tundra. 4 eggs is typical.

Natural History: These five species are all similar in their natural history and are confusingly alike in appearance. While serious birders and professional ornithologists take pride in being able to correctly identify any species, most casual observers are satisfied with calling these homogeneous birds simply "peeps." Food habits and feeding methods are also similar in these sandpipers, with mud dwelling benthic invertebrates making up the bulk of the diet in winter and during migration. Aquatic insect larva and some terrestrial insects are eaten on the breeding grounds. The hordes of mosquitoes for which the arctic tundra is famous in summer make up a high protein smorgasbord for both the adult birds and the newly hatched young. All the sandpipers are known for their epic migrations. Some species travel non-stop for a thousand miles or more over open ocean. Flights lasting as long as five days have been reported. Quite a feat of endurance for birds that can weigh as little as .75 to 1.5 ounces! Recent population declines have been reported for the Least Sandpiper and the Semipalmated Sandpiper. By contrast, the Western Sandpiper (despite being uncommon in Illinois) is one of the most abundant shorebirds in America with a total population estimate of 3.5 million birds.

Class - **Aves** (birds)		
Order - **Chariidriformes** (shorebirds)		
Family - **Scolopacidae** (sandpipers)		
Stilt Sandpiper *Calidris himantopus*	**Red Knot** *Calidris canutus*	**Upland Sandpiper** *Bartramia longicauda*

Summer

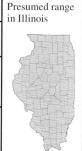

Size: 8.5 inches.	Presumed range in Illinois	**Size:** 10.5 inches.	Presumed range in Illinois	**Size:** 12 inches.	Presumed range in Illinois
Abundance: Fairly common.		**Abundance:** Rare in Illinois.		**Abundance:** Rare in Illinois.	
Migratory Status: Migrant. Seen mostly in fall.		**Migratory Status:** Spring/fall migrant in Illinois.		**Migratory Status:** Rare summer resident in northern Illinois.	
Variation: Winter birds are much paler, more grayish.		**Variation:** Winter plumage drab gray brown.		**Variation:** Fall and juvenile plumages paler than breeding adults.	

Habitat: Ponds, marshes, flooded fields, and lake shorelines. Uses salt marsh and brackish marshes in winter.	**Habitat:** Summer habitat is arctic tundra. Winter and migration habitat is intertidal areas and beaches/coastlines.	**Habitat:** An obligate of grasslands and prairies. Migrants will also use pastures and fields.
Breeding: Nests in lowland areas near the Arctic Ocean. Lays 4 eggs.	**Breeding:** Nest on tundra all the way to the Arctic Ocean. 4 eggs is typical.	**Breeding:** Nest is a shallow scrape on the ground lined with grass. Lays 4 eggs.
Natural History: The Stilt Sandpiper gets its name from its long legs. The long legs are an adaptation that allow it to feed in deeper water than most other *Calidris* sandpipers. Its body shape and habit of feeding in deeper water rather than on mud flats is unusual for its genus and mimics the yellowlegs sandpipers (genus *Tringa*, next page). The migratory routes for this sandpiper are mainly west of the Mississippi River, but some individuals will pass through Illinois. They nest along the northernmost coast of North America and will spend the winter in the interior of the South American continent. As with many other sandpiper species, the Stilt Sandpiper shows a remarkable fidelity to the nest site. After migrating thousands of miles from South America they often return to the same exact spot on the arctic coastline to lay their eggs.	**Natural History:** This is North America's largest member of the *Calidris* genus. Like many other Sandpiper species, the Red Knot is a remarkable traveler, covering nearly ten thousand miles in its round trip journey from southern South America to the Arctic and back each year. Some birds may fly non-stop for thousands of miles across great expanses of ocean, mountains, and deserts. Nesting is on the most northerly land masses in North America including northern Greenland and Canada's Arctic Archipelago. During the North American winter, they will be enjoying summer in the southern hemisphere as far south as Terra del Fuego on the southern tip of South America. Along the way these world travelers will sometimes stop for a brief rest somewhere in Illinois. Compared to many other Sandpiper species that travel through the state, the Red Knot is rather rare.	**Natural History:** The bulk of the Upland Sandpiper's summer range is in the northern Great Plains. A few summer very sparsely east of the Mississippi River into the Midwestern US. Unlike most other members of the sandpiper family, the Upland Sandpiper avoids coastal areas in favor of prairies and grasslands well into the interior of the continent. Historically, these birds were much more numerous. Market hunting in the late 19th century saw countless numbers of dead Upland Sandpipers shipped by rail from their nesting grounds on the northern plains to markets in the east. At the same time they were being hunted mercilessly on their winter habitats in the Pampas of South America. Even more devastating to their populations was the conversion of the native American prairie to cropland. Amazingly, the species survives. They are rare and declining in Illinois and are regarded as an Endangered Species.

Class - **Aves** (birds)

Order - **Chariidriformes** (shorebirds)

Family - **Scolopacidae** (sandpipers)

Greater Yellowlegs *Tringa melanoleuca*	**Lesser Yellowlegs** *Tringa flavipes*	**Solitary Sandpiper** *Tringa solitaria*

Size: 14 inches.

Size: 10.5 inches.

Size: 8.5 inches.

Presumed range in Illinois

Presumed range in Illinois

Abundance: Greater Yellowlegs is usually the less common of the two, but both species are fairly common during migration.

Migratory Status: Both species are transient spring and fall migrants but they can be seen in Illinois from March through October (except they are both absent through most of June). Peak spring migration is in late April and early May. Fall peak for Greater is August/September. Lesser begins fall migration as early as July.

Variation: Speckled appearance is less prominent on winter adults and juveniles of both species.

Abundance:
Fairly common.

Migratory Status:
Seasonal migrant. April and May. July to October. Peak fall migration is in August.

Variation: More white spots in winter.

Habitat: Both species are seen in a wide variety of wetland habitats during migration, including mudflats, flooded agricultural field and marshes.

Habitat: Pond margins, lake shores, and along creeks and rivers.

Breeding: Greater breeds in northern bogs, Lesser in drier, more upland habitats. Both species nest on the ground and 3 to 4 eggs is the typical clutch size for both.

Breeding: Nests in trees and uses old songbird nests. Lays 3 to 5 eggs, usually 4.

Natural History: These two related species are frequently seen together. When seen together they are easily recognized by size. When not in found in mixed flocks they are best identified by the shape of the bill. Greater's bill is longer and ever so slightly upturned at the tip. The Greater Yellowlegs is the least social of the two, and although it is seen in small flocks it can also be seen singly. Both species were once heavily hunted and during the days of market hunting both species experienced steep population declines. Hunting still occurs in some areas of their migratory range, especially in the Caribbean. Both spend the summer in the boreal regions of Canada and Alaska and winter from the Gulf Coast of the southeastern United States southward into South America. Food items for the Greater include both aquatic and terrestrial invertebrates as well as some small aquatic vertebrates like small frogs or fish. Lesser's food items are mainly invertebrates, both aquatic and terrestrial, but some small fish are also eaten. Both feed mostly by wading in shallows, but the Lesser is a more active feeder, wading rapidly and picking food from both the surface and the water column. It will also feed in this manner in terrestrial habitats such as grassy shorelines or meadow areas. Greater feeds both diurnally and at night, when it employs a sweeping motion of the bill back and forth through the water, apparently catching food by feel. The major threat to both species today is probably loss of habitat, both on wintering grounds in South America (loss of wetlands) and on summer range in North America, i.e logging in boreal forests (Greater), and loss of wetlands in Alaska (lesser).

Natural History: As implied by their name, the Solitary Sandpipers are nearly always seen alone during migration. In this respect they differ markedly from most other members of their family. They also differ in their nesting habits, as they are the only North American member of the Scolapacidae family that nests in trees. When feeding it wades in shallows and plucks its food from the surface or beneath the water. Rarely probes the mud with its bill. Food is mostly invertebrates, both aquatic and terrestrial. Insects make up the bulk of the terrestrial foods. They also take aquatic insects and their larva, small crustaceans, snails, and some vertebrate prey such as small minnows or tadpoles. Due to their solitary habits and the fact that they breed in trees in remote boreal forests, little is known about their population status, but it appears to be stable.

Class - **Aves** (birds)

Order - **Chariidriformes** (shorebirds)

Family - **Scolopacidae** (sandpipers)

Willet *Tringa semipalmata*	Wilson's Phalarope *Phalaropus tricolor*	Short-billed Dowitcher *Limnodromus griseus*

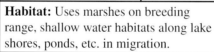

Willet	Wilson's Phalarope	Short-billed Dowitcher
Size: 15 inches.	**Size:** 9.5 inches.	**Size:** 11 inches.
Abundance: Rare in Illinois.	**Abundance:** Rare in Illinois.	**Abundance:** Fairly common.
Migratory Status: Spring/fall migrant.	**Migratory Status:** Spring/fall migrant.	**Migratory Status:** Spring/fall migrant.
Variation: No sexual dimorphism but does exhibit seasonal plumage variations. Winter plumage lacks brown speckling.	**Variation:** Sexual, seasonal, and ontogenetic variations. Nonbreeding birds are gray above and all white beneath. Juveniles mottled brown.	**Variation:** Breeding birds are rich brown. Winter birds uniformly gray with whitish belly. Sexes are alike (see photos above).

Presumed range in Illinois (shown for each species)

Habitat: In migration uses pond banks, mud flats, lake shores, riverbanks, and flooded fields.	Habitat: Uses marshes on breeding range, shallow water habitats along lake shores, ponds, etc. in migration.	Habitat: In inland migrations dowitchers use mud flats and lake shores. Many migrate along the coasts.
Breeding: Lays 4 eggs in nest on the ground. Does not nest in Illinois. Migrants nest on the northern plains.	**Breeding:** Breeds on inland marshes and wetlands in the west-central US and Canada. Always lays 4 eggs.	**Breeding:** Breeds in bog and muskeg habitats of northern Canada and Alaska. Both species lay 4 eggs.

Natural History: The Willet is a true "shorebird" that is quite familiar to those who frequent America's seashores. Both coasts of America are home to Willets during the winter, and some will nest in coastal marshes. Others fly into the interior of North America and nest as far north as the central Canadian prairie. It is these migrants that can sometimes be seen in Illinois. Crustaceans, mollusks, insects, small fish and polycheate worms are listed as food items. Feeds both day and night. In the 1800s, they were hunted for food and for their eggs which were also eaten, resulting in a significant decrease in populations. Today these are fairly common shorebirds whose population appears stable at an estimate of about a quarter of a million birds. In Illinois the most likely place to see this rare migrant is along lake shorelines.

Natural History: Phalaropes are known for the unique role reversal of the sexes. In these birds the female is the most vividly colored while the male has drab plumage. Even more unusual, it is the male that incubates the eggs in the nest. These birds are salt lake specialists and during migration they congregate in large flocks around alkaline and highly saline lakes of the interior of North America. The winter habitat is similar saline lakes in the Andes Mountains of South America. Birds seen in Illinois are mostly migrants or rare wanderers, but there is evidence of rare nesting occurring in the state. The slightly smaller (8 inch) **Red-necked Phalarope** (*P. lobatus*) may also be seen in Illinois on rare occasions during migration periods.

Natural History: The nearly identical **Long-billed Dowitcher** (*Limnodromus scolopaceus*-not shown) can also be seen in Illinois during spring and fall migrations, though it is less common than the Short-billed Dowitcher. Distinguishing between the two in the field is difficult even for experts. The Long-billed is slightly larger at 11.5 inches. It migrates earlier in the spring and later in the fall than the Short-billed. In Illinois, the Long-billed is seen mostly in the far northern portion of the state. The Short-billed may be seen anywhere in the state. Like many shorebirds both species of dowitcher were heavily hunted during the days of market hunting. At that time, it was not known that the two similar dowitchers constituted two distinct species. The existence of two species was not finally confirmed until 1950.

Class - **Aves** (birds)

Order - **Chariidriformes** (shorebirds)

Family - **Scolopacidae** (sandpipers)

Woodcock *Scolapax minor*	**Wilson's Snipe** *Gallinago delicata*	**Ruddy Turnstone** *Arenaria interpres*
		 Summer

Woodcock	Wilson's Snipe	Ruddy Turnstone
Size: 11 inches.	**Size:** 10.5 inches.	**Size:** 9.5 inches.
Abundance: Fairly common.	**Abundance:** Fairly common.	**Abundance:** Uncommon.
Migratory Status: Summer resident, seasonal migrant.	**Migratory Status:** Mostly a winter migrant. Rare winter resident.	**Migratory Status:** Seasonal migrant, late spring and early fall.
Variation: No plumage variations. Females are significantly larger.	**Variation:** No significant sexual or seasonal plumage differences.	**Variation:** Seasonal plumage variations. Breeding plumage shown above.

Presumed range in Illinois  — for each species

Habitat: Swamps, regenerative woodlands, thickets, and weedy fields in bottomlands or uplands with moist soils.	**Habitat:** Mudflats, flooded grassy fields, marshes, river bars, water-filled ditches, temporary pools and grassy pond banks.	**Habitat:** Winters on sandy beaches along both coasts. May use lake shores, mud flats, or river banks during inland migrations
Breeding: Nest is on the ground and not concealed. Lays 4 eggs as early as late February.	**Breeding:** Nesting takes places to north of Illinois. Lays 4 eggs in nest on a hummock within marsh or swamp.	**Breeding:** Breeds in the arctic tundra and coastlines from Siberia and Alaska across Canada to Greenland.
Natural History: The Woodcock is unique among American sandpipers in that it is strictly an inland species. It is also the most common member of its family that breeds widely throughout the state. Woodcock are known for their elaborate courtship flights that consist of an upward twisting corkscrew accompanied by a twittering call. The long beak is used to probe moist soils for invertebrates. Among its unique features are a flexible upper bill that aids in extracting the favorite food, earthworms, and eyes which are situated far back on the head, allowing for backward vision while feeding. One of the most remarkably cryptic of the sandpipers, Woodcocks are nearly impossible to detect when motionless on the forest floor. Woodcock are classified as a game bird and hunted in many states.	**Natural History:** As with other members of the sandpiper family, the beak of the Wilson's Snipe contains sensory pits near the tip which helps to locate invertebrate prey hidden in the mud. It also shares the Woodcock's rearward positioned eyes for watching behind and above while feeding. This is another highly camouflaged species that is nearly invisible when immobile. It is one of the most common and widespread members of the sandpiper family that often relys on its cryptic coloration when approached. Sitting quietly until nearly trod upon it will burst from the grass with a twisting, erratic flight while emitting a raspy call. Like the Woodcock the Wilson's Snipe is regarded as a game bird, but few people hunt them. Their populations have been negatively impacted by loss of wetland habitats.	**Natural History:** Most Ruddy Turnstones travel up and down America's coastlines during migration, but a few migrate through inland regions of the continent. This is one of the most northerly ranging birds in America, traveling to the northernmost extreme of the continent to breed each summer. Its name comes from its habit of using its beak to overturn pebbles and stones on beaches in search of small invertebrate prey. It also feeds on ocean carrion found on beaches. On the breeding grounds the primary food source is mosquitoes and other dipeteran insects. The unusual genus (*Arenaria*) contains only 2 species and their position in the phylogeny of the shorebirds is unclear. Migrants may rarely be seen statewide or most along the Lake Michigan shoreline.

Class - **Aves** (birds)		
Order - **Chariidriformes** (shorebirds)		
Family - **Scolopacidae** (sandpipers)		
Spotted Sandpiper *Actitis macularia*	**Buff-breasted Sandpiper** *Tryngites subruficollis*	**Whimbrel** *Numenius phaeopus*

Size: 7.5 inches.	Presumed range in Illinois	**Size:** 7.5 inches.	Presumed range in Illinois	**Size:** 17.5 inches.	Presumed range in Illinois
Abundance: Fairly common.		**Abundance:** Rare in Illinois.		**Abundance:** Very rare in Illinois.	
Migratory Status: Summer resident.		**Migratory Status:** Seasonal migrant.		**Migratory Status:** Seasonal migrant.	
Variation: Winter birds lack the spots on the breast and are grayer on the back. Most birds seen in Illinois will be in summer plumage.		**Variation:** No sexual dimorphism in this species. Juvenile birds are similar to adults but tend to be paler on the breast.		**Variation:** No sexual dimophism and no seasonal variation. Juveniles are very similar to adults but with slightly darker head and neck.	

Habitat: In migration uses edges of ponds, lake shores, stream courses and river bars. Nesting habitat in Illinois is mostly along major rivers.	**Habitat:** Unlike most sandpipers, Buff-breasted favors dry habitats. Likes short grass fields. Prairies, pastures, golf courses, etc.	**Habitat:** In migration will use meadows, pastures and crop fields. Also mud flats and shorelines. Winter habitat is coastlines.
Breeding: Nests on the ground in grassy situations. Lays 2 to 4 eggs. Widespread nester in glaciated Illinois.	**Breeding:** Nest is a shallow scrape on the tundra. Lays 3 to 4 eggs. Has elaborate courtship behavior.	**Breeding:** Breeds in the far north in Arctic tundra and Taiga forests. Typically 4 eggs in nest on ground.
Natural History: Unlike most sandpipers that exhibit strong flocking tendencies, the Spotted Sandpiper is always seen singly or in very small groups. This is one of the most widespread sandpipers in America and one of the few that nests in the lower forty-eight. The distinctly spotted breast along with a habit of constantly bobbing up and down makes the Spotted Sandpiper one of the most recognizable members of the Scolapacidae family. Feeds on a wide variety of aquatic and terrestrial invertebrates, especially dipteran (fly) larva. Also eats significant quantities of mayflies, crickets, grasshoppers, caterpillars, beetles, and mollusks, crustaceans, and worms. In Illinois this species is fairly common along the major rivers of the state in summer.	**Natural History:** Males perform breeding displays that consist of spreading wings and leaping and fluttering. These displays usually occur in a confined area (known as a Lek). They are one of the few sandpipers that exhibit this behavior. These birds are great travelers. They winter in the pampas region of southern South America and fly to the shores of the Arctic Ocean for breeding in the spring. Most transit through the US in the Great Plains region, but in fall a few will move southward through the eastern half of the country. Their tame behavior and unusual tendency to return to a wounded flock member made them easy targets for market hunting in the late 1800s. This, coupled with the destruction of the native American prairies devastated this species and they have never fully recovered.	**Natural History:** The likelihood of seeing this species in Illinois is not great, but those who do see it will have no trouble recognizing it. Its large size and long, downcurved bill is quite distinctive. On wintering grounds they feed mostly on crabs and the long, crescent shaped bill is thought to be an adaptation for penetrating the burrows of Fiddler Crabs in marine intertidal zones. On arctic breeding grounds insects are the major food but some berries are also eaten. Most of these birds migrate along the coastlines of America, but a few travel inland. Most inland migration is through the western Great Plains but a few migrate through the Mississippi flyway and thus through Illinois.

Class - **Aves** (birds)
Order - **Chariidriformes** (shorebirds)
Family - **Laridae** (gulls & terns)

Franklin's Gull *Leucophaeus pipixcan*	**Little Gull** *Hydrocoloeus minutus*	**Glaucus Gull** *Larus hyperboreus*

Franklin's Gull

Size: 14.5 inches.

Presumed range in Illinois

Abundance: Uncommon in Illinois.

Migratory Status: Migrant. Most migrate through the Great Plains but a few wanderers may be seen in Illinois.

Variation: In winter and juveniles, the black hood is replaced by a gray head and black bill.

Habitat: Migrants use lakes, rivers, marshes, flooded fields and pastures.

Breeding: Breeds in marshes in the Great Plains of Canada and north central US Nest is on floating mats of vegetation amid marshland. Lays 2 to 4 eggs. Breeds in large colonies.

Natural History: Adults in breeding plumage have a faint pinkish blush on the breast and belly feathers. A few of these breeding birds may pass through Illinois in spring and early summer, but most Franklin's Gulls seen in Illinois appear during southward migration in the fall. As with other gull species, the Franklin's Gull matures slowly and it takes three years to achieve the mature adult plumage shown in the photo above. Like other gulls the Franklin's is an opportunistic feeder that will eat both plant and animal matter. Most foods are invertebrates (insects, worms, crustaceans, etc.). The bulk of this bird's range is west of the Mississippi.

Little Gull

Size: 11 inches.

Presumed range in Illinois

Abundance: Rare in Illinois.

Migratory Status: Summer migrant on Lake Michigan. Winter along the east coast of North America.

Variation: Adults in breeding plumage have an all black head. Nonbreeding above.

Habitat: In Illinois, this gull is seen only in the vicinity of Lake Michigan.

Breeding: There are only a few dozen records of this species breeding in America. Most breed in the Old World. Nest is in marsh on floating mats of vegetation. Lays 3 to 4 eggs.

Natural History: A native of the Old World, the Little Gull apparently become established in North America as recently as recently as a few decades ago. They are most common along the northeast coast of the US, but are rare even there. In Illinois this species is seen only on Lake Michigan where it is extremely rare. Very few studies have been conducted into the natural history of this species in North America and less in known about it than any other gull in America. It usually occurs in small flocks or in the company of other gull species such as the Bonapartes Gull. At only 11 inches long it is the world's smallest gull species. It feeds on small fishes and insects and will also scavenge. Probably consumes aquatic invertebrates as well.

Glaucus Gull

Size: 27 inches.

Presumed range in Illinois

Abundance: Fairly common.

Migratory Status: Winter resident on Lake Michigan and shoreline. Summers along the Arctic Ocean coast.

Variation: Juvenile show above Adults are pure white with pale gray wings.

Habitat: Northern coastlines of both coasts. Habitat in Illinois is Lake Michigan.

Breeding: Nest is on the ground in open tundra. Often on ledges or atop steep cliffs. Usually lays 3 eggs.

Natural History: This is a northern gull that breeds far to the north on arctic coasts. Winters on northern coastlines, both Pacific and Atlantic and also throughout the Great Lakes region. They are rarely seen inland from Lake Michigan in Illinois. As with most gull species they are opportunistic predators as well as unashamed scavengers. The list of food items includes most types of aquatic organisms that are small enough to be swallowed as well as terrestrial foods such as the eggs and chicks of other birds that may be nesting nearby. These gulls are circumpolar in distribution and are fairly common in arctic regions. They are rare in Illinois however, seen only on Lake Michigan in winter. Other northern Gull species that winter on Lake Michigan are the **Thayer's Gull** (*Larus thayeri*) and the **Iceland Gull** (*Larus glaucoides*).

Class - **Aves** (birds)

Order - **Chariidriformes** (shorebirds)

Family - **Laridae** (gulls & terns)

Ringed-billed Gull *Larus delawarensis*	Herring Gull *Larus argentatus*	Bonapartes Gull *Chroicocephalus philadelphia*

Ringed-billed Gull

Size: 17.5 inches.

Presumed range in Illinois

Abundance: Very common.

Migratory Status: Mostly a migrant, but may be seen most anytime of the year.

Variation: Juveniles are brownish gray, two year olds like adults but greenish legs and bill.

Habitat: Primarily in the vicinity of lakes and rivers, but also in rural crop fields and in urban areas.

Breeding: Nest is usually on the ground on sandbars or rocky beaches. May nest on rooftops in urban areas. Lays 2 to 4 eggs.

Natural History: The Ring-billed Gull is one of the most common and widespread gull species in America. Most population estimates put their number in the millions, and they may be increasing. This is the gull commonly seen around inland lakes in summer and along coastal beaches in winter. They are also seen in urban parking lots or hanging around fast food restaurants ready to swoop in and grab a dropped french fry. They are can be common in garbage dumps and may be seen foraging with starlings and other urban birds around dumpsters. These are highly gregarious birds that travel in flocks and nest in colonies. Food is almost anything, from carrion to insects, fish, rodents, earthworms, and human refuse. Not known to nest in Illinois, but does nest on some of the Great Lakes.

Herring Gull

Size: 25 inches.

Presumed range in Illinois

Abundance: Common.

Migratory Status: Both a winter resident and a migrant. Can be seen statewide.

Variation: Younger birds are dark brownish gray with dark eyes and get lighter with age.

Habitat: In Illinois these birds are most common around large lakes. But they do occur statewide.

Breeding: Nest is on the ground in a bowl shaped scrape lined with vegetation. Also nest on rooftops in urban areas. 2 or 3 eggs are laid.

Natural History: Like the smaller Ring-billed Gull, the Herring Gull is an opportunistic feeder that will eat almost anything, including human garbage. This fact may account in part for their population rebound in recent decades. Like other gull species, they are gregarious and they often nest in large colonies. Only about 50 percent of the young gulls hatched each year reach adulthood, but the species seems to be thriving. Their numbers were drastically reduced during the 1800s but they have recovered completely and may be more numerous now than in historic times. The presence of man-made garbage dumps that serve as a smorgasboard for these birds may explain their recent population expansion. They are widespread in their distribution and are common on both of America's coastlines.

Bonapartes Gull

Size: 13.5 inches.

Presumed range in Illinois

Abundance: Fairly common.

Migratory Status: Year-round in southern tip of state. Seasonal migrant elsewhere.

Variation: Summer plumage adults have a black head. Juveniles resemble winter adults.

Habitat: Frequents large rivers and larger lakes when in Illinois. Summer habitat is wetlands in boreal forests.

Breeding: The only gull that nests in trees, using conifers bordering remote lakes in Canada and Alaska. Typically lays 3 eggs.

Natural History: Many people tend to lump all gull species together and refer to them all as "seagulls." Most species however, including the Bonaparte's Gull, are often inland birds during the breeding season. Like other gulls, many Bonaparte's Gulls will spend the winter along America's coastlines and sometimes far out to sea. Small to moderately large flocks can be seen on inland rivers and lakes in Illinois during migration and through early winter. One of America's smallest gulls, they feed mostly on small fish such as shad and shiners, but like other gulls they are highly opportunistic feeders and will eat a wide variety of insects and other invertebrates. Unlike other gull species however, they are not typically seen around towns or dumps. Gathers in large flocks in winter.

Class - **Aves** (birds)

Order - **Chariidriformes** (shorebirds)

Family - **Laridae** (gulls & terns)

Common Tern
Sternula hirundo

Caspian Tern
Hydroprogne caspia

Black Tern
Chlidonias niger

Transitional

Summer

Common Tern	Caspian Tern	Black Tern
Size: 15 inches.	**Size:** 21 inches.	**Size:** 9.75 inches.
Abundance: Common.	**Abundance:** Uncommon.	**Abundance:** Uncommon
Migratory Status: Seasonal migrant statewide. Nests along the shores of Lake Michigan.	**Migratory Status:** Migrant. Most common April and May and again in August/September. Rare in summer.	**Migratory Status:** Summer resident of Great Lakes marshes. Rare migrant elsewhere in the state.
Habitat: Migrating birds usually associate with major rivers and large lakes.	**Habitat:** Mainly coastal birds in winter, they use rivers, large lakes, and marshes in migration.	**Habitat:** Summer habitat is shallow, freshwater marshes, mostly in the western US.
Presumed range in Illinois	*Presumed range in Illinois*	*Presumed range in Illinois*
Variation: 1st year juveniles and winter birds have white foreheads and all black bill. White on forehead reduced on 2nd year juvenile in summer colors.	**Variation:** In winter birds, the black cap becomes mottled with white. Juveniles are similar to winter adults. Sexes are alike.	**Variation:** In winter and in juvenile birds, the dramatic black color of the breast and belly is replaced by white. Transitional plumage shown above.
Breeding: Nests mostly in Canada and along the Atlantic coastline. A few nest in Illinois in the vicinity of Lake Michigan. Lays 2 or 3 eggs.	**Breeding:** North American populations nest both on coasts and large bodies of water in the interior of the continent. Does not nest in Illinois. 1 to 3 eggs.	**Breeding:** Nest is built upon floating vegetation or muskrat platforms. Nests can be vulnerable to flooding. 2 or 3 eggs is typical.
Natural History: The Common Tern is well known to conservationists. They are symbolic of the fight to save many of America's bird species from wanton slaughter. From the early European settlement of North America to the late 1800s, unregulated overhunting of America's wildlife nearly wiped out many species. Millions of herons, egrets, waterfowl, and shorebirds were killed for food and for the millinery trade. Today the Common Tern is endangered in Illinois, but it is more common that two other similar terns found in the state. The **Forster's Tern** (*S. forsteri*) and the **Least Tern** (*S. antillarum*) are both endangered in Illinois and the latter is regarded as a federally endangered species.	**Natural History:** The worlds largest tern and also the most widespread. Found all over the world, the Caspian Tern breeds on every continent except Antarctica. Despite its wide range it is not as common in North America as many other terns. Feeds almost entirely on fish. Feeds by hovering and diving. When diving often submerges completely. Food is mostly fish. This is the only large tern regularly seen inland. They are found along the southern coastlines as well and in winter stay along the coasts. They are also seen inland in winter throughout the Florida peninsula. Although they will nest in some of the Great Lakes farther to the north, they do not nest in Illinois. These large terns are known to live up to 26 years.	**Natural History:** Winters along coastlines from Central America to northern South America. There is a European subspecies that winters in Africa. Like most terns, these birds are highly social and usually seen in flocks. Unlike other terns, however, they feed heavily on insects, especially in summer. This is the only tern seen in Illinois that has a dark breast and belly. Although the number of Black Terns today is estimated to be in the hundreds of thousands, this figure is paltry compared to the size of the population that existed before modern agricultural practices destroyed much of their breeding habitat.

Class - **Aves** (birds)

Order - **Pelecaniformes** (pelicans)	Order - **Gaviiformes** (loons)	
Family - **Pelecanidae**	Family - **Gaviidea**	
White Pelican *Pelecanus erythrorhynchos*	**Common Loon** *Gavia immer*	**Red-throated Loon** *Gavia*

White Pelican	Common Loon	Red-throated Loon
Size: 62 inches.	**Size:** 62 inches.	**Size:** 33 inches.
Abundance: Uncommon.	**Abundance:** Fairly common.	**Abundance:** Uncommon.
Migratory Status: Summer resident.	**Migratory Status:** See below.	**Migratory Status:** Winter migrant.
Variation: Juvenile birds are duskier and have a dusky gray bill. Breeding birds develop a projection on the bill.	**Variation:** Sexes are alike but exhibits significant seasonal plumage changes. See photos above.	**Variation:** Exhibits seasonal plumage changes but birds seen in Illinois will be in winter plumage.

Presumed range in Illinois

Presumed range in Illinois

Presumed range in Illinois

White Pelican	Common Loon	Red-throated Loon
Habitat: Restricted to larger lakes and rivers in Illinois. Elsewhere commonly uses large marshlands, natural and man-made lakes, large rivers and coastlines.	**Habitat:** Highly aquatic. In inland areas the Common Loon lives on lakes. They may also be seen along the coast in winter.	**Habitat:** Thoroughly aquatic. In inland areas in summer or on migration they may be seen on lakes and rivers. In winter they use mostly coastlines.
Breeding: Nests in colonies in protected areas such as islands on large lakes. Does not nest in Illinois. Lays 2 eggs.	**Breeding:** Nests is built on small islands in northern lakes. Usually lays 2 eggs. Chicks often ride on adults' back.	**Breeding:** Breeds in small ponds in remote tundra. Nest is a large mound of aquatic vegetation. 2 eggs.
Natural History: Although wandering flocks of White Pelicans may suddenly appear on almost any large body of water in Illinois, they are most commonly seen along the large rivers and lakes. Unlike their cousin the Brown Pelican which feeds by plunging into the water, White Pelicans feed in a more placid manner. Flocks of feeding White Pelicans corral fish by swimming in a coordinated group and dipping the head beneath the surface in perfect unison. The appearance of a feeding flock is that of a perfectly choreographed ballet. Competition between baby White Pelicans in the nest is fierce, and the strongest nestling often kills its sibling. Thus, usually only one of the two young survive. Primarily a bird of the southern coasts in winter and the Great Plains region in summer.	**Natural History:** On lakes and marshes in the far north the call of the Common Loon echoes through the wilderness. The sound is so distinctive and unique that it has inspired many poetic depictions. "Haunting," "ethereal," and "lonely" are words that are often used in conjunction with describing its yodeling cry that can carry for a great distance. They call both day and night on the breeding grounds in the northern half of the continent, but they are rarely heard calling on their winter range. Remarkable swimmers, they dive beneath the surface and propel themselves through the water with their powerful webbed feet. Fish caught in this manner are the main food item. In Illinois the Common Loon is a winter migrant and these migrant birds may be seen statewide on rivers and lakes.	**Natural History:** These birds occur mostly along the coastlines in winter. Migrants are not uncommon on the Great Lakes from fall thorugh spring. Winter migrants can show up on almost any large body of water throughout the state, but they are rare. In winter plumage they are very similar to the Common Loon but are smaller and have white spots on the back. These are mostly northern birds that summer all the way to the Arctic Ocean. They are circumpolar in distribution and occur throughout Scandinavia. The legs of loons are situated very far back on the body which works well for propelling through water, but makes movement on land very difficult. This species appears to be in decline in North America. No explanation for this decline is known at this time.

Class - **Aves** (birds)

Order - **Podicipediformes** (grebes)

Family - **Podicipedidae**

Red-necked Grebe	Pied-billed Grebe	Horned Grebe
Podiceps grisegena	*Podilymbus podiceps*	*Podiceps auritus*

Size: 18 inches.	**Size:** 13 inches.	**Size:** 14 inches.
Abundance: Rare in Illinois.	**Abundance:** Fairly common.	**Abundance:** Uncommon.
Migratory Status: Spring and fall migrant.	**Migratory Status:** Year-round in south. Summer in north.	**Migratory Status:** Winter migrant.
Variation: Winter plumage is gray and white (similar to Horned Grebe photo).	**Variation:** Winter birds are grayer and lack the prominent dark ring on bill.	**Variation:** Seasnal plumage changes. Winter plumage (shown) is usually seen in Illinois.

Presumed range in Illinois

Habitat: Summers on shallow lakes, marshes, and bays of large lakes across Canada and Alaska. Winters in marine habitats. Bays, esturaries, and offshore.

Habitat: Completely aquatic, the Pied-billed Grebe uses everything from large lakes to small farm ponds. Also open water areas of swamps and marshes.

Habitat: In Illinois, this species uses the larger lakes as well as large marshes with open water. They are not usually seen on small ponds.

Breeding: Nesting is on northern lakes. 4 to 5 eggs is typical (as many as 9).

Breeding: Nests on floating platform among emergent vegetation. 4 to 8 eggs.

Breeding: Nests on floating platform among emergent vegetation. 5 to 7 eggs.

Natural History: By midwinter, most of these grebes are along the coasts. Some will linger in the Great Lakes into winter. In Illinois, these birds are mostly restricted to the immediate area of Lake Michigan. But in severe winters when the Great Lakes freeze over, large numbers may irrupt southward and at these times they may be seen on open water anywhere in the state. They are circumpolar in distribution in the northern hemisphere. The grebes are known for their elaborate courtship displays and "dances." As many as a dozen different postures may be displayed during one of these courtship dances. The pair often engage in a mutually responsive movements that does give the appearance of two highly choreographed dancers. Most feeding is in shallows but they are capable swimmers and divers and may feed in deep water. Food items include fish, crustaceans, and aquatic insects.

Natural History: A nighttime migrator, this little grebe evades potential threats by submerging and they sometimes swim with just the head sticking out the water. They feed on a wide variety of small fish and other aquatic vertebrates as well as crustaceans and insects. This is the most widespread and common grebe in North America and they range from coast to coast. They are most common during summer in the "Prairie Pothole" habitats of the west-central US and Canada. In winter they move as far south as Central America. They can be seen all winter across the southern half of the US, but tend to concentrate along the Gulf Coast in winter. Most breed in more northerly regions of the continent, but there are a widespread records of Pied-billed Grebes breeding throughout Illinois. These little grebes escape threats by diving and swimming.

Natural History: As is the case with other grebes (and loons), their adaptations for an aquatic lifestyle include the legs being positioned far back on the body. The legs can also be flared outward to a remarkable degree to facilitate underwater swimming maneuvers. As a result of this adaptation, these birds are very clumsy on land and walk with difficulty. Breeding on marshes and lakes in the northernmost portions of the continent, these birds are a transient migrant in Illinois. Breeding birds are handsomely marked with chestnut neck and flanks and golden brown head stripe that flares out to form "horns." The specimen shown above is in winter plumage and is typical of fall migrants. Food is small fish, crustaceans, insects, etc. Most of their breeding range is west and north of Illinois, but they may be seen anywhere in the eastern US during migration and in winter.

Class - **Aves** (birds)
Order - **Anseriformes** (waterfowl)
Family - **Anatidae** (ducks, geese & swans)

Mallard *Anas platyrhynchos*	Black Duck *Anas rubripes*	Northern Pintail *Anas acuta*

Size: 23 inches.

Presumed range in Illinois

Abundance: Very common.

Migratory Status: Year-round resident and a seasonal migrant.

Variation: Pronounced sexual plumage variation (see photos above).

Habitat: Found in aquatic situations everywhere, from deserts to tundra to southern swamplands, ponds, lakes, etc.

Breeding: Nests on the ground in close proximity to water. Lays up to 13 eggs and will renest if nest is destroyed.

Natural History: By far the most familiar duck in America. The Mallards has been widely domesticated but it is also the most common wild duck in the United States. Many parks and public lakes around the country have semi-wild populations that are nonmigratory. Highly adaptable, this is the most successful duck species in America, perhaps in the world. It is the source of all breeds of domestic duck except the Muscovey and they are thus an important food source for humans. They are also a highly regarded game bird and they are hunted throughout North America. They range throughout the northern half of the globe and their range in the western hemisphere closely coincides with the North American continent. Between wild ducks and semi-tame populations in urban parks, breeding probably occurs in every county.

Size: 23 inches.

Presumed range in Illinois

Abundance: Uncommon.

Migratory Status: Seasonal migrant and winter resident.

Variation: Sexes are very similar, females have a darker bill than males.

Habitat: Fond of estuaries and coastal marshes. Inland will use other aquatic habitats (lake, marshes, swamps, etc.).

Breeding: For breeding favors coastal marshes and beaver ponds and bogs in boreal forests. Lays up to 14 eggs.

Natural History: The Black Duck is very similar to the Mallard in size, shape, and voice, and the two species are known to hybridize. In appearance and other traits however they are quite different. This is one of the few puddle ducks that does not range throughout the continent, being restricted to the eastern half of America. Like many of America's duck species, the Black Duck has been impacted negatively by human related changes to the landscape and environment in America. Drainage of wetlands, urbanization along northeastern coastlines, and deforestation have hit this species harder than most other ducks and the population has declined significantly in the last half-century. Interbreeding with the more adaptable Mallard may also be a threat to this uniquely American Duck. They may be seen throughout the state as a migrant or winter resident, but does not breed in Illinois.

Size: To 25 inches.

Presumed range in Illinois

Abundance: Uncommon.

Migratory Status: Seasonal migrant and winter resident.

Variation: Profound sexual dimorphism (see photos above). Male larger.

Habitat: Open country. In Illinois uses large flooded bottomland fields and marshes along river valleys.

Breeding: Breeds in marshes, potholes and tundra in the northern and western portions of the continent. 3 to 12 eggs.

Natural History: Northern Pintail populations are in decline. Modern agricultural practices on the Great Plains of the US and Canada are the greatest threat. They are also highly susceptible to droughts in the prairie regions, which limit breeding habitat. Food is mostly plant material but some aquatic invertebrates are also eaten. On wintering grounds waste grain from farming operations has become an important food source. In recent decades the species has benefited from a number of conservation efforts by state and federal agencies as well as private organizations, most notably Ducks Unlimited, an organization funded by duck hunters. Conservation efforts that have recently benefited the species are reduced hunter harvest and changing agricultural practices in the in the prairie pothole region. Though large numbers may migrate through the state, they are not common.

Class - **Aves** (birds)

Order - **Anseriformes** (waterfowl)

Family - **Anatidae** (ducks, geese & swans)

Gadwall	American Wigeon	Green-winged Teal
Mareca strepera	*Mareca americana*	*Anas crecca*

Size: 20 inches.

Abundance: Fairly common.

Migratory Status: Winter resident, seasonal migrant and rare year-round.

Variation: Significant sexual dimorphism (see photos above).

Presumed range in Illinois

Habitat: Marshes and potholes of the Great Plains in summer. Uses all aquatic habitats in winter.

Breeding: Nests among thick vegetation near water, often on islands in marshes or lakes. Lays 7 to 12 eggs.

Natural History: Gadwalls breed and summer largely in the Great Plains region. In the winter, they are seen all across the southern half of America, with the greatest numbers wintering along the western Gulf Coast coastal plain. Populations of this duck can fluctuate significantly depending upon water levels in the prairies of Canada and the north-central US. Droughts and poor agricultural practices that eliminate habitat can cause populations to plummet. Conversely, good rainfall and good wildlife conservation practices by farmers have shown to be a real boon to this and many other duck species that depend on the marshes and potholes on the Great Plains for nesting habitat. Adult Gadwalls feed mostly on plant material. Ducklings rely heavily upon high protein invertebrates for growth and development.

Size: 19 inches.

Abundance: Fairly common.

Migratory Status: Winter resident, seasonal migrant and rare year-round.

Variation: Significant sexual variation. See photos above.

Presumed range in Illinois

Habitat: Winter range includes all types of aquatic habitats in the state (swamps, marshes, lakes, ponds, etc.).

Breeding: Nests near shallow freshwater wetlands and potholes mostly in the North American prairie. Lays 3 to 12 eggs.

Natural History: The American Wigeon also goes by the name "Baldpate," a reference to the white crown of the male. This duck has a very similar Old World counterpart, the Eurasian Wigeon, which ranges throughout much of Europe and Asia. American birds feed mostly on plant material, but females when breeding opt for a higher protein diet of invertebrates. One of the more northerly ranging members of the "puddle duck" group, some individuals will summer as far north as the Arctic coastal plain of Alaska. These ducks may be seen in Illinois from September through April, but peak numbers occur in late fall or early spring. Some merely pass through the state during north-south migrations, but a few may reside in throughout the winter. As with other puddle ducks, this species is susceptible to population declines during droughts.

Size: 14 inches.

Abundance: Fairly common.

Migratory Status: Spring/fall migrant very rare breeder and rare winter resident.

Variation: Significant sexual variation. See photos above.

Presumed range in Illinois

Habitat: Winter range includes all types of aquatic habitats in the state (swamps, marshes, lakes, ponds, etc.).

Breeding: Nest is in dense vegetation in wetland habitats of the far north. 6 to 9 eggs are laid as early as May.

Natural History: This is the smallest of America's "puddle ducks," and also one of the more common. They range throughout the northern hemisphere, with a distinct subspecies being found in Eurasia. They are fast and agile fliers and flocks of Green-winged Teal move back and forth across the southern half of the continent all winter in response to weather patterns. Populations of this duck appear stable and may even be increasing. About 90 percent of the population breeds in Canada and Alaska where they favor river deltas and boreal wetlands over the typical "pothole" habitats used by many puddle ducks. Their remote nesting habitats in the far north are largely undisturbed by man, which may account in part for this species' abundance. As with many species, the increasing daylight hours of spring triggers migration and breeding instincts.

Class - **Aves** (birds)

Order - **Anseriformes** (waterfowl)

Family - **Anatidae** (ducks, geese & swans)

Blue-winged Teal *Anas discors*	**Shoveler** *Spatula clypeata*	**Wood Duck** *Aix sponsa*
		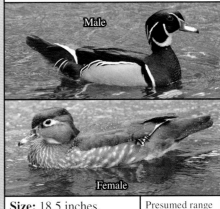

Size: 15.5 inches.

Presumed range in Illinois

Abundance: Fairly common.

Migratory Status: Spring through fall resident. March to November.

Variation: Significant sexual dimorphism (see photos above).

Habitat: Marshes, beaver ponds, bays, and other shallow water habitats.

Breeding: Nest is concealed in dense vegetation near water but above high water line. Lays 6 to 12 eggs.

Natural History: The food of this species is mostly plant material including algae and aquatic greenery. Many seeds and grains are also eaten, especially in winter when they converge on rice fields and other flooded agricultural areas in America's lower coastal plain. Breeding females will consume large amounts of invertebrates during the breeding season. These ducks are early fall migrators and one of the last to migrate back north in the spring. Many will winter as far south as South America, but substantial numbers can be seen along the lower coastal plain of North America all winter. Most breed and spend the summer on the central prairies of the US and Canada. But widespread breeding has been documented in Illinois. Young ducks are typically highly precocial, and babies will leave the nest within hours of hatching.

Size: 19 inches.

Presumed range in Illinois

Abundance: Fairly common.

Migratory Status: Mostly September through May. A few remain year round.

Variation: Significant sexual dimorphism (see photos above).

Habitat: Prefers shallow habitats. Swamps, marshes, flooded fields, bays.

Breeding: Breeds in northern and western United States (including Alaska) and in Canada. Averages 10 to 12 eggs.

Natural History: The Shoveler's name is derived from the unique shape of its bill, which is a highly effective sieve for straining tiny organisms from water. They are often observed swimming along with the bill held under water or skimming the surface. Like several of America's duck species, the Shoveler is holarctic in distribution and is breeds in Europe and Asia as well as North America. Eurasian birds winter southward to north Africa and the Pacific region. All ground nesting birds are vulnerable to mammalian predators and the Shoveler is no exception. Red Foxes and Mink are significant predators on the nesting females, while skunks are a major threat to the eggs. The nationwide population of these ducks seems to be on the increase, but waterfowl populations tend to be subject to significant annual variations.

Size: 18.5 inches.

Presumed range in Illinois

Abundance: Common.

Migratory Status: Year-round resident. Becomes scarce in north during winter.

Variation: Significant sexual dimorphism (see photos above).

Habitat: Beaver ponds, swamps, flooded woodlands, and farm ponds.

Breeding: Nests in tree hollows and takes readily to artificial nest boxes. Lays about 8 to 12 eggs typically.

Natural History: Male Wood Ducks are one of the most brilliantly colored birds in America. The bulk of the Wood Duck population in America occurs in the forested eastern half of the country. Populations plummeted during the latter half of the 19th century as America's forests were felled and swamplands drained. Populations began to recover by the 1950s and today the species is thriving. Most state wildlife agencies in America began placing Wood Duck nest boxes in suitable habitat many decades ago. The ducks responded favorably and a very high percentage of babies hatch in the man-made nests annually. Wood Ducks are widely hunted and make up a significant number of ducks killed by hunters annually. Although they are a small duck, they are considered by many as highly palatable. Along with the Mallard, the Wood Duck is the most common breeding duck in Illinois.

Class - **Aves** (birds)		
Order - **Anseriformes** (waterfowl)		
Family - **Anatidae** (ducks, geese & swans)		

Lesser Scaup *Athya affinis*	**Ring-necked Duck** *Athya collaris*	**Redhead** *Athya americana*

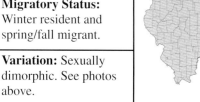

Size: 16.5 inches.	Presumed range in Illinois	**Size:** 17 inches.	Presumed range in Illinois	**Size:** 19 inches.	Presumed range in Illinois
Abundance: Common.		**Abundance:** Uncommon.		**Abundance:** Fairly common.	
Migratory Status: Winter resident and spring/fall migrant.		**Migratory Status:** Winter resident and spring/fall migrant.		**Migratory Status:** Winter resident and spring/fall migrant.	
Variation: Sexually dimorphic. See photos above.		**Variation:** Pronounced sexual dimorphism. See photos above.		**Variation:** Pronounced sexual dimorphism. See photos above.	

Habitat: Likes larger bodies of water and deeper water than many other ducks. Regularly uses large lakes and rivers in the state as well as flooded river bottoms.	**Habitat:** Open water habitats including shallow bays and flooded river bottoms. Also uses open marshes and large rivers and lakes, where it tends to use mostly shallow-water areas.	**Habitat:** Primarily a marshland species that alternates between prairie potholes and Gulf Coastal marshes. In migration they will use a variety of wetland habitats, especially the bays of large lakes.
Breeding: 8 to 10 eggs is typical. Nests in west-central US, Canada, and Alaska.	**Breeding:** Nests in subarctic regions of Canada and the northern Rockies in the United States. Lays 6 to 14 eggs.	**Breeding:** Breeds almost entirely in the "prairie pothole" region. Females often lay their eggs in other ducks nests.
Natural History: These ducks are the most widespread and common of the "diving ducks." Diving ducks are capable of diving deeper and prefer deeper waters than the "puddle ducks." They are also more clumsy on land and need a running start on the water to get airborne. They thus favor larger lakes and rivers over small ponds and swamplands. These ducks often gather in large flocks on open water. These large flocks are called "rafts." Rafts of Lesser Scaup are a common sight on large lakes in winter. A slightly larger version of the Lesser Scaup, known as the **Greater Scaup** (*Athya marila*) can also be seen in Illinois in winter. Both species like open water. The Greater Scaup tends to favor coastal areas and salt or brackish marshes, but it does migrate through much of the eastern US	**Natural History:** Closely related to and very similar in appearance to the scaups, the Ring-necked Duck should be called the Ring-billed duck. Although there is a brownish ring around the neck of the male, it is only visible when the bird is in the hand. The broad white ring near the tip of the bill and the narrow white ring at the base of the bill are both readily discernible on birds in the field. Unlike its relatives, the Scaups, which will feed on crustaceans, insects, and other aquatic invertebrates, the diet of the Ring-necked Duck is mostly vegetarian. Ring-necked Ducks favor small lakes, ponds and swamps over large rivers and lakes. Like other North American ducks, their movements in winter are determined by weather. Freeze ups will instigate movement.	**Natural History:** An entirely North American species, the Redhead is mostly a vegetarian and feeds heavily on tubers and aquatic vegetation. Most Redhead's congregate in winter on the western Gulf Coastal of Louisiana, Texas and northwest Mexico. In fact hundreds of thousands will concentrate in this region each winter. Here they feed mostly on the roots of shoalgrass. They will also eat some animal matter, mostly aquatic invertebrates. Redheads are easily decoyed and during the days of the market hunting their populations suffered dramatic declines. Recovery in the last few decades has been significant and in a good year the population may reach a million birds. There are records of breeding in Illinois, but most breeding takes place in the Western Plains and Northern Rockies.

Class - **Aves** (birds)

Order - **Anseriformes** (waterfowl)

Family - **Anatidae** (ducks, geese & swans)

Canvasback *Athya valisineria*	Bufflehead *Bucephala albeola*	Common Goldeneye *Bucephala clangula*

Size: 21 inches.	Presumed range in Illinois	**Size:** 13.5 inches.	Presumed range in Illinois	**Size:** 18.5 inches.	Presumed range in Illinois
Abundance: Uncommon.		**Abundance:** Common.		**Abundance:** Uncommon.	
Migratory Status: Winter resident and spring/fall migrant.		**Migratory Status:** Winter resident and spring/fall migrant.		**Migratory Status:** Winter resident and spring/fall migrant.	
Variation: Strong sexual variation. See photos above.		**Variation:** Significant sexual variation. See photos above.		**Variation:** Significant sexual variation. See photos above. Juvenile like female.	

Canvasback	Bufflehead	Common Goldeneye
Habitat: The primary breeding habitat for this species is known as "Aspen Parkland" habitat, which is found mostly in Canada. Winters mostly in marshes and bays along both coasts.	**Habitat:** Most winter in saltwater habitats on the coast but a few overwinter on inland lakes and rivers. In summer they use boreal forests and parklands in Canada.	**Habitat:** In winter, this species uses large lakes and rivers. They are also fairly common in winter in coastal regions. In summer they are a bird of the boreal forests.
Breeding: The large nest is built from grasses and hidden vegetation. Clutch size averages around 7 or 8.	**Breeding:** Cavity nester. Nest is often an old woodpecker hole. Clutch size ranges from a few to over a dozen eggs.	**Breeding:** Cavity nester that will use artificial nest boxes. May nest over a mile from water. 7 to 12 eggs.
Natural History: One of the most adept of the diving ducks, Canvasbacks have been known to dive to a depth of 30 feet. Feeds mostly on plant material including roots and rhizomes, but will also eat mud-dwelling invertebrates. This is strictly a North American species and is one of the least common duck species in America. They are vulnerable to droughts, habitat loss (mostly from agriculture) and water pollution that can impact the abundance of aquatic food plants. The Canvasback population is closely monitored by the US Fish and Wildlife Service and in years of low numbers hunting of this species may be banned. Even in years when hunting is allowed, the bag limits are typically very low (1 per day).	**Natural History:** America's smallest of the diving ducks, the Bufflehead is one of the few duck species that will remain with the same mate year after year. Breeding pairs usually return to the same pond or marsh to breed each year as well. With the exception of some seeds, these ducks are mostly carnivorous, feeding on aquatic insects, crustaceans, and mollusks. Unlike the puddle ducks which often feed on the surface, the Bufflehead finds all its food by diving. Although they are often seen on deep water lakes, they feed in the shallows along the banks or in the backs of bays. Although rarely seen in large flocks, this is one of the few duck species that has actually increased in numbers in the last few decades.	**Natural History:** As with other diving ducks the Common Goldeneye is an excellent swimmer that feeds by diving beneath the surface. They propel through the water using only the feet, with the wings held tight against the body. They are mostly carnivorous but they do eat some plant material in the form of tubers and seeds. Aquatic invertebrates are the main food and include (in order of importance) crustaceans, insects, and mollusks. Fish constitute only a small portion of the diet. Male Common Goldeneyes engage in a complex courtship display to attract females or reinforce the pair bond. These ducks are holearctic in distribution, breeding in boreal forests throughout the northern hemisphere.

Class - **Aves** (birds)
Order - **Anseriformes** (waterfowl)
Family - **Anatidae** (ducks, geese & swans)

Ruddy Duck	Long-tailed Duck	Surf Scoter
Oxyura jamaicensis	*Clangula hyemalis*	*Melanita perspicillata*

Size: 15 inches.

Abundance: Fairly common.

Migratory Status: Winter resident and spring/fall migrant.

Variation: Significant sexual variation. See photos above.

Presumed range in Illinois

Habitat: Marshes, ponds, lakes and to a lesser extent rivers. This is a true "Prairie Pothole" species and nearly 90 percent of nesting occurs in the prairie pothole habitats in the northern plains.

Breeding: Nest is usually built in cattails or other aquatic vegetation. 7 or 8 eggs is average.

Natural History: Ruddy Ducks are primarliy western birds that range generally from the Great Plains to the west coast. Winter range includes most of the eastern US and a few individuals are regularly seen in Illinois in winter. The larvae of aquatic insects of the order Diptera (flies, mosquitos, midges) are the primary food of these ducks. Although these are small ducks, their eggs are quite large and are in fact the largest eggs (relative to body size) of any North American duck. This species seems to be expanding its breeding range eastward into the Great Lakes region. Breeding has been recorded in northeastern Illinois.

Size: To 21 inches.

Abundance: Rare in Illinois.

Migratory Status: Winter resident and spring/fall migrant.

Variation: Males have very long tails and are more strikingly colored.

Presumed range in Illinois

Habitat: Summer habitat is arctic wetlands and seashores and deep water lakes. Winter habitat mostly coastal marine environments, but also large freshwater lakes, especially the Great Lakes.

Breeding: Nests in the arctic region on islands and peninsulas of freshwater lakes or in wetland tundra. 6 to 8 eggs.

Natural History: Also known as "Oldsquaw" these are primarily northern ducks that often wander far south in winter. Although they have been recorded in a variety of localities around the state, they are most likely to be seen around Lake Michigan. Rare individuals may go as far south as the Ohio River. These little ducks are great divers, and can dive to depths over 150 feet to reach marine invertebrate foods consisting mostly of benthic crustaceans. Also eats insects and their larva and to a lesser extent fish and fish eggs. This is one of the most northerly breeding ducks in the world and they nest well into the arctic. They often roosts in large "rafts" well offshore along coastlines or in large inland lakes.

Size: 21 inches.

Abundance: Rare in Illinois.

Migratory Status: Winter resident and spring/fall migrant.

Variation: Significant variation. Females and juveniles are brownish.

Presumed range in Illinois

Habitat: They are most common in winter in coastal regions. Some may be seen on the Great Lakes in the winter. In summer they are a bird of the boreal forests.

Breeding: Nests near shallow inland lakes in the far north, often well into the Arctic Circle. 7 to 12 eggs.

Natural History: There are a total of three Scoter species in North America and all three have been seen in Illinois during winter months. They are most likely to be seen on Lake Michigan. But they usually associate with coastal waters and they are often collectively referred to as "Sea Ducks." They will summer inland in the far north of northern Canada and Alaska. Waterfowl of all species are well known for wandering widely and sometimes appearing in areas far from their normal habitats. Two other scoter ducks, the **Black Scoter** (*M. nigra*) (not shown) and the **White-winged Scoter** (*M. fusca*) can also be seen in Illinois. Of the three scoter species the Surf Scoter is the most commonly seen in Illinois.

Class - **Aves** (birds)

Order - **Anseriformes** (waterfowl)

Family - **Anatidae** (ducks, geese & swans)

Common Merganser *Mergus merganser*	Red-breasted Merganser *Mergus serrator*	Hooded Merganser *Lophodytes cucullatus*
 Nonbreeding male	 Male / Female	 Male / Female

Size: 25 inches.	Presumed range in Illinois	**Size:** 23 inches.	Presumed range in Illinois	**Size:** 18 inches.	Presumed range in Illinois
Abundance: Uncommon.		**Abundance:** Fairly common.		**Abundance:** Fairly common.	
Migratory Status: Winter resident and spring/fall migrant.		**Migratory Status:** Winter resident and spring/fall migrant.		**Migratory Status:** Year-round resident and migrant.	
Habitat: In winter uses large lakes and rivers and larger reservoirs. Small creeks in summer.		**Habitat:** Uses larger lakes and rivers during migration. Boreal wetlands in summer.		**Habitat:** In winter uses swamps, shallow bays of lakes and river floodplains.	

Variation: Exhibits pronounced sexual dimorphism in breeding plumage with males having dark greenish head and white breast. Winter plumages (seen in Illinois) are similar in both sexes.	**Variation:** Significant plumage variations between the sexes during the breeding season. Also exhibits seasonal variation with winter males (and juveniles) resembling females.	**Variation:** Shows strong sexual dimorphism. Males are strikingly marked, having black heads with white "hood" and black wings and back. Females are more subdued (see above).
Breeding: Nests in tree cavities or sometimes in root crevices on the ground. 10 or 12 eggs is average.	**Breeding:** Nests on the ground. Nest is well hidden beneath overhanging vegetation or in cavities. 5 to 24 eggs.	**Breeding:** Cavity nester. Most nesting is to the north, but some nesting occurs in Illinois. Lays 12 eggs maximum.
Natural History: Most Common Mergansers seen in Illinois will be in nonbreeding plumage (shown above). A bird of northern climates and cold waters, the Common Merganser spends the summer on lakes in the boreal forests of Canada, Alaska and in the cold-water streams of the Rocky Mountains. They are also found throughout Eurasia. Fish is the primary food for this species. Their bill is serrated for holding slippery prey and they are excellent divers and underwater swimmers. They are excellent fishermen and can dive to a depth of tens of yards and have been known to stay submerged up to two minutes. They use their bill to probe in mud or gravel for aquatic insects, mollusks, crustaceans, and worms.	**Natural History:** During winter these birds show a preference for coastal regions where they use estuaries and saltwater bays and salt/brackish water marshes. Like its larger relative the Common Merganser, the Red-breasted has a holarctic distribution and is found in Europe and Asia as well as North America. In summer this species ranges even farther north than its larger cousin, being found as far north as the Arctic Ocean and southern Greenland. Food is mostly small fish that are grasped with the serrated bill. Also eats aquatic invertebrates and amphibians. Feeds both in shallow water and in deep water up to at least 25 feet deep. Flocks may feed cooperatively, with all the birds diving together to corral schools of minnows.	**Natural History:** Unlike our other two merganser ducks, both of which are holarctic in distribution, the Hooded Merganser is strictly a North American duck. Another odd distributional trait is the fact that these birds are rare in the Great Plains region, where many North American duck species are most common. They have a more diverse diet than the larger mergansers, feeding less on fish and more on aquatic invertebrates that are located by means of well developed underwater vision capability. Winter waterfowl surveys indicate that over 50 percent of the population winters in the Mississippi flyway. Many will winter to the south of Illinois, but they can be seen year-round throughout the state.

Class - **Aves** (birds)
Order - **Anseriformes** (waterfowl)
Family - **Anatidae** (ducks, geese & swans)

Snow Goose *Chen caerulescens*	**Canada Goose** *Branta canadensis*	**Greater White-fronted Goose** *Anser albifrons*

Size: 30 inches.	**Size:** 36 to 45 inches.	**Size:** 28 inches.
Abundance: Common.	**Abundance:** Very common.	**Abundance:** Uncommon.
Migratory Status: Winter migrant.	**Migratory Status:** Resident and migrant.	**Migratory Status:** Winter migrant.
Variation: Two distinct color phases occur. Juveniles are uniformly gray.	**Variation:** No variation. Sexes and juveniles are all alike.	**Variation:** Juveniles lack black spots on belly. Sexes are alike.

Presumed range in Illinois (×3)

Habitat: In Illinois, these geese are mostly seen in the western part of the state where they use very large agricultural fields. May be seen statewide.	**Habitat:** Habitat includes all types of aquatic situations, from urban parks to remote and inaccessible marshes, swamps or beaver ponds.	**Habitat:** When migrating through Illinois they will use large agricultural fields for feeding and roost on open water or bays in large lakes.
Breeding: Nests only in the high Arctic Tundra of Canada and Alaska.	**Breeding:** Nests above the water line but near water. 4 to 8 eggs is typical.	**Breeding:** Breeds in the Arctic Coastal Plain. Average clutch size is 4 or 5.
Natural History: Snow Goose populations have exploded in the last few decades, probably as a result of having so much habitat and food available throughout migration routes and on wintering grounds. The grain fields of Midwestern and southern United States provides more than an adequate food source. Mid-continent populations are expanding their migration routes eastward from their historical range west of the Mississippi River. Today they can be found every winter in Illinois and they are sometimes seen as far east as the Appalachian Plateau. There is also an east coast population that winters the along the Atlantic coast from New Jersey to the Carolinas. Snow Geese often occur in huge flocks numbering thousands of birds. The **Ross's Goose** (*C. rossii*) is a is a smaller version of the Snow Goose that may rarely be seen in Illinois in the company of Snow Geese.	**Natural History:** This is the most recognized wild goose in America, due in large part to the fact that tame and semi-tame populations are found in parks and on rivers, ponds and lakes in both urban and rural regions. Resident Canada Geese are numerous, but their numbers are swelled dramatically during winter, as birds from farther north visit the state for either a brief stopover or a months long stay . The characteristic "V formation" of Canada Geese in flight is a familiar sight and their musical, honking call is to many a symbol of wild America. They are heavily hunted throughout America both for sport and for food. They are long-lived birds and have been known to survive over forty years. There are several races of Canada Goose and they vary in size. An identical dwarf species of goose called the **Cackling Goose** (*B. hutchinsii*) is the size of a Mallard.	**Natural History:** Although they may migrate throughout the much of state, White-fronted Geese are found in their greatest numbers west of the Mississippi River. While they are holarctic in distribution, they are not as common in North America as the Canada Goose or Snow Goose. Most of the North American populations of these geese use the Mississippi and Central Flyways, but a smaller population occurs in the Pacific Flyway. Oddly, they are rarely seen in the Atlantic Flyway. Mississippi Flyway birds will usually winter along the Gulf Coast from Louisiana and Texas to northeastern Mexico. During migration small flocks may be seen traveling with larger flocks of Canada or Snow Geese, but they tend to segregate themselves when resting or feeding. They may be expanding their migration routes eastward.

Class - **Aves** (birds)
Order - **Anseriformes** (waterfowl)
Family - **Anatidae** (ducks, geese & swans)

Mute Swan *Cygnus*	Tundra Swan *Cygnus*	Trumpeter Swan *Cygnus buccinator*

Size: 60 inches.

Presumed range in Illinois

Abundance: Fairly common.

Migratory Status: Year-round resident.

Habitat: Ponds, lakes, marshes and swamps in both urban and rural areas. Most often seen in urban parks.

Variation: Some juveniles are brownish for the first year.

Breeding: Nest is platform of grasses up to 6 feet wide. Near water but above floodplain. About 6 eggs per clutch.

Natural History: The Mute Swan is a Eurasian species that is common in parks, zoos, farms, and private preserves all across America. Many have become feral or semi-feral and the species seems to be increasing in the wild in America. The impact of this exotic species on native wildlife populations is unclear, but some state wildlife agencies regard them as a nuisance animal. Many state wildlife agencies have active removal programs. In some other states they are protected. These large waterfowl are primarily vegetarians, but they will eat small amounts of animal matter. When threatened Mute Swans arch the wings over the back and pull the long neck back between the wings in a display known as "busking." They are graceful and elegant in flight or on the water, but rather clumsy on land due to the fact that the legs are located so far back on the body.

Size: 52 inches.

Presumed range in Illinois

Abundance: Rare in Illinois.

Migratory Status: Seasonal migrant.

Habitat: Large lakes and large, open agricultural fields are used in migration. In summer found on tundra.

Variation: Juveniles are "dingy" white with orange bill.

Breeding: Breeds on the tundra of the Arctic Coastal Plain. 3 to 5 eggs are laid.

Natural History: Although the Tundra Swan is America's most common swan species, these large swans are rare in IL. But they do pass through the state during migration. Most winter along the Atlantic coast from the Chesapeake Bay south to North Carolina and on the Pacific Coast from Washington to central California. In winter they use coastal estuaries and will fly inland to forage on waste grain in agricultural fields. Young swans stay with the parents throughout the first year until returning to their arctic breeding grounds the following spring. Prior to the passage of the first migratory bird protection legislation in 1918, these birds had become quite rare. Today their numbers have recovered substantially and a few states now allow a limited harvest during waterfowl season. Migratory flights over Illinois may include flocks numbering hundreds of swans, but smaller groups one or two dozen is more common.

Size: 60 inches.

Presumed range in Illinois

Abundance: Very rare in Illinois.

Migratory Status: Year-round resident.

Habitat: Uses wetlands, lakes, etc. In western US found on rivers, lakes, and freshwater marshes.

Variation: None in adults. Juveniles are grayish.

Breeding: Nest is a hummock in wetland area. May use muskrat house or beaver lodge. 4 to 6 eggs.

Natural History: Trumpeter Swans were eradicated from the eastern United States by European settlers about 200 years ago. They managed to cling to existance in northern and western North America but were highly endangered until recent decades. Today the species has recovered significantly and populations in the western half of North America appear secure. In Illinois they are still quite rare but occasional individuals may wander into northern Illinois. Despite the fact that this species is increasing in numbers it still faces an uncertain future. The main threats to the species today are probably loss of habitat, pollution, and ingestion of lead sinkers used by fishermen. Food is mostly plant material, mainly aquatic plants but also some terrestrial plants. Adult birds often show a reddish wash on the head and neck as a result of foraging for tubers in mud that is rich in iron.

Class - **Aves** (birds)
Order - **Siluiformes** (tropical sea birds)
Family - **Phalacrocoracidae** (cormorants)

Double-crested Cormorant
Phalacrocorax auritus

Size: 33 inches.

Abundance:
Fairly common.

Migratory Status:
Season migrant through the state and rare winter resident in southern tip of Illinois.

Variation: Juveniles are much browner and have whitish throat and breast.

Presumed range in Illinois

Habitat: Lakes, rivers, estuaries, and swamplands. In Illinois, they are most common on larger lakes and rivers.

Breeding: Some nesting occurs in northern Illinois. Bulky nest of sticks and floating debris. Lays 2 to 4 eggs.

Natural History: Cormorants are rarely seen far from water. They are thoroughly aquatic birds that have webbed feet and frequently submerge and swim underwater in search of fish. Their exclusive diet of fish and their uncanny aquatic abilities have caused these birds to come into conflict with man. Occurring in large flocks, they will concentrate in areas where food is most readily available. Under natural conditions, they catch a wide variety of fish species and thus do not impact significantly upon fisheries. However, around fish farms or hatcheries they can become quite a nuisance. In some regions they have become an ecological problem by crowding out other colonial nesting species such as herons and egrets.

CHAPTER 5

THE TURTLES OF ILLINOIS

— THE ORDERS AND FAMILIES OF ILLINOIS TURTLES —

Note: The sequence of turtle families shown in the table below is a representation of the order in which they appear in the book, and may not be an accurate representation of the phylogentic relationships of the turtles.

Class - **Chelonia** (turtles)

Order - **Cryptodira** (straight necked turtles)

Family	**Chelydridae** (snapping turtles)
Family	**Kinosternidae** (mud & musk turtles)
Family	**Emydidae** (sliders & box turtles)
Family	**Trionychidae** (softshell turtles)

Class - **Chelonia** (turtles)
Order - **Cryptodira** (straightneck turtles)
Family - **Chelydridae** (snapping turtles)

Common Snapping Turtle *Chelydra serpentina*	**Alligator Snapping Turtle** *Macrochelys temminckii*

Size: Maximum length 20 inches. Record weight 86 pounds.

Variation: No variation occurs in Illinois specimens. Specimens found on the Florida peninsula differ slightly.

Abundance: Very common.

Habitat: Found in virtually every aquatic environment in the state. Ponds, lakes, rivers, creeks, swamps, and marshes.

Breeding: Eggs are deposited in underground chambers excavated by the female turtle. A typical clutch contains 25 to 50 eggs. Hatchlings are about the size of a quarter.

Presumed range in Illinois

Size: Maximum length 31 inches. Record weight 251 pounds.

Variation: No variation in Illinois Males attain a larger size than females and all the really large specimens are males.

Abundance: Very rare in Illinois.

Habitat: Large rivers and their impoundments. Also oxbow lakes and small tributaries near their confluence with rivers.

Breeding: Adult females leave the water to lay up to 50 eggs in an underground chamber dug by the turtle. The leathery shelled eggs hatch in 3 or 4 months.

Presumed range in Illinois

Natural History: These common turtles can be found in any aquatic habitat in the state, including tiny farm ponds or tributaries narrow enough for a person to step across. They even can exist in waters that are heavily polluted with sewage. They will feed on some plant material but are mainly carnivorous and will eat virtually anything they can swallow. Fish, frogs, tadpoles, small mammals, baby ducks, crayfish, and carrion are all listed as food items. Hatchlings turtles often must travel long distances to find a home in a pond or creek, and adults occasionally embark on long overland treks, presumably in search of a more productive habitat after depleting the food source in a small pond or creek. These long hikes overland usually occur in the spring. The ferociousness of a captured snapping turtle is legendary and their sharp, powerful jaws can inflict a serious wound. When cornered on land they will turn to face an enemy and extend the long neck in a lunging strike that is lighting fast and so energetic that it may cause the entire turtle to move forward several inches. By contrast when under water they almost never bite.

Natural History: Alligator Snapping Turtles are the most completely aquatic of any American freshwater turtle. In fact, they never leave the water except for egg laying excursions by the female. Unlike most aquatic turtles, they do not bask and rarely show more than the tip of the snout when coming up to breath. They spend most of their time "bottom walking" or lying in ambush in the muck or mud. They possess a specialized structure on the tongue that resembles a worm and can be wriggled to effectively lure fish into striking distance. They also eat other turtles, carrion, crayfish and in fact probably any type of animal matter that can be swallowed. Mussels are reportedly an important food item, the hard shell being no match for the powerful jaws of these huge turtles. The longevity of this turtle in the wild is unknown, but some specimens have been in captivity for over 70 years, suggesting a long life span. These interesting and unique animals have declined significantly throughout their range. In Illinois the Alligator Snapping Turtle is now regarded as an Endangered Species.

Class - **Chelonia** (turtles)
Order - **Cryptodira** (straightneck turtles)
Family - **Kinosternidae** (mud & musk turtles)

Common Musk Turtle *Sternotherus oderatus*	**Common Mud Turtle** *Kinosternum subrubrum*

Size: Mature adults are about 4 inches in length.

Abundance: Fairly common.

Variation: In some regions females are larger than males, but there is no variation in Illinois specimens.

Habitat: Primarily a stream dweller, but can be found in a variety of aquatic habitats including swamps, oxbows, lakes, etc. They reach their highest densities in waters with abundant aquatic vegetation.

Presumed range in Illinois

Size: Adults range from 4 to 4.75 inches in length.

Abundance: Fairly common.

Variation: There are 3 subspecies. Specimens from Illinois are probably Mississippi Mud Turtles (*K. s. hippocrepis*).

Habitat: Found in all aquatic habitats withing its range, but prefers shallow water areas with abundant aquatic vegetation. They are turtles of the lower elevations and are most common in Illinois in the Gulf Coastal Plain.

Presumed range in Illinois

Breeding: Female lays 2 to 5 eggs under leaf litter or sometimes merely on top of the ground. Eggs hatch into tiny turtles that are barely an inch in length.

Breeding: Reaches breeding age at about 5 to 7 years old. Breeds in the spring. Females dig a hole and deposit an average of 2 to 4 eggs, sometimes as many as 8.

Natural History: Nocturnal and crepuscular and completely aquatic in habits. Unlike most aquatic turtles in Illinois, the Musk Turtle rarely basks, but when it does it may climb several feet up into branches that overhang the water. When disturb while basking they will launch themselves clumsily into the safety of the water. Since they seldom leave the water, the carapace is often covered with a thick growth of algae. Their name comes from the presence of musk producing glands that emit an unpleasant odor when the turtles are handled. This musk also accounts for their other common name "Stinkpot." The Common Musk Turtle is widespread throughout the eastern US, being found from the Gulf Coast north to the Great Lakes, but they are absent from most of the higher elevations of the Appalachian Plateau. They are an omnivorous species that feeds on a variety of aquatic plant and animal matter. Like many turtle species, the Eastern Musk Turtle is a long lived species and one captive zoo specimen lived for 55 years.

Natural History: Although this is a are very aquatic turtle, they sometimes embark on overland treks, presumably to find new habitats or seek a mate. These aquatic turtles have a double hinged plastron, a characteristic that is rare in North American turtles and shared with the Box Turtles (genus *Terrepene*). Their diet is omnivorous. A variety of aquatic plants are eaten and animal foods include crustaceans, aquatic insects, mollusks, amphibians and carrion. Locates food by "bottom walking" when in water, but may also feed on land near the waters edge. They can remain under water for up to twenty minutes. These small turtles have been known to live up to 40 years and perhaps can survive even longer. A nearly identical species known as the **Yellow Mud Turtle**, *Kinosternon flavescens* can be found in a few places along the Illinois and Mississippi Rivers in Illinois. It is quite rare and regarded as an Endangered Species in Illinois.

Class - **Chelonia** (turtles)

Order - **Cryptodira** (straightneck turtles)

Family - **Emydidae** (water & box turtles)

Red-eared Slider *Trachemys scripta*	Spotted Turtle *Clemmys guttata*	Painted Turtle *Chrysemys picta*

Red-eared Slider	Spotted Turtle	Painted Turtle
Size: 6 to 8 inches. **Abundance:** Very common. **Variation:** Males are smaller than females and have longer claws on the front feet. Hatchlings have a yellowish carapace boldly marked with green and black lines or circular patterns.	**Size:** To 4.5 inches. **Abundance:** Very rare in Illinois. **Variation:** Yellow spots are most vivid on young specimens and tend to fade with age. Very old Spotted Turtles may be nearly solid black.	**Size:** 4 to 6 inches. **Abundance:** Very common. **Variation:** At least two forms can be seen in Illinois. Some recognize a third subspecies in the southern tip of the state. Other experts regard Illinois specimens as being a single subspecies.
Presumed range in Illinois	*Presumed range in Illinois*	*Presumed range in Illinois*
Habitat: Most common in large bodies of water but can be found in any aquatic habitat in the state except for very small streams.	**Habitat:** Prefers sluggish waters. Inhabits lakes, marshes, swamps and slow-moving rivers. Sometimes found in wet meadows or wet woods.	**Habitat:** Avoids fast flowing streams in favor of still or slow-moving waters. Common in swamps, marshes, ponds, and lakes throughout its range.
Breeding: Females leave the safety of the water and crawl hundreds of yards to upland areas to deposit their eggs in an underground nest chamber dug with the hind legs. Large females may lay 20 eggs, younger females lay fewer.	**Breeding:** Mating takes place in early spring through early summer with eggs being laid from May to July. Female digs a flask shaped hole and deposits from 1 to 8 eggs. 2 clutches per year is not uncommon.	**Breeding:** Females lay 10 to 15 eggs within a flask shaped underground nest chamber dug with the turtles hind legs. Egg laying occurs from late May to early July. Eggs hatch in about 10 weeks. Hatchlings are the size of a quarter.
Natural History: Highly aquatic but sometimes seen far from water. Omnivorous. Eats a variety of water plants as well as mollusks, minnows, dead fish, aquatic insects, crustaceans, etc. Young are more carnivorous, while mature turtles will consume more plants. Old specimens tend to darken with age and very old specimens can be nearly all black (see inset). These are hardy turtles that will emerge from the mud to bask on logs on warm, sunny days throughout the winter. There are 3 subspecies of slider turtles in America, one of which, the **Red-eared Slider** (subspecies *elegans*) is found in Illinois.	**Natural History:** These handsome little turtles range throughout the Atlantic slope of the eastern United States from southern Maine to northern Florida. A disjunct population is found throughout the Great Lakes region, and it is to this population that the Illinois Spotted Turtles belong. The Great Lakes population is in decline and this species is regarded as endangered in Illinois. The Spotted Turtle is both an omnivore and a scavenger. Aquatic grasses and algea make up the vegetarian diet with insects, crustaceans, snails, amphibian larva, and fish listed as food items. Opportunistic feeding on carrrion is also reported. They are shy and docile and rarely attempt to bite when captured.	**Natural History:** The Painted Turtles are among the most common and widespread of the Emydidae turtles in America. Like other members of their family they spend a great deal of time basking on floating logs and they are quick to slide into the water if approached too closely. These are omnivorous turtles that eat a very wide array of plant and animal foods as well as carrion. There are as many as three geographic morphs of Painted Turtle in Illinois. Experts disagree as to whether they constitute disinct species or are merely subspecies. The current prevailing attitude (based on DNA evidence) is that they are distinct species.

Class - **Chelonia** (turtles)
Order - **Cryptodira** (straightneck turtles)
Family - **Emydidae** (water & box turtles)

Eastern River Cooter *Pseudemys concinna*	**Blanding's Turtle** *Emydoidea blandingii*

Old adult

Size: 10 to 12 inches.

Abundance: Fairly common.

Variation: Males are smaller than females and have long, needlelike claws on the front feet. There is no geographic variation in Illinois specimens (see Natural History section below).

Habitat: Primarily a turtle of large rivers and lakes, but they can also be common in swamps and oxbows that are adjacent to larger streams. Range in Illinois is along the major river valleys in the southern half of the state.

Presumed range in Illinois

Breeding: Lays about 20 eggs in an underground chamber dug with the females hind legs. Egg deposition is in late spring or early summer with the eggs hatching in August or September. Babies are slightly larger than a quarter.

Natural History: The largest member of the Emdidae family in Illinois. They primarily eat aquatic plants, including large quantities of algae. Some animal matter is consumed usually in the form of aquatic invertebrates or fish, especially so with younger turtles that need a higher protein diet. In habits they are strictly diurnal. Like many other aquatic turtles, they spend the winter buried in the mud at the bottom of a body of water. Their metabolic processes slowed significantly by cold temperatures, they absorb oxygen throught the lining of the cloaca. These large turtles are often utilized as food by humans. The phylogeny of the *Pseudemys* genus has undergone repeated revisions in recent years. Today most experts consider all *Pseudemys* found in Illinois to be Eastern River Cooters.

Size: Maximum of 11.25 inches

Abundance: Uncommon in Illinois.

Variation: Amount of light, irregular spots and lines on carapace is variable. Some individuals have spots significantly faded or no spots at all. Newly hatched babies tend to lack spots.

Habitat: The habitat is marshes and wetlands. Especially along the margins of glacial lakes. Also uses wet meadows or to a lesser extend mesic woodlands. Though semi-aquatic, they are commonly seen on land, sometimes far from water.

Presumed range in Illinois

Breeding: 10 to 15 eggs are laid by the female in an underground nest chamber that she digs at night. Only 1 clutch per year is produced.

Natural History: The oldest known wild specimen of Blanding's Turtle was calculated to be 77 years old. Crayfish are reported to be the favorite food item. Among aquatic foods listed are insects, fish, fish eggs, and frogs are along with algae. On land they will eat earthworms, slugs, insect larva, leaves, grasses and berries. It is thought that the Blanding's Turtle is closely related to the more terrestrial Box Turtle. Like the Box Turtle the Blanding's does posses a hinged plastron. Like their cousin the Box Turtle, the greatest threat to adult Blanding's Turtles is the automobile. Their nests are raided by a variety of predators including foxes, Oppossums, Raccoon and especially Striped Skunks. A Threatened Species in Illinois.

Class - **Chelonia** (turtles)
Order - **Cryptodira** (straightneck turtles)
Family - **Emydidae** (water & box turtles)

False Map Turtle *Graptemys pseudogeographica*	**Common Map Turtle** *Graptemys geographica*	**Ouachita Map Turtle** *Graptemys ouachitensis*

Female

Male top, female bottom

Size: Maximum of 11 inches.

Abundance: Fairly common along major rivers.

Variation: Two very similar subspecies recognized in Illinois. Males have longer claws on the front feet. Pattern fades with age.

Presumed range in Illinois

Size: Males 6.5 inches. Females 11 inches.

Abundance: Fairly common, especially in northern Illinois.

Variation: In mature adults, females are larger and have larger heads. No subspecies known from Illinois. Young resemble adults.

Presumed range in Illinois

Size: Males to 5 inches. Females to 10 inches.

Abundance: Fairly common, especially in the Wabash watershed.

Variation: Males are smaller than females and have longer front claws. Young resemble adults but have markings on the plastron.

Presumed range in Illinois

Habitat: The habitat is mostly in rivers and large creeks with mud bottoms. Abundant basking sites in the form of floating logs or down trees favored.

Habitat: Primarily found in larger rivers and lakes, but also found in smaller tributaries near their confluence with larger streams.

Habitat: Primarily lives in rivers and river impoundments. They can also be found in the oxbows and swamps associated with major rivers.

Breeding: 10 to 15 eggs are laid by the female in an underground nest chamber that she digs at night. Only 1 clutch per year is produced.

Breeding: Breeds in early spring and eggs are laid in June. Most egg laying occurs in the morning. The average clutch size is about 10 eggs.

Breeding: Breeds in spring and fall. Eggs are laid in early summer and average about 10 per clutch. May lay 2 clutches per year.

Natural History: When not feeding or breeding these turtles spend most of their time basking. They are quite wary and will dive into the water at the slightest disturbance. They eat mainly insects but also eat other aquatic invertebrates and will scavenge on dead fish. They eat less plant material than other aquatic turtles. The longevity record for this species is 35 years. With the exception of the three map turtle species shown on this page, this genus of turtles are mostly animals of America's Lower Gulf Coastal Plain. It is here that they reach their greatest diversity and some have very small geographic ranges. The range of some species in the Gulf Coast region is restricted to a single small river drainage.

Natural History: Diurnal and crepuscular in activity. These turtles are fond of basking on logs but are very wary and will disappear into the water if approached. Food items include, crustaceans, fish, insects, and aquatic plants. They also eat mollusks and the thick, crushing surface of the jaws suggests that small mussels may be an important element in the diet. The Common Map Turtle is one of the more widely distributed of the map turtles and can be found from the Great Lakes southward into Arkansas and Alabama. They also range widely throughout Illinois and they may occur statewide, although they have not been documented from every county in the state. They have a life span in the wild of at least 20 years.

Natural History: Food includes insects, dead fish, aquatic invertebrates, and plant material, especially algae. The carapace (top shell) of this species has a rough, serrated appearance that is more pronounced in younger turtles. They are good climbers and will bask on steep trunks or limbs overhanging water. This turtles name is derived from the Ouachita Mountains of Arkansas, where the first specimen described to science was found. This species is more widespread to the west of Illinois but occurs along most of the major rivers of the state. The map above is at best an approximation, as the exact range of this species in the state may not be fully known.

Class - **Chelonia** (turtles)

Order - **Cryptodira** (straightneck turtles)

Family - **Emydidae** (water & box turtles)

Eastern Box Turtle *Terrapene carolina*	Ornate Box Turtle *Terrapene ornata*

Size: Averages 4 to 6 inches. The record is just under 8 inches.

Abundance: Very common.

Variation: There are four subspecies of this common land turtle. Only the eastern race occurs in Illinois. It is a highly variable subspecies. In fact, no two specimens look exactly alike (see photos above). The color and pattern on each specimen is as individual as a fingerprint. Sexes can be differentiated by examination of the bottom part of the shell (plastron). Males have a concave plastron and females a flat plastron. In adult turtles, males tend to be slightly larger than females.

Presumed range in Illinois

Habitat: Occupies a wide variety of habitats from open fields and pastures to deep woods. Can be found in both upland areas and lowlands, but is most common in damp woods, edge areas near creeks and streams, and wooded bottom lands.

Breeding: Breeding takes place in late April and May with egg deposition in late June or early July. Up to 6 eggs may be laid but 2 or 3 is more common. Young hatch in late fall and some may overwinter in their underground nest chamber before emerging the following spring. Newly hatched baby Box Turtles do not possess the hinged plastron and are thus unable to tightly close themselves within their shell.

Natural History: These familiar turtles often go by the name "Terrapin." They are primarily diurnal and are most active in the morning and the late afternoon. They sometimes burrow into the mud during hot weather, and overwinter by burrowing themselves into loose soil or deep leaf litter. The hibernation burrow is quite shallow, only a few inches deep. Studies have shown that they are tolerant of some freezing, a trait that enables survival of such a shallow hibernator. Still, hibernation is a significant source of mortality among adults. Their diet is omnivorous and they consume berries, fruits and mushrooms as well as a wide variety of insect prey and other invertebrates. Earthworms and snails are a favorite animal food and blackberries and mulberries are among the favorite plant foods. Box Turtles are known for their longevity and reports of their living up to a century are common but difficult to verify. Some researchers report a life span of 80 years, while others say 30 to 40 years is probably the average in the wild. When threatened they will retract the head and feet into the shell which can then close tightly by means of hinges on the front and back of the plastron. The muscles that close the shell are remarkably strong and efforts to pry open the shell of a frightened Box Turtle are futile. They are tough little turtles that can sometimes survive serious injury such as the shell being cracked open by a glancing blow from an automobile tire. Turtles with badly deformed but completely healed shells are sometimes found. In regions where wildfires are common many are seen with shells that are completely scarred by fire. There is some concern among conservationists that commercial collecting of these turtles for foreign markets may be threat to their long term survival. Habitat degradation and automobiles are a much more imminent threats.

Size: Max 6.5 inches.

Abundance: Rare.

Variation: Male has concave platron (females is flat) and red eye. Amount of yellow spotting in head is variable as is the prominence of light markings on the carapace.

Presumed range in Illinois

Habitat: Seems to prefer more xeric conditions than the Eastern Box Turtle. Inhabits remant prairie and dry woods.

Breeding: Lays up to 6 eggs in midsummer. Eggs hatch in fall. Baby turtles are tiny replicas of the adult, but lack the ability to close the plastron completely until several inches long.

Natural History: This turtle could be regarded as a western, dry land version of the Eastern Box Turtle. They range throughout the Great Plains and well into the desert southwest. Illinois populations (and those in nearby Indiana) represent the easternmost extension of the species range in America. They are more carnivorous than their eastern cousins, but they do consume some vegetable matter. Insects, snails, and earthworms are probably the main food items. Some small vertebrate prey may be consumed and they are known to scavenge for carrion as well. There are two subspecies recognized, but only the nominate form is found in Illinois. The other is the Desert Box Turtle which ranges well into the Chihauhau Desert region as far west as Arizona. For unknown reasons, the Ornate Box Turtle spends more time in hibernation than the Eastern Box Turtle.

Class - **Chelonia** (turtles)

Order - **Cryptodira** (straightneck turtles)

Family - **Trionychidae** (softshell turtles)

Smooth Softshell Turtle	Spiny Softshell Turtle
Apalone mutica	*Apalone spinifera*

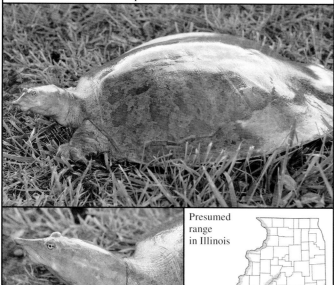

Underwater

Close-up of head showing tubular snout

Sunning on streambank

Presumed range in Illinois

Presumed range in Illinois

Size: 12 to 14 inches.	**Size:** Maximum of 18 inches.
Abundance: Uncommon to rare in Illinois. Endangered.	**Abundance:** Fairly common.
Variation: No significant species variation in Illinois There are two other Smooth Softshell species found in parts of the southeast. Females attain a much larger size than males.	**Variation:** No subspecific variation among Illinois specimens, but there are a total of five subspecies in America. Adult females may be twice the size of males.
Habitat: Essentially an inhabitant of streams, both large rivers and small creeks. Flowing water is a requirement for this species, but it is found in large river impoundments.	**Habitat:** Occurs in both large and small steams and in impoundments. May also be found in farm ponds in some areas. Shows a preference for habitats with sandy substrates.
Breeding: Eggs are laid in excavated chambers on exposed sandbars in late spring or early summer. About a dozen eggs is typical.	**Breeding:** A dozen or more eggs are laid between May and August (most in June or July). Nests are often on sandbars of creeks or rivers.
Natural History: The Smooth Softshell is found mostly in flowing streams with fine gravel or sand bottoms. They are capable of great speed in the water and will actively forage for fish and other small aquatic animals. They are also ambush predators that burrow into the soft substrate of streams and extend their long necks with blinding speed to grab passing fish. Insects are also an important food item, along with various small aquatic animals and some plant material such as seeds and berries. Because of their permeable skin and requirement of clear streams and rivers these turtles may be under significant threat from water pollution. Damming of major rivers can also impede their natural movements and dispersal. Siltation from agricultural runoff alters preferred stream substrates of sand or fine gravel All species of softshell turtles have elongated, snorkel-like snouts which they will use to breath when buried in sand or mud at the waters edge.	**Natural History:** Crayfish, fish, and insects are the primary food items, but dead fish and other carrion can be an important food item, especially in lakes where fishing is common. Spiny Softshells are active from April to October in Illinois. They hunt both by ambush and by active pursuit. When immobile they can remain under water or several hours. Because of the soft, permeable shells and skin, softshells are more susceptible to dehydration than other turtle species and thus they seldom stray far from water. These turtles are harvested as food in many parts of their range, and much of this harvest is to date unregulated. Some believe this practice may pose a long term threat to the species. Like all softshell turtles the Spiny has a long and flexible neck, which makes handling these turtles without being bitten difficult. Wild adults may bite savagely if handled.

CHAPTER 6

THE REPTILES OF ILLINOIS

— THE ORDERS AND FAMILIES OF ILLINOIS REPTILES —

Note: The sequence of reptile orders and families shown in the table below is a representation of the order in which they appear in the book, and may not be an accurate representation of the phylogenetic relationships of the reptiles.

Class - **Reptilia** (reptiles)

Order - **Squamata** (lizards & snakes)
Suborder - **Lacertilia** (lizards)

Family	**Phrynosomatidae** (spiny lizards)
Family	**Teiidae** (whiptail lizards)
Family	**Anguidae** (glass lizards)
Family	**Scincidae** (skinks)

Suborder - **Serpentes** (snakes)

Family	**Colubridae** (harmless egg laying snakes)
Family	**Dipsadidae** (rear-fanged snakes)
Family	**Natricidae** (harmless live-bearing snakes)
Family	**Crotalidae** (pit vipers)

THE REPTILES OF ILLINOIS

PART 1: LIZARDS

Class - **Reptilia** (reptiles)

Order - **Squamata** (snakes & lizards)

Suborder - **Lacertilia** (lizards)

Family - **Phrynosomatidae**	Family - **Teiidae** (whiptails)	Family - **Anguidae** (glass lizards)
Eastern Spiny Lizard *Sceloperus undulatus*	**Six-lined Racerunner** *Aspidoscelis sexlineatus*	**Slender Glass Lizard** *Ophisaurus attenuatus*

Size: Maximum of 7.25 inches.	**Size:** From 6 to 10 inches.	**Size:** 2–3 feet. Record 43 inches.
Abundance: Very common.	**Abundance:** Uncommon.	**Abundance:** Rare in Illinois.
Variation: Males have bright blue patches on each side of the belly. There are no variants in Illinois, but several subspecies occur in the western US.	**Variation:** Males and subadults are a bit more vividly colored than mature females. Two subspecies occur in Illinois (see photos above).	**Variation:** Males (inset) have light and dark speckling. Juveniles resemble females but longitudinal stripes are more vivid on younger lizards.
Habitat: Dry, upland woods. Found in both pure deciduous woods and in pine dominated woodlands.	**Habitat:** Habitat requirements are sandy or gravelly soils in dry upland areas with prolonged exposure to the sun.	**Habitat:** Dry soils with an open canopy seem to be important factors in this lizards habitat. Woods, fields and edge.
Breeding: Egg layer. Deposits 6 to 15 eggs in rotted logs, stumps, etc. 2 clutches per year are common.	**Breeding:** Breeds in April or May. 6 or 8 eggs are laid in and underground nest chamber in sandy soil.	**Breeding:** Females lay as single clutch of eggs in late June or early July. Average clutch size is about 10 eggs.
Natural History: A woodland species, the Eastern Fence Lizard spends much of its time on tree trunks and fallen logs. Its color and pattern perfectly matches the bark of most trees within its range. This is one of the most common lizards in Illinois. They are quite arboreal in habits an will regularly climb trees to great heights. Feeds on insects, spiders, etc. Both sexes are often seen perched on rocks, logs, or stumps in wooded areas. Breeding males are especially conspicuous as they attempt to attract females by sitting atop rocks or stumps and methodically raising and lowering their body to show off the bright blue patches on the undersides. This is the only representative of its family in eastern North America.	**Natural History:** The Teiidae lizards are a common and diverse family in the southwestern United States, but they are represented in the east by this single species. The Teiidae lizards are famous among biologists because in some species there are no males and reproduction is accomplished by parthenogenesis (the development of unfertilized eggs into embryos). These speedy lizards are aptly named as they can reach a speed of up to 20 mph. They are active at higher temperatures than many reptiles and they will spend the first few minutes of the day basking in the sun to raise their body temperature. At night they retreat to an underground burrow dug into loose soil. Food is insects and other invertebrates.	**Natural History:** These lizards are often confused with snakes due to their lack of limbs. They are easily recognized as lizards however by the presences of ear openings and eyelids. When grasped these lizards will thrash about wildly and break off their tail. The tail is quite long, making up about two-thirds of their total length. The apparent fragility of these lizards and the shiny appearance of their skin has led to the common name "glass lizard." The highly specialized escape mechanism of breaking off the tail is shared with many other lizard species, as is the rare ability to regenerate a new tail. Regenerated tails never attain the original length. Like other Illinois lizards they prey on small invertebrates.

Class - **Reptilia** (reptiles)

Order - **Squamata** (snakes & lizards)

Suborder - **Lacertilia** (lizards)

Family - **Scincidae** (skinks)

Ground Skink	Five-lined Skink	Broad-headed Skink
Scincella lateralis	*Plestiodon fasciatus*	*Plestiodon laticeps*

Size: 3 to 5 inches.

Presumed range in Illinois

Abundance: Common in southern Illinois.

Variation: Color may vary from reddish to golden brown or chocolate brown. Color has a metallic quality. Some have small dark flecks on the back.

Size: 5 to 7 inches.

Presumed range in Illinois

Abundance: Very common.

Variation: Young are brightly colored with distinct pale yellow stripes and bright blue tails. Females resemble faded young. Males are plain brown above with reddish cheek patches.

Size: To 13 inches.

Presumed range in Illinois

Abundance: Fairly common.

Variation: Young have blue tails and yellow stripes and resemble Five-lined Skinks. In adults females have indistinct lines and males are brown with bright red cheeks.

Habitat: Dry upland woods and pine woodlands. Microhabitat consists of leaf litter and detritus on the forest floor. Avoids permanent wetlands.

Habitat: Most common in damp woodlands but also found in swamps and in drier upland areas. Patches of sunlit areas for basking is important.

Habitat: Mesic woodlands, wetland areas and also dry upland woods with moist microhabitat. Requires some open areas for sunning.

Breeding: Small clutches of 3 to 5 eggs is typical. May lay two clutches per year. Unlike other skinks, the female Ground Skink does not remain with the eggs until hatching.

Breeding: Eggs (6 to 12) are laid in May or early June in rotted logs, stumps, sawdust, mulch or other moisture retaining material. Female remains with eggs until hatching.

Breeding: Females will vigorously defend their eggs that are usually laid on the ground in a hollowed out depression beneath sheltering log or inside a hollow stump.

Natural History: These tiny ground dwellers dive quickly beneath leaf litter when approached and they are easily overlooked. Often, their presence is revealed by the rustling sound made as they forage through the dry leaves. Despite being rarely observed, they can be quite common in many areas. Foods are tiny insects and other small invertebrates living among the leaf litter on the forest floor. They also go by the name "Little Brown Skink." They are widespread throughout the southeastern half of America and are most common in the Deep South. They are the smallest lizard found in Illinois.

Natural History: The young of this species are strikingly colored with bright blue tails and they sometimes are mistaken by lay persons as being another species going by the name "Blue-tailed Skink." These common and well known lizards are fond of sunning on decks, porches, sidewalks and patios of homes in rural areas. They can often be found in suburban environments as well, particularly older neighborhoods with abundant large trees and shrubbery. They feed on a wide variety of insects, spiders and arthropods and they are a useful species in controlling invertebrate pests around the home. Like the male Broad-headed Skink, breeder male Five-lined Skinks develop bright red cheeks.

Natural History: These very large skinks are quite arboreal and often den in tree hollows many feet above the ground. These arboreal dens are used only during summer and hibernation takes place underground. In much of the southeast they are known as "Scorpion Lizards" and some believe the myth that they are dangerously venomous. Although they will bite if handled, they are totally harmless to humans. This is Illinois' largest lizard species and the largest individuals can barely exceed a foot in length. Insects are the main food but they will also eat small mammals such as baby mice.

THE REPTILES OF ILLINOIS

PART 2: SNAKES

Class - **Reptilia** (reptiles)
Order - **Squamata** (snakes & lizards)
Suborder - **Serpentes** (snakes)
Family - **Colubridae** (harmless snakes)

Racer *Coluber constrictor*	Coachwhip *Coluber flagellum*

Southern Black Racer Young Blue Racer

Size: Average about 4 feet. Maximum 6 feet.

Abundance: Very common.

Variation: 9 subspecies of *Coluber constrictor* are found across North America. 2 occur in Illinois, the Southern Black Racer and the Blue Racer. As a rule, the Blue Racer is much lighter in color. Young racers have a pattern of distinctive saddles (see inset photo).

Habitat: Racers are habitat generalists that may be found in most natural habitats within the state. They favor dry upland woods and overgrown fields. They are most common in ecotone areas.

Presumed range in Illinois

Size: Max of 8.5 feet.

Abundance: Rare.

Variation: Young have a blotched pattern similar to young racers (see inset photo of young racer).

Habitat: Uplands. Xeric woods, overgrown fields, brush.

Presumed range in Illinois

Breeding: Females lay about a dozen (from 5 to 20) eggs in rotted logs, humus, or frequently in sawdust piles around old sawmills. Eggs are laid in early summer and hatch in about two months. Like most egg layers, the Racer reproduces annually (some live bearing snakes breed only every other year).

Breeding: Breeds in late spring or early summer and female will deposit up to two dozen eggs. Eggs are laid in moist places beneath rocks, logs, etc.

Natural History: Racers are alert, active snakes that relentlessly prowl in search of almost any type of animal prey that can be swallowed. They will eat insects, amphibians, lizards, other snakes (including the young of venomous species), nestling birds, eggs, and small mammals. They are also adept at catching fish trapped in drying pools of streams and swamps. Unlike many snake species, the Racer is a diurnal animal and may be active even during the heat of the day in midsummer. They are apparently intelligent, curious snakes that will follow livestock and other large animals in hopes of capturing insects and other prey that may be disturbed by the larger animals passing. This is probably how they gained the reputation as aggressive snakes that will chase a human. Their name is appropriate as they are probably the on of the fastest snakes in Illinois and one of fastest in America. Quite speedy for a snake, they can reach a blazing 12 to 15 mph. Due to their catholic feeding habits and ability to adapt to a wide variety of habitats, the racers are among the most successful snakes in America. When threatened these snakes can use their speed to literally disappear into thick cover. When hard pressed out in the open they will climb into bushes or shrubs to escape. If captured they will bite vigorously and spray the captor with feces and musk.

Natural History: The Coachwhip is the longest snake species in Illinois. Most are about 6 feet when grown but the record is 8.5 feet. This is also perhaps the rarest snake in Illinois, found only in a single county (Monroe). They are widespread and common across the river in the Missouri Ozarks, and the Illinois population may represent a relict population that was "cut off" from the rest of the Ozark Plateau by a change in the flow of the Mississippi River. Like their relatives the racers, coachwhips are fast and agile snakes that hunt by sight during the day. Any animal small enough to be swallowed can be prey. Like their relatives the racers, these snakes are fierce fighters when captured.

Class - **Reptilia** (reptiles)
Order - **Squamata** (snakes & lizards)
Suborder - **Serpentes** (snakes)
Family - **Colubridae** (harmless snakes)

Midland Rat Snake *Pantherophis spiloides*	**Great Plains Rat Snake** *Pantherophis emoryi*

Size: Average 5 to 6 feet as adults. Record 8 feet 4 inches.

Abundance: Common

Presumed range in Illinois

Variation: These snakes exhibit some variation in the dorsal pattern of adults. Most show a blotched pattern on the back, but in some individuals this pattern is obscured by an overall dark coloration. The color between the dorsal blotches also varies. It may be cream or yellowish, brownish, or varying shades of gray. Specimens from the southern tip of the state typically exhibit distinct blothes. Those from farther north may be solid black. Young are light gray with charcoal blotches.

Habitat: Found in virtually all habitats within it range in Illinois, but most common in woodlands, woodland edges, and swamps. Also occurs in riparian habitats in grassland or agricultural regions. They are least common in areas of intensive agriculture or urbanized areas, but they can persists in urban regions if there is some cover and large trees.

Breeding: An egg layer that breeds in the spring and lays up to twenty (average about a dozen) eggs. Eggs are laid in old woodpecker holes or hollow limbs above ground or on the ground in rotted stumps, beneath logs, or any sheltered place where some form of humus is present to prevent dessication. Breed annually. Eggs are laid in early summer and hatch in late summer or early fall.

Natural History: This is the most arboreal snake species in Illinois and adults spend a great deal of time in trees. They often choose a regular den site in old woodpecker holes or hollows of trees and may be seen sunning with the forepart of the body emerged from a hole. Excellent climbers, they can ascend straight up a tree trunk using only the bark to gain a purchase with their belly scales. They will climb to great heights in search of bird nests. In addition to baby birds and eggs they will also eat rodents, squirrels, and other small mammals up to the size of a rabbit. They are also quite fond of barns and derelict buildings as a habitat. In Illinois, these large snakes are well known to rural dwellers and they often go by the nickname "Chicken Snake," a reference to their historical habit of raiding hen houses for eggs and chicks. They are also call "Cowsuckers" in some parts of the state. This name comes from the erroneous belief rural people once had that they would enter barns to suck milk from cows. In fact, they enter barns to hunt rodents.

Size: Max of 8.5 feet.

Abundance: Rare.

Presumed range in Illinois

Variation: Very little variation is exhibited by this species and the specimen shown above is typical. Even the young of this snake show the same color and pattern as adults.

Habitat: Dry upland woods, old fields, successional areas and most of all ecotone areas. A western species that exists in Illinois only along the Salem Plateau.

Breeding: Breeds in spriing and lays up to 30 eggs about a month later. Eggs hatch in about two months into 12-inch replicas of the adult. Young eat tiny vertebrates and some invertebrates.

Natural History: A Threatened Species in Illinois, the Great Plains Rat Snake is widespread across the Ozark Plateau, the southern Great Plains, and the desert southwest. Its occurrence in Illinois is likely the result of a historical shift in the flow of the Mississippi River that left a small slice of the Ozark Plateau on the Illinois side of the river. Food is mostly small mammals and ground nesting birds and their eggs. More nocturnal than the Midland Rat Snake.

Class - **Reptilia** (reptiles)

Order - **Squamata** (snakes & lizards)

Suborder - **Serpentes** (snakes)

Family - **Colubridae** (harmless snakes)

Eastern Fox Snake *Pantherophis vulpina*	**Bullsnake** *Pituophis catenifer*	**Flat-headed Snake** *Tantilla gracilis*

Size: Record length 5 feet 10 inches.

Presumed range in Illinois

Abundance: Fairly common in northern Illinois.

Variation: Shows little variation. Ground color varies somewhat, light brown to reddish. Juveniles are grayer in ground color.

Habitat: Inhabits woodlands, marshes, and prairies. Found in both mesic and xeric soils. Most common in ecotones where woodlands meet open fields.

Breeding: Breeding occurs in spring or early summer with egg deposition following fertilzation by about a month. Clutch size is about a dozen eggs, though it can be twice that amount.

Natural History: Interestingly, there is a population of Eastern Fox Snakes that exists around the western end if Lake Erie in Ohio that is disjunct by many miles from the main population to which Illinois Fox Snakes belong. This probably represents a "relict" population that was cut off from the rest of this snakes contiguous range by habitat changes at some time in the geological/climatological history of the region. In Illinois, these snakes are endemic to the northern half of the state, mostly in the Central US Plains Level II ecoregion. The food of this species is primarily endothermic vertebrates, mostly hatchling birds, bird eggs and small mammal such as mice and voles.

Size: Record length 8 feet 3 inches.

Presumed range in Illinois

Abundance: Fairly common in northwest Illinois.

Variation: Very little variation in Illinois specimens. Sexes are alike and young resemble adults. Males may grow slightly larger.

Habitat: Old fields and remant prairies are the primary habitat. Prefers xeric soils that are loose and friable and allow easier burrowing. Avoids mesic soils.

Breeding: The eggs are quite large and the baby bullsnakes are over a foot in length at hatching. Clutch size can be up to two dozen but is usually about half that amount.

Natural History: Also goes by the name "Gopher Snake," an appropriate name since they are apparently a major predator of the Plains Gopher. Like the Plains Gopher, the range of this species in Illinois probably originally coincided with the state's prairie habitats. In addition to gophers and ground squirrels the Bullsnake will eat any type of warm blooded prey that is small enough to be swallowed, which can include animals the size of tree squirrels and young rabbits. Small rodents probably make up the bulk of its diet but birds and their eggs are also eaten and this species will sometimes climb trees in search of bird nests. When cornered these snakes will hiss loudly and strike repeatedly.

Size: Record length 9.75 inches.

Presumed range in Illinois

Abundance: Very rare in Illinois.

Variation: No significant variation in Illinois. Sexes are alike and young are tiny replicas of the adult snakes.

Habitat: Macrohabitat in Illinois is wooded bluffs along the Mississippi River Valley. Microhabitat is mesic leaf litter or beneath rocks, logs, etc.

Breeding: Clutch size is small (2 to 4 eggs usually). Eggs are laid in a moist, protected environment such as beneath a rotten log or under a rock. Baby snakes are tiny!

Natural History: The genus *Tantilla* consists of at least 75 species of very small snakes that range from the southeastern United States to southern South America. These are the smallest snakes in America, and the Flat-headed Snake is the smallest snake in Illinois. They feed on small, soft-bodied invertebrates of all types. Most species that in the US live in the southwestern portion of the country and the bulk of the Flat-headed Snakes range is west of the Mississippi River. This is another species that owes its existence in Illinois to the wanderings of the Mississippi River, which changed course and left a small slice of the Ozark Plateau east of the river channel in what is today Illinois.

Class - **Reptilia** (reptiles)
Order - **Squamata** (snakes & lizards)
Suborder - **Serpentes** (snakes)
Family - **Colubridae** (harmless egg layers)

Common Kingsnake - *Lampropeltis getulus*		Prairie Kingsnake *Lampropeltis calligaster*
Speckled Kingsnake (formerly subspecies - *L. g. holbrookii*)	**Black Kingsnake** (formerly subspecies - *L. g. nigra*)	

Size: Average about 4 feet. Maximum 74 inches.

Abundance: Both subspecies are fairly common within their respective ranges.

Habitat: Mature woodlands, successional areas, weedy fields and edge habitats in uplands, bottom lands, swamps and marshes. Nearly all habitats within their range are utilized except areas where large amounts of land has been converted to row crops. They are absent as well from intensively urbanized regions.

Breeding: An annual breeder that lays 8 to 12 eggs in early summer. Eggs are laid in moisture retaining medium, often inside rotted stumps or logs. Eggs hatch in about 60 days. Young Black Kingsnakes have a chain-like pattern of white spots.

Presumed range in Illinois

Size: Record 58 inches.

Abundance: Fairly common.

Habitat: Open fields overgrown with weeds, brush and briers, but can also be found in woodland edges.

Breeding: Females produce about a dozen eggs that are laid underground.

Presumed range in Illinois

Variation: Two forms of Common Kingsnakes occur in Illinois. These two vary in the amount of white or cream colored spots on the body. Specimens from farther west have more light spotting, with individuals from the Mississippi Alluvial Plain typically have a spot on every dorsal scale (Speckled Kingsnake). Black Kingsnakes have fewer spots and older snakes from farther to the east may be nearly solid black. More recent research has resulted in the merging of the two subspecies in Illinois into a single species (the Black Kingsnake, *L. nigra*). Some experts question this merger as an error caused by inadequate sampling. Young specimens always have easily discernible light spots.

Variation: Two color phases occur in Illinois. A dark morph and a spotted morph (see photos above). Young specimens resemble the spotted morph. Dark morph specimens are usually older adults. Their are two other subspecies of *Lampropeltis calligaster* that are found in the southeastern United States and Florida.

Natural History: Common Kingsnakes are best known for their habit of killing and eating other snakes, including venomous species. These powerful constrictors are immune to the venom of pit vipers and will kill and eat any snake that is small enough to be swallowed whole. They also eat rodents, birds, lizards and baby turtles. They are mainly terrestrial in habits but have been found inside of standing dead trees several feet off the ground. They may be active both day and night but are mostly crepuscular and during hotter months tend to become more nocturnal. This species is a favorite captive pet of many reptile enthusiasts in America. After some time in captivity they will become quite tame and rarely bite. When the do bite however, they do so with very strong jaws! They are common in many areas of their range but like many other snakes they can be quite secretive. They will begin to emerge from hibernation in mid- to late April. The controversy between herpetologists as to whether to regard all Common Kingsnakes in Illinois as a single species is an example of the tug of war that exists in biology between the "splitters", who favor the subspecies concept; and the "groupers" who tend to regard subspecies as merely geographical color morphs.

Natural History: Three subspecies are found in the southern United States but only one of those occurs in Illinois (the Prairie Kingsnake – *L. c. calligaster*). This is a subterranean species that is only rarely seen above ground, usually in early spring. It feeds mostly on small mammals which it hunts in their underground burrows. They also eat bird eggs and nestling's, but they are a threat only to those that nest on or near the ground. Despite the fact that this is a fairly common snake in the southern half of Illinois, they are rarely observed due to their burrowing habits.

Class - **Reptilia** (reptiles)
Order - **Squamata** (snakes & lizards)
Suborder - **Serpentes** (snakes)
Family - **Colubridae** (harmless egg layers)

Milksnake - *Lampropeltis triangulum*		**Rough Green Snake** *Opheodrys aestivus*
Eastern Milksnake (formerly subspecies - *L. t. triangulum*)	**Red Milksnake** (formerly subspecies - *L. t. syspila*)	

Size: The record for the Eastern Milk is 52 inches. Red Milk record is 42 inches.

Abundance: Generally uncommon in Illinois, but both subspecies can be fairly common in some habitats within their range.

Variation: Milk Snakes are one of the most wide-ranging and diverse snake species in America. Experts once recognized as many as 8 subspecies in the US, and several more south of the Mexican border. The two pictures above show typical examples of Illinois' two forms. Some intermediate forms between the Eastern and Red Milk Snakes can be expected to be seen where their ranges meet across the central portion of the state.

Presumed range in Illinois

Size: Record is 3 feet, 11 inches.

Abundance: Fairly common.

Variation: This species is remarkably uniform in appearance. A very rare blue morph can occur with an abnormality omitting yellow pigments.

Presumed range in Illinois

Habitat: Eastern Milk Snakes are found in the northern third of Illinois. Like the rat snakes, Eastern Milk Snakes often enter barns and outbuilding in search of mice. Red Milk Snakes range in the southern third of Illinois and can be found in both dry woodlands and in wetland areas. Both subspecies are drawn to fallen logs and dead snags with loose bark as a microhabitat.

Habitat: Open fields, pastures, and edges of woods and fields. Often common in wetlands where there are low bushes and shrubs overhanging water. Found in the southern third of Illinois.

Breeding: Both forms are egg layers. Eggs are deposited in rotten logs, stumps, or beneath a flat rock. Eastern Milk lays from 6 to 24 eggs. Red Milks lay few eggs (from 2 or 3 up to about a dozen).

Breeding: 3 to 12 eggs are laid in late spring or early summer. The babies are slender, miniature replicas of the adult.

Natural History: The name comes from the habit these snakes have of entering stock barns in search of mice. Early settlers erroneously thought the snakes were there to suckle from the milk cow (that every pioneer family kept on the farm). These snakes eat many lizards and will also consume other, smaller snakes. Reptile eggs may also be eaten along with amphibians and small mammals like mice. Like the Common Kingsnakes, the Milk Snakes enjoy a resistance to snake venom and baby copperheads, cottonmouths or rattlesnakes may be eaten by large adults. Young snakes feed mostly on skinks. Additionally, eggs and nestling's of ground nesting birds may be a food item on occasion. Both races of milk snake found in Illinois are primarily nocturnal snakes that usually remain hidden during daylight hours beneath rocks, logs, and other woodland debris. They are thus not as readily observed as many other snakes in the state. A recent evaluation of the Milk Snake complex by herpetologists regards both the above snakes as Eastern Milk Snakes and disregards subspecies status for the forms found in Illinois. Some herpetologists do not accept this new designation and retain the concept of subspecies in Illinois populations. Populations of this snake in central Illinois are aptly described as "intergrades" and are intermediate in morphology between the two subspecies.

Natural History: Rough Green Snakes live in dense bushes and shrubs where their bright green color renders them invisible. Arthropods of many varieties are their prey. Food includes spiders, caterpillars, crickets, and grasshoppers to name a few of their favorites. These snakes are sometimes called "grass snakes" in reference to their bright green coloration. There is a widespread belief that they have become extremely rare and endangered. In fact their populations are probably fairly stable, although they are certainly vulnerable to habitat destruction wrought by modern agricultural practices as well as the widespread use of insecticides.

Class - **Reptilia** (reptiles)		
Order - **Squamata** (snakes & lizards)		
Suborder - **Serpentes** (snakes)		
Family - **Colubridae** (harmless egg layers)	Family - **Dipsadidae** (rear-fanged snakes)	

Smooth Green Snake *Opheodrys vernalis*	**Mudsnake** *Farencia abacura*	**Wormsnake** *Carphophis amoenus*

Size: Average 18 inches. Record 31 inches.	Presumed range in Illinois	**Size:** Average 3 to 4 feet. Maximum 6 feet.	Presumed range in Illinois	**Size:** Average about 8 inches. Maximum 11.	Presumed range in Illinois
Abundance: Uncommon in Illinois.		**Abundance:** Uncommon in Illinois.		**Abundance:** Fairly common.	
Habitat: Open fields, pastures, meadows and edges of lakes, ponds, or marshes. Generally a snake of open habitats but may be found in open woods.		**Habitat:** This is a snake of swamps, marshes and wetland areas. In Illinois they are found exclusively in the floodplains of the southern tip of the state.		**Habitat:** Found in a variety of habitats, but mostly in woodlands. Its microhabitat is beneath the leaf litter, rocks, logs, old stumps, etc.	

Variation: No variation.	**Variation:** No variation in Illinois.	**Variation:** No variation in Illinois.
Breeding: Clutch size is relatively small and may be as few as three or four eggs or as high as a dozen. Egg laying has been reported from June to August.	**Breeding:** Lays very large clutches of eggs (the record is over 100). Eggs are place in hollows of floating logs or stumps above the water line.	**Breeding:** From 1 to 12 eggs are laid in late June or July and hatch in 2 or 3 months. Hatchlings are only about 3 inches in length.
Natural History: Like the similar Rough Green Snake the Smooth Green Snake often goes by the common name "Grass Snake" or "Green Grass Snake." These small snakes eat a variety of invertebrate prey including slugs, spiders, millipedes, crickets, grasshoppers and caterpillars, to name a few. This diet makes them exceptionally vulnerable to insecticides and widespread applications of chemicals on agricultural fields may pose a serious threat to this handsome little snake. Unlike the larger Rough Green Snake that climbs into bushes and small trees, the Smooth Green Snake tends to stay close to the ground. The range of the two Green Snakes in Illinois is mutually exclusive. They are easily identified by the presence of keeled scales (Rough Greensnake), or the absence of keels (Smooth Greensnake).	**Natural History:** Few people who are not actively seeking this species will ever see one. Living among the tangled mass of vegetation and plant roots in the muck of swamps and marshes, they prey primarily on several species of aquatic vertebrates including frogs and fish. But it specializes in feeding on a number of large, totally aquatic salamanders that inhabit the swamps and floodplains of the deep south (i.e. sirens and amphiumas). The tail of this snake terminates in a stiff, sharp spine that is erroneously believed to be able to sting. Some also believe these snakes to be the mythical "hoop snake," that according to legend can take its tail into its mouth forming a hoop and then roll down hills. This fable also sometimes includes the myth that the spine on the tail is used as a deadly stinger.	**Natural History:** A confirmed burrower that lives under leaf litter, logs, rocks and even man made debris such as old boards, discarded shingles, etc. Feeds almost exclusively on earthworms, but some experts list tiny soft-bodied invertebrates such as insect larva or termites as food. The aptly named worm snakes do in fact resemble earthworms. Their tiny, conical head and smooth glossy scales help to facilitate burrowing through tiny tunnels created by earthworms, termites or insect larva. These snakes are often turned up in backyards by people gardening, raking leaves, or doing other types of yard work. Like other Dipsadidae snakes, Wormsnakes possess tiny grooved teeth in the rear of the jaw that serve to introduce a mild venom into the bodies of prey. These tiny teeth are too small to penetrate human skin and they are harmless to man.

Class - **Reptilia** (reptiles)
Order - **Squamata** (snakes & lizards)
Suborder - **Serpentes** (snakes)
Family - **Dipsadidae** (rear-fanged snakes)

Eastern Hognose Snake *Heterodon platirhinos*	**Plains Hognose Snake** *Heterodon nasicus*

Black Morph

Spotted Morph

Orange Morph

Size: Averages about 2.5 feet. Maximum 45 inches.

Presumed range in Illinois

Abundance: Generally uncommon in Illinois. It may be fairly common however in regions of dry, sandy, uplands.

Habitat: Hognose Snakes are most common in habitats with sandy soils which facilitate easy burrowing. They tend to be more common in sandy creek bottoms and river valleys. But can be found in upland woods and fields with less friable soils.

Breeding: Hognose snake breed in early spring and lay up to two dozen eggs. Nests are probably in an underground chamber in sandy soil. Young snakes are about 8 inches in length and always have a spotted pattern. Babies are grayish brown with well defined dark gray or black blotches.

Size: Record length 3 feet.

Abundance: Fairly common.

Habitat: Prefers more xeric soil conditions than the Eastern Hognose Snake.

Breeding: Clutch size is around 8 to 10 eggs that are laid in early summer and hatch in late summer/early fall.

Variation: Highly variable (see photos above). Individuals range from solid black to uniform olive green. Others may be variously spotted or blotched with dark saddles on a yellowish or orange background. Often one color morph will be dominant in a given area. The young always exhibit a spotted pattern.

Variation: Compared to the Eastern Hognose, this species exhibits very little variation among adults. Even juveniles will resemble the specimen above.

Natural History: The Eastern Hognose Snake is famous for the elaborate performance it puts on when threatened. First, they will spread the neck like a cobra (hence the nickname "Spreading Adder"), and with the mouth wide open they will strike repeatedly. They always intentionally miss with the strike and never bite even when picked up and handled. The initial "cobra display" is always accompanied by loud hissing. When their complicated bluff fails to deter the threat they will roll onto their backs, stick out their tongue and give a convincing impression of being dead. They do have one behavioral trait that betrays their antics however. If rolled onto their belly while they are feigning death they will immediately flip over onto their backs once again! Their primary food is frogs and toads. They possess enlarged teeth in the back of the upper jaw that are used to puncture the bodies of toads that have gulped air and inflated themselves in an attempt to become to large to be swallowed. The saliva of these snakes is mildly toxic, but is not considered to be a threat to humans. The food is almost entirely toads and frogs, making them one of the more specialized feeders among Illinois snakes. Salamanders are reported to have been found in the stomachs of a few individuals as well. Mice are also sometimes listed as prey items. Anecdotal evidence suggests they may be declining. Their habit of feeding on toads and frogs almost exclusively may make them vulnerable to insecticides, as frog and toads are primarily insect eaters and poisoning through secondary ingestion is a possibility.

Natural History: As its name implies this is a snake of the plains. Except for a few disjunct populations occurring in Tallgrass Prairies in the Midwest (including in Illinois), the range of this snake coincides almost exactly with the Mixed and Short Grass Prairies of the the Great Plains Province (see Figure 2). This snake is more catholic in its diet and will regularly include reptile eggs, birds, and small mammals along with the more typical amphibian foods. Like the Eastern Hognose the Western has enlarged rear teeth (fangs) and a mildly toxic saliva that may help to subdue prey. This species is less likely to "play dead" but will sometimes exhibit that behavior. All types of hognose snakes have a specialized rostral scale on the snout that assists in burrowing. The snout is slighty upturned, thus the name.

Class - **Reptilia** (reptiles)

Order - **Squamata** (snakes & lizards)

Suborder - **Serpentes** (snakes)

Family - **Dipsadidae** (rear-fanged snakes)	Family - **Natricidae** (harmless live bearing snakes)	
Ringneck Snake *Diadophis punctatus*	**Kirtland's Snake** *Clonophis kirtlandii*	**Lined Snake** *Tropidoclonion lineatum*

Size: Average about 14 inches. Max 2 feet.	Presumed range in Illinois	**Size:** Record length is 24 inches.	Presumed range in Illinois	**Size:** Record length is 21.5 inches.	Presumed range in Illinois
Abundance: Common.		**Abundance:** Rare in Illinois.		**Abundance:** Very rare in Illinois.	
Variation: A highly variable species with twelve subspecies nationwide, three of these subspecies can be found in Illinois.		**Variation:** There is no significant variation in Illinois and no subspecies. In fact, most specimens are remarkably similar.		**Variation:** Ground color varies from brown to olive to grayish. Dark spots bordering pale dorsal vary in prominence.	

Habitat: A woodland species that lives in rotted logs, stumps, and beneath rocks and leaf litter on the forest floor.	**Habitat:** Usually associates with moist environments both in woodlands and fields. Also swamps and marshes.	**Habitat:** Native to prairie regions, in Illinois today uses old fields, vacant lots in urban areas.
Breeding: Lays up to a dozen eggs, usually fewer in rotted logs or other moisture retaining places. Young are about 5 inches long at hatching.	**Breeding:** Live-bearer. Litters may be as small as 3 or 4 or as many as 10 or 15. Young are born in late summer to early fall.	**Breeding:** Live-born young number 5 to 10. Babies are quite small, usually only about 4 inches in length. Breeds in late summer and births a year later.
Natural History: Ringneck snakes are are often uncovered by humans beneath boards, stones, leaves, or other debris. The distinctive yellow or cream-colored collar around the neck readily identifies them, and even those unfamiliar with reptiles have no trouble recognizing this species. They feed mostly on soft-bodied insects and other invertebrates. Earthworms are a favorite food. When threatened they will often hold aloft the tightly curled up tip of the underside of their bright yellow tail to distract a predator. This defense mechanism is probably designed to direct an attackers attention away from the vulnerable head to the less vulnerable tail. Despite having enlarged grooved teeth in the rear of the jaw for envenoming small prey, they are harmless to man.	**Natural History:** The Kirtland's Snake is an enigmatic species. It is found in several widely dispersed areas in the the Midwest and populations are apparently highly fragmented. This is usually the sign of a species in decline and indeed the Kirtland's Snake does appear to be disappearing. It probably once ranged across most of the glaciated regions of the Midwest. It is regarded as a Threatened Species in Illinois. It apparently is at least as common in urban areas as it is in more natural habitats within its range. Earthworms and slugs are listed as its primary prey. It is mostly a nocturnal hunter and hides by day beneath boards, stones or other structures. When threatened these snakes will flatten the body to such an extreme as to create a ribbonlike appearance to the snake.	**Natural History:** This species has a long gestation period than can be as much as a year. Like many species indigenous to the prairie, the Lined Snake may have historically been a much more common animal in Illinois. Today they are most common in places like Kansas, Oklahoma, and Texas where ample praire habitat remains. The range in Illinois consists of several disjunct populaitons that are many miles apart. Many small snakes relish earthworms, but the Lined Snake apparently eats them almost exclusively. In appearance the Lined Snake closely resembles the garter and ribbon snakes of the genus *Thamnophis,* but its exact relationship to those snakes in unknown. The behavior of curling the end of the tail when threatened is reminiscent of the Ringneck Snakes.

Class - **Reptilia** (reptiles)

Order - **Squamata** (snakes & lizards)

Suborder - **Serpentes** (snakes)

Family - **Natricidae** (harmless live-bearing snakes)

Brown Snake *Storeria dekayi*	**Red-bellied Snake** *Storeria occipitomaculata*	**Smooth Earth Snake** *Virginai valeriae*

Size: Average 12 inches, record 19.	Presumed range in Illinois	**Size:** 10 to 12 inches, record 16.	Presumed range in Illinois	**Size:** Usually around 10 inches. Record 15.	Presumed range in Illinois
Abundance: Very common.		**Abundance:** Common.		**Abundance:** Fairly common.	
Variation: None in Illinois.		**Variation:** None in Illinois		**Variation:** None in Illinois.	
Habitat: Woodlands, grassy fields, and wetlands. Found even in urban areas, especially vacant lots littered with old boards or scrap tin.		**Habitat:** Mostly found in wooded areas, in both lowland and uplands. They can also be found in fields around the edges of woods.		**Habitat:** Smooth Earth Snakes are basically a forest species but they can also be found in open fields near forests and edge areas.	

Breeding: Gives birth to 5 to 20 young (rarely more, as many as 40). Baby snakes are about 3 inches long with the girth of a matchstick.	**Breeding:** Live-bearer. Litters number from 5 to 15. Newborn babies are only about three inches in length an no bigger around than a matchstick.	**Breeding:** These snakes are live bearers that give birth to from 4 to 12 young. The young snakes resemble the adults and measure about three inches.
Natural History: This diminutive snake is often found in vacant lots of large cities and towns, where it hides beneath boards, trash, even small pieces of cardboard. It feeds primarily on earthworms and slugs, but also reportedly eats insects, amphibians eggs, and tiny fishes. Brown Snakes are known to hibernate communally, an odd behavior for a tiny snake that should have no trouble finding adequate crevices in which to spend the colder months. These snakes are sometimes called "Dekay's Snake," in honor of an early American naturalist. These little snakes make interesting pets and will readily eat earthworms in captivity.	**Natural History:** Redbelly Snakes usually remain hidden by day beneath rocks, logs, etc., and emerge at night to hunt insects and small soft-bodied invertebrates such as earthworms, slugs, beetle larva, isopods, etc. These snakes sometimes exhibit a peculiar behavior when threatened. If voiding of feces and musk fails to discourage a handler, they will curl their upper lip in an strange expression of apparent ferocity. It is a purely fallacious display however as their tiny teeth could never penetrate human skin. Although these little snakes are widespread across much of Illinois, they are less common than many other small snake species.	**Natural History:** The Smooth Earth Snake is a tiny, docile snakes that could not manage to bite a human even if they were so inclined, which they are not. They have tiny heads, even for their size, and thus their food consists of small invertebrates. Insects, snails, and mostly, earthworms. These are secretive little serpents that sometimes emerge to prowl about on the surface after summer rains. Otherwise they are easily overlooked except by herpetologists who know where to find them beneath logs, stones, or amid accumulated humis on the forest floor. As with other small snakes that burrow beneath detritus on the floor of woodlands, these little snakes are occasionally turned up by rural residents as they rake mulch from flower beds in the spring.

Class - **Reptilia** (reptiles)		

Order - **Squamata** (snakes & lizards)		

Suborder - **Serpentes** (snakes)		

Family - **Natricidae** (harmless live-bearing snakes)		

Mississippi Green Water Snake *Nerodia cyclopian*	**Plainbelly Water Snake** *Nerodia erythrogaster*	**Diamondback Water Snake** *Nerodia rhombifer*

Young

Northern Copperbelly Water Snake

Mississippi Green Water Snake	**Plainbelly Water Snake**	**Diamondback Water Snake**
Size: Record length 50 inches.	**Size:** Record length 45 inches.	**Size:** Average 4 feet. Record 69 inches.
Abundance: Rare. Threatened in Illinois.	**Abundance:** Fairly common.	**Abundance:** Fairly common.
Variation: Little variation exists in this snake in Illinois. Young specimens do tend to be lighter in color and old adults may have dorsal markings obscured.	**Variation:** Two subspecies in Illinois. The **Yellow-bellied Water** Snake (*N. e. flaviventris*) and the **Copperbelly Water Snake** (*N.e. neglecta*).	**Variation:** The dorsal pattern is more evident on young snakes and freshly molted specimens. Females are grow much larger than males.

Presumed range in Illinois

Presumed range in Illinois

Yellowbelly light gray

Copperbelly dark gray

Presumed range in Illinois

Mississippi Green Water Snake	**Plainbelly Water Snake**	**Diamondback Water Snake**
Breeding: The 15 to 20 young are born in late summer and are about 6 to 8 inches long at birth,	**Breeding:** Large females will produce litters numbering over forty babies. young are born in late summer or fall.	**Breeding:** Produces very large litters of up to 30 or 40 babies in late summer. Babies are 8 to 10 inches long.
Habitat: These snakes are totally aquatic and inhabit large bodies of water. Large lakes, oxbows, rivers and the mouths of larger creeks. In Illinois they occur only in a thin strip of the Mississippi Alluvial Plain in southern Illinois.	**Habitat:** Although all subspecies of this snake are primarily aquatic, they are less tied to water than any of their kin and they will often wander far from permanent water. They are found in creeks, rivers, lakes, ponds, etc.	**Habitat:** Diamondback Water Snakes frequent most aquatic habitats within their range except for small ponds and smaller streams. They show a definite preference for large swamps and marshes, lakes and reservoirs.
Natural History: Primarily nocturnal in habits in summer. In the spring it may be seen sunning by day atop drift, beaver lodges, or branches overhanging water. Green Water Snakes feed mainly on fish but they may also eat frogs and salamanders. This is a rare snake in Illinois and they are seen in the state only in the lower Mississippi Alluvial Plain in Alexander and Union counties. They are much more piscivorous than most other water snakes and show a definite preference for large bodies of water. Unlike many other water snakes that sometimes wander far overland, the Mississippi Green rarely ventures far from water.	**Natural History:** These snakes feed primarily on aquatic and semi-aquatic vertebrates such as frogs, toads, salamanders, and fish. They are active both day and night in the spring but are more nocturnal or crepuscular during hot weather. Like many other water snakes, they are fierce fighters if caught and will bite and smear the attacker with foul smelling feces and a pungent musk. In Illinois, the Yellow-bellied is found mostly in the Coastal Plain and it may be quite common many lowland areas. The Copperbelly on the other hand is an uncommon animal that may be in decline in much of its range. The range of the Copperbelly in Illinois coincides closely with Wabash River drainage.	**Natural History:** The water snakes have a reputation among herpetologists for their pugnacious attitudes and none is more deserving of that reputation than the Diamondback Water Snake. When captured they will thrash wildly and bite savagely and repeatedly. The bite, though harmless, can be painful and may bleed profusely due to an anti-coagulant property in the saliva. These snakes attain an impressive size and can be very heavy bodied. A large female may have a girth the size of a man's wrist. Like all water snakes they are mainly nocturnal during hot summer months. But in the early spring they can be very obvious as they bask on logs, beaver lodges, stumps, and branches.

Class - **Reptilia** (reptiles)
Order - **Squamata** (snakes and lizards)
Suborder - **Serpentes** (snakes)
Family - **Natricidae** (harmless live-bearing snakes)

Common Watersnake - *Nerodia sipedon*		Queen Snake
Northern Watersnake *N. s. sipedon*	**Midland Water Snake** *N. s. pleuralis*	**Queen Snake** *Regina septemvittata*

Size: Average about 3.5 feet. Record is 59 inches (Midland Water Snake).

Abundance: Both subspecies are common within their respective ranges.

Habitat: These snakes are aquatic animals but they do sometimes wander away from water in search of a mate or as a result of natural dispersal. They are very fond of small farm ponds or small streams as habitat, but they can also be found in large lakes and in swamps and marshes.

Breeding: Females may mate with several males in the spring. Birthing occurs in late summer to early fall. Live born young can number two or three dozen, but the largest females may produce nearly 100 babies. Young females may have as few as 6 or 8.

Presumed range in Illinois

Size: Average 2 feet. Maximum 3 feet.

Abundance: Uncommon in Illinois.

Habitat: Creeks with flat stones are a favorite habitat They will also occupy lakes or larger streams.

Breeding: Queen Snakes arelive-bearers that will produce up to a dozen young per litter.

Variation: There are four subspecies nationwide and two can be found in Illinois. Both vary somewhat in color, ranging from brown, tan, reddish brown, or gray-brown. They will always exhibit a pattern of darker bands across the back that contrasts with the lighter color between the bands. In the Northern Water Snake, the light spaces between the bands are much narrower than in the Midland Water Snake.

Variation: There are no subspecies of the Queen snake and there is very little variation among specimens. Even the young snakes are remakably similar and are miniature replicas of the adult.

Natural History: Northern Water Snakes adapt well to man-made environments like large lake impoundments where they can thrive in the rip-rap of dams and levees. Frogs and fish are the two favorite food items for these snakes. Around man-made impoundments they can become very numerous near boat docks and fishing areas where they scavenge on dead or dying fish and fish heads left behind by fishermen. Like most other water snake species, they are fond of basking in the sun atop debris and limbs overhanging water. As with other water snakes they are commonly confused with the venomous Cottonmouth, even in areas of the state where the Cottonmouth does not occur (see page 163). Their dorsal pattern of dark brownish bands on a lighter brown background also causes them to be mistaken for another venomous species, the Copperhead. But Copperheads are terrestrial snakes that only rarely enter water. Thus snakes seen in the water are almost invariably not Copperheads, but Northern/Midland Water Snakes.

Natural History: The Queen Snake is a specialized feeder that preys almost exclusively on recently molted, soft-bodied crayfish. In one study, over 95 percent of stomach contents examined contained crayfish (Branson and Baker 1974). As a result their distribution is limited to areas where this common crustacean is abundant. They are often found hiding beneath flat stones in creeks throughout their range. Like other water snakes they may be seen basking from limbs and branches overhanging water.

Class - **Reptilia** (reptiles)
Order - **Squamata** (snakes & lizards)
Suborder - **Serpentes** (snakes)
Family - **Natricidae** (harmless live-bearing snakes)

Graham's Crayfish Snake *Regina grahamii*	**Plains Garter Snake** *Thamnophis radix*	**Eastern Garter Snake** *Thamnophis sirtalis*

Size: Average 2 feet. Record 47 inches.

Presumed range in Illinois

Abundance: Uncommon in Illinois.

Habitat: Aquatic. Prefers lentic waters over flowing streams. Found in lakes, swamps and backwaters, marshes and streams with low flow rates.

Size: Record length 43 inches.

Presumed range in Illinois

Abundance: Fairly common in northern Illinois.

Habitat: Prairies primarily and historically. In Illinois today uses vacant lots, neglected fields, pastures, meadows, marshes and to a lesser degree farmlands.

Size: Record just under 41 inches.

Presumed range in Illinois

Abundance: Very common statewide.

Habitat: The dorsal pattern is more evident on young snakes and freshly molted specimens. Females are grow much larger than males.

Breeding: Gives birth to about a dozen (as many as 20) young in late summer.

Variation: None.

Natural History: The range of the Graham's Crayfish Snake is enigmatic. They are widespread in the central and southern plains and in the lower Mississippi River Valley and the western Gulf Coastal Plain. Their range also includes much of the western portion of what was once the great Tallgrass Prairie region. But their range today is fragmented with many small pockets of disjunct populations and they are not found in some regions where their absence is not easily explained. Probably they were once more continuously distributed and have retreated from many areas due to alterations or total loss of suitable local habitats. Their food is ectothermic vertebrates including fish and frogs, but mainly soft bodied crayfish. In many ways they are a western version of the Queen Snake, but instead of inhabiting flowing streams they live quiet, still waters.

Breeding: Live-born young can number over two dozen, but usually fewer.

Variation: Some variation (see below).

Natural History: Yet another prairie species whose range extends eastward from the Great Plains into historical prairie regions of Illinois and northern Indiana. Very widespread across the Great Plains region from Oklahoma to the prairie provinces of Canada. This species is well adapted to the cold environments of the northern plains and they are among northern Illinois earliest snakes to emerge in the spring. Prey species are typical of the Garter Snake/Ribbon Snake clan; i.e. frogs, toads, insects and earthworms. Some experts recognize an eastern subspecies (*T. r. radix*) ranging from Indiana across Illinois and into eastern Iowa; and a western subspecies (*T. r. haydeni*) throughout the rest of the range in the Great Plains region. The differences between the two are very slight and today most experts consider them to be conspecific.

Breeding: Live-bearer that gives birth to enormous litters of up to 60 babies.

Variation: Some variation (see below).

Natural History: There are two subspecies of Garter Snake in Illinois. The Eastern Garter (*T. s. sirtalis*) ranges across more than 90 percnet of the state but is replaced in the vicinity of Lake Michigan by the Chicago Garter Snake (*T. s. semifasciatus*). The Chicago Garter has the lateral stripes interrupted on the neck by black bars, otherwise the two are very similar. Garter snakes are non-specialized feeders that will eat insects, earthworms, frogs, toads,, salamanders, fish and rarely small mammals such as baby mice or voles. Their name is derived from their resemblance to the old fashioned "garters" that were used to hold up men's socks. The name has been widely familiarized to "Garden Snake" in many places. Still an appropriate name, as they are often seen in rural gardens. This is a ubiquitous species that may be found in both wilderness or urban regions. They are most common in edge habitats.

Class - **Reptilia** (reptiles)
Order - **Squamata** (snakes & lizards)
Suborder - **Serpentes** (snakes)
Family - **Natricidae** (harmless live-bearing snakes)

Western Ribbon Snake *Thamnophis proximus*	**Eastern Ribbon Snake** *Thamnophis sauritus*

<table>
<tr><td>Size: 20 to 30 inches. Record 39.</td><td rowspan="3">Presumed range in Illinois
</td><td>Size: 18 to 28 inches. Record 38.</td><td rowspan="3">Presumed range in Illinois
</td></tr>
<tr><td>Abundance: Fairly common where found in IL.</td><td>Abundance: Uncommon.</td></tr>
<tr><td>Variation: The color of the stripes may vary from greenish to bluish, yellow, or orange. There are 4 subspecies but only (T. p. proximus) occurs in Illinois.</td><td>Variation: A total of 3 subspecies are found in the eastern United States. The Eastern Ribbon Snake (T. s. sauritus), shown above, is found in Illinois</td></tr>
</table>

Habitat: Lives in semi-aquatic habitats, i.e. wet meadows, swamps, marshes, and edges of streams and lakes. Also damp, weedy fields in bottoms.	**Habitat:** Occupies aquatic and semi-aquatic habitats from swamps and marshes to streams, stream edges and mesic bottomland woodlands.
Breeding: Live bearing. Gives birth to between 10 and 20 young. Births usually occur in August.	**Breeding:** 10 to 20 young is typical. Birthing occurs in late summer following breeding in the early spring.
Natural History: Frogs, toads, fish and lizards are listed as some to this snakes prey. During certain times of the year tadpoles and the recently transformed young of frogs and toads are a primary food item. During periods of drought these snakes will gorge on small fishes trapped in drying pools. Insects and earthworms are also important in the diet. The range of the Western Ribbon Snake lies mostly west of the Mississippi River and this snake is most common in Illinois mainly in the narrow strip of land bordering the Mississippi River (the Mississippi Alluvial Plain). Ribbon Snakes are extremely elongated, slender-bodied snakes and they have exceptionally long tails.	**Natural History:** Eastern Ribbon Snakes are both diurnal and nocturnal in habits. They often climb into low shrubs and vines. They are alert snakes that hunt by both smell and with their excellent eyesight that is attuned to quick movements of fleeing prey. Food items include insects, frogs, and minnows, crayfish and tadpoles. Although these snakes are nearly always found near water, they tend to live near the edges of wetlands rather than within them. In many ways the ribbon snakes occupy a niche that is halfway between an aquatic and a terrestrial species. Common Kingsnakes are one of their major predators, along with many other carnivorous vertebrates.

Class - **Reptilia** (reptiles)
Order - **Squamata** (snakes & lizards)
Suborder - **Serpentes** (snakes)
Family - **Crotalidae** (pit vipers)

Eastern Copperhead - *Agkistrodon controtrix*		Northern Cottonmouth *Agkistrodon piscivorous*
Southern Morph (formerly subspecies - *A. c. controtrix*)	**Northern Morph** (formerly subspecies - *A. c. mokasen*)	

Size: Average 2.5 to 3 feet. The record is 58 inches.

Abundance: Can be fairly common in suitable habitat, especially in the mountains.

Habitat: Copperheads are primarily woodland animals, but they do wander into overgrown fields and thickets where rodent prey is abundant. Edge areas and small woodland openings choked with briers, saplings, and weeds are prime habitat. They will inhabit both upland and lowland regions, but avoid permanently wet areas such as swamps and marshes. Steep, wooded bluffs adjoining overgrown fields are a favorite habitat.

Presumed range in Illinois

Size: Record 50 inches

Abundance: Fairly common.

Habitat: A highly aquatic species, the cottonmouth inhabits mostly swamps and marshes, but they can also be found in creeks, lakes, or ponds.

Presumed range in Illinois

Variation: Illinois specimens can be quite variable in color but always exhibit the same pattern of dark bands on a lighter background. The background color is some shade of brown, tan, orange or grayish with darker brown or gray-brown hourglass shaped crossbands across the back. Most specimens from Southern Illinois resemble the photo above on the left. The specimen on the right is typical of snakes of the northern subspecies. Until recently the two color morphs were regarded as distinct subspecies called Southern and Northern Copperheads. Some experts still consider that to be the case. Baby copperheads are identical to the adults but have a bright yellow tail tip that is wriggled to lured prey.

Variation: Adults vary from uniform brown to nearly black. Freshly molted specimens often show a pattern of dark bands on an olive or grayish background. Young have a strongly banded pattern and and resembles their cousin the Copperhead. Like the Copperhead young Cottonmouths have a bright yellow tail tip used to lure prey.

Breeding: Breeds in spring or in the fall. From 4 to 12 young are born in late August through September. The resources required to produce a litter by a live-bearing snake are considerable and can be quite stressful on the female. Thus many copperheads likely produce litters only ever other year.

Breeding: Produces 3 to 12 babies in late August or early September. Unlike the copperhead, female cottonmouths may reproduce annually.

Natural History: Like most pit vipers copperheads are primarily nocturnal, especially during hotter months. In early spring and fall they may be seen abroad during the day. Young snakes eat some invertebrates and small vertebrates such as young frogs, lizards and small snakes. Larger snakes prey on small mammals (mice and voles), and the young of ground nesting birds. Insects are also taken, especially cicadas and during years when the Periodic Cicada emerges by the millions they will stuff themselves with these high protein, high fat insects. In areas of undisturbed habitat these can be common snakes but they are secretive and discreet. Because they are the state's most common venomous snake, they account for more snakebites than any other venomous snake in Illinois. Fortunately, their venom is not highly toxic and deaths from copperhead bites are extremely rare.

Natural History: The name "Cottonmouth" is derived from the habit these snakes have of gaping open the mouth when threatened. The inside of the mouth is white, hence the name. Cottonmouths attain a large size and have powerful venom that is capable of killing a human, but most victims of their bite do survive. Frogs, fish, salamanders, and small mammals are the main prey. Carrion is also eaten at times.

Class - **Reptilia** (reptiles)

Order - **Squamata** (snakes & lizards)

Suborder - **Serpentes** (snakes)

Family - **Crotalidae** (pit vipers)

Timber Rattlesnake *Crotalus horridus*	Eastern Massassauga *Sistrurus catenatus*

Size: Averages about 4 feet. Record length is 6 feet 2 inches. Few Illinois specimens will exceed 5 feet.

Presumed range in Illinois

Abundance: Uncommon to rare in Illinois. Regarded as a Threatened Species by IDNR.

Variation: Timber Rattlesnakes can be highly variable. Yellow and brown "light morphs," along with very dark (nearly black) morphs occur in some regions of their range in the Appalachians. A southern form from the coastal plain of the southern United States was once regarded as a distinct subspecies known as the "Canebrake" Rattlesnake. Illinois specimens will usually resemble the photos above.

Size: Record 39.5 inches.

Presumed range in Illinois

Abundance: Very rare in Illinois.

Variation: Varies from very dark (nearly black) to light, smokey gray. In some regions ground color may be brownish, tan, or reddish.

Habitat: As their name implies Timber Rattlesnakes are forest animals. Within their woodland habitats they are most common in upland areas with rocky outcrops and talus slopes. They inhabit both mature forests and second growth woodlands, as well as forest edges. In some areas they may occur in bottomland woods as well, but usually only when the lowland areas are in proximity to ridges and uplands.

Habitat: Wetlands primarily. Inhabits swamps, marshes, wooded floodplains. Historically probably ranged across much of glaciated Illinois but has been extirpated from most areas in the state.

Breeding: Timber Rattlesnakes in Illinois typically breed in August and the females delay implantation of embryos until the following spring. The young snakes are then born in late summer or early fall, about a year after breeding. Females will produce young only every other year. Average litter is 6 to 12.

Breeding: Young are born in late July, August or September. 5 or 6 babies is common but can be as many as 14. Babies are 8 to 10 inches in length. for

Natural History: This is one of the largest rattlesnake species in America and their bite is quite capable of killing a human. Fortunately they are peace loving animals that only strike as a last resort. Timber Rattlesnake populations are declining in many areas of their range, including in Illinois and they are now regarded as Threatened Species in the state of Illinois. Though they are still present in healthy numbers in some areas of the Appalachians and the southern United States, they are less numerous than in earlier times and are now rare or extirpated from much of their former range. Today they are absent from many areas of their former range in Illinois. As a result, the Illinois Department of Natural Resources now protects them against exploitation and wanton slaughter. These large snakes feed mostly on mammals, with squirrels and chipmunks being a favorite food. They are known to lie in ambush beside fallen logs that are frequently traveled by ground foraging chipmunks and squirrels. Almost any type of small mammal can be food and many types of mice and voles are eaten. Nestlings of ground dwelling birds can also be prey. Mice are probably the main food for the young and a even a newborn Timber Rattlesnake is large enough to swallow a young mouse. This is a dangerously venomous snake, but the treat they pose to the average outdoorsman is negligible.

Natural History: The name Massassauga comes from the Chippewa Indian name for a marshy area at the mouth of a river. Which is one of this snakes primary natural habitats. During summer months they may leave the sanctity of the swamp or marsh and venture into nearby fields or uplands. Food items include rodents, amphibians, birds, crayfish and insects. In some regions of Illinois they are known to hibernate in crayfish burrows. Today this is one of the rarest rattlesnakes in America and their remaining populations are highly fragmented and isolated from one another. They are regarded as a Threatened Species in Illinois.

CHAPTER 7

THE AMPHIBIANS OF ILLINOIS

— THE ORDERS AND FAMILIES OF ILLINOIS AMPHIBIANS —

Note: The sequence of Amphibian orders and families shown in the table below is a representation of the order in which they appear in the book, and may not be an accurate representation of the phylogenetic relationships of the Amphibians.

Class - **Amphibia** (amphibians)

Order - **Anura** (frogs & toads)

Family	**Ranidae** (true frogs)
Family	**Hylidae** (treefrogs)
Family	**Microhylidae** (narrowmouth toads)
Family	**Bufonidae** (true toads)
Family	**Scaphiopodidae** (spadefoots)

Order - **Caudata** (salamanders)

Family	**Ambysotmatidae** (mole salamanders)
Family	**Salamandridae** (newts)
Family	**Plethodontidae** (lungless salamanders)
Family	**Proteida** (mudpuppies)
Family	**Cryptobranchidae** (hellbenders)
Family	**Sirenidae** (sirens)

THE AMPHIBIANS OF ILLINOIS

PART 1: FROGS & TOADS

Class - **Amphibia** (amphibians)
Order - **Anura** (frogs & toads)
Family - **Ranidae** (true frogs)

Green Frog - *Lithobates clamitans*		**Bullfrog** *Lithobates catesbeianus*
Bronze Morph (formerly subspecies - *L. c. clamitans*)	**Green Morph** (formerly subspecies - *L. c. melanotus*)	

Size: 2 to 4 inches. Record 4.5 inches.

Abundance: Both color morphs are very common within their respective ranges.

Variation: There are 2 color morphs and both can be found in Illinois. The difference between the 2 is slight and usually relates to the color of the snout (see photos). Historically experts regarded the two morphs as different subspecies. Today most experts consider them to be a single species with 2 color morphs.

Habitat: Found in virtually every aquatic habitat type within the state, from small ponds and large lakes to streams and wetlands. Often found in uplands in temporary puddles on dirt roads and logging lanes or in the vicinity of springs or seeps. Less commonly can be found in wet meadows or damp woodlands.

Presumed range in Illinois

Size: Record 8 inches.

Abundance: Fairly common.

Variation: Females grow larger. Males have a larger tympanum and a yellow throat, white in female.

Habitat: All aquatic habitats are used. Ponds, lakes, and streams as well as swamps and marshes.

Presumed range in Illinois

Breeding: Breeding can begin as early as May and continue until August. As with other frogs, eggs are fertilized externally by the male who clasps onto the females back and deposits sperm onto the eggs as they are extruded by the female. Up to 4,000 eggs may be deposited. Two clutches per year can occur. Eggs hatch in as little as a week and larva (tadpoles) metamorphose in 2 to 3 months. Young frogs may disperse up to a mile or more.

Breeding: Breeding and egg laying occurs from late spring through midsummer. Several thousand eggs can be laid and two clutches per year is not uncommon. Tadpole metamorphosis does not occur until the following summer.

Natural History: A drive through a wetland on a rainy night in late summer when the tadpoles of *Lithobates clamitans* are emerging onto land will reveal astounding numbers of small frogs crossing the roadway as they disperse into new territories. Adult frogs feed on insects primarily but other arthropods including small crayfish are frequently eaten. Minnows and other small aquatic vertebrates are also potential prey. These frogs are easily confused with the much larger Bullfrog, but are distinguished by the presence of a fold of skin (known as a dorso-lateral fold) that runs along each side of the back. These frogs require smaller bodies of water than the larger Bullfrog and they can be found in almost any moist environment. Like other aquatic frogs they sometimes wander away from water on rainy nights to forage for insects in grassy areas. Despite the fact that this species is still very common, frogs in general are in a steep decline in North America. The much larger Bullfrog (next column) was extremely common in Illinois just a few decades ago, but that species has experience a decline in some populations. The filling of small stock ponds for row cropping and use of herbicides and pesticides may be the cause.

Natural History: These are the largest frogs in Illinois (and in fact in the US). Their hind legs are considered to be a delicacy by many. They are regarded as a game animal and are hunted for food during the annual "frog season." In some places they are raised commercially for food and for research or teaching laboratories. They may venture far from water and will travel from pond to pond during rainy weather. Food is almost any animal small enough to be swallowed, including other frogs. There is even a record of a large Bullfrog eating a baby rattlesnake!

Class - **Amphibia** (amphibians)

Order - **Anura** (frogs & toads)

Family - **Ranidae** (true frogs)

Wood Frog *Lithobates sylvatica*	Northern Leopard Frog *Lithobates pipiens*	Southern Leopard Frog *Lithobates sphenocephalus*

Wood Frog		Northern Leopard Frog		Southern Leopard Frog	
Size: About 3 inches. Record 3.25 inches.	Presumed range in Illinois	**Size:** 3 to 4 inches. Record 4.375 inches.	Presumed range in Illinois	**Size:** Average 3 inches. Record 5 inches.	Presumed range in Illinois
Abundance: Fairly common.		**Abundance:** Fairly common.		**Abundance:** Common.	
Variation: There is single, wide-ranging species of Wood Frog found across the entire northern half of the continent. Varies from light tan to dark brown.		**Variation:** The color of the skin between the dark spots varies from greenish to brown or tan. Always has a spot on the snout.		**Variation:** Individuals vary from bright green to light tan (see photos above). Very similar to the preceding species but without a spot on the snout.	

Habitat: This is a forest species that is most common in Illinois in forested areas. It prefers mesic woods near streams.	**Habitat:** Wet meadows, vegetated fields, wetland, and stream edges. This species wanders extensively into grassy fields in bottom lands.	**Habitat:** Found in virtually all aquatic habitats within its range. Like the Northern Leopard Frog they often wander in to grassy fields far from water.
Breeding: Breeds in winter. This is one of the earliest breeding frogs and they may breed as early as January. Eggs are laid in ephemeral pools and small fishless bodies of water.	**Breeding:** Breeding occurs in the early spring in ponds, marshes and swamps. Females will lay 2,000 to 5,000 eggs. Tadpoles grow from less than an inch to nearly 4 inches before transforming.	**Breeding:** Breeds mostly in April and May Breeding localities are ponds, ditches, marshes, and swamps. Lays up to 5,000 eggs in several clumps. Young frogs emerge in midsummer.
Natural History: Despite the fact that this is the most widespread frog species in America, there is but a single species that shows little variation. Wood frogs from Canada and Alaska are identical to those found northern Alabama or northern Georgia. This is the most cold tolerant frog species in Illinois and it ranges farther to the north than any of its kin. They can be frozen solid and recover without harm when thawed. Food is a variety of small invertebrates. Like many frogs, Wood Frogs migrate overland during periods of heavy rainfall. They can be commonly seen on roadways at night during the breeding season.	**Natural History:** Insects and spiders are the mainstay of this frogs diet. It is not uncommon for these frogs to be seen far from water during the summer months. But they retun to ponds and wetlands in the late fall to hibernate in the mud underwater. These are familiar animals to anyone who has dissected frogs in a biology class. In recent years, their numbers in the wild have experienced an unexplained decline. In many regions specimens are being found with deformities to limbs. Some possible causes include chemical pollutants, acid rain, a pathogenic fungus that attacks frogs, or a combination of these and other, as yet unknown factors.	**Natural History:** Leopard frogs are frequently found some distance from permanent water sources in meadows and overgrown fields. They can even be seen in rural lawns on occasion, especially in late summer. Southern Leopard Frogs can be told from their northen cousin by the lack of a dark spot on the snout. They are easily discerned from the Pickeral Frog by their round rather than squarish spots; while the Northern Crayfish Frog is much stouter with a more rounded snout. A wide variety of insects, spiders, and other invertebrates are eaten. Like most frogs, they spend the winter in the mud at the bottom of a pond, creek, or other permanent water.

Class - **Amphibia** (amphibians)

Order - **Anura** (frogs & toads)

Family - **Ranidae** (true frogs)

Plains Leopard Frog *Lithobates blairi*	**Pickerel Frog** *Lithobates palustris*	**Crayfish Frog** *Lithobates areolatus*

	Presumed range in Illinois 		Presumed range in Illinois 		Presumed range in Illinois 
Size: To 3.75 inches. Record 4.375 inches.		**Size:** Average about 3 inches.		**Size:** Average 3–4 inches. Record 4.5 inches.	
Abundance: Widespread but uncommon.		**Abundance:** Uncommon.		**Abundance:** Uncommon in Illinois.	
Variation: Ground color (skin color between the spots) varies from tan to brown or greenish. There are no subspecies.		**Variation:** Ground color (skin color between the spots) varies from tan to brown. There are no subspecies of this frog.		**Variation:** Ground color between the spots varies from light gray to brown or tan. Two subspecies, but only *L. a. areolatus* in Illinois.	

Habitat: Mainly a prairie species. In Illinois occupies lowlands, river valleys, and remnant prairie near water.	**Habitat:** Prefers spring fed streams and clear, cool waters in woodland areas. May also occur in fields near streams.	**Habitat:** Floodplains, bottomland fields, and other low-lying areas with mesic substrates supporting crayfish.
Breeding: Breed in Illinois is in March and April. Lays up to 6,500 eggs. Tadpoles transform into froglets by mid- to late summer.	**Breeding:** Breeds in ponds, ditches or permanent streams. Lays 2,000 to 4,000 eggs. Tadpoles transform in about 3 months.	**Breeding:** An early breeder. Most breeding apparently occurs during periods of heavy rainfall in March. Up to 7,000 eggs may be laid.
Natural History: The bulk of this frog's range is far to the west and north in the Great Plains region. There it can be a common species. It was perhaps once more common in Illinois before the states extensive praires went under the plow. Loss of many small ponds that once dotted the landscape in the days of subsistance farming has also probably impacted this and other frog species. Todays large crop fields can be deserted of wildlife, especially amphibians. In places it shares its range with the more common Southern Leopard Frog and hybrids between the two species are known. Food is mostly insects and other invertebrates. In Kansas this species has been reported to sometimes emerged from hibernation during warm spells in midwinter.	**Natural History:** Pickerel Frogs are distinguished from Leopard Frogs by their square rather than round spots. These frogs secrete a toxin from the skin that protects them from many predators and is strong enough to kill other frogs kept with them in a small container. Among the predators that are able to eat them however is another frog species, the Bullfrog. Pickerel Frogs show a preference for clean water and an intolerance for pollution. In this respect the Pickerel Frog may be an indicator species that can provide an early warning regarding environmental threats like water pollution. Sadly for those who appreciate nature, populations of this frog, (and in fact frogs in general) may be declining in the state. Populations are being monitored by IDNR.	**Natural History:** This frog's name is derived from their habit of utilizing crayfish burrows as a home. They are quite secretive and are rarely observed except during the breeding season when they will travel overland in search of suitable breeding ponds or pools in wetland areas. Crayfish, other amphibians, small reptiles, and of course insects are food items. This frog appears to be another species in decline Modern agricultural practices such as tiling of wetland meadows to remove water and thus enable row cropping, along with the filling of small isolated ponds is possibly the cause of this decline. Remaining populations appear to be fragmented and isolated from each other, which is never a good thing for the survival of a species.

Class - **Amphibia** (amphibians)
Order - **Anura** (frogs & toads)
Family - **Hylidae** (treefrogs)

Blanchard's Cricket Frog *Acris blanchardi*	**Green Treefrog** *Hyla cinerea*	**Bird-voiced Treefrog** *Hyla avivoca*
	 Rare blue morph	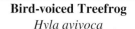 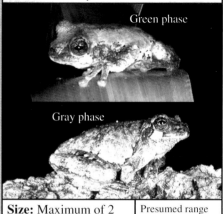 Green phase / Gray phase

Blanchard's Cricket Frog

Size: Tiny, usually less than 1 inch.

Abundance: Very common.

Variation: Varies from brown to reddish brown or tan. May also be green. Many will have markings on the back that may be greenish or brownish.

Presumed range in Illinois

Habitat: Shorelines of ponds, along creeks, temporary pools, marshes, swamps, wet meadows, and uplands.

Breeding: Breeds from spring through late summer. Up to 400 eggs are laid in small clusters of 10 to 15 per cluster. Tadpoles and froglest are tiny.

Natural History: These tiny frogs are most commonly seen along the receding shorelines of ponds and lakes in late summer or early fall. When startled by a passing human they will often jump into the water and then immediately swim back to shore. This may be an "out of the frying pan into the fire" behavior intended to keep them from the jaws of hungry fish. They are often seen far from water in fields and woodlands, but are always more common in wetland habitats and permanently damp areas. Their name comes from their call which resembles that of a cricket, but is more accurately described as sounding like two small stones being rapidly clicked together. This is one of the most common frog species in Illinois, but they are easily overlooked.

Green Treefrog

Size: Record size 2.5 inches.

Abundance: Rare in Illinois.

Variation: Varies in the amount of yellow spots on the back. May have several or none at all. In cold weather, color will turn dark brown.

Presumed range in Illinois

Habitat: Green Treefrogs are lowland animals that are found in swamps and marshes mostly.

Breeding: Breeds in early to midsummer. Lays up to 1,500 eggs in shallow waters of swamps or marshes. Multiple clutches may be produced in a summer.

Natural History: Similar to green phase of the Gray Treefrog but has smooth skin and usually a yellow stripe on the side. One of this frogs favorite daytime perches are the stems of cattails and sedges where its deep green color renders it almost invisible. Its primary prey consists of caterpillers, spiders, grasshoppers, and other insects. Green Treefrogs are primarily nocturnal in habits but they are sometimes seen during the day, especially during rainy weather. As with most other treefrogs of the genus *Hyla* this is another mainly southern species. Its range extends northward through western Kentucky and into southern Illinois where the Gulf Coastal Plain Province reaches its northernmost extension. May have been introduced farther to north in Jersey and Clinton Counties.

Bird-voiced Treefrog

Size: Maximum of 2 inches.

Abundance: Rare in Illinois.

Variation: Changes color from solid gray with a lichen pattern to gray with a bright green back.

Presumed range in Illinois

Habitat: Wetlands. Found mainly in swamps and marshes or in their immediate vicinity.

Breeding: Breeds in spring or summer in shallow, vegetated waters of swamps and marshes. Metamorphosis of tadpoles occurs in about 4 weeks.

Natural History: These handsome little treefrogs are easily confused with the frogs of the Gray Treefrog complex (see next page). Bird-voiced Treefrogs have a greenish wash on the inner thighs as opposed to the orange or yellow inner thigh seen on the Gray Treefrogs. These are mainly southern animals that reach the northernmost limits of their range in the upper Coastal Plain region. Their name comes from the sound of the male's breeding call, which resembles the whistling song of a bird. This species survival is dependant upon wetlands. The range of these frogs in Illinois is restricted to the southern tip of the state where lower elevations and the presence of wetland habitats mimic habitat conditions common farther to the south. A threatened Species in Illinois.

Class - **Amphibia** (amphibians)

Order - **Anura** (frogs & toads)

Family - **Hylidae** (treefrogs)

Gray Treefrog complex *Hyla chrysoscelis & Hyla versicolor*	Illinois Chorus Frog *Pseudacris streckeri*

Size: Averages about 2 inches. Maximum of just under 2.5 inches.

Presumed range in Illinois

Abundance: Fairly common to common.

Variation: There are actually two identical species in the Gray Treefrog complex. They can only be reliably differentiated by the sound of their call or by laboratory examination of the number of cell chromosones. The two species are known as the Cope's Gray Treefrog (*Hyla chrysoscelis*), and the Gray Treefrog (*Hyla versicolor*). Both species have the ability to change color from gray to green. Additionally, the shade of gray can range from a dark sooty gray to a light smoky gray (see photos above).

Habitat: Habitat is chiefly woodlands. These treefrogs are more adapted to dry uplands than most members of their genus and they can be found far from water in dry upland woods.

Breeding: Breeds from late spring through summer in small bodies of water ranging from small ponds to roadside ditches. Up to 2,000 eggs are laid.

Natural History: These highly arboreal treefrogs are rarely seen on the ground and they often climb high into treetops to forage for insects. They are mainly nocturnal but they may be active by day on cloudy or rainy days or in cooler weather. They shelter by day in small hollows in tree trunks or limbs and have been known to take up residence in small bird nest boxes such as a wren box or bluebird box. They will also live in the rain gutters of house roofs. They can sometimes be seen sitting in the opening of their hiding place with the head and front feet exposed. They possess remarkable camouflage abilities and the gray, lichen like pattern of their skin will perfectly match the bark of the tree they occupy. They can produce a natural anti-freeze in the blood which allows them to hibernate in tree hollows above the ground, or in leaf litter on the forest floor. Most members of the genus *Hyla* are southern animals, but these frogs range far into the northern states and even into parts of southern Canada. Food items are small insects and arthropods. Differentiating between these two species is very difficult. Those with a "good ear"can tell the difference between their calls. Other researchers must resort to a laboratory analysis of chromosones. Cope's Gray Treefrog has a the typical dipoliod set of chromosones (2 chromosones) while the Gray Treefrog is tetraploid (4 chromosones) in its chromosone count.

Size: Under 2 inches. Record 1.75 inches.

Abundance: Rare.

Variation: Ground color varies from tan to gray. Dark markings on the back can be black or dark brown. Dark markings can be vivid or obscure and vary in amount.

Habitat: Remant prairies with sandy soils are the primary habitat in Illinois. Persists in fallow fields in croplands.

Breeding: Breeds in early spring. Eggs are contained ina gelatinous mass.

Natural History: In many respects the Illinois Chorus frog behaves more like a toad than a treefrog. They are ground dwellers that will burrow into loose soil in the manner of toads and they spend much of their adult life burrowed into the ground. But they burrow headfirst into loose soil using its stout front legs rather than digging in with back legs the way a toad would. They emerge from the ground on rainy nights to forage for small insect prey. They may once have been more widespread in Illinois but today are found mainly in the area shown on the map above. At least three other disjunct populations occur in southeast Missouri. They are a Threatened Species in Illinois.

Class - **Amphibia** (amphibians)

Order - **Anura** (frogs & toads)

Family - **Hylidae** (treefrogs)		Family - **Microhylidae** (narrowmouth toads)

Upland Chorus Frogs
Pseudacris species

Upland Chorus Frog

Size: 0.75 to 1.25 inches.	Presumed range in Illinois 
Abundance: Very common.	
Habitat: Low wet fields, bottomland woods, swamps, marshes, ponds, or bogs. Also found in uplands that are in close proximity to bottomlands or creeks.	

Variation: Variable. Ground color varies from brown to grayish. Dorsal pattern can be stripes or spots.

Breeding: Very early breeders that may begin breeding as early as February. Breeding is in ephemeral pools in flooded fields, roadside ditches, etc.

Natural History: Breeding may be interrupted several times by cold snaps and freezing weather. The name comes from their "chorus" of breeding calls that carries over quite a long distance. Standing water in flooded bottomlands and shallow, water filled depressions in croplands are favorite breeding sites for this frog. Though amazingly common during the brief breeding season, most of the rest of the year they seem to disappear. There are three nearly identical Chorus Frog species in Illinois and their collective ranges include the entire state. The three species found in Illinois are the **Boreal Chorus Frog** (*P. maculata*); the **Midland Chorus Frog** (*P. triseriata*) and the **Upland Chorus Frog** (*P. feriarum*). Some experts regard them as a single species with three subspecies.

Spring Peeper
Pseudacris crucifer

Size: About 1 inch.	Presumed range in Illinois 
Abundance: Common.	
Habitat: Woodlands and thickets, usually near water. Most common in lowlands (swamps, marshes, etc.), but also found in upland areas adjacent to creek bottoms or wetlands.	

Variation: Ground color varies. Usually tan or brown. Sometimes grayish or reddish.

Breeding: Spring Peepers begin breeding activity as early as late winter and continue into early spring. Several hundred eggs are laid in shallow water.

Natural History: Another diminutive frog that is heard more often than seen. The name comes from the sound made when breeding frogs are calling. The call is a rapidly repeated "peep, peep, peep." Despite being members of the treefrog family they live mostly on the ground. The species name "*crucifer*" is latin for "cross bearer" and refers to the x-shaped mark that is always present on this frogs back. These little frogs, along with their cousins the Chorus Frogs, are a true harbinger of spring throughout much of the eastern United States. They may breed in the same flooded field pools with Chorus Frogs or even in the same pool. They are widely distributedthroughout the Eastern Temperate Forest Level I Ecoregion but in Illinois are absent from regions that were historically prairie.

Narrowmouth Toad
Gastrophryne carolinensis

Size: About 1 inch.	Presumed range in Illinois 
Abundance: Rare in Illinois.	
Variation: Ground color may vary from various shades of gray to olive, or reddish brown. No subspecies are recognized despite being widespread in the southeastern US.	

Habitat: Can be found both in dry upland and in more mesic bottomlands. Primarily a woodland animal.

Breeding: Breeding: From 500 to 800 eggs are laid in late spring or summer. Eggs hatch in two days and tadpoles transform in 2 to 4 weeks.

Natural History: Narrowmouth Toads are confirmed burrowers that are occasionally found hiding beneath flat rocks, boards, etc. Their call is a nasal "baaaa" and sounds like the cry of a young lamb. Ants and termites are recorded as prey and it is likely that other diminutive insects and other arthropods are eaten. The tiny mouth on this frog precludes eating anything larger than the average termite. Despite their name they are not true toads but are the sole representatives in the eastern United States of a specialized family of anurans known as Microhylidae. Microhylidae frogs are much more common in tropical regions. Their are over 300 species in the family and they can be found on every major continent except Europe and Antarctica. Known for their very rapid development of eggs and tadpoles.

Class - **Amphibia** (amphibians)

Order - **Anura** (frogs & toads)

Family - **Bufonidae** (toads)		Family - **Scphiopodidae** (spadefoots)

American Toad
Anaxyrus americanus

Fowler's Toad
Anaxyrus fowleri

Eastern Spadefoot
Scaphiopus holbrookii

Size: To 6 inches.

Presumed range in Illinois

Abundance: Common.

Habitat: Uses a wide variety of habitats from woodlands and fields to urban lawns and gardens.

Variation: There are two subspecies and both occur in Illinois.

Size: 3.75 inches.

Presumed range in Illinois

Abundance: Common.

Habitat: Uses a wide variety of habitats from woodlands and fields to urban lawns and gardens.

Variation: Variable. Dark brown, reddish brown, tan, or grayish.

Size: 2 to 3 inches.

Presumed range in Illinois

Abundance: Rare in Illinois.

Habitat: The main habitat requirement is loose, sandy soil that facilitates easy burrowing.

Variation: Color varies from brown or olive through gray to black.

Breeding: Breeds as early as March. Eggs are laid in long strings of clear gelationous material. Breeds in small ponds, water filled ditches, or temporary pools in seasonally flooded lowlands.

Breeding: Breeding is in May in shallow ponds, flooded ditches, creeks, Inudated fields (including crop fields), creeks, etc. From 5,000 to 10,000 eggs are laid.

Breeding: Breeds explosively during periods of heavy rainfall from late spring throughout the summer. Up to 5,000 eggs hatch within a few days. Spadefoot tadpoles transform rapidly.

Natural History: American Toads eat a wide variety of insects and other small arthropods. They are adept burrowers and like other toads possess hardened spade-like structures on the hind feet that are used for digging. These toads can be told from the similar and sympatrically occurring Fowler's Toad by the their larger warts and the fact that the dark spots on the back never have more than 2 warts per spot. The similar Fowler's Toad may have up to six warts per dark spot. Although they are sometimes active by day, these toads are primarily nocturnal in habits. They usually spend the day at least partially buried in loose soil or beneath leaf litter or other debris. When attacked by a predator they will inflate their bodies by gulping air. This behavior sometimes works if the predator is an animal like a snake that must swallow its food whole.

Natural History: The natural history of the Fowler's Toad is similar to that of the American Toad. Fowler's Toads breed later in the spring and young toadlets do not emerge from the tadpole stage until late summer. Like many toads (and many treefrogs) the Fowler's Toad secretes a toxic substance from the skin when threatened. While this toxin can cause irritation to sensitive areas and membranes, the old wives' tale that toads cause warts is a fallacy. Food is insects and other small invertebrates and toads are recognized by many for the valuable role they play in controlling destructive insect pests around the yard and in the garden. Savvy gardeners encourage toads by placing shallow water dishes in the garden. Many predators avoid toads due to their toxic secretions.The common Eastern Garter Snake along with the Eastern Hognose Snake are two of the major predators of toads.

Natural History: The name "Spadefoot" come from a sickle-shaped horny structure on the hind feet that is used for digging into the ground. They spend much of their lives in burrows only a few inches deep and emerge only on rainy nights. During dry weather they may spend weeks in the burrow without feeding. They secrete a toxic substance which is highly irritant to mucus membranes, thus making these anurans unpalatable to many potential predators. Touching the face or other sensitive skin after handling a Spadefoot will result in an uncomfortable burning sensation. Although widespread and quite common farther to the south, in Illinois the Spadefoot is restricted to the southernmost tip of the state. Spadefoots are known for the rapid trasition of tapoles into baby spadefoots. Metamorphis can occur in 2 weeks.

THE AMPHIBIANS OF ILLINOIS

PART 2: SALAMANDERS

Class - **Amphibia** (amphibians)

Order - **Caudata** (salamanders)

Family - **Ambystomatidae** (mole salamanders)

Tiger Salamander *Ambystoma tigrinum*	**Spotted Salamander** *Ambystoma maculatum*

Mature adult / Recently transformed adult

Size: Averages about 8 inches. Maximum length is around 14 inches.

Abundance: Fairly common in some areas of Illinois. Uncommon to rare in regions of intensive agriculture and urban development.

Variation: A good deal of variation occurs in this species. The light markings can appear as irregular spots, blotches, or stripes. The color of the light pigments can vary as well and may be yellow, orange, or greenish. Juveniles are uniformly olive green or dark gray (see photo above). Tigers are easily confused with the Spotted Salamander, but that species has spots that are more rounded.

Presumed range in Illinois

Size: Average 6 inches. Maximum 9 inches.

Abundance: Common in southern Illinois.

Variation: The spots on the Spotted Salamander may be yellow or orange. The number of spots varies widely. Rarely spots are absent.

Presumed range in Illinois

Habitat: Woodlands and fields, in both upland an lowland areas. This species seems more common in regions where a mosaic of woodlands and fallow fields or prairie remain. Least common in agricultural areas.

Habitat: Primarily woodland areas, but also found in overgrown fields and edges bordering agricultural lands.

Breeding: Breeds in small, fishless bodies of water like stock ponds, vernal pools and "borrow pits." Breeding occurs in midwinter, with a few hundred to several thousand eggs produced by the female. Males meet females in breeding ponds and fertilize the eggs as they are laid, much like fish. Eggs are encased in a ball of jellylike material and hatch in about a month.

Breeding: Breeds during periods of heavy rainfall in late winter. Eggs are deposited in large gelatinous masses in ponds or wetland pools. Larvae transform in 2 to 4 months.

Natural History: The large size of the Tiger Salamander allows it to feed on much larger prey than most salamander species. Although invertebrates such as earthworms and insect larva are the major foods, small vertebrates may also eaten and captive specimens will eat baby mice. The apparent decline of this salamander in Illinois (and elsewhere withing its range) may be traced to the draining and filling of small ponds and wetlands and the destruction of vernal pools by modern agricultural practices. Many amphibians in Illinois require small bodies of water that do not hold significant numbers of aquatic predators such as predaceous fish that will eat amphibian larva. Amphibians are also vulnerable to toxins released into the environment by farming operations where both insecticides and herbicides are widely used. In fact, the amphibians are in decline throughout the globe and many scientists regard their diminishing populations as an environmental alarm call. Despite their large size, Tiger Salamanders are rarely seen except during the late winter breeding season when they make their nocturnal overland treks to breeding ponds. At this time they can sometimes be seen on rural roadways on stormy, rain-soaked nights. During these annual migrations they have been known to stumble into basement stairwells, old cisterns, etc., and become trapped.

Natural History: Primarily subterranean in habits. Lives in underground burrows and beneath rocks, logs, or leaf litter on the forest floor. During periods of hot, dry weather retreats deeper underground or stays in the vicinity of perennially wet areas. Feeds on a wide variety of insects and invertebrates as well as a few small vertebrates. This is one of the most common members of the "mole salamander" group in Illinois. In the late-winter breeding season they are easily observed on rural roads at night during rainy weather as they make the migration to breeding ponds. If the habitat and timing are right, dozens may be observed on a few miles of roadway.

Class - **Amphibia** (amphibians)

Order - **Caudata** (salamanders)

Family - **Ambystomatidae** (mole salamanders)

Small-mouthed Salamander *Ambystoma texanum*	Blue-spotted Salamander *Ambystoma laterale*	Jefferson Salamander *Ambystoma jeffersonianum*

	Presumed range in Illinois		Presumed range in Illinois		Presumed range in Illinois
Size: 4 to 5 inches as an adult.		**Size:** 4 to 5 inches average. Record 6.25.		**Size:** Up to 8 inches.	
Abundance: Fairly common.		**Abundance:** Fairly common within range.		**Abundance:** Very rare in Illinois.	
Variation: Varies in color from uniform dark gray to blue-gray with varying amounts of silver or light gray flecking Some have no light flecking at all.		**Variation:** Considerable variation in the amount of blue spotting present. Hybrid "unisexual" forms can be confusingly similar (see below).		**Variation:** There is some variation in the number of light blue spots that are present. Older adults tend to lose their spots and become darker.	

Habitat: Found in a variety of habitats from woodlands to grassy meadows. Most common in lowlands and stream bottoms but also in upland areas.

Habitat: Another forest species. May also be found in wet meadows and swamps. Favors areas with loamy soils.

Habitat: An upland forest species mostly. This is primarily an eastern species that reaches the westernmost limits of its range in eastern Illinois.

Breeding: Breeds in late winter or very early spring. May lay up to several hundred eggs in large clumps. Ponds, wetland pools or flooded roadside ditches may be used for egg deposition. Larvae transform into adults in about 6 to 8 weeks, sooner in warmer weather.

Breeding: Breeds in early spring. Courtship activity involves the male grasping the female from above and rubbing the nose across her body. The male then deposits sperm packets which are picked up by the female's cloaca.

Breeding: Breeding occurs in late winter or early spring, with eggs being deposited in woodland ponds. As with all *Ambystoma* salamanders, the eggs hatch into larva that spend up to a year as thoroughly aquatic, gilled salamanders before transforming into adults.

Natural History: Like other members of its genus the Smallmouth Salamander spends most of its time in underground burrows or beneath rocks, logs, or leaf litter. They will emerge on rainy nights to forage above ground. Feeds on a wide variety of soft-bodied invertebrate prey such as earthworms, slugs, and grubs. The Smallmouth Salamander is very similar in appearance to the other salamanders shown on this page and one clue to identification between the species is to refer to their respective range maps.

Natural History: Hybridization with the Jefferson Salamander regularly occurs. All hybrids have triploid chromosones and all are females, hence the term "Unisexual Salamander." Hybrids were once regarded as distinct species. Those with more chromosones from the Blue-spotted were known as "Tremblay's Salamander." Hybrid individuals with more chromosones from the Jefferon's were called "Silvery Salamander." Food is small insects and other invertebrates such as worms, sow bugs, snails, spiders, etc. The Blue-spotted is a boreal salamander that ranges well to the north in eastern Canada. It is the most northerly ranging of the *Ambystoma*.

Natural History: Most of this species's range is to the east of Illinois in Indiana, Ohio, West Virginia, Pennsylvania, New York, and Kentucky. In Illinois, they are known from only two counties (Clark and Edgar). Like all terrestrial salamanders in Illinois, this is mainly a fossorial species. They will surface at night or on rainy, heavily overcast days with dim light and forage on the forest floor. They regularly hybirdize with the Blue-spotted Salamander in regions where their ranges overlap. Hybrids have tripoid chromosones are always females. These hybrids are known as "Unisexual Salamanders."

Class - **Amphibia** (amphibians)

Order - **Caudata** (salamanders)

Family - **Ambystomatidae** (mole salamanders)		Family - **Salamandridae** (newts)

Marbled Salamander
Ambystoma opacum

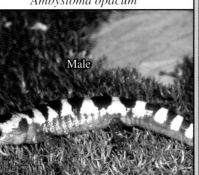

Mole Salamander
Ambystoma talpoideum

Eastern Newt
Notophthalmus viridescens

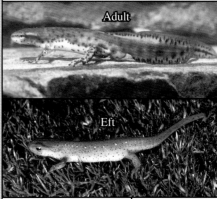

Size: 3 to 4 inches. Record 5.25 inches.

Presumed range in Illinois

Abundance: Fairly common.

Variation: Sexually dimorphic. Light colors are grayish or silver in the female and whiter in the male.

Habitat: Most fond of bottomlands (especially during breeding) but also common in upland woods.

Breeding: Breeds in the fall during rainy weather. Overland migration is common. Eggs are laid on land under rocks, logs, etc. in low lying areas subject to flooding. Hatching is delayed until eggs are flooded by fall rains.

Natural History: This is one of the few salamanders to exhibit sexual dimorphism. The light markings are wider and whiter on the male and narrower and more silver or grayish on the female. Like other members of the "mole salamander" family, Marbled Salamanders are fossorial in habits. In fact, this species may be even more secretive than many of its kin. Thus, though they are fairly common they are not readily observed. They can reportedly produce a noxious secretion from the tail which may help to ward off some predators. Adults probably feed on most any small animal they can swallow. Larvae have been known to eat the eggs of small frogs.

Size: Adult to 4 inches. Record nearly 5 inches.

Presumed range in Illinois

Abundance: Uncommon in Illinois.

Variation: Some are uniformly dark gray. Others have a significant amount of light gray flecking on the sides.

Habitat: Swamps, marshes, and bottomland woods prone to seasonal flooding. Less commonly in upland woods.

Breeding: Breeding occurs in late fall or early winter and overland treks to breeding areas are made. Eggs are laid in the waters of swamps and marshes. After a few months the gill-breathing larvae develop into air-breathing adults.

Natural History: This decidedly fossorial salamander is the namesake of the "mole salamander" family. This species is rarely seen above ground except during the breeding season when they will emerge on rainy nights and travel to areas of breeding congregations. They can sometimes be turned up beneath logs or other objects in low, perennially moist areas. These salamanders have a stout bodied appearance and a large head which distinguishes them from the similarly colored Small-mouthed Salamander and Streamside Salamander. When captured they will sometimes assume a defensive posture that consists of raising the body off the ground while lowering the head.

Size: Adults 5 inches. Efts 3 inches.

Presumed range in Illinois

Abundance: Fairly common within range.

Variation: 2 subspecies. Only 1 in Illinois. Significant ontogenetic variation (see Natural History section below).

Habitat: Adults are found in ponds, swamps, or other permanent water. Eft stage is a terrestrial animal of woods.

Breeding: Breeds in spring. Males deposit packages of sperm which are taken up by the females into the cloaca where fertilization occurs internally before eggs are laid. Hatchlings metamorphose into efts in 4 to 5 months.

Natural History: Newts are unique among Illinois salamanders in having an extra stage in their life cycle. Following hatching the young spend the summer as gill breathing larva then undergo a transformation to an air breathing semi-adult that lives on land for up to three years. Newts in this terrestrial stage are call "efts." After 1 to 3 years the eft returns to the water and undergoes another metmorphosis into a totally aquatic adult. After returning to the water the coarse skin of the eft becomes smooth and the round tail flattens vertically to become finlike. Their life span can be up to 15 years. Newts produce a neurotoxin in their skin that protects them from many predators.

Class - **Amphibia** (amphibians)

Order - **Caudata** (salamanders)

Family - **Plethodontidae** (lungless salamanders)

Northern Zigzag Salamander *Plethodon dorsalis*	**Eastern Redback Salamander** *Plethodon cinereus*	**Northern Slimy Salamander** *Plethodon glutinosus*

Size: Average 3 to 4 inches.

Presumed range in Illinois

Abundance: Fairly common.

Variation: Varies somewhat in ground color and in the intensity of the zigzag strip. Some are uniformly gray above and lack the dorsal stripe altogether.

Habitat: Both are forest species (mesic woodlands) and are most common in regions with a limestone substrate.

Breeding: Lays only a few eggs (as few as 4 or 5). Eggs are deposited into an underground nest chamber.

Natural History: The Northern Zigzag Salamander (*P. dorsalis*) and the Southern Zigzag Salamander (*P. ventralis*) where once regarded as single species with two subspecies. They were separated into two distinct species based on DNA analysis. For the layman identifying individual specimens is best accomplished by way of geography (only the Northern Zigzag is found in Illinois). These are terrestrial salamanders that spend much of their life beneath leaf litter, logs, or other cover on the forest floor. They do emerge at night and forage for small invertebrate prey. They also capture worms and tiny insects beneath the leaf litter. Like all members of the *Plethodon* salamanders, young salamanders hatch fully formed.

Size: 3 to 4 inches. Maximum 5 inches.

Presumed range in Illinois

Abundance: Uncommon in Illinois.

Variation: Considerable variation in the dorsal pattern. Some Redback Salamanders are not red on the back at all, but uniformly gray.

Habitat: Chiefly woodlands. This is another terrestrial but retiring species that hides beneath leaf litter, logs, etc.

Breeding: Female lays about 10 eggs on land and guards them until they hatch. Babies hatch fully formed.

Natural History: Most of this salamanders range is to the north and east of Illinois, as far north as the Canadian provinces of Quebec, Nova Scotia, and New Brunswick. In the heart of its range this is not only the most common salamander species, but one of the most common vertebrate species. Ironically, in Illinois this is an uncommon species and their range barely enters the our area in northernmost region of the state. The Illinois range of this salamander consists of a region where natural habitats have been radically altered by agriculture and urbanization. Thus this is regarded as an uncommon species in Illinois. They are very similar to the Zigzag Salamanders and can be difficult to differentiate. Range is the best clue to identity.

Size: To 8 inches.

Presumed range in Illinois

Abundance: Common in southern Illinois.

Variation: Ground color is consistantly black or very dark gray. Varies considerably in amount of light flecking. Color of flecks white, silver or golden.

Habitat: Another woodland species. More common in upland woods and hillsides than in bottomlands.

Breeding: 12 to 15 eggs seems to be the average. As with other *Plethodon* Salamanders, young hatch fully formed.

Natural History: The name is derived from the fact that slimy salamanders exude a thick, sticky mucus from the skin when handled. This material is difficult to wash off and once dried becomes black and crusty. Herpetologists capturing slimy salamanders sometimes wear the residue of salamander mucus on their hands for days before it finally wears off. The food of these woodland species is undoubtedly a wide variety of soft bodied insects, insect larva, annelids, small crustaceans and other tiny invertebrate life found among the leaf litter on the forest floor. Until the advent of DNA technology there was only one ubiquitous species of Slimy Salamander that ranged across most of the eastern United States. There are now over dozen individual species. Only one (Northern) occurs in Illinois.

Class - **Amphibia** (amphibians)

Order - **Caudata** (salamanders)

Family - **Plethodontidae** (lungless salamanders)

Long-tailed Salamander *Eurycea longicauda*	Southern Two-lined Salamander *Eurycea cirrigera*	Cave Salamander *Eurycea lucifuga*

Long-tailed Salamander	Southern Two-lined Salamander	Cave Salamander
Size: Record length 7.75 inches.  Presumed range in Illinois	**Size:** Maximum 4 inches, average 2 to 3 inches.  Presumed range in Illinois	**Size:** Record 7.125 inches.  Presumed range in Illinois
Abundance: Fairly common within range.	**Abundance:** Fairly common within range.	**Abundance:** Fairly common within range.
Variation: Two subspecies in Illinois. *E. l. longicauda* in southern Illinois. *E. l. melanopleura* in more northerly regions along the Mississippi River.	**Variation:** Ground color varies slightly from bright yellow to dingy brownish. Dorsal stripes are usually quite vivid, but can be obscure on dark specimen.	**Variation:** Varies somewhat in the amount of dark spots on the dorsum. Ground color varies from bright red to reddish brown or orange.
Habitat: Spring runs, small clear creeks, in the vicinity of seeps, and near cave openings.	**Habitat:** Streams, wetlands and seeps. Mostly a lowland animal but also found in mesic upland environments.	**Habitat:** Although frequently found in caves, this salamander also lives in upland woods beneath rocks, logs, etc.
Breeding: Breeds in late winter or early spring. Eggs are deposited in streams and springs or often in caves. Larvae metamorphose in about a year.	**Breeding:** Several dozen eggs are attached to the underside of rocks and brooks. Eggs hatch into aquatic larvae that transform in one or two years.	**Breeding:** Several dozen eggs are attached to the underneath side of rocks underwater in springs or waterways both inside and outside of caves.
Natural History: These salamanders can often be found beneath rocks within small clear streams. They also live in mesic woodland environments, usually in the vicinity of a permanent stream. Here they may be found hiding beneath or within rotted logs or stumps. On rainy nights they can be encountered on roads as they roam around in search of tiny invertebrate prey. Although they can reach an impressive length of over 7 inches, they are a slim bodied animal and over half their length is tail. The two subspecies in Illinois are the Long-tailed Salamander (*longicauda*) and the Dark-sided Salamander (*melanopleura*). Autotomy (breaking off of the tail) is a common defense use by these and other *Eurycea* salamanders.	**Natural History:** The members of this genus (*Eurycea*) are often called "Brook Salamanders," in reference to their propensity to inhabit small, clear streams. Other habitats are also utilized and the Southern Two-lined Salamander is often found in swamps or bottomland woodlands in the vicinity of seeps. Springs and seeps that emerge from ridges and upland areas that border bottomlands and swamps are good places to find this small and secretive salamander. Brook Salamanders differ from their family relatives the "Woodland Salamanders" (genus *Plethodon*) in that their affinity to aquatic stream habitats persists as adults. They are also different in another important respect. Brook Salamanders must undergo an aquatic larval stage in their life cycle while "Woodland Salamanders" hatch fully formed.	**Natural History:** The distribution of this species is restricted to regions with predominantly limestone substrates. Thus in Illinois they are absent from all but the southern tip of the state. Adults of this species have prehensile tails and they are good climbers. They are sometimes seen clinging to the walls inside caves. Despite their name these salamanders are not true troglodytes (cave dwellers). They inhabit mostly the twilight zone of caves as well as more typical terrestrial habitats in mesic upland woods. They can be found beneath rocks, logs, etc., and can be common near springs and seeps in upland areas. Like other salamanders on this page, the tail may break off if grasped.

Class - **Amphibia** (amphibians)

Order - **Caudata** (salamanders)

Family - **Plethodontidae** (lungless salamanders)

Family - **Proteidae** (waterdogs)

Spotted Dusky Salamander *Desmognathus conanti*	**Four-toed Salamander** *Hemidactylum scutatum*	**Mudpuppy** *Necturus maculosus*

Female with eggs

Size: 2.5 to 5 inches. Average about 3.5 inches.

Presumed range in Illinois

Abundance: Very rare in Illinois.

Variation: Color varies from gray through many shades of brown. Yellowish spots on the dorsum or spots may coalesce into stripe.

Habitat: Springs, seeps, and spring fed brooks in wooded areas. Beneath rocks, detritus or in the muck of forest streams.

Breeding: Eggs are laid under rocks in the vicinity of streams. The eggs (average 15 to 30) are laid in clusters of individual eggs that are not contained in a gelatinous mass like the mole salamanders.

Natural History: The Spotted Dusky and its kin are salamanders that are often well known to rural folk in the southern US. Many a youngster has amused themselves on a hot summer day by rolling stones and logs in streams to try and catch these slippery and quick moving salamanders. They are often collected for fish bait in many areas within their range and sometimes go by the name "Spring Lizards." Other members of the genus are frequently sold in bait stores in the Appalachian region. Although this practice probably has no significant impact on this common species, accidental "by catch" of some rarer species may have an negative impact on those less common species. Mainly nocturnal, they will emerge at night to forage.

Size: Average 2 to 3 inches. Record of 4 inches.

Presumed range in Illinois

Abundance: Uncommon in Illinois.

Variation: Dorsal ground color varies from brown to gray or orange.

Habitat: Mature woodlands, usually near woodland bogs, springs or seeps. Or near small woodland ponds.

Breeding: Eggs are laid in winter at the edges of streams, ponds, or other permanent wetlands. Females remain with the eggs until they hatch in about 4 weeks.

Natural History: The name comes from the fact that they have only four toes on the hind foot (other terrestrial salamanders in Illinois have five). There is also an obvious constriction at the base of the tail that is unique to this species. It is at this constricted location that the tail will be broken off as a defensive maneuver. The most readily identifiable characteristic of this species is its white belly with black spots. No other Illinois salamander is similarly colored and patterned ventrally. This species has a greater geographic range than most other American Salamanders, being found from Nova Scotia to the gulf coast and west to Minnesota and Arkansas. But like many amphibians it is threatened by habitat destruction and has been in decline for decades. The disappearance of vernal pools, bogs and streamside habitats to agriculture and urban development is probably the most significant threat.

Size: Average 2 to 3 inches. Record 4.

Presumed range in Illinois

Abundance: Locally can be fairly common.

Variation: There is no variation in this species. Adults and young are similar but young often have a dark dorsal stripes.

Habitat: Utilizes most aquatic habitats in the state. Prefers clean waters but can persist in turbid waters.

Breeding: Breeding and egg laying occurs in the fall. Female Mudpuppys hollow out a nest beneath a sunken log or rock where they will lay from a few score to over a hundred eggs. The eggs attach to the underside of a rock or log.

Natural History: Mudpuppys have extensive external gills that resemble downy feathers. Some think the gills are reminiscent of the ears of a dog, thus the name "Mudpuppy." These are totally aquatic salamanders that never lose the gills of the larva. This condition of permanent larval characteristics is known scientifically as "neotony" and is a phenomenon that is not rare in salamanders of several species. Mudpuppys prey on fish eggs, insects, mollusks small crustaceans and annelids. The female remains with eggs during incubation.

Class - **Amphibia** (amphibians)
Order - **Caudata** (salamanders)
Family - **Cryptobranchidae** (giant salamanders)
Hellbender - *Cryptobranchus allegheniensis*

Size: Up to 30 inches in length and very heavy bodied.

Abundance: Very rare in Illinois. Populations throughout its range are in decline.

Variation: Some variation in ground color. Reddish, brown, tan, or chocolate. A very similar but distinct species occurs in the Ozarks region.

Habitat: Clear pure streams. Once found throughout the Appalachians and much of the Interior Plateau. Populations now restricted to remote, unpolluted streams. Large underwater rocks are used as a refuge.

Breeding: Fertilization is external and eggs are laid in a nest guarded by the male. Lays over 400 eggs.

Presumed range in Illinois

Natural History: These huge, totally aquatic salamanders have deep folds and wrinkles in the skin. They have very large, dorso-ventrally flattened heads and laterally flattened, finlike tails. They are completely aquatic and feed on crustaceans, minnows, and invertebrates with crayfish reported as a primary prey. They require clean, unpolluted flowing waters and they are in decline throughout their range due to stream degradation, impoundments, and chemical pollutants. This is one of America's largest salamander species, but it is dwarfed by its larger relative from Japan. The world's largest salamander, the Pacific Giant Salamander, is native to pristine streams in the mountains of Japan, where it can reach 5 feet in length. Many streams throughout America lack their original water quality and can no longer support this bizarre and interesting creature.

Class - **Amphibia** (amphibians)
Order - **Caudata** (salamanders)
Family - **Sirenidae** (sirens)
Lesser Siren - *Siren intermedia*

Presumed range in Illinois

Size: Average 12 to 16 inches. Can reach a maximum length of up to 20 inches.

Abundance: Uncommon in Illinois. More common farther to south in the lower coastal plain where swamps are common.

Variation: No variation in Illinois. There are two subspecies. The Western subspecies (*nettingi*) is native to Illinois.

Habitat: Wetlands. Swamps, marshes, oxbows, sloughs, slow-moving streams and low lying areas along stream courses.

Breeding: Lays several hundred eggs in a nest hollowed out in the mud. Probably breeds in late winter or early spring.

Natural History: Another completely aquatic salamander that breathes through external gills that are easily visible just in front of the forelimbs. Known food items include insects, crustaceans, mollusks, and worms, as well as some plant material such as algea. Capable of surviving drought periods by secreting slime which hardens into a cocoon-like structure, creating a sealed chamber in the mud. Like many wetland species the Lesser Siren has been negatively impacted by the conversion of wetlands to agricultural land. Sirens have elongated bodies with very small front legs and lack hind limbs completely. They are often mistaken for eels, but the feathery external gills of the sirens are diagnostic (eels are fish and have internal gills). This is one of the few salamanders that is capable of vocalization. They are reported to communicate with each other using clicking sounds and when captured they sometimes emit a yelping sound.

CHAPTER 8

THE RIVERS AND STREAMS OF ILLINOIS

As a preface to the next chapter (Chapter 9, The Fishes of Illinois), this short chapter is intended to provide a brief introduction into the waterways of Illinois, which are home to the state's fish species. Many people are surprised to learn that the state of Illinois boasts over 87,000 miles of rivers and streams within its borders. Eight hundred eighty of these miles make up the state's borders. The entire western border of Illinois is defined by the Mississippi River, the state's southern border is marked by the Ohio River, and the southeastern border from Clark County south to the Ohio River is delineated by the Wabash River.

In additon, another aquatic ecosystem, Lake Michigan, defines a portion of the state's northeastern border.

With so many miles of waterways, it is not surprising that Illinois is also home to more than 200 fish species. The number of native fish species that can be found in Illinois' waters numbers 191 (plus 20 introduced species), making the fishes the second most diverse group of vertebrates in the state.

Figure 8 below shows how completely the state of Illinois is partitioned by waterways.

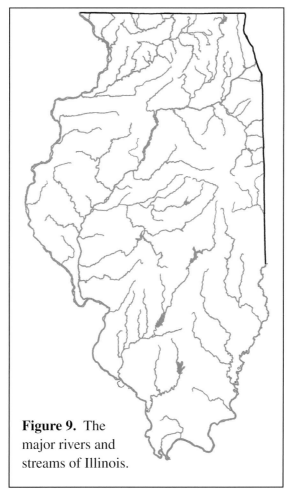

Figure 9. The major rivers and streams of Illinois.

With the exception a few tiny creeks in a small strip of land bordering Lake Michigan, the entire state of Illinois is within the Mississippi River drainage basin. Figure 9 below shows how much of the North American Continent is contained within the Mississippi River Level I Watershed. The St. Lawrence River Level I Watershed is shown in green. Since the Great Lakes are contained within the St. Lawrence River Level I watershed, a tiny sliver of land in extreme northeastern Illinois bordering Lake Michigan is actually within the St. Lawrence River Level I Watershed. Although that sliver of land along Lake Michigan is too small to be seen in Figure 10 below, it can be seen in Figure 11 on the next page.

Meanwhile Figure 11 below shows how the Mississippi River Level I Wastershed is divided into smaller Level II Watersheds, 2 of which, the Mississippi River and Ohio River Watersheds, impact the state of Illinois.

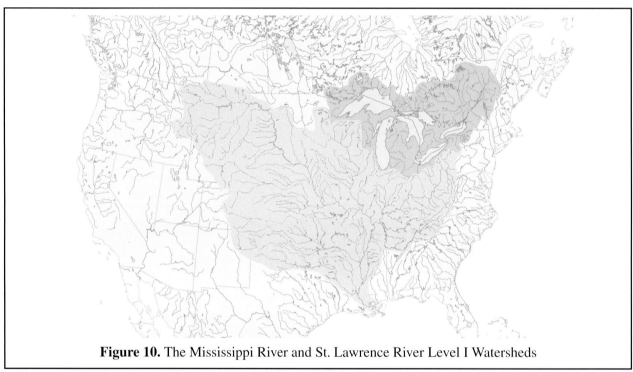

Figure 10. The Mississippi River and St. Lawrence River Level I Watersheds

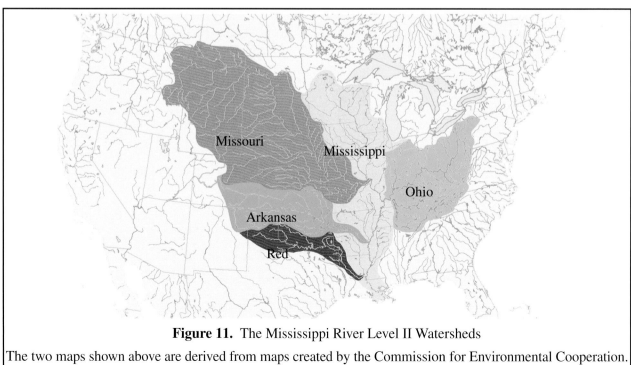

Figure 11. The Mississippi River Level II Watersheds

The two maps shown above are derived from maps created by the Commission for Environmental Cooperation.

Figure 12 below shows the rivers and streams of Illinois and the Level II Watersheds within which those Illinois streams reside. On this map, the Mississippi River Level II Watereshed is in gray and the Ohio River Level II Watershed in Orange. The sliver of green in the northeastern portion of the state represents small creeks that drain directly into Lake Michigan, which is actually a part of the St. Lawrence River Level I Watershed (shown in Figure 10 on the previous page).

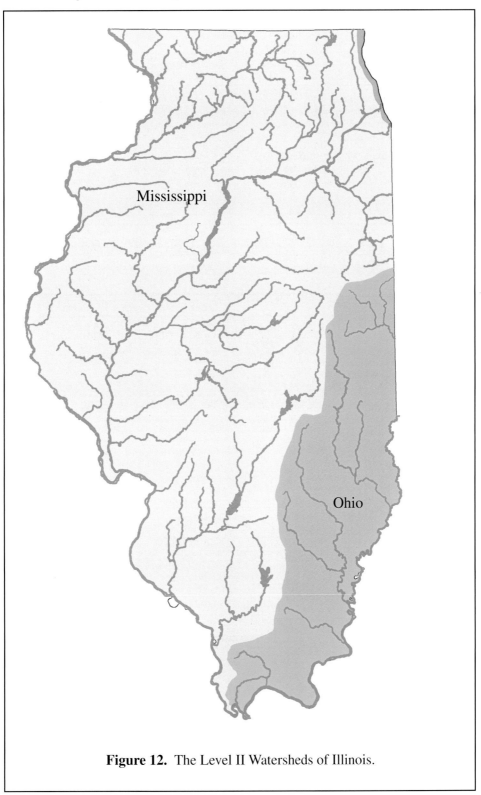

Figure 12. The Level II Watersheds of Illinois.

Both the Ohio River watershed and the Mississippi River watershed naturally consist of increasingly smaller tributaries, each of which constitutes its own drainage area. The next level of watershed designation after Level II of course is Level III. The Ohio and Mississippi watersheds consist of a total of 9 Level III Watersheds in Illinois. Figure 13 below shows those Level III Watersheds. The bold black line on the map designates the division between the state's Level II Watersheds (Mississippi and Ohio). The sliver of red seen in the northeastern portion of the state represents the area which drains directly into Lake Michigan. As was explained in the description of Figure 10, this region is a part of the St. Lawrence Watershed.

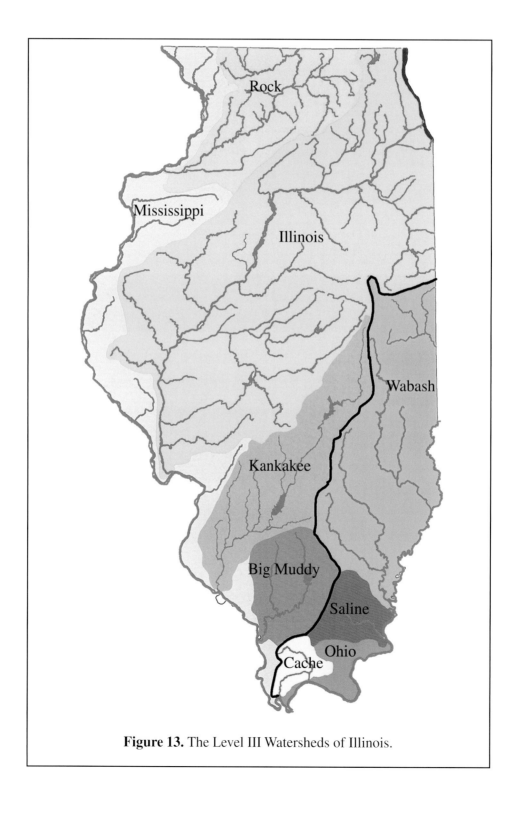

Figure 13. The Level III Watersheds of Illinois.

The watershed divisions illustrated in the series of maps shown in this chapter are useful to natural scientists in many ways. For the purposes of this book, an appreciation of these drainage basins (or watersheds) can provide insight into the distribution of Illinois's fish species. More importantly, conservation organizations can monitor these various watersheds for pollution and other factors that may impact upon the health of fish populations contained within them. Figure 14 below shows the Level IV watersheds of the state. Even the relatively small watersheds shown in Figure 14 can be divided into subsequently smaller and smaller designations, with each smaller watershed providing a more concise view of the local ecosystem represented by that smaller designation.

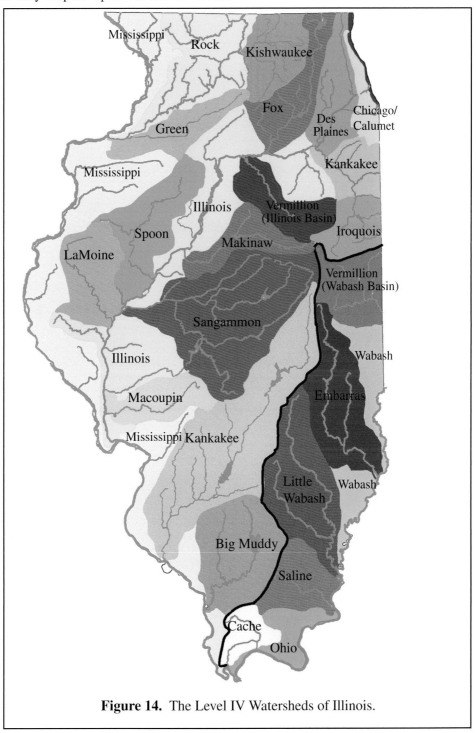

Figure 14. The Level IV Watersheds of Illinois.

Although the state of Illinois still boasts an abundance of fish species, a few species no longer exist in the state. At least 9 species of fishes native to Illinois are now extirpated. A total of 28 more are now regarded as endangered or threatened and still others are regarded as species for which there is cause for concern regarding their continued survival in Illinois waters.

Like all other habitat types within the eastern United States, the waterways of Illinois have been highly altered by man. There are a number of major impoundments on Illinois's larger river systems. Countless smaller dams have inundate portions of many small creeks. Direct pollution from industry and urbanization is an important source of stream degradation in the state. But of equal importance is indirect contamination from agriculture. Agricultural-related pollution and stream degradation can come in the form of chemical runoff from herbecides, pesticides, and chemical fertilizers. Also important is the destruction of vegetated buffer zones by farmers needing to maximize the production area of their land. Erosion and siltation from row cropping operations impact nearly every stream in the state. To a lesser extent, livestock operations statewide can also have negative impacts as cattle destroy creek banks and stir up silt from stream bottoms.

Add to these problems the presence of nearly 13 million people, and you have a significant threat to our fresh waters. All Illinoisans use prodigious amounts of water and collectively we produce many of tons of sewage and waste water, some of which in rural areas may wind up entering the state's waterways.

Many of Illinois's rivers and streams no longer support the high diversity of fish and other aquatic species that once was abundant within their banks and the future for many of the state's fish species is uncertain. If we regard this fact as a warning sign relating to the health of our aquatic ecosystems, and surely they are just that, then all Illinoisans should be acutely concerned about the future of our waterways. We often hear reasonable people argue against stringent protections of our environment. But few things are more important than these protections. Humans can survive for a maximum of 4 minutes without air and maximum of 4 days without water. It follows then that our paramount priorities should be to ensure that we all always have clean air to breath and pure water to drink!

The series of maps shown on the previous pages gives a good representation of how smaller streams and their watersheds are integrated into larger streams and larger watersheds. What also becomes apparent from these maps is that when it comes water, everything (and everyone) downstream is affected by the quality of the water and the overall environmental health of the waters upstream. The environmental quality of that tiny creek in your backyard or on your farm affects not only the life of organisms living within that stream, but also organisms within the larger streams into which it flows. And ultimately, the wildlife living in Louisiana's coastal marshes, the fishes living in the depths of the Gulf of Mexico, and the magnificent coral ecosystems of the great reefs of the Caribbean.

CHAPTER 9

THE FISHES OF ILLINOIS

— THE ORDERS AND FAMILIES OF ILLINOIS FISHES —

Note: The sequence the orders and families of fishes shown in the table below is a representation of the order in which they appear in the book, and may not be an accurate representation of the phylogeny of the fishes.

Class - **Actinopterygii** (ray-finned fishes)

Order - **Perciformes** (typical fishes)

Family	**Centrarchidae** (sunfishes)
Family	**Elassomatidae** (pygmy sunfishes)
Family	**Scianidae** (drums)
Family	**Moronidae** (true basses)
Family	**Gobidae** (gobies)
Family	**Percidae** (perches & darters)

Order - **Salmoniformes**

Family	**Esocidae** (pikes)
Family	**Umbridae** (mudminnows)
Family	**Osmeridae** (smelts)
Family	**Salmonidae** (salmonids)

Order - **Percopsiformes** (pirate perch & cavefish)

Family	**Percopsidae** (trout perch)
Family	**Aphredoderidae** (pirate perch)
Family	**Amblyopsidae** (cavefishes)

Order - **Acipenseriformes** (primitive fishes)

Family	**Acipenseridae** (sturgeons)
Family	**Polyodontidae** (paddlefish)

Order - **Lepisosteiformes** (gar)

Family	**Lepisosteidae** (gars)

Order - **Amiiformes** (bowfin)

Family	**Amiidae** (bowfin)

Order - **Osteoglossiformes** (bonytongues)

Family	**Hiodontidae** (mooneyes)

Order - **Anguilliformes** (eels)

Family	**Anguillidae** (freshwater eels)

Order - **Gadiformes**

Family	**Gadidae** (codfish)

Order - **Atheriniformes**

Family	**Atherinidae** (silversides)

Order - **Cyprinodontiformes** (topminnows & livebearers)

Family	**Fundulidae** (topminnows)
Family	**Poeciliidae** (livebearers)

Order - **Clupeiformes** (sardines, herrings, & shads)

Family	**Clupeidae** (herring & shad)

Order - **Gasterosteiformes** (mostly small marine fishes)

Family	**Gasterosteidae** (sticklebacks)

Order - **Siluriformes** (catfishes)

Family	**Ictaluridae** (American catfishes)

Order - **Cypriniformes** (minnows & suckers)

Family	**Catastomidae** (suckers)
Family	**Cyprinidae** (minnows)

Order - **Scorpaeniformes**

Family	**Cottidae** (sculpins)

Class - **Actinopterygii** (bony fishes)

Order - **Perciformes** (typical fishes)

Family - **Centrarchidae** (sunfishes)

Largemouth Bass *Micropterus salmoides*	**Smallmouth Bass** *Micropterus dolomieui*	**Spotted Bass** *Micropterus punctulatus*

Size: May reach 38 inches and 22 pounds. Illinois record size is just over 13 pounds and 10 ounces.

Abundance: Very common in all Level II watersheds.

Natural History: This is probably America's most popular freshwater game fish, pursued by anglers throughout the country. Indeed an entire sporting industry has evolved around the pursuit of this fish. Found in virtually any body of water in the state, including streams and small farm ponds.

Size: Maximum of 11 pounds. Illinois record size is 6 pounds and 7 ounces; it was caught in 1985.

Abundance: Common. Range restricted to northern half of state.

Natural History: Prefers clearer, cooler, more highly oxygenated waters than the Largemouth Bass. Crayfish are a preferred prey, especially for stream dwelling Smallmouth Bass. Like its cousin the Largemouth Bass, this is an important game species. It is renowned for its tenacious fighting abilities.

Size: Maximum of 8 pounds. Average adult is about 3 to 4 pounds Ohio record size is 5.5 pounds and 21 inches.

Abundance: Fairly common.

Natural History: Intermediate between the 2 previous species in both the size of the mouth and in its habitat preferences. Primarily a fish of flowing waters but can tolerate warmer conditions than the Smallmouth. Avoids the still waters favored by the Largemouth. Tongue feels rough to the touch.

Bluegill *Lepomis macrochirus*	**Longear Sunfish** *Lepomis megalotis*	**Warmouth** *Lepomis gulosus*

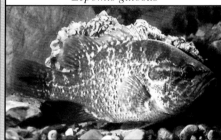

Size: Record of 4 pounds, 12 ounces. Illinois record is 3 pounds, 8 ounces from a farm pond. Most are under 0.5 pounds.

Abundance: Very common.

Natural History: The Bluegill is Illinois's best known sunfish. This is the first fish caught on hook and line by many a young angler. It is an important game fish throughout the state. They are regularly stocked in new impoundments and are found in virtually every significant body of water in the state.

Size: World record size is 1 pound, 12 ounces. No records are available for this species in Illinois. Most are about 6 inches in length.

Abundance: Common.

Natural History: Breeding males are one of the most brilliantly colored of the sunfishes. Clear streams with gravelly or sandy substrates are habitat. Two very similar species in Illinois. The **Northern Sunfish** (*L. peltastes*) is found on map in dark gray, while the Longear range is the light gray areas.

Size: Record of 2 pounds 7 ounces. Illinois record 1 pound, 13 ounces. Most are about 6 to 7 inches as adults.

Abundance: Uncommon in Illinois.

Natural History: A fish of lowland creeks and swamps, the Warmouth is most common in the southern United States. Although it occurs statewide, it is sporadically distributed and may be absent from many areas. It prefers waters with thick growths of aquatic plants. Teeth are present on the tongue.

Class - **Actinopterygii** (bony fishes)

Order - **Perciformes** (typical fishes)

Family - **Centrarchidae** (sunfishes)

Redear Sunfish *Lepomis microlophus*	**Pumkinseed** *Lepomis gibbosus*	**Green Sunfish** *Lepomis cyanellus*

Size: Record 4 pounds 13 ounces. Illinois record is 2 pounds and 12 ounces. Averages about 8 to 10 inches.

Abundance: Uncommon in most of Illinois.

Natural History: These fish also go by the name "Shellcracker," a reference to their habit of eating small freshwater mollusks such clams and snails. The natural distribution of this fish was originally the southeastern United States. Today it has been widely introduced throughout much of the eastern US.

Size: The maximum length for this species is 16 inches. There are no angling records available for Illinois.

Abundance: Uncommon in Illinois. Northern Illinois only.

Natural History: Found mainly in the northern United States and along the eastern seaboard. Inhabits still or slow-moving waters. Snails and bivalves are a major food source. The Pumpkinseed is similar to the Redear Sunfish in both habits and appearance and is the northern counterpart of that species.

Size: Maximum recorded size is 2 pounds 2 ounces and 12 inches in length. No size records available for Illinois.

Abundance: Common. Found in statewide in all watersheds.

Natural History: This is a fairly common fish throughout the state. It may be found in ponds and lakes but its natural habitat is quiet pools of slow-moving streams. It is known to hybridize readily with other *Lepomis* sunfishes, especially the Bluegill. Tolerates warm, low-oxygen waters.

Orange-spotted Sunfish *Lepomis humilis*	**Bantam Sunfish** *Lepomis symmetricus*	**Rock Bass** *Ambloplites rupestris*

Size: Average adult size is only 2 to 3 inches. Maximum reported length is about 4 inches. No records available for this species in Illinois.

Abundance: Fairly common.

Natural History: Inhabits creeks and rivers where it favors quiet water pools with cover in the form of brush. When it occurs in lakes and impoundments it is found in shallow bays. Nests in gravel. Eats mainly small aquatic insect larva and small crustaceans. Female is less colorful than the male.

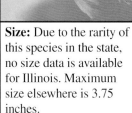

Size: Due to the rarity of this species in the state, no size data is available for Illinois. Maximum size elsewhere is 3.75 inches.

Abundance: Very rare in Illinois. Threatened.

Natural History: The smallest of Illinois *Lepomis* sunfishes. In Illinois the Bantam Sunfish is an inhabitant of the lowlands near the confluence of the Big Muddy and the Mississippi Rivers. Swamps with clean, clear water and ample aquatic vegetation are the favored habitats. Common in the Deep South.

Size: Record size is 3 pounds. Largest recorded specimen from Illinois is 1 pound and 10 ounces from Aux Sable Creek.

Abundance: Common in northern Illinois.

Natural History: Also known as the "Goggle Eye," the Rock Bass is a fish of clear, cool waters. They are primarily a stream fish that is found in clear streams with good water quality mostly in the northern portion of the state. The natural distribution is from the Great Lakes region south into northern Alabama.

Class - **Actinopterygii** (bony fishes)

Order - **Perciformes** (typical fishes)

Family - **Centrarchidae** (sunfishes)

Flier *Centrachus macropterus*	White Croppie *Pomoxis annularus*	Black Croppie *Pomoxis nigromaculatus*

Flier — *Centrachus macropterus*

Size: Averages about 5 inches. Maximum of about 8 inches. No record size data is available for Illinois.

Abundance: Uncommon in Illinois, Lower Mississippi, and Ohio.

Natural History: The Flier is a lowland species that is usually found in natural lakes, oxbows, swamps, or sluggish streams. Most often occurs in waters with mud bottom. In Illinois this species is most common in the swamps of the Mississippi and lower Ohio River valleys.

White Croppie — *Pomoxis annularus*

Size: Maximum size about 5 pounds, 3 ounces. Illinois angling record 4 pounds, 7 ounces.

Abundance: Common in all Level III watersheds in Illinois.

Natural History: The White Croppie is more tolerant of turbid warter conditions than the Black Croppie, though both are often found in the same waters. White Croppie is usually much lighter, but not always. Positive ID can be made by counting the stiff spines on the dorsal fin. White Croppie has only 6.

Black Croppie — *Pomoxis nigromaculatus*

Size: Maximum size about 5 pounds and 19 inches in length. Illinois record 4 pounds, 8 ounces.

Abundance: Found statewide but less common than White Croppie.

Natural History: The Black Croppie likes clearer waters than the White Croppie, though they may occur together. Black Croppie are native to the Atlantic slope but have been widely introduced across the eastern US. Usually shows more black pigment than white. Has 7 or 8 stiff spines on dorsal fin.

Family - **Elassomatidae** (pygmy sunfishes)	Family - **Sciaenidae** (drums)
Banded Pygmy Sunfish *Elasoma zonatum*	Freshwater Drum *Aplodinotus grunniens*

Banded Pygmy Sunfish — *Elasoma zonatum*

Size: Maximum 1.75 inches. Most are barely over an inch in length. Exhibits sexual dimorphism (see photos above) and males grow slightly larger than females.

Abundance: Rare in Illinois. Lower Ohio, lower Mississippi, lower Big Muddy, and Cache watersheds only. They are widespread throughout the Coastal Plain from Texas to North Carolina where they live in swamps, oxbows, and slow-moving streams. In Illinois, they are restricted to the southern of the state.

Natural History: These tiny fishes are unknown to most Illinoisans. They are southern species that can be quite common in the swamps and bayous of the Deep South. Like many southern animals and fishes they range northward in the Mississippi Valley as far as the southern tip of Illinois. The extreme southern tip of Illinois between the Shawnee Hills and the Ohio River is a region characterized by flat floodplains and historically was mostly swamp and marsh. Ecologically, this region has more in common with the southern US than it does with the rest of the state.

Freshwater Drum — *Aplodinotus grunniens*

Size: Record size 54 pounds. Illinois record is 35 pounds.

Abundance: Very common and found in all watersheds throughout the state. Most common in large streams and lakes.

Natural History: This is the only member of the drum family that lives in fresh water. Most are saltwater fishes and several are important food and sport fishes. By contrast, the Freshwater Drum is not highly regarded by sport anglers.

Class - **Actinopterygii** (bony fishes)

Order - **Perciformes** (typical fishes)

Family - **Moronidae** (true basses)

Yellow Bass *Morone mississippiensis*	White Bass *Morone chrysops*	Striped Bass *Morone saxatilis*

  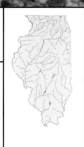

Yellow Bass
Morone mississippiensis

Size: Record size is 2 pounds 4 ounces. Illinois record is 2 pounds.

Abundance: Fairly common in larger rivers in the state. Recorded from all Level III watersheds in Illinois.

Natural History: A clear water fish, the Yellow Bass avoids muddy rivers and streams in favor of lakes, oxbows, and other still waters. Natural lakes with abundant vegetation are its main habitat but it has adapted well to man-made lakes.

White Bass
Morone chrysops

Size: Illinois record 4 pounds, 14 ounces. Record 5 pounds, 9 ounces.

Abundance: Fairly common in larger rivers in the state. Recorded from all Level III watersheds in Illinois.

Natural History: These important game fish are famous for forcing schools of bait fish to the surface then attacking them in a feeding frenzy. Bait fish leaping indicate the presence of feeding bass. Savvy fishermen look for these eruptions of bait fish known as "jumps."

Striped Bass
Morone saxatilis

Size: World record 78.5 pounds. Illinois record 31.5 pounds.

Abundance: Uncommon to rare in Illinois. Widely introduced into impoundments across the state.

Natural History: Striped Bass were anadromous fish that lived in salt water but migrated into freshwater rivers to spawn. Now widely stocked in lakes by wildlife agencies, they have adapted to a freshwater existence. Hybrid Striped/White Bass are known as "Rockfish."

Family - **Moronidae** (true basses)	Family - **Gobiidae** (gobies)	Family - **Percidae** (perch & darters)
White Perch *Morone americana*	Round Goby *Neogobius melanostomus*	Eastern Sand Darter/Western Sand Darter *Ammocrypta pellucida/Ammocrypta clara*

Eastern Sand Darter

White Perch
Morone americana

Size: No size records available for Illinois. Maximum size attained is about 22 inches.

Abundance: Uncommon in Illinois. Introduced.

Natural History: The White Perch is native to streams and brackish waters east of the Appalachian Plateau. They have been introduced into Illinois in the Ohio, Mississippi and Illinois Rivers as well as in Lake Michigan. They are important game fish within their native range on the Atlantic slope.

Round Goby
Neogobius melanostomus

Size: Averages about 5 or 6 inches but can reach a maximum length of 10 inches.

Abundance: They are quite common in Lake Michigan.

Natural History: The gobies are exotic invasive species native to Eurasia that appeared in the Great Lakes sometime around 1990. As is often the case with exotic species, these fish have not been good for the Great Lakes. Though relatively small, they are voracious predators of fish eggs and fry.

Eastern Sand Darter/Western Sand Darter
Ammocrypta pellucida/Ammocrypta clara

Size: The Eastern Sand Darter can reach a maximum of 3.25 inches. Western Sand Darter 2.75 inches.

Abundance: Rare. Western is Endangered. Eastern is Threatened.

Natural History: The aptly named Sand Darters are associated with sandy substrates of medium to large streams. When not swimming about in search of food or a mate they stay buried in the sand except for the top of their heads. Their translucent colored bodies render them effectively invisible.

Class - **Actinopterygii** (bony fishes)

Order - **Perciformes** (typical fishes)

Family - **Percidae** (perch & darters)

Yellow Perch *Perca flavescens*	Walleye *Sander vitreus*	Sauger *Sander canadensis*

Yellow Perch — *Perca flavescens*

Size: World record 4 pounds 3 ounces. Illinois record 2 pounds and 8.75 ounces. Averages less than a pound.

Abundance: Most common in northern Illinois.

Natural History: Native to the northern and eastern United States, Yellow Perch have recently expanded their range into more southerly regions. They are a popular pan fish in the north. In Illinois they are found in both man-made and natural lakes throughout the state, and are common in Lake Michigan.

Walleye — *Sander vitreus*

Size: World record is 25 pounds. Average is 2 to 4 pounds. Illinois record is 14 pounds from Kankakee River.

Abundance: Fairly common in large rivers and lakes.

Natural History: Walleye live in larger rivers, impoundments, and natural lakes where deep water provides the cool temperatures these fish require. They are regarded as one of the most palatable of the game fishes. Found statewide in large rivers and lakes. Most common in northern Illinois and Lake Michigan.

Sauger — *Sander canadensis*

Size: World record 8 pounds 12 ounces. Average about a pound. Illinois record is 5 pounds, 12.5 ounces.

Abundance: Fairly common in large rivers and lakes.

Natural History: Found throughout the Midwest and northward to Canada, the Sauger is a smaller relative of the Walleye that is more adapted to turbid waters. Hybridization between the Walleye and the Sauger results in a fish known as the "Saugeye," which can attain a much larger size than the Sauger.

Logperch *Percina caprodes*	Dusky Darter *Percina sciera*	Blackside Darter *Percina maculata*

Logperch — *Percina caprodes*

Size: Averages 3 to 5 inches with a maximum of about 7 inches.

Abundance: Fairly common. Probably occurs in suitable habitats in all Level III watersheds in Illinois.

Dusky Darter — *Percina sciera*

Size: Averages 3 to 4 inches with a maximum of 5 inches.

Abundance: Uncommon in Illinois. Occupies only the Wabash, lower Saline, and Ohio Level III watersheds.

Blackside Darter — *Percina maculata*

Size: 2 to 3 inches typically. Maximum length 4.5 inches.

Abundance: Fairly common. Probably occurs in suitable habitat in every Level III watershed in the state.

Natural History: The darters of the genus *Percina* were originally represented by a total of 9 species in Illinois. Today, 3 species have been extirpated, leaving 6 extant species in the state. Several of these are uncommon or rare, and only the Blackside Darter and the Logperch can be regarded as fairly common fish in Illinois. There as many as 40 *Percina* species in the US and collectively they range throughout much of the eastern United States. All occur east of the Rocky Mountains and most are found east of the Great Plains. The infamous Snail Darter, which was the subject of a great environmental controversy that arose over the construction of the Tellico Dam in Tennesse, is a member of this genus. Most tend to inhabit the larger creeks (or even rivers), but some can be found in small (even tiny) creeks. The three species occurring in Illinois that are not shown above are the **Channel Darter** (*P. copelandi*); **River Darter** (*P. shumardi*); and **Slenderhead Darter** (*P. phoxocephala*).

Class - **Actinopterygii** (bony fishes)

Order - **Perciformes** (typical fishes)

Family - **Percidae** (perch & darters)

The True Darters - genus *Etheostoma* - 17 species in Illinois (15 shown below and on next page)

Mud Darter	Bluebreast Darter	Bluntnose Darter
Etheostoma asprigne	*Etheostoma camurum*	*Etheostoma chlorosum*

Size: Maximum total length is 2.75 inches.

Abundance: Fairly common. Absent from the Chicago/Calumet, Des Plaines, Kankakee, and most of the Fox and Kishwaukee watersheds.

Size: Maximum total length is 3.5 inches.

Abundance: Very rare in Illinois. Occurring in Illinois only in the lower reaches of theVermillion watershed of the Wabash Basin.

Size: Maximum total length is 2.25 inches.

Abundance: Fairly common but absent from much of upper Illinois, the Rock, and the upper Wabash Level II watersheds.

Cypress Darter	Fantail Darter	Fringed Darter
Etheostoma proeliare	*Etheostoma flabellare*	*Etheostoma crossopterum*

Male / Female

Male / Female

Size: Maximum total length is 2 inches.

Abundance: Rare in Illinois. Restricted to the southern tip of state in Ohio, Cache, lower Big Muddy, and lower Mississippi.

Size: Maximum total length is 3.25 inches.

Abundance: Fairly common in northern half of Illinois. Disjunct population in the southern tip of the state along the Mississippi.

Size: Maximum total length is 4 inches.

Abundance: Rare in Illinois. Found in Illinois only in the Cache River Watershed in the southern tip of the state.

Rainbow Darter	Johnny Darter	Orangethroat Darter
Etheostoma caerulum	*Etheostoma nigrum*	*Etheostoma spectabile*

Breeding male

Breeding male

Size: Up to 3 inches.

Abundance: Fairly common in northeastern Illinois. Disjunct population in southeastern corner of state.

Size: Up to 2.75 inches.

Abundance: Common and found statewide. A common darter in the US and probably the most common darter in Illinois.

Size: Up to 2.75 inches.

Abundance: Fairly common and widespread but absent from northern Illinois and southeastern Illinois.

Class - **Actinopterygii** (bony fishes)
Order - **Perciformes** (typical fishes)
Family - **Percidae** (perch & darters)
The True Darters - genus *Etheostoma* - 17 species in Illinois

Greenside Darter	Iowa Darter	Slough Darter
Etheostoma blennoides	*Etheostoma exile*	*Etheostoma gracile*

Size: Maximum total length is 6.75 inches.

Abundance: Fairly common. Occurs in Illinois only in the upper portions of the Wabash River Level III watershed.

Size: Maximum total length is 2.75 inches.

Abundance: A northern species whose range extends southward into northernmost Illinois. Rock, upper Illinois, and upper Mississippi.

Size: Maximum total length is 2.25 inches.

Abundance: Mainly a southern fish but ranges northward into Illinois as far north as the Kankakee and the Little Wabash watersheds.

Banded Darter	Least Darter	Spottail Darter
Etheostoma zonale	*Etheostoma microperca*	*Etheostoma squamiceps*

Size: Maximum total length is 3 inches.

Abundance: Fairly common in northeastern Illinois. Upper Illinois, Rock and uppermost Wabash Level III watersheds.

Size: Maximum total length is 1.75 inches.

Abundance: Restricted to upstream portions of the Illinois and Rock River Level III watersheds in Illinois.

Size: Maximum total length is 3.25 inches.

Abundance: Rare in Illinois. Occurs in the state only in the Ohio watershed and the lower portion of the Saline River watershed.

Natural History: With at least 148 species distributed across North America, this genus boasts more species than any other genus of freshwater fish in the US. Among them are some of America's rarest fish and some of our most common. In coloration they range from a cryptic mottled brown to remarkably colorful. In many species the breeding males rival the most colorful of tropical aquarium fishes. Most species are strongly sexually dimorphic, with the females being more subdued in color and sometimes outright drab. The stunning breeding color of the male is temporary and replaced by a much more faded appearance through the rest of the year following spring breeding. The females of these fishes are often so similar that even expert ichthyologists can have difficulty identifying them. New species have been recently described and there are most likely new species yet to be discovered. Unlike most fishes, they lack air bladders for flotation and they are mostly bottom dwellers that hug the sand and gravel bottoms of flowing streams. When startled they will move in quick, short dashes, hence the common name "darter." Illinois boasts 17 species of *Etheostoma*. Collectively their habitats include probably every drainage within the state and they are found in waterways ranging from swamps to large rivers to small creeks. A few species have a very restrictive distribution, being confined to a single drainage. Many species require pristine water conditions and these little fish can be a barometer to help determine the quality of Illinois waterways. Like "the canary in the coal mine" they are often the first fishes to suffer from the effects of water pollution, siltation, and other forms of stream degradation. In addition to those species pictured, tow other *Etheostoma* darter occurs in Illinois. The **Harlequin Darter** (*E. histrio*) and the **Stripetail Darter** (*E. kennicotti*).

Class - **Actinopterygii** (bony fishes)

Order - **Salmoniformes**

Family - **Esocidae** (pikes)

Grass Pickerel *Esox americanus*	**Northern Pike** *Esox lucius*	**Muskellunge** *Esox masquinongy*
		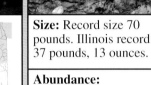
Size: Size: Average 8 to 10 inches. Maximum length 14 inches. 	**Size:** World record size of 62.5 pounds is from Europe. 	**Size:** Record size 70 pounds. Illinois record 37 pounds, 13 ounces. 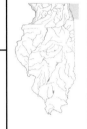
Abundance: Fairly common. Recorded from all Level III watersheds in Illinois. Least common in western IL.	**Abundance:** Uncommon. Range includes all of Illinois from about one-third up the way up the Illinois river north.	**Abundance:** Uncommon to rare in Illinois except in Lake Michigan where it may be fairly common.
Natural History: Inhabits swamps and streams. In smaller creeks it usually is found in quite pools. This fish likes clear waters and avoids muddy streams. This is the smallest of the pike family and thus feeds on smaller prey. Minnows and other small fish are prey.	**Natural History:** The Northern Pike is a fish of clear waters with abundant aquatic vegetation. Like all members of the pike family it is a highly carnivorous ambush predator with a very large mouth. The jaws are equipped with rows of sharp, barracuda-like teeth.	**Natural History:** Known as the "Muskie" by fishermen, this largest of the pikes is a prized game fish and one of the most difficult to catch. They live in both man-made lakes and clear water rivers where they favor the deep pools containing boulders, logs, etc.

Family - **Umbridae** (mudminnows)	Family - **Osmeridae** (Smelts)	Family - **Salmonidae** (salmonids)
Central Mudminnow *Umbra limi*	**Rainbow Smelt** *Osmerus mordax*	**Cisco** *Coregonus artedii*

Size: Maximum length of 5.25 inches. Average about 2 to 3 inches. 	**Size:** Adults average 8 to 10 inches with a maximum of 14 inches. 	**Size:** Maximum length of 20 inches and up to 3 pounds. 
Abundance: Fairly common. Range in Illinois avoids most of the central prairie region of the state.	**Abundance:** Found only in Lake Michigan and its immediate tributaries.	**Abundance:** Now rare in Illinois. Occurs only in Lake Michigan. Was once much more common.
Natural History: The Central Mudminnow is the only Illinois representative of a very small family of fishes found in both North America and in Europe. They live in swamps and still waters of oxbows or slow flowing lowland creeks. Prefers areas with mucky bottom and can tolerate waters with low oxygen.	**Natural History:** Although they are a small fish the Rainbow Smelt is an important food fish in the Great Lakes region, where they are usually served fried with the bones intact. Many people in the region would be surprised to learn that this is not a native species. Rainbow Smelt were introduced into the Great Lakes in the early 1900s.	**Natural History:** These fish were once so common that a single fisherman might catch over a hundred in days fishing on the Great Lakes. They are now a Threatened Species. A northern fish that reaches the southernmost limits of its range in Lake Michigan. Cisco sometimes go by the name "Lake Herring."

Class - **Actinopterygii** (bony fishes)

Order - **Salmoniformes**

Family - **Salmonidae** (salmonids)

Lake Whitefish *Coreagonus clupeaformis*	Lake Trout *Salvelinus namaycush*	Chinook Salmon *Onchorhynchus tshawytscha*

Size: Can reach a maximum of 15 pounds and 30 inches. No records available for Illinois.

Abundance: Uncommon in Illinois waters but has seen an increase from historic lows a few decades ago.

Natural History: A northern species that reaches its southern distribution limits in the Great Lakes. Inhabits deep, cold waters with high dissolved oxygen content. In summer this species retreats to depths of more than 200 feet. Although not rare, they are much less common than in historical times before the impact of human activities.

Size: Illinois record is 38 pounds, 4 ounces. Maximum length is 4 feet.

Abundance: Uncommon in Illinois waters but has seen an increase from historic lows a few decades ago.

Natural History: The Lake Trout is a northern species that reaches its southern limits in the Great Lakes region. Historically they were more common but they have suffered from parasitism by the Sea Lamprey and from degradation of the Great Lakes water quality. These are fish of deep, cold waters and they are usually found well offshore.

Size: The Illinois record of 37 pounds was taken from Lake Michigan.

Abundance: Uncommon. Despite annual restocking efforts populations are currently low.

Natural History: This species is popular game fish and it is stocked annually in Lake Michigan by state wildlife agencies. Like most American Salmon, they are naturally anadromous fishes of the Pacific Northwest. They are an introduced species that has adpated to life in the Great Lakes but populations in Lake Michigan fluctuate.

Coho Salmon *Onchorhynchus kisutch*	Pink Salmon *Onchorhynchus gorbuscha*

Size: World record for hook and line is 33 pounds, 7 ounces. Illinois record is 20 pounds and 9 ounces.

Abundance: Fairly common in Lake Michigan.

Natural History: Another anadromous species native to the Pacific. Has been stocked in the Great Lakes since the 1970s and now enjoys a limited amount of spawing in New York waters in the tributaries of lakes Erie and Ontario. The sport fishery for this and other non-native salmon in New York is maintained by continuous restocking by NYDEC. These fish often go by the name "Silver Salmon" a reference to the color of non-spawning fishes. This is an important commercial fish species, but its flesh is not as highly rated as the Sockeye.

Size: Illinois record is 3 pounds, 4 ounces. World record of 14.5 pounds is from the Skykomish River in Washington.

Abundance: Fairly common in Lake Michigan.

Natural History: An anadromous species native to the Pacific Northwest of America. Introduction into the Great Lakes was unintentional but has since become an important game fish species in Lake Superior and Lake Michigan. First seen in Lake Erie in 1979. Great Lakes populaitons have now adapted to a freshwater existence. Adults move out of the lakes and into the lower reaches of some eastern Great Lakes drainages to spawn. Sometimes called "Humpback Salmon."

Class - **Actinopterygii** (bony fishes)

Order - **Perciformes** (typical fishes)

Family - **Salmonidae** (salmonids)

Rainbow Trout *Onchorhynchus mykiss*	**Brown Trout** *Salmo trutta*	**Brook Trout** *Salvelinus fontanalis*
Size: World record is 42 pounds, 2 ounces. Illinois record is just over 31 pounds.	**Size:** World record 40 pounds 4 ounces. Illinois record is 36 pounds, 11 ounces.	**Size:** Illinois record is 7 pounds, 5 ounces. World record is 14.5 pounds.
Abundance: Most common in northern Illinois. Stocked irregularly around the state.	**Abundance:** Extreme northern Illinois only. Stocked irregularly around the state.	**Abundance:** Extreme northern Illinois only. Native to Lake Michigan, stocked in streams.
Natural History: The Rainbow Trout is originally native to Pacific drainages of the Northwest. Today they have been widely introduced across much of America. They require cold, clear waters and thus are limited in distribution. Several streams in Illinois along with some lakes are stocked by IDNR.	**Natural History:** Like the Rainbow Trout this species has been introduced into Illinois where cool, clear waters allow for its survival. In the most ideal waters, some natural reproduction may occur, but most of the Brown Trout caught by anglers in Illinois were hatched in fish hatcheries and stocked.	**Natural History:** The Brook Trout is the only trout native to the eastern United States. This fish requires cooler water temperatures than our other trouts and is less tolerant of changes in stream conditions. It is not native to any streams in Illinois, but is today stocked in some locations in the state by IDNR.

Order - **Percopsiformes**

Family - **Percopsidae** (trout-perches)	Family - **Aphredodidae** (pirate perches)	Family - **Amblyopsidae** (cavefishes)
Trout Perch *Percopsis omiscomaycus*	**Pirate Perch** *Aphredoderus sayanus*	**Spring Cavefish** *Forbesichthys agassizii*
Size: Reaches a maximum of 7.75 inches.	**Size:** Reaches a maximum of 5.5 inches.	**Size:** Reaches a maximum of 3.25 inches.
Abundance: This is a species of high latitudes that approaches the southernmost limits of its range in Illinois.	**Abundance:** Fairly common. Range in Illinois is south of the Illinois River and mirrors that of the Trout Perch (north of river).	**Abundance:** Rare in Illinois. Found only in the Shawnee Hills region of southern Illinois where it has very restrictive habitat.
Natural History: The Trout Perch lives in lakes and quite pools of larger streams. It feeds on insects, crustaceans, and small fish. Mainly nocturnal, it spends the day in deep water	**Natural History:** The Pirate Perch is endemic to North America. It lives in swamps and spring-fed wetlands among heavy aquatic vegetation. May also be found in backwaters of streams.	**Natural History:** The Spring Cavefish lives in the mouths of caves and in springs emanating from underground waterways and is thus heavily pigmented and has small eyes.

Class - **Actinopterygii** (bony fishes)

Order - **Acipenseriformes** (primitive fishes)

Family - **Acipenseridae** (sturgeons)

Shovelnose Sturgeon *Scaphirynchus platorynchus*	**Pallid Sturgeon** *Scaphirynchus albus*

Size: Maximum of 43 inches. Illinois record is 5 pounds, 2 ounces.

Abundance: The most common sturgeon in Illinois, but still an uncommon fish. Mississippi River population is Endangered.

Natural History: Lives in the deep channels of the Mississippi, Ohio, Missouri, Tennessee, Arkansas and Red Rivers. Extirpated from the Rio Grande. The Shovelnose Sturgeon is a fish of flowing water rivers, thus they cannot live in lakes.

Size: Up to 67 pounds and 6 feet. No size records available for Illinois.

Abundance: A rare fish throughout most of its range and quite rare in Illinois. Federally Endangered.

Natural History: Found only in the deep channels of the Mississippi and Missouri Rivers. Today this is one of America's most endangered fishes. Locks and dams hinder movement and dredging of river channels eliminates sandbars.

Family - **Acipenseridae** (sturgeons)	Family - **Polydontidae** (paddlefish)
Lake Sturgeon *Acipenser fulvescens*	**Paddlefish** *Polyodon spathula*

Size: Record 310 pounds. Maximum length 8 feet.

Abundance: Rare. An Endangered Species in Illinois.

Natural History: Now highly endangered, the Lake Sturgeon inhabits the deep channels of the large rivers draining the middle of America. Range includes the Mississippi (except near the mouth), the Missouri, the Ohio, the Cumberland, the Arkansas and the Tennessee rivers as well as the Great Lakes. Lives for up to 150 years. Large females will lay up to 3 million eggs. Females attain a greater size than males.

Size: Can reach at least 180 pounds and over 7 feet.

Abundance: Fairly common in larger rivers.

Natural History: Paddlefish often go by the name "Spoonbill Catfish," but in fact they are not related to the catfishes. They are a member of a very small, primitive order of fishes that contains only 2 species (the other is a giant found in China that can reach lengths of over 20 feet). Paddlefish have skeletons that are mostly cartilage. Lives in larger rivers with turbid waters. Flesh is edible and is commercially valuable.

Class - **Actinopterygii** (bony fishes)

Order - **Lepisosteiformes** (gar)

Family - **Lepisosteidae**

Longnose Gar *Lepisosteus osseus*	**Shortnose Gar** *Lepisosteus platostomus*

Size: Record 50 pounds (6 feet in length). Illinois record 31 pounds, 8 ounces.

Abundance: Fairly common and probably the most common gar in Illinois.

Natural History: America's most widespread gar species, the Longnose Gar can be found in both large and medium sized rivers as well as large creeks. Also common in natural lakes and oxbows and in man-made impoundments. Females average larger than males and can live over 20 years. Highly piscivorous, feeding mostly on shad and other forage fishes.

Size: Maximum of about 5 pounds and 33 inches. Illinois record 6 pounds, 4 ounces.

Abundance: Widespread and probably fairly common in most areas.

Natural History: An inhabitant of quiet pools and floodplains of rivers and large creeks. Also found in swamps and oxbows and can tolerate waters with high turbidity. During periods of severe drought can survive for days in the mud of drying pools. In addition to fish also eats insects and crayfish.

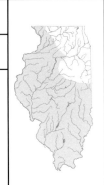

Spotted Gar *Lepisosteus oculatus*	**Alligator Gar** *Atractosteus spatula*

Size: Illinois bowfishing record 10 pounds, 2 ounces. Maximum length about 3.5 feet.

Abundance: Fairly common in the southern tip of the state.

Natural History: Habitat is swamps, sloughs, oxbows, natural lakes, and slow-moving creeks. In Illinois, they are most common in the southern tip of the state. This gar prefers clearer waters with less siltation than the similar Shortnose Gar. Heavily vegetated waters are preferred. Best differentiated from the Shortnose Gar by the presence of dark spots on the snout. Food is mostly fishes.

Size: Can reach 10 feet and 300 pounds. No size records are available for Illinois.

Abundance: Very rare in Illinois. State Endangered.

Natural History: Alligator Gar once ranged well up the Ohio and Mississippi Rivers and their major tributaries into Illinois, Missouri, and southern Indiana and southern Ohio. Today this is a highly endangered fish and efforts to restore the species are being undertaken by the IDNR. Adult Alligator Gars are highly predaceous and known to eat small mammals and birds as well as fish and even carrion.

Class - **Actinopterygii** (bony fishes)

Order - **Amiiformes**	Order - **Osteoglossiformes** (bony tongues)	
Family - **Amiidae** (bowfin)	Family - **Hidontidae** (mooneyes)	

Order - Amiiformes — Family - Amiidae (bowfin)

Bowfin
Amia calva

Size: Record size 21.5 pounds.

Abundance: Fairly common and widespread in Illinois. Absent from the Sangammon, Iroquois and upper Wabash basins.

Natural History: This is the only surviving species of an ancient family of primitive fishes that dates back to the age of the dinosaurs. Found in swamps and oxbow lakes. They sometimes go by the nickname "Grinnel." These fish are capable of gulping air into the swim bladder to breath and burrowing into the mud to survive during droughts.

Order - Osteoglossiformes — Family - Hidontidae (mooneyes)

Mooneye
Hiodon tergisus

Size: Maximum 17 inches and 2.5 pounds

Abundance: Has declined signifcantly in Illinois waters. Probably as a result of siltation. This fish like clear, flowing waters.

Natural History: The Mooneye is one of only two species in the family Hiodontidae, which is endemic to North America. Their appearance is very similar to their distant relatives the shads and herrings. They live in large rivers and lakes and feed on a wide variety of invertebrate and small vertebrate prey.

Goldeye
Hiodon alasoides

Size: Reaches 20 inches and 3 pounds.

Abundance: Uncommon in Illinois. Has probably declined from historical numbers in the state. Tolerates turbitity better than Mooneye.

Natural History: Similar to the Mooneye but found in rivers with higher turbidity. Unlike the Mooneye, this species does not thrive in impoundments, but does exist in natural lakes and backwaters of large rivers. It is an important food fish in parts of Canada, where it is eaten smoked.

Order - **Anguilliformes** (eels) — Family - **Anguillidae**

American Eel
Anguilla rostrata

Size: Up to 4 feet.

Abundance: Rare and in decline.

Natural History: Eels have one of the most remarkable life cycles of any fish. After hatching far out in the Atlantic Ocean tiny larva migrate to the coast and swim hundreds of miles upstream in inland rivers. After up to 15 years, adults return to the sea to spawn and die. Dams hinder migrations.

Order - **Gadiformes** — Family - **Gadidae**

Burbot
Lota lota

Size: Record size 18.5 pounds.

Abundance: Uncommon.

Natural History: A relative of the saltwater cod, haddock, and pollock, all of which are important food fishes. The Burbot is the single freshwater species of the entire order. They are cold-water fish that inhabit large rivers. They are primarily nocturnal and usually confined to deep waters.

Order - **Atheriniformes** — Family - **Atherinidae**

Mississippi Silverside
Menidia audens

Size: About 5 inches maximum length.

Abundance: Common.

Natural History: Silversides travel in large schools near the surface of lakes and rivers and are important prey for larger fish species, including many game fish. Another species known as the Brook Silverside (*Labidesthes siculus*) is widespread in Illinois.

Class - **Actinopterygii** (bony fishes)

Order - **Cyprinidontiformes** (topminnows & livebearers)

Family - **Fundulidae** (topminnows)

Blackspotted Topminnow *Fundulus olivaceus*	**Blackstripe Topminnow** *Fundulus olivaceus*

Starhead Topminnow *Fundulus dispar*	**Banded Killifish** *Fundulus diaphanus*

Size: Blackspotted Topminnow 3.75 inches maximum. Blackstripe Topminnow maximum of 3 inches. Banded Killifish can reach up to 5 iches. Starhead Minnow has a record length just over 3 inches.

Natural History: The topminnows get their name from the fact that they are always seen right at the water's surface. They feed on both emerging aquatic insects and tiny terrestrial insects that fall or fly onto the water. The characteristic white spot on the top of the head of many species is easily visible as they suspend at the surface. Most species are found in the Mississippi River Watershed, and in Illinois only one species is widesrpead across the state. The Blackstripe Topminnow is the most widely distributed *Fundulus* species in Illinois, being found everywhere *except* for the northern portion of the Mississippi Valley. It is one of the few species to occupy upland streams. Most topminninows are lowland species. Although they are found in flowing streams, all topminnows prefer quite pools and backwaters, including beaver ponds, swamps, and low gradient streams throughout their range. The Banded Killifish is a Threatened Species in Illinois. One other *Fundulus* species, the **Northern Studfish** (*F. catenatus*), has been recorded at a few localities along the lower Mississippi in southern Illinois.

Family - **Poeciliidae** (livebearers)

Western Mosquitofish *Gambusia affinis*

Size: Females 2.5 inches, males 1.25.

Natural History: True to their name, these tiny fish eat large numbers of mosquito larva. Uniquely among Illinois fishes, they give birth to fully-formed young. They live in the shallows of swamps and backwaters, where they will forage in water less than an inch deep. A close relative of the aquarium Guppy.

Class - **Actinopterygii** (bony fishes)

Order - **Clupieformes** (sardines, herrings, shad)

Family - **Clupiedae** (shad & herring)

Threadfin Shad *Dorosoma petenense*	**Gizzard Shad** *Dorosoma cepedianum*

Skipjack Herring *Alosa chrysochloris*	**Alewife** *Alosa psuedoharengus*

Size: Threadfin Shad is the smallest with a maximum of about 9 inches. Both the Gizzard Shad and the Skipjack Herring can get well over 3 pounds (3.5 and 3.75, respectively). Meanwhile the Alewife can reach 15 inches, although most are about 10 inches in length as adults.

Natural History: Threadfin Shad are filter feeding fishes occurring in large schools and they are a major food for many important game fishes in America. They are not very tolerant of cold temperatures and severe winter cold fronts can cause major die-offs. **Gizzard Shad** are another plankton feeder that filters tiny organisms from the water through specialized gill rakers. These fish occur in major rivers and their large impoundments throughout the eastern United States, including all the larger rivers in Illinois. They are an important forage species for many popular game fishes. The **Skipjack Herring** is originally an anadromous species that is now mostly landlocked due to the presence of dams on most major rivers. Although they are sometimes caught by fishermen they are not regarded as good table fare. Their range is restricted mostly to larger rivers and their impoundments. **Alewife** are also anadromous fishes by nature, but they have been introduced into the Great Lakes where they have adapted to a year-round life in fresh water.

Order - **Gasterosteiformes**

Family - **Gasterosteidae** (sticklebacks)

Brook Stickleback
Culaea inconstans

Size: Up to 3.5 inches.

Natural History: Most members of this fish order (Gasterosteiformes) are marine and include such strange fishes as the pipefish, tubenoses, and trumpetfishes to name a few. There are a total of 3 stickleback species in Illinois and all are northern fishes. The **Ninespine Stickleback** (*C. pungitiuss*) the **Threespine Stickleback** (*C. aculeatus*) are found in Lake Michigan and the immediate vicinity. The **Brook Stickleback** (*C. inconstans*, shown above) ranges across northern Illinois.

Class - **Actinopterygii** (bony fishes)

Order - **Siluiformes** (catfishes)

Family - **Ictaluridae** (American catfishes)

Yellow Bullhead *Ameiurus natalis*	**Black Bullhead** *Ameiurus melas*	**Brown Bullhead** *Ameiurus nebulosus*

Size: Maximum of 19 inches. Illinois record is 5 pounds, 4 ounces from the Fox River back in 1955.

Abundance: Very common. Probably the most common catfish in Illinois.

Natural History: Widespread, common and easily caught on hook and line the Yellow Bullhead is a familiar fish to many Americans. They are often known by the nickname "Mudcat." Ranges from the central Great Plains eastward, including all of Illinois. Told from other bullheads by yellow chin barbels.

Size: Maximum length of 24 inches and record weight of 8 pounds. Illinois record is 5 pounds, 6 ounces.

Abundance: Common and widespread but probably less common that Yellow Bullhead.

Natural History: Black Bullheads are mainly nocturnal fishes that do not feed during the day. They live in still water pools in streams or in natural lakes and man-made impoundments. They can be distinguished from the Yellow Bullhead by their dark chin barbels. Brown Bullhead has darker caudal fin (see photos).

Size: Maximum of 21 inches and 5 pounds, 11 ounces. Illinois record is only 1 pound and 10 ounces.

Abundance: Restricted to the main channel and uper tributaries of the Illinois River.

Natural History: The least common of the Illinois' *Ameiurus* catfishes. As with other bullheads, the parent fish stay with the eggs until hatching and the newly hatched young swim in schools near the surface with the mother bullhead in attendance. Found in ponds, lakes, sloughs, creeks, and small rivers.

Channel Catfish *Ictalurus punctatus*	**Blue Catfish** *Ictalurus furcatus*	**Flathead Catfish** *Plylodictus olivaris*

Size: Maximum of about 65 pounds. Illinois record is 45 pounds.

Abundance: Common and widespread in Illinois. Our most common large catfish.

Natural History: A popular game species. Grown commercially as a food fish on fish farms in the south and sold in groceries and restaurants. Specimens in clear water are uniformly dark (as in photo above). Individuals from turbid waters are light gray with black spots.

Size: Maximum size 150 pounds and 5 feet. Illinois record is 124 pounds.

Abundance: Fairly common in deep channels of larger rivers in the state.

Natural History: This is America's largest catfish and old (unverified reports of specimens in excess of 300 pounds exist). This is an important game fish and also important commercially. Most common in the larger rivers and their impoundments.

Size: Maximum of about 100 pounds. Illinois record is 78 pounds from Carlyle Lake.

Abundance: Fairly common but less common than the Channel Catfish.

Natural History: Second in size only to the Blue Catfish. Found mostly in rivers and in impoundments of larger rivers. Adults are mainly nocturnal and spend the day hidden among submerged structure such as logs or rocks. Often hides in caves in steep banks.

Class - **Actinopterygii** (bony fishes)

Order - **Siluiformes** (catfishes)

Family - **Ictaluridae** (American catfishes)

Genus - *Noturus* (madtoms)

Stonecat *Noturus flavus*	**Brindled Madtom** *Noturus miurus*
Tadpole Madtom *Noturus gyrinus*	**Freckled Madtom** *Noturus nocturnus*
Mountain Madtom *Noturus eleutherus*	**Slender Madtom** *Noturus exilis*

Size: These are small catfishes. The largest example of the genus is the widespread Stonecat (*N. flavus*) which can reach a length of 12 inches. Most are much smaller. The maximum recorded length for each of Illinois' madtom species is as follows: Brindled Madtom and Northern Madtom, 5.25 inches; Brown Madtom 5.34 inches; Tadpole Madtom, 5 inches; Freckled Madtom, just under 6 inches; and Mountain Madtom, 5 inches.

Natural History: There are 26 species total in this genus. 7 occur in Illinois but one of these is extremely rare and limited in distribution in the state (Northern Madtom, not shown). All Madtoms are secretive and nocturnal, and are thus relatively unknown to the general public. Most Madtom species occur in the eastern portion of America, but a few species range well into the Great Plains and the Stonecat can be found as far west as Wyoming and Montana. Like other American catfishes the Madtoms have spiny dorsal and pectoral fins that produce a mild venom. A puncture from one of these spines can result in a significant amount of pain and swelling, but it is not life threatening. Like all catfishes, madtoms have a fleshy fin between the dorsal fin and the tail known as an "adipose fin." In the most madtoms this fin connects to the caudal (tail) fin, a character that immediately separates madtoms from the rest of the catfish family. These are predaceous fish that feed on a wide variety of aquatic life consisting of both invertebrates and very small fishes. They feed and are active mostly at night, and spend the days hidden beneath overhanging root wads or burrowed into detritus of deep pools. Most madtoms are stream fishes that inhabit creeks and small to medium sized rivers. The Mountain Madtom, Stonecat and Northern Madtom can also be found in large rivers.

Class - **Actinopterygii** (bony fishes)

Order - **Cypriniformes** (minnows & suckers

Family - **Catastomidae** (suckers)

Quillback *Carpiodes cyprinus*	Highfin Carpsucker *Carpiodes velifer*	River Carpsucker *Carpiodes carpio*

Quillback
Carpiodes cyprinus

Size: Maximum about 2 feet and 12 pounds. No size records available for Illinois specimens.

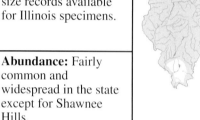

Abundance: Fairly common and widespread in the state except for Shawnee Hills.

Natural History: Though found statewide the Quillback is least common in the Coastal Plain. Food is benthic invertebrates sucked from the substrate. Occurs both in rivers and impoundments but may be less tolerant of turbid conditions than its larger cousin the River Carpsucker. Like the River Carpsucker, this is a commercial food fish.

Highfin Carpsucker
Carpiodes velifer

Size: Maximum length about 15 inches and maximum weight about 2 pounds. No size records for Illinois.

Abundance: Uncommon. Requires clear, flowing waters with gravel or sand substrate.

Natural History: This is the smallest of the Carpsuckers and is therefore not highly valued by commercial fishermen. This species inhabits medium to large rivers and favors clearer waters with some gravel substrates. Highfin Carpsukers are less common than our other two species. Siltation and lake impoundments may be to blame.

River Carpsucker
Carpiodes carpio

Size: Maximum length 25 inches. Record weight 10 pounds. No size records are available for Illinois.

Abundance: Fairly common and widespread except in northeastern Illinois.

Natural History: Found in the larger rivers and their reservoirs. Most common in the Ohio and Mississippi Rivers and also in the lower reaches of Illinois' other larger river systems. Food is tiny invertebrates sucked from mud of the bottom of a river or lake. Known to live at least 10 years. Valued as a commercial food fish.

Smallmouth Buffalo *Ictiobus bubalus*	Largemouth Buffalo *Ictiobus cyprinellus*	Black Buffalo *Ictiobus niger*

Smallmouth Buffalo
Ictiobus bubalus

Size: Maximum probably about 30 pounds. No size data is available for Illinois.

Abundance: Common in larger rivers. Uncommon in smaller streams.

Natural History: A river fish that also thrives in lakes and impoundments. Less likely to be found in turbid water than the Largemouth Buffalo and also is more fond of waters with some current. Feeds on bottom dwelling invertebrates and plants. Like other *Ictiobus* (buffalo fishes), this fish commercially fish.

Largemouth Buffalo
Ictiobus cyprinellus

Size: Can reach a maximum of 80 pounds. No size data is available for Illinois.

Abundance: Fairly common and widespread throughout the state.

Natural History: Largemouth Buffalo are important commercial food fishes. Found in large rivers and their backwaters and in impoundments and is more accepting of silt laden waters than others of its genus. Breeds during spring in flooded fields and backwaters. Dams restrict movement.

Black Buffalo
Ictiobus niger

Size: To at least 30 pounds, probably more. Illinois record is 23 pounds, 2 ounces.

Abundance: Probably the least common of Illinois 3 species of *Ictiobus* suckers.

Natural History: Least common of the Buffalo fishes and regarded as a species of concern in places. Morphologically somewhat intermediate between the two previous species. In habits, feeding, etc., most similar to the Smallmouth Buffalo. Found in large and medium size rivers.

Class - **Actinopterygii** (bony fishes)

Order - **Cypriniformes** (minnows & suckers)

Family - **Catastomidae** (suckers)

Longnose Sucker	White Sucker	Blue Sucker
Catastomus catastomus	*Catastomus commersonii*	*Cycleptus elongatus*

Size: Maximum length is thought to be about 25 inches. No size data is available for this rare species in Illinois.

Abundance: Rare in Illinois and probably was never a common species in the state.

Natural History: The Longnose Sucker is mainly a fish of the far north and the bulk of the population occurs in Canada. It does occur in the Great Lakes. This fish favors cool streams and lakes with gravel substrates. Its range includes most of Canada and all of Alaska as far north as the Arctic where it appears to be secure.

Size: Maximum of 25 inches and about 7 pounds. No size records are available for Illinois.

Abundance: .Common. Occurs in streams statewide as well as in Lake Michigan.

Natural History: Name comes from the white belly of the breeding male. They inhabit a wide variety of small rivers and creeks as well as natural and man-made lakes. A bottom feeder that eats mostly benthic insects. Although bony, their flesh is quite palatable and they are sought for food and sport in some regions.

Size: Can probably reach 20 pounds. Current world record is 18 pounds and 14 ounces from the Missouri River.

Abundance: Uncommon in Illinois. This species is in decline throughout its range.

Natural History: A unique member of the sucker family, the Blue Sucker is the only species of its genus. Although its range includes all of the Mississippi, Ohio, Missouri, and western Gulf Coast rivers, this is today a rare fish throughout most of its range. It prefers fast flowing channels over hard bottom. Dams and siltation impact negatively.

Northern Hogsucker	Spotted Sucker	Chubsuckers
Hypentelium nigricans	*Minytrema melanops*	*Erimyzon claviformes & Erimyzon sucetta*

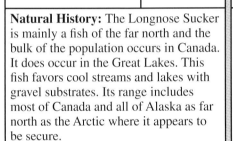  

Western Creek Chubsucker

 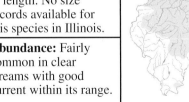 

Size: Up to about 2 feet in length. No size records available for this species in Illinois.

Abundance: Fairly common in clear streams with good current within its range.

Natural History: This species is found mostly in large, clear creeks with rocky or gravel substrates. In the Ozarks region, it is common in large rivers. This is a bottom dweller that hugs the substrate and sucks small aquatic invertebrates from sand, gravel or silt. They are very cryptically patterned.

Size: Maximum of about 18 inches. Most are about a foot in length.

Abundance: Widespread but not a common species anywhere within its range.

Natural History: Lives in pools and slow-moving waters of large and small rivers, as well as larger creeks. Moves into smaller creeks in spring to spawn over gravel or rocks. Feeds on small aquatic invertebrates. Although fairly widespread, this is not a common fish and it may be decreasing.

Size: Both species grow to about 15 inches, although most are about half that length.

Abundance: Creek Chubsucker is common. Lake Chubsucker is less common in Illinois.

Natural History: There are two nearly identical chubsucker species in Illinois. On the map above the Creek Chubsuckers (*claviformes*) range is in light gray and the Lake Chubsucker (*sucetta*) in dark gray. Lake Chubsucker has 11 or 12 dorsal fin rays as opposed to 9 or 10 in the Creek Chubsucker.

Class - **Actinopterygii** (bony fishes)
Order - **Cypriniformes** (minnows & suckers)
Family - **Catastomatidae** (suckers)

Redhorse Suckers - genus *Moxostoma* (6 species in Illinois, 5 shown)

Golden Redhorse *Moxostoma erythrurum*	**Black Redhorse** *Moxostoma duquesnii*	**Shorthead Redhorse** *Moxostoma macrolepidotum*

Size: Maximum of about 26 inches and 4.5 pounds.		**Size:** Record size 26 inches and 7 pounds. No size data for Illinois.		**Size:** Can reach 19 inches and just over 3 pounds.	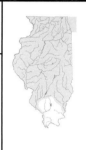
Abundance: Widespread and perhaps the most common redhorse sucker in Illinois, but has declined significantly in some areas.		**Abundance:** Uncommon in Illinois. Requires unpolluted streams with ample current and was probably never common.		**Abundance:** Fairly common but less so than the Godlen Redhorse. Favors larger rivers and tends to avoid small streams.	

River Redhorse - *Moxostoma carinatum*	**Silver Redhorse** - *Moxostoma anisurum*
	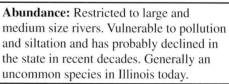

Size: The largest of the redhorse suckers reaches at least 29 inches and 10.5 pounds.		**Size:** Official record 25 inches and 8.25 pounds. Unconfirmed reports of 10 pounds. Illinois record 7 pounds, 11 ounces.	
Abundance: Uncommon to rare in Illinois. Restricted to larger rivers in the northeastern portion of the state (Upper Illinois, Rock, and Vermillion Rivers). Listed as a Threatened Species in Illinois by the IDNR.		**Abundance:** Restricted to large and medium size rivers. Vulnerable to pollution and siltation and has probably declined in the state in recent decades. Generally an uncommon species in Illinois today.	

Natural History: The Redhorse Suckers are the most diverse group within the sucker family, with 20 species found in North America. The genus ranges across much of the eastern United States and their are 6 species that range into Illinois. All are similar in appearance and can be difficult to properly identify. Collectively, they range throughout most of the state and nearly ever major drainage has at least one species. Their flesh is described as good but bony, and they are sometimes pursued by anglers both for food and sport. In some regions of their range there are "gigging seasons" for these species, and they are hunted at night with lights and gigs from specialized boats. This practice is fairly common in the clear rivers of the Ozark Plateau in Missouri. Some anglers will use bow-fishing techniques for these species as well. Although they will persist in reservoirs they always spawn in small to medium sized streams with gravel substrates. These are stream fishes that are typically found in clear waters. Pictured above are 5 of Illinois's *Moxostoma* species. The other species (not shown) is the **Greater Redhorse** (*M. valenciennesi*), a rare and endangered species found in Illinois only in the upper reaches of the Illinois River Watershed. This species may be extirpated from Illinois. Collectively, these fishes are often mistaken for Carp. Unlike the Carp, which is a non-native species from the Old World that can live in waters of poor quality, the redhorse suckers require unpolluted waters. In this manner their presence is an indicator of the overall health of a stream. Hybridization between species makes proper identification even more challenging.

Class - **Actinopterygii** (bony fishes)
Order - **Cypriniformes** (minnows & suckers)
Family - **Cyprinidae** (minnows)

Grass Carp *Ctenopharyngodon idella*	**Silver Carp** *Hypophthalmichthys molitrix*	**Bighead Carp** *Hypophthalmichthys nobilis*

Grass Carp	Silver Carp	Bighead Carp
Size: 4 feet and 100 pounds (in Asia). 	**Size:** Can reach 60 pounds. 	**Size:** Up to 3 feet and 90 pounds.
Abundance: Generally uncommon but widely distributed in the state. Introduced into ponds and lakes to control aquatic plants.	**Abundance:** Currently restricted to the Ohio River but spreading rapidly. May be more widespread than shown on map.	**Abundance:** Currently restricted to the Ohio River but spreading rapidly. Highly invasive and may soon invade Lake Michigan.
Natural History: Inhabits pools and backwaters of large rivers and both man made and natural lakes. Introduced into the United States from Asia to control aquatic plant growth in commercial minnow ponds. As with most alien species, the Grass Carp probably does more harm than good to the environments where it has become established.	**Natural History:** Native to China, the Silver Carp has become established in the larger rivers of the eastern United States. These fish consume tiny zooplankton and algae that is filtered from the flowing water of large river channels. Originally imported into Arkansas along with the Bighead Carp to control algae blooms in fish ponds.	**Natural History:** Like the previous species this fish is native to China. Now widespread in the major rivers of the eastern US, this is a filter feeder that inhabits the flowing waters of large river channels. Though both species of *Hypophthalmichthys* were intentionally introduced, they are now regarded as environmentally harmful aliens.

Common Carp *Cyprinus carpio*	**Goldfish** *Carassius auratus*	**Golden Shiner** *Notemigonus crysoleucas*

Common Carp	Goldfish	Golden Shiner
Size: Angling record is 55 pounds. Illinois record is 51 pounds. 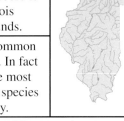	**Size:** Maximum 20 inches and up to 5 pounds. 	**Size:** Maximum size 14.5 inches. Most are about 8 inches as adult. 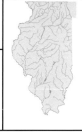
Abundance: Common and widespread. In fact this is one of the most widespread fish species in America today.	**Abundance:** Uncommon but widely distributed. Released bait can be found almost anywhere.	**Abundance:** Common and widespread. A bait minnow that is now one of the most widely distributed minnows.
Natural History: Many people are surprised to learn that the Common Carp is an invasive species in America. Native to Eurasia, they were first brought to the US in the early 1800s. They are now widespread and common in most aquatic habitats in America. A benthic feeder that "roots" like a hog in muddy bottoms and increases water turbidity.	**Natural History:** Native to Asia, the Goldfish is now widely established across most of North America. The gaudy colors commonly seen in fish ponds and pet stores rarely survive in wild populations. Found in most rivers and lakes and can survive in tiny ponds. More tolerant of pollution and siltation than many native species.	**Natural History:** This minnow is well known among fishermen and is sold as a bait fish in many regions of the US. In their natural habitat they are fish of still water pools of streams and backwaters of rivers. They will also thrive in impoundments and small farm ponds. Millions are raised commercially each year to be sold in bait stores.

Class - **Actinopterygii** (bony fishes)
Order - **Cypriniformes** (minnows & suckers)
Family - **Cyprinidae** (minnows)

Creek Chub
Semotilis atromaculatus

Size:. Maximum length 12 inches.

Abundance: Very common. Probably every stream in Illinois capable of supporting fish life will have a population of Creek Chubs.

Natural History: One of the most widespread and common creek fishes in America. Like many minnows, breeding males develop tubercles on the head and snout, leading to the common nickname "Hornyhead." In the days when most Americans lived on the farm, fishing in small creeks for Creek Chubs was commonplace entertainment for youngsters.

Lake Chub
Couesius plumbeus

Size: Can reach a length of up to 9 inches.

Abundance: Fairly common within it range. In Illinois it occurs only in Lake Michigan and possibly in its feeder streams.

Natural History: Lake Chubs are northern fishes. They are common across Canada from the east coast to British Columbia and the Yukon. They also occur in Montana and Wyoming in the western US. Lake Michigan represents the southernmost extension of their range in the eastern US.

Stonerollers
Genus - *Campastoma*

Size: Maximum of about 11 inches.

Abundance: Central Stoneroller is very common throughout the state. Large-scale Stoneroller is found in northernmost Illinois.

Natural History: 2 nearly identical species in Illinois. They are the Central Stoneroller (*C. anomalum*) and the Largescale Stoneroller (*C. oligolepis*). To the laymen they are indistinguiable. Their name comes from their habit of aggressive bottom feeding in gravelly stream beds, moving small stones in the process.

Southern Redbelly Dace
Chrosomas erythrogaster

Size: Maximum of 4.5 inches. Most are about 3 to 4 inches.

Abundance: Fairly common. Illinois population is disjunct from other populations to the east and south.

Natural History: Can be found in very small streams only a few feet across. Requires clean, unpolluted waters with moderate to fast current and abundant riffles and pools. Often very common in small streams in forested regions, especially those that are fed by springs or seeps. This species is an indicator of good water quality. The breeding males are one America's colorful minnows.

Redside Dace
Clinostomus elongatus

Size: Can reach a maximum length of 4.5 inches.

Abundance: Very rare in Illinois. Occurs only in a few streams inhe upper Rock River drainage.

Natural History: Lives in clear water creeks or small, clear rivers with gravel, sand, or rock substrates. Although fairly common and widespread in nearby Wisconsin, the Redside Dace has been documented in Illinois in only a single stream (Racoon Creek) near the Wisconsin border. Despite being very rare in Illinois, this species is widespread in Wisconsin and in southeast Minnesota.

Gravel Chub
Erimystax x-punctatus

Size: Can reach a maximum length of 4.5 inches.

Abundance: Possibly extirpated from central Illinois. Still fairly common in the Rock River drainage.

Natural History: These small minnows live in small and medium size rivers in highland regions. They favor flowing water over gravel bottoms. There are apparently 2 subspecies in Illinois, one in the Wabash River drainage and the other elsewhere in the state. Food is both algae and invertebrates.

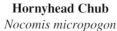

Class - **Actinopterygii** (bony fishes)

Order - **Cypriniformes** (minnows & suckers)

Family - **Cyprinidae** (minnows)

River Chub *Nocomis bigutatus*	Hornyhead Chub *Nocomis micropogon*	Pugnose Minnow *Opsopoeodus emiliae*

 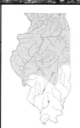 

Size:. River Chub can reach 13 inches.

Abundance: Very rare in Illinois. An Endangered species that occurs in Illinois only in portions of the upper Wabash River.

Natural History: Inhabits medium to large rivers in areas of swift currents. Like the many other chubs breeding males have grossly enlarge heads with horny tubercles. During the breeding season the males head also turns pupleish or pink. Males gather pebbles with their mouths and stack them to create large spawning mounds that may be several inches high.

Size: Maximum length about 10 inches.

Abundance: Fairly common across the northern half of the state and in the upper Wabash River watershed.

Natural History:. Large adults are quite carnivorous and feed on small crayfish, snails, and aquatic insects. They will readily take worms on hook and line and many a young fishermen learned their trade by catching river chubs from nearby rivers and streams. All species of *Nocomis* develop tubercles on the snout and head.that are especially apparent on the males, thus the common name.

Size: Maximum of about 2.5 inches.

Abundance: Although widespread this minnow has declined in many areas of its range. Its abundance in Illinois is not known.

Natural History: This tiny minnow is widespread across the southeast from South Carolina to eastern Texas. It also ranges northward up the Mississippi and Ohio drainages as far as the southern Great Lakes. Habitat is backwaters and pools of low gradient streams having some aquatic vegetation. Also found in swamps and natural lakes with abundant plant life.

Suckermouth Minnow *Phenacobius mirabilis*	Blacknose Dace *Rhinichthyes atratulus*	Longnose Dace *Rhinichthyes cataractae*

Stream form

Size: Reaches a maximum length of 4.5 inches.

Abundance: Common. Found nearly statewide but absent from extreme northeastern Illinois. A prairie species mainly.

Natural History: This minnow is a habitat non-specialist that occurs in both small creeks and large rivers. It is tolerant of a wide variety of conditions from clear flowing waters to still waters with some turbidity. The common name "Suckermouth" is derived from the sub-terminal position of the mouth which is typical of the sucker family.

Size: Reaches a maximum length about 4 inches.

Abundance: Fairly common throughout its range in Illinois, but only in clear, fast flowing, gravelly streams.

Natural History: Found in springs and in small (sometimes tiny) spring fed creeks. Its intolerance for siltation and warm water limits its distribution in the state and it has disappeared from some areas due to degradation of water quality. Breeding males developed a bright red stripe along the side. Spawns in gravelly, rapid flowing water.

Size: Reaches a maximum length of 6.5 inches.

Abundance: The Lake Michigan population is common, stream populations are rare in Illinois.

Natural History: This is a widespread fish across the northern portions of North America. In fact it the most widespread minnow in North America. Two forms occur in Illinois. The inland, stream form is a the typical widespread form. The population found in Lake Michigan is a much paler colored fish than the stream population.

Class - **Actinopterygii** (bony fishes)

Order - **Cypriniformes** (minnows & suckers)

Family - **Cyprinidae** (minnows)

Fathead Minnows - genus *Pimephales* (3 species in Illinois)

Bluntnose Minnow *Pimephales notatus*	**Bullhead Minnow** *Pimephales vigilax*	**Fathead Minnow** *Pimephales promelas*
	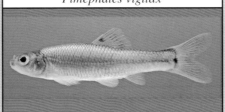	

Size:. 4 inches is the maximum length for these small minnows. Males are larger than females.

Abundance: The Bluntnose minnow is the most widespread *Pimaphales* minnow in the state, found in all watersheds. It also probably the most common of the three species in Illinois. The Bullhead Minnow can be found in all of the state except for perhaps the Chicago/Calumet and Des Plaines watersheds in the northeastern corner of Illinois. The Fathead Minnow is fairly widespread across the state but appears to be absent from much of southeastern Illinois.

Natural History: These are very common minnows that may be found in rivers, creeks, reservoirs, and even ponds occasionally. They are tough little fishes that can survive warm, low-oxygen waters and waters with high turbidity. Breeding males of all three species have very dark, nearly black heads and tubercles on the snout. Their resilience, rapid reproductive capacity, and ease in rearing in captivity has led to the Bluntnose Minnow and the Fathead Minnow being widely used as a bait minnows, where they are often sold under the nickname "Tuffy." A reddish colored strain of the Fathead Minnow known as "Rosy Red" has also been bred for sale in bait stores. Because of their prolific use for bait, these minnows have become widely established across the United States and Canada and they are today perhaps the most common fish species in North America. These minnows are mostly bottom feeders that eat a variety of tiny invertebrates as well as algae.

Macrhybopis Chubs - genus *Macrhybopsis* (4 species in Illinois, 2 shown below)		**Hybopsis Minnows** - genus *Hybobpsis*
Shoal Chub *Macrhybopsis hyostoma*	**Silver Chub** *Macrhybopsis storeiana*	**Bigeye Chub & Pallid Shiner** *Hybopsis amblops & Hybopsis amnis*

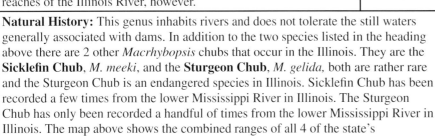

Bigeye Chub

Size: Silver Chub can reach 9 inches. Sicklefin Chub to 4.5 inches; Sturgeon Chub has a maximum length of about 3.25 inches; and Shoal Chub only to about 3 inches.

Abundance: Shoal Chub has been documented from the Mississippi, Illinois, and Wabash Rivers in Illinois. Silver Chub is a river fish that probably occurs in the main channels of all the Level II rivers in the state. But it has likely been exitrpated from the upper reaches of the Illinois River, however.

Natural History: This genus inhabits rivers and does not tolerate the still waters generally associated with dams. In addition to the two species listed in the heading above there are 2 other *Macrhybopsis* chubs that occur in the Illinois. They are the **Sicklefin Chub**, *M. meeki*, and the **Sturgeon Chub**, *M. gelida*, both are rather rare and the Sturgeon Chub is an endangered species in Illinois. Sicklefin Chub has been recorded a few times from the lower Mississippi River in Illinois. The Sturgeon Chub has only been recorded a handful of times from the lower Mississippi River in Illinois. The map above shows the combined ranges of all 4 of the state's *Machrybopsis* fishes.

Size: Reaches a maximum length of 4 inches in length.

Abundance: Very rare in Illinois. Listed as an Endangered Species by the Illinois Department of Conservation.

Natural History: A fish of small rivers and large creeks. In decline over much of its range, probably due to dams and siltation. A similar species, the **Pallid Shiner** (*H. amnis*), also occurs in Illinois. The latter is another extremely rare and endangered species in the state. The map above shows the ranges of the two species in Illinois. The Bigeye Chub is in light gray and the Pallid Shiner in dark gray.

Class - **Actinopterygii** (bony fishes)
Order - **Cypriniformes** (minnows & suckers)
Family - **Cyprinidae** (minnows)

Silvery Minnows - genus *Hybognathus* (5 species in Illinois, 3 shown below)

Mississippi Silvery Minnow *Hybognathus nuchalis*	Brassy Minnow *Hybognathus hankinsoni*	Western Silvery Minnow *Hybognathus argyritis*

Size:. Mississippi Silvery Minnow is the largest and can reach 7 inches in length. The Plains Minnow grows up to 5 inches; the Western Silvery Minnow and Cypress Minnow both grow to about 4.5 inches; and the Brassy Minnnow is the smallest at 3.75 inches maximum.

Abundance: Mississippi Silvery Minnow is common and is the most widespread of the *Hybognathus* minnows in Illinois. The Cypress Minnow is extremely rare in Illinois and is an Endangered Species. The Brassy Minnow is also rare and Endangered in the state. Western Silvery Minnow and the Plains Minnow are uncommon fishes in Illinois.

Natural History: The **Cypress Minnow** is known from only a single locality in extreme southern Illinois. The **Plains Minnow** (*H. placitus*) and **Western Silvery Minnow** (*H. placitus*) barely occur in Illinois in the lower portions of the Mississippi River. **Brassy Minnow** (*H. hankinsoni*) is found in the upper Mississippi, upper Rock, Kishwaukee and Fox Rivers. These fish are bottom feeders that ingest tiny algae and detritus from the silt of sloughs and backwaters. The map shows the combined ranges of all 5 species in Illinois.

Bloodtail Shiners - genus *Lythrurus*

Redfin Shiner *Lythrurus umbratilis*		Ribbon Shiner *Lythrurus fumeus*
Breeding male	Female	

Size: Redfin Shiner grows to a maximum length of 3.5 inches.	**Size:** Maximum length is 2.5 inches.
Abundance: Common. Found in all Level IV watersheds in the state. Capable of thriving in turbid waters. This species may increasing in population as competive species that require clear waters dissappear from streams impacted by excessive runoff from agricultural operations and urbanization.	**Abundance:** Range in Illinois includes the Wabash, Big Muddy, all streams in the southern tip of the state and also most of the upper Kankakee.
Natural History: Redfin Shiner is a stream fish that occurs in small to medium size creeks. Their reproduction habits are noteworthy due to the fact that they often spawn in the nests of other fish species, often using the nest of one of the sunfishes. Food is small aquatic insect larva such as mayfly and midge nymphs supplemented by filamentous algeas. Habitats include a wide variety of streams from still water oxbows to faster flowing creeks. Redfin Shiners tolerate both clear and turbid conditions. Longivity for individuals of this genus is short, and most will not survive beyond 3 years. 	**Natural History:** The Ribbon Shiner is mostly a lowland species of the lower Gulf Coastal Plain that ranges north into much of southern Illinois. Inhabits creeks and small rivers over mud or sandy substrates. 

Class - **Actinopterygii** (bony fishes)

Order - **Cypriniformes** (minnows & suckers)

Family - **Cyprinidae** (minnows)

Carp Minnows - genus *Cyprinella* (4 species in Illinois)

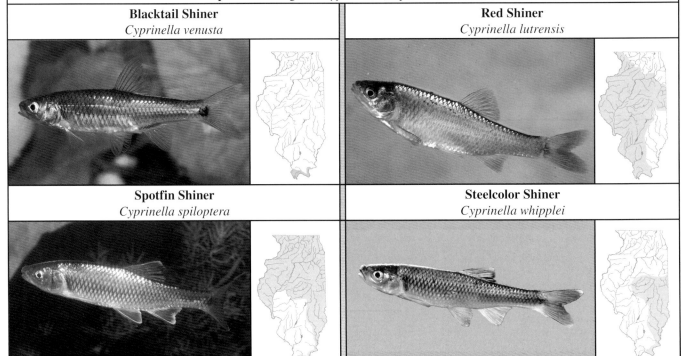

Blacktail Shiner	Red Shiner
Cyprinella venusta	*Cyprinella lutrensis*

Spotfin Shiner	Steelcolor Shiner
Cyprinella spiloptera	*Cyprinella whipplei*

Size: Members of this genus are typically larger than the similar *Notropis* shiners (next page) The Red Shiner is the smallest at 3.5 inches. Maximum sizes for the other species are as follows: Steelcolor Shiner 5.5 inches; Blacktail Shiner 5 inches; Spotfin Shiner 4.75 inches.

Abundance: Collectively these are common and widespread minnows in Illinois. At least one species occurs in every watershed in the state.

Natural History: These minnows are very similar to the *Notropis* shiners (next page) and many species were once included in that group. This is a fairly large genus with 27 total species ranging throughout the eastern half of North America from southern Canada to northern Mexico. The group name "Carp Minnow" comes from the genus name which translates as "little carp." Like many minnows, immatures and females can pose a difficult identification challenge, especially for nonprofessionals. The adult males (especially in breeding colors) are usually fairly distinctive in color and morphology and much easier to recognize. All *Cyprinella* are mainly insectivorus but some plant material is also eaten. Some species are quite opportunistic and larger invertebrates or even tiny fish fry are taken on occasion. Hybridization can be common among these minnows where their ranges overlap, adding to the already difficult task of identification.

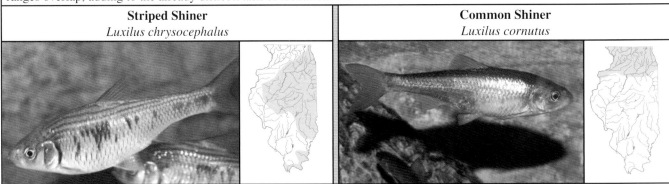

Striped Shiner	Common Shiner
Luxilus chrysocephalus	*Luxilus cornutus*

Size: Both species can reach a maximum length of 8 inches.

Abundance: Both species are common within their respective ranges in Illinois.

Natural History: 2 very similar species that often hybridize where their range overlaps. Both are stream fishes that live in small to medium sized creeks with clear water and sand or gravel substrates. Common Shiner is found in northern Illinois only.

Class - **Actinopterygii** (bony fishes)

Order - **Cypriniformes** (minnows & suckers)

Family - **Cyprinidae** (minnows)

True Minnows - genus *Notropis* - 17 species in Illinois (15 shown below and on next page)

Emerald Shiner *Notropis atherinoides*	**River Shiner** *Notropis blennius*	**Sand Shiner** *Notropis stramineus*

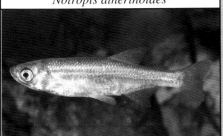

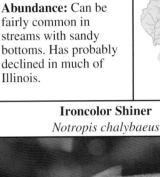

Size: Maximum length about 5 inches.

Abundance: Presumably occurs statewide. One of the few *Notropis* minnows found in the Great Lakes, including Lake Michigan.

Size: Can reach a total length of 5 inches.

Abundance: Common in the major rivers of the state, i.e., Mississippi, Illinois, Wabash, and Ohio. Uncommon in the Rock.

Size: Maximum length about 3.5 inches.

Abundance: Can be fairly common in streams with sandy bottoms. Has probably declined in much of Illinois.

Silverjaw Minnow *Notropis buccata*	**Ghost Shiner** *Notropis buchanani*	**Ironcolor Shiner** *Notropis chalybaeus*

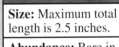

Size: Maximum total length is 3.75 inches.

Abundance: Uncommon in Illinois and very rare in the southern portions of it range in the state.

Size: 2 to 2.5 inches.

Abundance: Occurs in the states 4 largest rivers, the Mississippi, Ohio, Illinois, and the Wabash. Also in the mouths of tributaries.

Size: Maximum total length is 2.5 inches.

Abundance: Rare in Illinois. A Threatened Species. 2 disjunct populations. One in the Iroquois and one in the lower Sangammon.

Mimic Shiner *Notropis volucellus*	**Bigeye Shiner** *Notropis boops*	**Spottail Shiner** *Notropis hudsonius*

Size: To 3 inches.

Abundance: Historically found in the lower Mississippi, Ohio, and Wabash Rivers but now probably extirpated from those waterways.

Size: To 5 inches.

Abundance: Rare and Endangered in Illinois. Found in upper Wabash. Disjunct populations in the upper Illinois and along the Mississippi.

Size: To 5.75 inches.

Abundance: Range in Illinois is from the Illinois River northward. Also can be found in Lake Michigan along sandy shorelines.

Class - **Actinopterygii** (bony fishes)

Order - **Cypriniformes** (minnows & suckers)

Family - **Cyprinidae** (minnows)

True Minnows - genus *Notropis* - continued

Bigmouth Shiner *Notropis dorsalis*	Blackchin Shiner *Notropis heterodon*	Blacknose Shiner *Notropis heterolepis*

Size: Maximum length about 5 inches.

Abundance: Common. Range in Illinois is generally from the Kankakee River northward.

Size: Can reach a total length of 2.75 inches.

Abundance: Rare in Illinois and a Threatened Species in the state. Found only in the Fox and Des Plaines watersheds in Illinois.

Size: Maximum length about 3.75 inches.

Abundance: Rare in Illinois. Regarded as endangered by IDNR. Found only in a few localities in northern Illinois.

Ozark Minnow *Notropis nubilis*	Weed Shiner *Notropis texanus*

 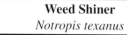 

Size: Maximum length about 3.75 inches.

Abundance: Uncommon to rare in Illinois.

Size: Maximum length about 3.5 inches.

Abundance: Rare in Illinois. A state Endangered Species.

Natural History: In the sense that most people think of minnows as being tiny fishes, these are the "true minnows." Members of this genus are among the smallest of Illinois fishes. Several *Notropis* are quite diminutive with a maximum length of only about 2.5 inches. The largest species will barely exceed 5.5 inches. *Notropis* is largest genus of minnows in North America with as many as 83 species across the continent. In fact, this is the second largest generic group of fishes in North America, surpassed only by the darters of the *Etheostoma* genus. The exact status some species included in this genus is problematic and taxonomic changes occur frequently within the group, with occasional species being reassigned to another genus and some being added from other genera. Their distribution is generally east of the Rocky Mountain Continental Divide, and most species occur within the Gulf of Mexico Drainage Basin. There are at least 17 species in Illinois but 5 are regarded as endangered in the state and two others are threatened. Collectively, the Shiner Minnows are found in virtually all aquatic habitats within the state and their combined ranges encompass all of Illinois. The breeding males of many *Notropis* species are quite colorful. Even those species that don't acquire significant color on the body will typically acquire yellow, orange, or red color in the fins of nuptial males. At least 1 species, the Emerald Shiner (*N. atherinoides*) is widely used as a bait minnow.

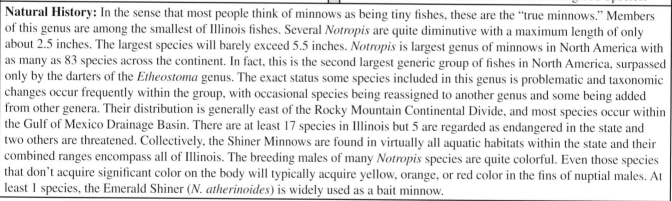

Class - **Actinopterygii** (bony fishes)

Order - **Scorpaeniformes** (scorpion fish)

Family - **Cottidae** (sculpins)

Banded Sculpin *Cottus carolinae*	**Mottled Sculpin** *Cottus bairdi*

Size: May rarely reach 7 inches. Most adults are about 4 to 5 inches in length.

Abundance: In Illinois, the Banded Sculpin is restricted to the southern tip of the state and to a few tributary streams in the lower portions of the Illinois River watershed. Also in a few high gradient, gravel-bottomed streams in the lower Mississippi River watershed.

Natural History: Most of the 250-plus members of this order of fish (Scorpaeniformes) are cold-water marine species. About 30 species inhabit freshwater streams in America. Most are found in the western United States and in the northern portions of the continent. In Illinois, two species are among the few that range east of the Mississippi and south of the Great Lakes. The Banded Sculpin is a stream fish that favors fast flowing water and riffle areas of very small to large streams. A substrate of rock or gravel is a habitat requirement for this species.

Size: Can reach a maximum of 6 inches in length.

Abundance: Although generally uncommon, the Mottled Sculpin is a fairly common fish in suitable habitat of clear, cool streams and in Lake Michigan. Watersheds in Illinois include the Rock, Des Plaines, Kishwaukee, and the Great Lakes/St. Lawrence.

Natural History: Typically a fish of upland streams and spring fed runs where they inhabit the fast-flowing regions with gravel or rocky substrates. Also found in Lake Michigan. Requires cold waters. All Sculpins have large mouths that enable them to take larger prey than would be suspected for such a small fish. They are highly cryptic and their color and pattern always matches the substrate of their stream. They are thus nearly nearly impossible to see when motionless on the gravel of stream beds. In addition to the 2 species shown on this page, there are 3 other sculpin species that inhabit Lake Michigan. Those species are the **Slimy Sculpin** (*C. cognatus*); the **Spoonhead Sculpin** (*C. ricei)* and the **Deepwater Sculpin** (*Moxocephalus thomposonii*).

REFERENCES

Chapters 1 and 2

Print

Bailey, Robert G. 2009. *Ecosystem Geography, From Ecoregions to Sites.* Springer Science & Business Media, New York, NY.

Hunt, Charles B. 1974. *Natural Regions of the United States and Canada.* W.H. Freeman and Company, San Francisco, CA.

Ricketts, Taylor, H., Eric Dinerstein, David M. Olson, and Colby J. Loucks, et al. 1999. *Terrestrial Ecoregions of North America.* World Wildlife Fund and Island Press. Washington, DC.

Internet

US Environmental Protection Agency/Ecoregions of North America - www.epa.gov/wed/pages/ecoregions.htm

The Encyclopedia of Earth - www.eoearth.org

USGS - www.usgs/science/geology/regions

Commission for Environmental Cooperation - www.cec.org

Mammal References

Print

Barbour, Roger W. and Wayne Davis 1974. *Mammals of Kentucky.* University Press of Kentucky. Lexington, KY.

Bowers, Nora, Rick Bowers and Kenn Kafuman. 2004. *Mammals of North America.* Houghton Mifflin Company. New York, NY.

Hoffmeister, Donald F. 2002. *Mammals of Illinois.* University of Illinois Press. Urbana, IL.

Kays, Roland W. and Don. E. Wilson. 2009. *Mammals of North America.* Princeton University Press. Princeton, NJ.

Trani, Margaret K., Mark Ford and Brian R. Chapman. 2007. *The Land Manager's Guide to Mammals of the South.* The Nature Conservancy, Southeast Region. Durham, NC.

Walker, E.P. 1983. *Walkers Mammals of the World.* The John's Hopkins University Press. Baltimore, MD.

Whitaker, John O. Jr. and W. J. Hamilton Jr. 1998. *Mammals of the Eastern United States.* Cornell University Press. Ithaca, NY.

Wilson, Don E. and Sue Ruff. 1999. *North American Mammals.* Smithsonian Institution.

Internet

Illinois Department of Natural Resources - www.dnr.illinois/gov

Illinois Natural History Survery - www. inhs.edu

Kentucky Department of Fish and Wildlife Resources - www.kdfwr.state.ky.us

Kentucky Bat Working Group - www.biology.eku.edu/bats

International Union of Concerned Naturalists - www.iucnredlist.org
Nature Serve Explorer - www.natureserve.org
Ohio Department of Natural Resources - www.wildlife.ohiodnr.gov
Smithsonian National Museum of Natural History - www.mnh.si.edu
Mammalian Species, American Society of Mammologists species accounts - www.science.smith.edu
Encyclopedia of Life - www.eol.org

Bird References

Print

Clark, William S. and Brian K. Wheeler. 1987. *A Field Guide to Hawks-North America.* Peterson Field Guides, Houghton Mifflin Co. Boston, MA.

Dunn, John L., Kimball Garret, Thomas Shultz, and Cindy House. *A Field Guide to Warblers of North America.* Peterson Field Guides, Houghton Mifflin Co. Boston, MA.

Farrand, John, Jr. 1998. *An Audubon Handbook, Eastern Birds.* McGraw Hill Book Co. New York, NY.

Floyd, Ted. 2008. *Smithsonian Field Guide to the Birds of North America.* Harper Collins Publishers. New York, NY.

Harlan, Robert N., Joseph W. Hammond, David C. Dister, Bernard F. Master, and Bill Whan. 2008. *Annotated Checklist of the Birds of Ohio.* Ohio Birds Records Committee, North Bend, OH.

Kaufman, Ken. 2000. *The Birds of North America.* Houghton Mifflin Co., New York, NY.

Mengel, Robert M. 1965. *The Birds of Kentucky.* American Ornithologist's Union Monogram, no. 3. The Allen Press, Lawrence, KS.

Palmer-Ball, Brainard. 1996. *The Kentucky Breeding Bird Atlas.* The University Press of Kentucky, Lexington, KY.

Johnsgard, Paul A. 1988. *North American Owls, Biology and Natural History.* Smithsonian Institution Press, Washington, DC.

Vanner, Micheal. 2003. *The Encyclopedia of North American Birds.* Parragon Publishing, Bath, UK.

Internet

Cornell University Lab of Ornithology, Birds of North America Online - http://birds.bna.cornell.edu.bna/species
Ebird - www.ebird.org
Encyclopedia of Life - www.eol.org
Environment Canada - www.ec.gc.ca
Illinois Department of Natural Resources - www.dnr.illinois.gov
Illinois Natural History Survey - www.inhs.illinois.edu
Illinois Ornithological Society - www.illinoisbirds.org
McGill Bird Observatory - www.migrationresearch.org
Waterfowl Hunting Management in North America - www.flyways.us
NatureServe Explorer - www.natureserve.org

Turtle References

Print

Buhlmann, Kurt. Tracey Tuberville, and Whit Gibbons. 2008. *Turtles of the Southeast.* The University of Georgia Press, Athens, GA.

Collins, Joseph T. and Travis W. Taggart. 2009. *Standard Common and Scientific Names for North American Amphibians, Turtles, Reptiles & Crocodilians.* The Center for North American Herpetology, Hays, KS.

Conant Roger, and Joseph T. Collins. 1998. *Reptiles and Amphibians of Eastern/Central North America.* Houghton Mifflin Co., Boston and New York.

Ernst, Carl H., Jeffrey E. Lovich, and Roger W. Barbour. 1994. *Turtles of the United States and Canada.* Smithsonian Institution Press, Washington and London.

Niemiller, Matthew L., R. Graham Reynolds, and Brian T. Miller. 2013. *The Reptiles of Tennessee.* The University of Tennessee Press, Knoxville, TN.

Trauth, Stanley E., Henry W. Robison, and Michael V. Plummer. 2004. *The Amphibians and Reptiles of Arkansas.* The University of Arkansas Press, Fayetteville, AR.

Internet

Encyclopedia of Life - www.eol.org

Illinois Department of Natural Resources - www.dnr.illinois.gov

Illinois Natural History Survey - www.inhs.illinois.edu

Kentucky Department of Fish & Wildlife Resources - www.kdfwr.state.ky.us

NatureServe Explorer - www.natureserve.org

Reptile References

Print

Collins, Joseph T. and Travis W. Taggart. 2009. *Standard Common and Scientific Names for North American Amphibians, Turtles, Reptiles & Crocodilians.* The Center for North American Herpetology, Hays, KS.

Conant Roger, and Joseph T. Collins. 1998. *Reptiles and Amphibians of Eastern/Central North America.* Houghton Mifflin Co., Boston - New York.

Meade, Les. 2005. *Kentucky Snakes. Their Identification, Variation, and Distribution.* Kentucky State Nature Preserves Commission.

Trauth, Stanley E., Henry W. Robison, and Michael V. Plummer. 2004. *The Amphibians and Reptiles of Arkansas.* The University of Arkansas Press, Fayetteville, AR.

Powell, Robert, Roger Conant and Joseph T. Collins. 2016. *Reptiles and Amphibians of Eastern/Central North America.* Houghton Mifflin Co., Boston and New York.

Niemiller, Matthew L., R. Graham Reynolds, and Brian T. Miller. 2013. *The Reptiles of Tennessee.* The University of Tennessee Press, Knoxville, TN.

Shupe, Scott. 2005. *US Guide to Venomous Snakes and Their Mimics.* Skyhorse Publishing, New York, NY

Trauth, Stanley E., Henry W. Robison, and Michael V. Plummer. 2004. *The Amphibians and Reptiles of Arkansas.* The University of Arkansas Press, Fayetteville, AR.

Internet

Encyclopedia of Life - www.eol.org

Illinois Department of Natural Resources - www.dnr.illinois.gov

Illinois Natural History Survey - www.inhs.illinois.edu

Kentucky Department of Fish & Wildlife Resources - www.kdfwr.state.ky.us

The Center for North American Herpetology - www.naherpetology.org

NatureServe Explorer - www.natureserve.org

Amphibian References

Print

Collins, Joseph T. and Travis W. Taggart. 2009. *Standard Common and Scientific Names for North American Amphibians, Turtles, Reptiles & Crocodilians.* The Center for North American Herpetology, Hays, KS.

Conant Roger, and Joseph T. Collins. 1998. *Reptiles and Amphibians of Eastern/Central North America.* Houghton Mifflin Co., Boston and New York.

Niemiller, Matthew L. and R. Graham Reynolds. 2011. *The Amphibians of Tennessee.* University of Tennessee Press, Knoxville, TN.

Trauth, Stanley E., Henry W. Robison, and Michael V. Plummer. 2004. *The Amphibians and Reptiles of Arkansas.* The University of Arkansas Press, Fayetteville, AR.

Powell, Robert, Roger Conant and Joseph T. Collins. 2016. *Reptiles and Amphibians of Eastern/Central North America.* Houghton Mifflin Co., Boston-New York.

Trauth, Stanley E., Henry W. Robison, and Michael V. Plummer. 2004. *The Amphibians and Reptiles of Arkansas.* The University of Arkansas Press, Fayetteville, AR.

Dodd, C. Kenneth. 2013. *Frogs of the United States and Canada.* Johns Hopkins University Press, Baltimore, MD.

Internet

Illinois Department of Natural Resources - www.dnr.illinois.gov

Illinois Natural History Survey - www.inhs.illinois.edu

International Union of Concerned Naturalists - www.iucnredlist.org

Kentucky Department of Fish & Wildlife Resources - www.kdfwr.state.ky.us

The Center for North American Herpetology - www.naherpetology.org

NatureServe Explorer - www.natureserve.org

Fish References

Print

Clay, William M. 1974. *The Fishes of Kentucky.* Kentucky Department of Fish & Wildlife Resources, Frankfort, KY.

Eddy, Samuel. 1969. *How to Know the Fresh Water Fishes.* Wm. C. Brown Company Publishers, Dubuque, IA.

Etnier, David A. and Wayne C. Starnes. 1993. *The Fishes of Tennessee.* The University of Tennessee Press, Knoxville, TN.

Goldstein, Robert J. with Rodney Harper and Ridchard Edwards. 2000. *American Aquarium Fishes.* Texas A&M University Press, College Station, TX.

Miller, Rudolph J. 2004. *The Fishes of Oklahoma.* The University of Oklahoma Press, Norman, OK.

Page, Lawrence M. and Brooks M. Burr. 2011. *Peterson Field Guide to Freshwater Fishes of North America North of Mexico.* Houghton Mifflin Harcourt, Boston - New York.

Pflieger, William L. 1975. *The Fishes of Missouri.* Missouri Department of Conservation, Springfield, MO.

Burr, Brooks M. & Melvin L. Warren, Jr. 1986. *A Distributional Atlas of Kentucky Fishes.* Kentucky Nature Preserves Commission.

Smith, Philip W. 2002. *The Fishes of Illinois.* University of Illinois Press. Urbana, IL.

Internet

FishBase - www.fishbase.org

Illinois Department of Natural Resources - www.dnr.illinois.gov

Illinois Natural History Survey - www.inhs.illinois.edu

North American Native Fish Association - www.nanfa.org

National Fish Habitat Action Plan - www.fishhabitat.org

NatureServe Explorer- www.natureserve.org

USGS Fact Sheets - www.search.usgs.gov

Kentucky Department of Fish & Wildlife Resources - www.kdfwr.state.ky.us

Encyclopedia of Life - www.eol.org

Land Big Fish - www.landbigfish.com

GLOSSARY

Amphipod	A Crustacean of the order Amphipoda. Includes the freshwater shrimps.
Anadromous	Ascending into freshwater rivers to spawn.
Annelid/Annalida	A class of invertebrate organisms commonly known as worms.
Anuran	A member of the amphibian order Anura (the frogs and toads).
Arboreal	Pertaining to trees.
Arthropod	A member of the invertebrate phylum Arthropoda.
Aspen Parkland	An open or semi-open area (usually grassland) that is intermingled with groves of Aspen.
Barbel	A long "whisker-like" appendage orginating near the mouth of fishes, often sensory.
Barrens	Open areas within normally forested or brusy habitats.
Benthic	Pertaining to the bottom of a stream or lake.
Bivalve	An organism of the phylum Molluska (mollusks) or Branchiopoda having a shell consisting of two halves.
Boreal	Northern.
Borrow Pit	Shallow ditches and ponds created by road construction when earth is "borrowed" from a nearby area to build up road beds.
Buteo	A hawk belonging to the genus Buteo. Also known as the "Broad-winged Hawks."
Cache	The act of storing or hiding food for future use.
Carapace	The top half of the shell of a turtle.
Carnivore	A meat eater.
Caudal	Pertaining to the tail.
Chromosone	Long strand of proteins and DNA found within the nucleus of a cell.
Circumpolar	Literally, around the poles. Usually used in reference to the geographic range of an organism, that is found throughout the northern hemisphere.
Cloaca	A common opening for reproductive and excretory functions in an organism. Typical for all animals except mammals.
Congeneric	belonging to the same genus.
Conspecific	belonging to the same species.
Contiguous	In contact with or adjoining.
Copepod	A group of tiny crustaceans belonging to the suborder Copapoda. Many are microscopic and aquatic and are important food for tiny fishes and other small aquatic organisms.
CRP	Conservation Reserve Program.
Crustacean	A member of the class Crustacea. A class of Arthropod organisms that includes the crayfish, lobsters, crabs, shrimps, barnacles, copepods, and water fleas.
Cryptic	Pertaining to concealment.

Diploid	having the normal set of two chromosones.
Dipteran	An insect of the order Diptera. Includes flies, mosquitos, gnats and midges.
Disjunct	Not attached to or not adjoining.
Dessicate/Dissication	Dry out.
Diurnal	Pertaining to day. Being active by day.
Dorsal	The top or back of an organism.
Dorso-ventral	The region between the side and the belly of an organism, or along the lower side adjacent to the belly.
Echolocate/Echolocation	The use of sound waves to navigate or move about. As in bats.
Ecoregion	A large unit of land or water containing a geographically distinct assemblage of species, natural communities, and environmental conditions.
Ecotone	The region where one or more habitats converge.
Embryo	A young animal that is developing from a fertilized egg. Embryonic stage ends at birth or hatching.
Endemic	Native to a particular area.
Endotherm/Endothermic	A organism that regulates its body tempaerature internally. Warm-blooded.
Ephemeral	Fleeting. Temporary.
Estivate/Estivation	Dormant state of inactivity usually brought on by hot, dry conditions. The opposite of hibernation, which is a wintertime dormancy.
Extirpated	No longer found within a given area.
Extant	Still present. Opposite of extirpated.
Fecund/Fecundity	Capable of producing abundant offspring.
Fin rays	The bony structures that support the membranes of a fishes fin.Fossorial Burrowing or living in underground burrows.
Fossorial	Burrowing.
Gastropod	A class of the animal phylum Molluska. Includes snails and slugs.
Herbaceous	A type of flowering plant which does not develop woody tissue.
Holarctic	The circumpolar region that includes North America, Europe, and Asia.
Homogeneous	Of the same kind.
Insectivorous	Insect-eating.
Invertivorous	Feeding on invertebrates.
Intergrade	An organism which possess morphological characteristics that are intermediate between two distinctly different forms.
Irruptive	The sudden movement of animals from one portion of their range to another, often very distant portion of their range. As in when Snowy Owls occasionally move down from the Arctic region into the southern half of North America.
Isopod	An order of Crustaceans that includes the familiar pillbugs.
Kames	hills or ridges formed by the deposition of sand and gravels from glaciers.
Keeled Scales	The presence of a small ridge down the middle of the dorsal scales on snakes.
Lentic	Non-flowing bodies of water, lakes, swamps, ponds, etc.
Mandible	The lower jaw of an animal or the bill of a bird.
Marine	Pertaining to living in a saltwater environment.

Mast	Seeds produced by plants in a deciduous forest. Usually means the cumulative production of acorns, nuts, berries, seeds, etc., which are widely utilized by wildlife as food.
Melanistic	A predominance of the dark pigment known as melanin. The opposite of Albinistic.
Mesic	Damp or moist.
Metabolic/Metabolism	The sum of the chemical activity that occurs within a living organism. Usually relates to the digestion of food and utilization of food compounds within the body.
Metamorphose	Change of the body. Usually refers to the change from an immature stage to a more mature stage (as in a tadpole to a frog).
Metamorphosis	Abrupt physical change of body form.
Millinery Trade	The sale of bird feathers.
Molt	The shedding of and renewal (replacement) of skin, hair, or feathers.
Moraine	Large mass of earth, sand, gravels, and rock bulldozed by glacial movement. Moraines usually accumulate along the sides and in the front of glaciers.
Morphology	The study of the body form, shape, and structure of organisms, including colors or patterns.
Muskeg	A Sphagnum bog occurring the boreal (northern) regions of North America.
Neotropical	Pertaining to the tropical regions of the western hemisphere.
Nuptial	Pertaining to breeding.
Obligate	In biology means occurring within a restricted environment.
Omnivore	Eats both plant and animal matter.
Ontogenetic	Related to the development or age of an organism.
Opercle flap	The bony structure on the side of a fishes head that covers the gills. Also sometimes called gill cover.
Organism	A living thing.
Orthopteran	A member of the insect order Orthoptera. Includes such well-known insects as crickets and grasshoppers.
Ossification	The formation of bone.
Palearctic	The geographic region that includes Europe and northern Asia.
Parthenogenesis	The development of an ovum (egg) without fertilization.
Passage Migrant	Refers to birds that merely migrate through an area without staying any appreciable amount of time.
Pectoral	Pertain to or located in the chest area.
Pelage	Fur.
Pelvic	Pertaining to or located in the region of the pelvis (hips).
Phylogeny	The evolutionary relationships and/or evolutionary history of organisms.
Physiography	Refers to the natural features of a landscape, i.e. mountians, rivers, plains, etc.
Piscivorous	Fish-eating.
Plastron	The ventral (bottom) portion of a turtle's shell.
Plumage	The feathers of a bird.
Polychaete worms	Annelid worms (Phylum Annelida) belonging to the class Polychaeta. Mostly marine but some are fresh water.

Precocious	Having adult (or highly developed) characteristics in the young. Precocial being highly precocious.
Predaceous	Feeding on other animals, being a predator.
Piscivorous	Fish eating.
Puddle Duck	Ducks belonging to the genus *Anas*.
Prehensile	Grasping. As in a prehensile tail that is able to wrap around and grasp a tree limb.
Regenerative	Refers to the ability to repair or replace damage or destroyed tissues or structures.
Riparian	Pertaining to the bank of a stream or river.
Sexual Dimorphism	Morphological differences between the sexes.
Species of Concern	A species or subspecies which might become threatened in Illinois under continued or increased stress.
Species of Special Interest	A species that occurs periodically and is capable of breeding in Illinois.
Successional woodlands/areas	Landscape areas (usually woodlands) that are undergoing change from an early stage of development to an older stage. As in woodlands regenerating following logging operations.
Sympatric/Sympatrically	A condition where more than one species occurs in the same or overlapping area or habitat.
Taiga	A type of forest occurring in the far north. Usually dominated by dwarfed spruces.
Tetraploid	Possessing four chromosones.
Topography	The configuration of the land surface. Literally, "the lay of the land."
Troglodyte	Cave dwelling. Usually refers to organisms that live in caves.
Turbid	Water that is opaque due to the high amount of suspended silt particles.
Tympanum	The circular ear structure on the side of the head of frogs and toads.
USF&WS	Acronym for the United States Fish & Wildlife Service.
Ventral	Pertaining to the belly or bottom side of an organism.
Vernal	Pertaining to spring. Also frequently used to describe temporary ponds and pools that hold water only during the wet season.
Vestigial	A rudimentary structure. Usually a remnant, degenerative structure that was once (in the evolutionary history of the organism) a fully functioning structure.
Xeric	Dry.
Zygote	A fertilized egg that has not yet begun to divide.

INDEX

PHOTO CREDITS

John R. MacGregor
Least Weasel, Golden Mouse, Southern Bog Lemming, Meadow Jumping Mouse, Masked Shrew, Hoary Bat, Eastern Red Bat, Gray Bat, Northern Bat, Silver-haired Bat, Rafinesque's Big-eared Bat, Slender Glass Lizard (male), Slender Glass Lizard (female), Eastern Redback Salamander, Four-toed Salamander, Helbender

Matthew R. Thomas
Eastern Sand Darter, Blackside Darter, Mud Darter, Bluntnose Darter, Cypress Darter (male), Cypress Darter (female), Fringed Darter (male), Fringed Darter (female), Fantail Darter (male), Fantail Darter (female), Goldeye, Starhead Minnow, Threadfin Shad, Skipjack Herring, Stonecat, Slender Madtom, Tadpole Madtom, Quillback, River Redhorse, Pugnose Minnow, Suckermouth Minnow, Shoal Chub, Silver Chub, Mississippi Silvery Minnow, Mimic Shiner

David Speiser, www.lilibirds.com
Yellow-bellied Flycatcher, Northern Shrike, Sedge Wren, Wilson's Warbler (male), Golden-winged Warbler, Mourning Warbler, Connecticut Warbler, Snow Bunting, Buff-breasted Sandpiper, Surf Scoters, Long-tailed Duck (male and female)

Don Martin Bird Photograpy
Olive-sided Flycatcher, Alder Flycatcher, Least Flycatrcher, Ruby-crowned Kinglet (male), Clay-colored Sparrow, Henslow's Sparrow, LeContes Sparrow, Virginia Rail, Western Sandpiper

Konrad Schmidt
Iowa Darter (female), Iowa Darter (male), Least Darter, Rainbow Smelt, Trout Perch, Silver Redhorse, Ghost Shiner, Spottail Shiner, Bigmouth Shiner, Blackchin Shiner, Blacknose Shiner

Nate Tessler
Pink Salmon, White Perch, Brassy Minnow, Western Silvery Minnow

James Kiser
Northern Short-tailed Shrew, Evening Bat, Bluebreast Darter

T. Travis Brown
Franklin's Ground Squirrel, Mottled Sculpin

Brian Zimmerman
Banded Killifish, Highfin Carpsucker

Phil Myers
Meadow Vole

Uland Thomas
Goldeye

Jeffrey Offermann, www.flickr.com/jphotos/jeff_offerman
Long-tailed Weasel

Dave Neely
Ribbon Shiner, River Shiner

Jeff Poklen
Glaucus Gull, Little Gull

John Williams
Eastern Woodrat

Nathan Petersen
Western Harvest Mouse

Michael Jeffords
Plains Pocket Gopher

Greg Lavaty
Short-eared Owl

Tom Murray
Goshawk

Peter Paplanus
Flat-headed Snake, Lined Snake, Illinois Chorus Frog

David Haggard
Green Treefrog (blue morph)

James H. Harding
Blue-spotted Salamander

Roger Tabor, USFWS
Chinook Salmon

ABOUT THE AUTHOR

Naturalist Scott Shupe began his professional career in 1971 at the famed Ross Allen Reptile Institute and Venom Laboratory in Silver Springs, FL. He later worked at the St. Augustine Alligator Farm in St. Augustine, FL, and with Reptile Gardens in Rapid City, SD. From 1992 to 2002, he enjoyed an association with the Knight & Hale Game Call company in Cadiz, KY, where he served as director of The Woods & Wetlands Wildlife Center, a private zoo/nature center. He is the founder and original owner of the Natural History Educational Company, an organization of professional naturalists that provided live-animal wildlife education programs to thousands of schools throughout the United States.

He has served as a host and narrator for wildlife related television programming ("In the Wild," Outdoor Channel), produced educational life science videos, and has appeared as a guest naturalist on a number of public television programs and satellite networks. He has been recognized for his contributions to conservation education by the US Fish & Wildlife Service, named naturalist of the year by the Kentucky Society of Naturalists, awarded the Jesse Stuart Media Award for his educational video productions, and received the Environmental Stewardship Award from the Kentucky Environmental Quality Commission. Since 1987, he has contracted annually with the Kentucky Department of Parks to provide naturalist programming in state parks across Kentucky. Since 2005, he has enjoyed an association with the Kentucky Reptile Zoo and Venom Laboratory, acting as an outreach ambassador for educational school programming.

He has written for outdoor and nature periodicals and scientific journals, and his wildlife photographs have appeared in dozens of nature magazines and books. This is his fourth book on nature and wildlife and his third book for Skyhorse Publishing. He also authored *US Guide to Venomous Snakes and their Mimics*, *Venomous Snakes of the World, A Handbook for Use by US Amphibious Forces,* and *Life List of North American Birds*. A professional naturalist with nearly forty years experience in a wide array of nature interpretation, wildlife tourism, education, writing and wildlife photography and videography, he lives in Murray, KY.

Contact Scott Shupe at kscottshupe@gmail.com.